www.wadsworth.com

www.wadsworth.com is the World Wide Web site for Wadsworth and is your direct source to dozens of online resources.

At www.wadsworth.com you can find out about supplements, demonstration software, and student resources. You can also send e-mail to many of our authors and preview new publications and exciting new technologies.

www.wadsworth.com
Changing the way the world learns®

Philosophical Thinking about Death and Dying

VINCENT BARRY
Professor Emeritus of Philosophy
Bakersfield College

Australia • Brazil • Canada • Mexico • Singapore
Spain • United Kingdom • United States

THOMSON

WADSWORTH

Publisher: Holly J. Allen

Philosophy Editor: Steve Wainwright

Assistant Editors: Lee McCracken,
  Barbara Hillaker

Editorial Assistant: Gina Kessler

Technology Project Manager: Julie Aguilar

Marketing Manager: Worth Hawes

Marketing Assistant: Alexandra Tran

Marketing Communications Manager:
  Stacey Purviance

Creative Director: Rob Hugel

Executive Art Director: Maria Epes

Print Buyer: Nora Massuda

Permissions Editor: Joohee Lee

Production Service: International Typesetting
  and Composition

Copy Editor: Kevin Broccoli

Cover Designer: Hatty Lee/Yvo Riezebos Design

Cover Image: Alan Thornton/Stone/
  Getty Images, Inc.

Compositor: International Typesetting
  and Composition

Text and Cover Printer: Transcontinental,
  Louiseville

Thomson Higher Education
10 Davis Drive
Belmont, CA 94002-3098
USA

For more information about our products,
contact us at:
**Thomson Learning Academic Resource
Center
1-800-423-0563**
For permission to use material from this text
or product, submit a request online at
http://www.thomsonrights.com
Any additional questions about permissions
can be submittted by e-mail to
thomsonrights@thomson.com

Library of Congress Control Number: 2005938148

ISBN 0-495-00824-9

To Jen-Li Rose,
my hedge against premature departure

Contents

Preface

Overwhelmingly, introductory texts on death and dying prefer the science of psychology or sociology to the wisdom of philosophy and religion. For all that is gained, and much it is, I expect that some enduring questions, as well some urgent ones, largely go muted. *What exactly is death? What are the implications of knowing that we will die? Do we naturally fear death, and if so, so what? Is death bad and the fear of it rational? Does life continue after bodily death? Are there good reasons to believe in an afterlife, including paranormal ones? How much control should we have over our own deaths? Is voluntary death always wrong? Should physician-assisted suicide be permitted? Can we ever have a duty to die?* And, perhaps most important: *What's the relation between death and life? Does one make the other more meaningful or less so?*

This text aims to give voice to such questions. While mining the contributions of other fields, it uniquely provides understanding and analysis of basic *philosophical* problems concerning death.

A convenient way to sort out fundamental philosophical questions about death is according to their curiosity about three things: (1) the nature of death, including questions about the consciousness, fear, and evil of death; (2) survival of death, including questions about the self and its relation to death, as well as various afterlife beliefs and their bases; and (3) voluntary death, including questions about suicide, euthanasia, and futile medical treatment. These categories of interest correspond to the three parts of the book, within which are covered a dozen foundational topics.

With no pretense to being comprehensive, the coverage is intended to provide a stimulative groundwork of thought and insight for further reflection and study. Braced with a solid Introduction and Conclusion, the tidy 12 chapters comprise a concise but sturdy guide to the basics of philosophical thinking about death and dying.

Although weighted to the thought of philosophers, the book requires no formal background in philosophy. Truth be told, it was written for a general audience unfamiliar with that subject and activity. This accounts for the descriptions of philosophy and philosophical thinking at the outset; and, throughout, the definition of key terms and identification of notable figures, as well as the avoidance of jargon and name dropping. Other friendly, orienting features are the part-opening introductions and the chapter-ending conclusions. Noteworthy, too, is the inclusion of interdisciplinary material.

The book, in fact, ventures freely across academic fields, for reasons both conceptual and practical. Conceptually, much that is not philosophy bears directly on philosophical analysis of death and dying. This explains the material from psychology and sociology, but also from other fields—literature, history, medicine. It also accounts for many of the extensive references located at the end of the chapters. Their reach and specificity are intended not only to support the text but direct further trans-curricular research in classical and contemporary sources. Practically, I hope the intended cross-fertilization enhances learning and sharpens critical thinking. Most of all, may it help fit philosophy into death studies by showing where philosophy fits in.

Any book that charts a new direction sets out, nonetheless, from the safe harbor of tradition. And so a sizable debt of gratitude is owed the great many writers and scholars in the field for their stellar constancy along the way.

For the successful launch of the book, credit and appreciation go to the crew at Wadsworth, especially: editor Steve Wainwright for his staunch support; and project manager Deepa Ghosh for yeomanly attention to details.

Finally, for keeping me afloat when I might otherwise have run aground, I salute the book's reviewers: Francis Degnin, University of Northern Iowa; Gerald A. Larue, University of Southern California; Bonnie Luft, Baylor University; Warren Shibles, University of Wisconsin, Whitewater; and Douglas Wall Shrader, Jr., SUNY Oneonta. They serve, as always, to error's edge, beyond which I sail alone

Philosophical Thinking
about Death and Dying

Introduction
Philosophical Thinking and Death

*T*he *Death of Ivan Ilyich* (1886) is the story of a 45-year-old opportunistic lawyer who, busy with mundane affairs, as if life will go on forever, never even considers the inevitability of his own death until forced to when suddenly stricken with a cruel disease. How will this successful and unreflective court judge confront the fact of his own mortality? In one of literature's major death explorations, author Leo Tolstoy's powerful answer takes us inside the mind of a hollow man transfigured by death, as he contemplates things both troubling and fascinating, and altogether alien to him. *What has my life meant? Did I make the right choices? What is death, now that it is I who must die? What will become of me? What, if anything, will I leave behind?*

It is thus that, as he lies dying, the worldly careerist Ivan Ilyich turns philosopher. What he spent a lifetime studiously avoiding, Ivan Ilyich no longer can escape: philosophical thinking about death and dying, the subject of this text.

If we ask what makes Ivan Ilyich's deathbed thinking "philosophical," words such as "serious," "deep," "intense," or "contemplative" likely come to mind. The problem with such terms, though, is they tend to be vague and indiscriminate. We can, after all, think "seriously" about politics, "deeply" about science, "intensely" about sports, "contemplatively" about a promising future—and yet not *philosophically*. So while such expressions may say something about the general quality of philosophical thinking, they still leave us asking: "But what makes Ivan Ilyich's serious (deep, intense, or contemplative) thinking *philosophical?*"

To answer that question, it helps to return briefly to the discipline of philosophy as it was first conceived and practiced in the West some 2,500 years ago. There we'll discover something about the nature and purpose of philosophical thinking, and its connection to death and this book.

PHILOSOPHY AND THE DEATH OF IVAN ILYICH

It is said that philosophy (from the Greek *philo* for "love" and *sophia* for "wisdom") begins in wonder. Every time we wonder about life and the world, about ourselves and our experience, perhaps even about our place in the universe, we reconnect with the origins of philosophy and wellspring of all the sciences. On any occasion that we ponder things, as Ivan Ilyich did as he lay dying, we journey back to ancient Greece, where some extraordinary people of immense curiosity puzzled over certain aspects of the world and their experience of them.

What the ancients wondered about still interests similarly curious people today—questions about reality, knowledge, and conduct. Now, as then, these broad categories of wonder and inquiry still comprise the three main branches of philosophy, termed metaphysics, epistemology, and ethics. We can see each in the travail of Ivan Ilyich, and allow their interests to shape our understanding of philosophical thinking about death and dying.

Metaphysics

"Meta" in Greek means "behind" or "after." The term metaphysics apparently owes its origin to the fact that the corresponding part of Aristotle's work came *after* the part called "physics." In his "metaphysics" Aristotle (384–322 BCE) engaged questions that went *beyond* the apparent nature of things to their true nature or ultimate reality. Metaphysics retains this ancient interest in questions of reality, including the nature of being and existence, and the study and development of the universe. Understanding the nature of mind, self, freedom, and consciousness are metaphysical concerns. So are issues about the nature of religion, the existence of God, the immortality of the soul, theories of afterlife, the destiny of the universe, and the meaning of life.

The very first questions of the ancients were metaphysical. One of these concerned the relation of appearance to reality, specifically whether reality is best described as change or constancy. Ivan Ilyich, for example, undergoes a profound transformation as he lies dying. His body, his mind, his emotions, his character—virtually every aspect of his personality undergoes change. Yet for all that he is still "Ivan Ilyich." How to explain this? What makes you or I the same person through all the years and changes of our lives—if, in fact, we are the same person? As for the ultimate change, death, that only amplifies such questions. *What awaits us when we die? Continued existence? If so, what will it be like? Or do we face annihilation? Does death bring extinction?* Little wonder that Ivan Ilyich silently asks, "What does it all mean?"[1]

Epistemology

The second of the three main branches of philosophy, epistemology (from the Greek *episteme* meaning "knowledge")deals with the nature, sources, and reliability of knowledge. What we can know and how we can know it are central epistemological concerns. Also of interest is the relationship between philosophy and science, as well as a variety of language concerns. Epistemology deals with questions such as: *How can we determine truth and validity? How are belief, truth, and knowledge related? What are the rules of logic?* Such matters are hardly foreign to a man who has spent years agilely practicing law. And yet to the dying Ivan Ilyich all the courtroom jousting now seems so vapid, at best a shallow exercise, at worst a cruel game full of deceit and vanity. He is convinced that it is all part of the web of lies designed by society to deny one thing: death. "Can *It* alone be true?" he is left to wonder.[2]

Ethics

Although Ivan Ilyich's agony has metaphysical and epistemological overtones, his is in the main a moral crisis. Morality (from the Latin *moralis* meaning "custom") consists of the standards that an individual or a group has about what is of value, including what is right and wrong, or good and evil. To term Ilyich's ordeal a "moral crisis" means that he is seriously questioning the values, standards, and rules by which he's lived. He's beginning to do ethics, the third major branch of philosophy.

Ethics (from the Greek *ethos* meaning "character") is the study of morality. In growing up, we absorb moral standards from our families and society. Later we may seriously question and test those standards by closely examining the reasons for and against them. "Why is this action right and that one wrong?" we may ask ourselves; or "Why is this character trait good, and that one bad?" When we undertake this inspection of our inherited moral customs, we're doing ethics.

One area of applied ethics with special relevancy to death and dying is bioethics (from the Greek *bios* meaning "life"). Bioethics is the study of morality in the life sciences, especially in medicine. Bioethical issues include abortion, human embryo and fetal research, human cloning, stem cell research, and assisted death.

An historical interest of ethics is Ivan Ilyich's deathbed obsession: how best to live. Determining the "good life" takes ethics into a lacework of issues, including the ultimate end(s) of human life; the proper relation of one person to another and of the individual to society; the nature of good and evil, right and wrong. A scratch on the surface of these and other ethical matters inevitably reveals two foundational questions of ethics: *"What ought I do?"* and *"What ought I be?"* These two questions—the first of conduct, the second of character—are at the heart of determining the good life. Answers to them form the core of how best to live. For never having engaged either question, Ivan Ilyich, by his own measure, has lived a hollow life.

The ancients who pursued wisdom in matters of reality, knowledge, and conduct were termed philosophers, "lovers of wisdom." To them we owe our understanding of philosophy as both content and activity. There is, on one hand, the sizable body of work of the philosophers, which constitutes the *subject* or *discipline* of philosophy. Then there is the *activity* of philosophizing, which involves a critical and logical response to the viewpoints advanced. It is in the process and activity of philosophizing that the content of philosophy offers us a chance to create and adopt for ourselves what Ivan Ilyich can but desperately grope for as he lies dying: meaningful belief.

PHILOSOPHICAL THINKING

Evident in the curiosity of the early philosophers was thinking appropriate to each area of inquiry. For example, striving to understand reality, metaphysics, generally entailed *speculative* or theoretical thinking. On the other hand, *practical* thinking more suited an inquiry into the human's place in that world, the concern of ethics. And, of course, whatever the products of metaphysical and ethical curiosity—i.e., the conclusions, hypotheses, positions, or principles reached—all needed to be grounded in reliable foundations and methods of thought, the concern of epistemology. For that, *critical* thinking was called for—thinking about thinking itself, including the processes, quality, and direction of one's own thinking and that of others. These three kinds of thinking, then—speculative, practical, and critical—characterized philosophical thinking in the beginning. They still do.

A less formal way to understand philosophical thinking is to follow its original impetus of wonder. Philosophical thinking continues to reflect an attempt to deal creatively with the things of experience. It is typically driven by a curiosity and self-doubt that poses some fundamental question of human existence. *Who am I? Where do I come from? Where am I going? What's the meaning of life? Is there a God? What is truth? How can I be happy?* Philosophical thinking strives to go beyond the common place to see what is not readily apparent, to think seriously about what most people unquestioningly accept, to conceive of possibilities and alternatives to what is thought obvious. Philosophical thinking aims for knowledge with understanding. So understood, virtually anyone can do philosophical thinking. Sometimes it even seems thrust upon us.

Recall that in the aftermath of the September 11, 2001, terrorist attack on the World Trade Center that killed nearly 3,000 people, most of us expressed an array of emotions—from shock and horror to anger and confusion to hatred and vengeance. But some likely went beyond these feelings to wonder "Why?" Not "Why?" in the sense of who did it, how, and with what motive. Rather, they asked "Why?" in a philosophical sense, in a metaphysical and moral sense.

Mulling 9/11 at that level of thought inevitably involves pondering the meaning of *any* perceived evil of which 9/11, presumably, was an extreme example. Thus: *Why do dreadful things happen at all? What kind of world do we live in where horrific things happen routinely to innocent people? How could a good God create a world so filled with cruelty and torture? Is it that we don't understand evil or can't comprehend God? Does God, in fact, exist? Is there or is there not some divinely ordained design, plan, and purpose for everything, including evil? And if there is, how do pain and suffering and death fit into this plan? How does 9/11? How does a killing earthquake, tsunami, or hurricane?*

Ivan Ilyich craved answers to his ultimate questions. So, too, with philosophical thinking. Philosophical thinking isn't only about asking questions and entertaining doubts, but also about finding answers. It's not interested only in raising questions about 9/11 or a natural disaster or the meaning of life and death; it wants to answer those questions. To accomplish this philosophical thinking employs rigorous, persistent analysis conducted at a high level of generality and abstraction that moves from the facts of experience to inspection of those facts. This method is sometimes called the Socratic method, after Socrates (470–390 BCE), who used it to arrive at defensible answers and correct belief. Philosophical thinking is still driven by two interdependent endeavors practiced by Socrates: (1) to clarify ideas and concepts; and (2) to present defensible answers to the issues.

In summary, philosophical thinking is speculative, practical, and critical thinking that aims for an understanding with knowledge based upon clear ideas and defensible answers. This makes philosophical thinking quite different from ordinary, everyday thinking.

PHILOSOPHICAL VS. ORDINARY THINKING

Although perfectly adequate in many common contexts, ordinary thinking tends to be vague and imprecise. It can be opinionated, to be sure, but uncompelling. Ordinary thinking also tends to be naive, uncritical, and unquestioning, even gullible. Philosophical thinking, by contrast, is sophisticated in the sense of being skeptical and searching. Reasoning—the process of following relationships from thought to thought to some ultimate conclusion—is crucial to philosophical thinking, peripheral to ordinary thinking. Philosophical thinking engages the fundamental questions of human existence in a disciplined, imaginative way; ordinary thinking does not.

Beyond this, ordinary thinking is superficial, whereas philosophical thinking is reflective. This means that ordinary thinking generally accepts the surface meaning of an idea, and doesn't see it in relation to other concepts. Also, ordinary thinking rarely turns inward to scrutinize its own thoughts, feelings, and experiences in relation to larger questions. In contrast, philosophical thinking seeks deeper meaning of concepts and wider connections of ideas as a basis for understanding and acceptance. It is introspective of the contents and qualities of its own thinking and thought processes in seeking answers to life's fundamental questions.

Finally, and perhaps most important, ordinary thinking is "ordinary" precisely because it is customary, established, popular, and conventional. There is nothing distinctively individual about it. It's basically "group think." By contrast, the knowledge with understanding that philosophical thinking aims for ideally separates the individual from the herd by moving one in the direction of rational autonomy. "Rational autonomy" basically refers to the freedom of being able to decide for oneself by using one's own mind. Rational autonomy means living one's own life, something that suddenly is of utmost importance to Ivan Ilyich.

It is only when he's dying that Ivan Ilyich painfully realizes that he didn't so much live his life as have it lived for him. The result is profound disappointment, but also regret and bitterness. No comparable feelings beset Socrates, who spent his final hours as he did his life: in philosophical contemplation and discourse with students and friends. A lifetime of philosophical thinking well prepared the gadfly of Athens for death; a lifetime of ordinary thinking left Ivan Ilyich pitifully unprepared.

PHILOSOPHICAL THINKING AND DEATH

The Death of Ivan Ilyich is about the importance of facing death. It teaches that unless we honestly deal with the fact of our mortality we're missing something very important about ourselves. Because philosophical thinking supports us in living our own lives, it inevitably engages this crucial though often denied aspect of our lives.

What does it mean to honestly face our own death? That's difficult to say. Different disciplines would give different answers. Many religions, for example, would answer within a larger view of creation, life, and destiny. Psychology, on the other hand, might frame an answer within a theory of human development. Both, conceivably, would help us deal with the fact that we will die, one by offering spiritual guidance, the other emotional support.

This book takes its cue from the nature of philosophy and philosophical thinking. Philosophical thinking about death and dying suggests something along the lines of being curious enough about our own mortality to ask basic questions about it suggested by the discipline of philosophy, and attempting to give plausible answers to those questions. When we do this we take a giant step toward honestly facing our own death.

Three Kinds of Fundamental Questions

A convenient way to categorize fundamental questions about death is according to their philosophical curiosity about three things:

1. the nature of death, including questions about the consciousness, fear, and evil of death

2. survival of death, including questions about the self and its relation to death, as well as various afterlife beliefs and their bases

3. voluntary death, including questions about suicide, euthanasia, and futile medical treatment

The branch of philosophy that each falls under is open to interpretation. In general, questions about (1) the nature and (2) survival of death tend to be metaphysical and invite speculative thinking; whereas questions about (3) voluntary death tend to be ethical and call for practical thinking. As for epistemology and critical thinking, in all three areas of interest we must think carefully and deliberately in order to decide rationally what to or what not to believe.

These divisions correspond to the three parts of this text: The Nature of Death, Survival of Death, and Voluntary Death. Together they raise a multitude of questions, such as: *What are the implications of the fact that human beings uniquely are aware that they will die? Is one's death something to fear? Is death an evil? Are there good reasons to believe in life after death? What are the competing views of afterlife? Why do most people believe in life after death? Is suicide ever a rational, justified act? Is deliberately hastening the death of someone who has requested it ever moral? How much control should we have over our own deaths? Does one ever have a duty to die?*

In philosophical thinking about these and other questions, we'll often cross disciplines. This is inevitable and desirable. How else to discuss afterlife theories without getting into religious beliefs, or deal with the consciousness of death without treading in psychology, or understand present attitudes toward death without a little history and even cultural anthropology? Whatever heightens understanding of a subject is grist for philosophical thinking, no more so than when the subject is death and dying.

One other point. Like philosophical thinking in general, philosophical thinking about death and dying tends to be driven by issues of meaning and acceptability. Issues of meaning include disputes over definition. Some of these definitional disputes really matter, such as those involving "human nature," "self," "soul," and even "death" itself. Issues of meaning also include disputes about purpose or goal, as in "What is the meaning of life?" or "Does death mean anything more than the biological termination of life?" Agreement on meaning, however, doesn't guarantee agreement of viewpoints. For example, even after agreeing on what constitutes an act of suicide, we might disagree on whether or not such an act is ever moral. Indeed, we might agree that, in theory, assisting a suicide may sometimes be okay, but object to its legalization.

This book is not intended to change your opinions or indoctrinate you. In the spirit of Socrates throughout his life and Ilyich at the end of his, it is designed to help you chart your own way, not set you on a predetermined course. It aims to stimulate philosophical thinking about death—to give you the opportunity to clarify your own ideas and concepts about death and dying and to formulate your own answers to some big questions. To support that goal, it samples the thought of a wide range of scholars and writers, physicians and nurses, and occasionally the dying and their families. While often in disagreement, the voices you will hear are of one mind on at least one point: the value of philosophical thinking about death and dying.

THE VALUE OF PHILOSOPHICAL THINKING
ABOUT DEATH AND DYING

When was your first death experience? If it was around age eight, you are like most people. According to researchers, eight is the average age of a person's first real-life death experience.

For some children the first is the death of a valued pet, for others a relative such as a grandparent. While some people may get to midlife without ever having personally experienced such a death, far more will have lost several significant others by then. With the passing of years, of course, these personal deaths mount. Add to these the public deaths of well-known figures, as well as victims of accidents, crimes, wars, political persecutions, and natural disasters. The point is that its very ubiquity makes death just about impossible *not* to think about. And sometimes, if only briefly, our thoughts wax philosophical: *Why did Grandpa have to die? Why did Mother have to suffer so? Why the death of one so young? Where have all the dead gone?* The point is that, since we probably can't avoid thinking about death, why not think about it for ourselves as well as we can?

Still, admittedly, we don't have to give philosophical questions about death and dying more than fleeting attention. We can, and most of us probably do, treat death as an abstraction, something that happens, will happen, but is of no concern to us right now. We can, in effect, live our lives much as Ivan Ilyich. For him for the longest time "everything went on without change and everything was fine." Of course, Ilyich discovers that everything was not fine and things do change.

All the same, Ivan Ilyich's fate may not be exactly ours. Who's to say that death will find us as philosophically naked as he? Perhaps we'll die suddenly, without time for reflection. In the event of a long, hard dying, perhaps our deeply ingrained beliefs, though unexamined, will anesthetize us to psychic pain. Maybe so.

But to so separate ourselves from the experience of Ivan Ilyich is to miss the point of the story, which has less to do with the circumstances than the fact of death. It is *that* more than *how* he is dying that brings Ivan Ilyich to admit that he might not have lived as he should have, and then to wonder: "But how can that be when I did everything one is supposed to?" This paradox—that the way we are supposed to live as not necessarily how we should live—ought to give us pause before disowning Ivan Ilyich's fate. It suggests how death awareness can positively affect how we live.

Consider the uniquely human capacity to grasp a future. College, marriage, family, career—whatever the possible futures we envision for ourselves, they can and do affect our choices and behavior in the present. We even invite them to, as when we make plans for the future. Of course, these plans aren't entirely of our own making. They are powerfully shaped by the values and the expectations of society, notably social conceptions of achievement and success. This means that we allow socially scripted future possibilities to help shape our present. And for so doing, we are praised for and feel good about being "mature" and "responsible."

Now, if we willingly and proudly permit *possible*—and therefore *uncertain*—futures to help shape the present, shouldn't we permit the *certain* future of inevitable death to do the same? We don't, probably because we'd prefer to contemplate good things more than bad, and death typically is considered a bad thing. Besides, there's nothing we can do about death except, perhaps, to take some practical measures—make out a will, purchase a pre-need burial plot, express what end-of-life medical treatment we want and don't want.

Such explanations for death *un*awareness certainly have a psychological and pragmatic appeal. But don't they ultimately beg the issue? After all, even if death is a bad thing that no one can avoid, it doesn't follow that we need not or should not permit it to help shape our so-called future plans. And it's this issue—the potential influence of our inevitable death on our lives—that addresses the paradox Ivan Ilyich raises, which is, again: *How can one live a life that one is supposed to while at the same time not live the life one should?*

If death is a bad thing, it is *uniquely* a bad thing in that, while it exists as an event in our future, there is nothing uncertain about it except time, place, and circumstance. This means that all of us *all the time* live in the light of our own mortality. The only question is how much and what degree of conscious awareness of our own death we allow into our lives. Ivan Ilyich allowed none till the end. We are led to believe that had he lived more consciously that he was mortal he would have made more of the uncertain amount of time he *always* had to live. In other words, he'd have given his possible futures more thought, especially respecting those social scripts he blindly followed. And in the encounter with his own mortality, he would have become aware of his uniqueness and individuality, something that is only revealed to him in and by his dying when, tragically, he no longer has *any* possible futures. As he poignantly laments, "I am taking leave of life with the awareness that I squandered all I was given and have no possibility of rectifying matters . . . ."[3] In other words, by *his own reckoning*, he foolishly lived as he was supposed to but not as he should have, and now that he realizes it, he can do nothing about it.

In the end, Ivan Ilyich sees that there actually is something he can do to salvage his life. What that is we'll take up in a later chapter. Here it's enough to point out that Ilyich ultimately realizes the great lesson lived and taught by Socrates: "The unexamined life is not worth living." If Socrates is correct, then examining death, philosophical thinking about it, is essential to a worthwhile life. To examine life without confronting death, frankly, is like ignoring the proverbial 800-pound gorilla in the middle of the room. As Ivan Ilyich discovered pitifully late, life is not comprehended truly or lived wholly unless the idea of death is grappled with honestly.

Now, of course, we can always reject Socrates by insisting or, as Ivan Ilyich did, simply living as if the unexamined life *is* worth living. Before so doing, however, we might remember, finally, why Socrates, all philosophers, and countless other thoughtful people think otherwise.

The unexamined life, a consensus of considered opinion holds, is deeply impoverished for failing to take into account the life proper to a human being considered as a human being, as opposed to, say, a creature of base animal appetites. When cultured voices remind us that the unexamined life is not worth living, they have in mind human beings as rational creatures, who, among other things, desire freedom; have beliefs and values; seek truth, knowledge, and happiness; cherish objects of beauty and ultimate loyalty; and, most notably here, are aware of their mortality and allow that awareness to act upon all the rest.

So framed the question now becomes: Which is the more worth living—the examined or unexamined life? To be or not to be with questions, wonder, curiosity, and open mindedness—which is more befitting the life of a human being? Each of us will have to decide for ourselves. But one thing is plain: If the examined life is to be preferred, than an honest confrontation with death is as inevitable as death itself.

REFERENCES

1. Leo Tolstoy, *The Death of Ivan Ilyich*, New York: Bantam Books, 1981, p. 120.
2. Ibid., p. 95.
3. Ibid., pp. 126–127.

PART I

The Nature of Death

Introduction: The 9/11 Memorial and Death Denial

> They are pretty.
> Soothing and smooth.
> Smooth and light.
> Light and watery.

*N*ew York Times columnist Maureen Dowd is describing the eight finalist-models for a memorial at Ground Zero. Each gleams, she writes, with "hanging candles and translucent tubes and reflecting pools and smiling faces of those killed on September 11." They're intended to transcend terror. And they succeed, offering as they do, "nothing raw, harsh, or rough on which the heart and mind can collide." Dowd likens the "prettified designs" variously to "spas," "fancy malls," "aromatherapy centers," "New Age pavilions," and "architectural Musak"—all designed to dull mass murder. In their blandness, the memorials turn us away from examining what went wrong and offer no lessons learned. "There's no darkness in the designs, literally or metaphorically. They have taken death and finality out of this pulverized graveyard."[1]

Students of American culture probably would find little surprise in making the "lightest memorials" of "the heaviest event in modern American history." We are, after all, largely a death-denying culture.

That we are inclined to deny death has been long and widely observed. As psychologist Herman Feifel (1916–2003) wrote nearly a half-century ago: "Denial and avoidance of the countenance of death characterize much of the American outlook."[2]

They still do, although perhaps not in the same way as in mid–twentieth century. But what is still not broadly addressed outside academic circles are the many questions that orbit that cultural denial of death.

Why, for example, *do we collectively and often individually deny death?* Fear springs to mind. What we fear, we tend to flee. *If fear explains our denial, is the fear of death natural or unnatural? Is it something we're born with or learn? If natural, what does that say about the kind of beings we are? Are we essentially death fearing? If so, so what? Can the fear of death affect us as individuals and as a society? Does it really matter that, individually and collectively, we tend to flee the reality of our own eventual death with purpose and persistence?* Perhaps we have good reason to run from death, since we probably consider our own prospective death a bad thing. But is it? *Is death a bad thing for the one who dies, or is it not?*

Questions like these pertain to the nature of death, which is the interest of this part of the book.

The first thing to note about these questions is their interdisciplinary character. While the questions themselves have fear of death as a common interest, no single field has all the answers to them. In the twentieth century, virtually every major discipline contributed to the formidable accumulated research and opinion on the denial and fear of death: history and sociology; psychology and cultural anthropology; religion, theology, and philosophy.

The work of some scholars and writers has resonated with the public. Among them, chronologically: novelist Evelyn Waugh's *The Loved One* (1948), which cast a sardonic eye on the American funeral industry; cultural critic Jessica Mitford's *The American Way of Death* (1963), which criticized Americans for both their obsessive denial of death and fixation on immortality; psychiatrist Elisabeth Kubler-Ross's *On Death and Dying* (1969), which opened a window on the emotional life of the dying within a culture of fear and denial.

Less popular, but more scholarly contributions include: Feifel's *The Meaning of Death* (1959), a pioneering work that established the field of death studies or *thanatology* (from the Greek *thanatos* for "death") and earned its author the sobriquet "founder of the modern death movement"; philosopher Jacques Choron's *Death and Western Thought* (1963), which depicted the influence of fear, hope, and even disregard of death down through the ages; sociologist Geoffrey Gorer's *Death, Grief and Mourning* (1965), which showed how death had become a taboo in the twentieth century; cultural anthropologist Ernest Becker's *The Denial of Death* (1973), which analyzed how far we'll go to deny death; social historian Philippe Aries's *Western Attitudes Toward Death* (1974) and *The Hour of Our Death* (1981), both of which traced Western attitudes toward mortality from medieval to modern times.

Then there are those eminent figures whose death insights must be sought amidst their larger body of work, among them: psychoanalysts Sigmund Freud (1856–1939), Carl Jung (1875–1961), and Otto Rank (1884–1939); and philosophers Soren Kierkegaard (1813–1855), Martin Heidegger (1889–1976), and Jean Paul Sartre (1905–1980).

In attempting to make sense of this abundance of diverse research and opinion, we will use the familiar feeling of fear for stringing together much of our coverage of the nature of death. Accordingly, Chapter 2 takes a historical view of death fear in Western civilization, while Chapter 3 deals with fear of death as it relates to human consciousness, and Chapter 4 considers fear as a human response to the presumptive evil of death. With no pretense at being comprehensive, these chapters are intended merely to provide a coherent groundwork of information and insight into the fear of death that will stimulate further reflection and study regarding its nature.

We begin, however, with where philosophical analysis always begins—with conceptual clarification. Fundamental to studying the nature of death—indeed, an aspect of it—is a definition of physical death, including the criteria of it. Far from an abstraction, these concerns, which we will consider in Chapter 1, loom large in an age like ours when medical technology instills wonder, to be sure, even at times wonder about whether a patient is alive or dead. That same life-prolonging technology that challenges us to clarify our concept of death also contributes to our fear of death.

REFERENCES

1. Maureen Dowd, "The Unbearable Lightness of Memory," *New York Times*, November 30, 2003, sec. 4, p. 9.
2. Herman Feifel, ed., *The Meaning of Death,* New York: McGraw-Hill Paperback Edition, 1959, p. xv.

Definition and Criteria
of Death

O n the evening of March 19, 2005, the U.S. Congress did something it had never done before. With time running out on how much longer she could remain alive, congressional leaders announced that they would allow the parents of a 41-year-old Florida woman to petition the federal courts to have a feeding tube replaced for their severely brain damaged daughter. The next day, President Bush flew back to Washington from his Texas ranch to sign the emergency legislation.

THE DEATH OF TERRI SCHIAVO

"The case of Terri Schiavo raises complex issues," the president had said in a statement three days earlier. "Those who live at the mercy of others deserve our special care and concern. It should be our goal as a nation to build a culture of life, where all Americans are valued, welcomed, and protected—and that culture of life must extend to individuals with disabilities."

Fifteen years earlier, Terri Schiavo had incurred severe neurological damage when a chemical imbalance stopped her heart, cutting the oxygen supply to her brain. Although her entire brain wasn't permanently destroyed, it was severely damaged. The 26-year-old was left in what physicians term a persistent vegetative state (PVS). PVS patients may exhibit spontaneous, involuntary movements such as yawns or facial grimaces. They are sometimes able to breathe without aid, but are unable to eat or speak. Their condition is often described as "awake but unaware," because, without higher brain functions, their apparent wakefulness does not represent awareness of self or environment.

Like that of other PVS patients, Terri Schiavo's condition was considered permanent and irreversible, but not terminal. With proper care, she could continue to live many years, a fate her husband and legal guardian, Michael Schiavo, didn't think she would want. Therefore, Michael requested that his wife's artificial feeding tube be removed. When her Catholic parents, the Schindlers, objected, the stage was set for a lengthy legal battle that culminated in a court order to remove Terri's feeding tube.

Once the feeding tube was removed, evangelical Christian conservatives sprang into action, precipitating the congressional intervention. Exploiting their pivotal role in reelecting President Bush and swelling Republican majorities in Congress, the "religious right" demanded and obtained emergency legislation allowing the Schindlers to petition federal courts to have the feeding tube reinserted. The legal tactic failed, however, and Terri Schiavo died on March 31, nearly two weeks after the removal of her life-sustaining feeding tube.

In a message to supporters and media shortly after her death, Terri Schiavo's brother was quoted as saying, "Throughout this ordeal we are reminded of the words of Jesus' message on the cross: 'Forgive them for they know not what they do.'" Bobby Schindler's allusion was to the bitter family feud between the Schindlers and Michael Schiavo. However, it implied something darker: that Terri was killed, not just let die.

Most people probably wouldn't agree with Bobby Schindler that his sister was killed. However, they would likely agree that she was alive when the feeding tube was removed. Was she? Or was she dead long before, as some would argue? Are the thousands of patients like Terri in the U.S. dead or alive? Any answer depends on an understanding of physical death.

This chapter deals with four main approaches to defining and determining death: heart-lung, whole brain, higher brain, and brainstem. All of these formulations assume that life requires the integrated functioning of an organism. When that is lost, so is life. But exactly when that occurs is debatable. Each gives an answer with implications for morally appropriate treatment for patients like Terri Schiavo. Each also directs our thinking about bioethical issues, such as abortion, human and fetal research, cloning, stem cell research, and assisted death. One of the four approaches to death—the higher-brain formulation—is especially provocative. As we will see, it implies not only that Terri Schiavo died long before March 31 but also that many of the currently ill or disabled are properly considered dead.

TRADITIONAL HEART-LUNG DEFINITION

A terrible auto accident. One of the cars is occupied by a husband and wife. Authorities on the scene pronounce the man dead and rush the unconscious woman to a hospital, where she spends the next seventeen days in a coma due to severe brain damage. On the morning of the 18th day she dies. Or did she? Some time afterward, a relative contesting the couple's estate claims that the two died simultaneously. Did they?

In an identical case about a half-century ago, the Supreme Court of Arkansas ruled that since the unconscious woman was breathing, she was alive.[1] In making its decision, the court relied on a time-honored understanding of death as "the cessation of life; the ceasing to exist; defined by physicians as a total stoppage of the circulation of blood and a cessation of the animal and vital function consequent thereon, such as respiration, pulsation, etc."[2] This can be termed the traditional definition of death.

Given this understanding, death is to be determined by the permanent absence of breathing and heartbeat. This time-honored formulation is variously termed "heart-lung," "cardiopulmonary," or "cardiorespiratory" definition of death. It's also called "clinical death." By whatever name, death occurs when circulation and respiration permanently cease. Through the years, different ways have been used to determine this kind of death, placing a stethoscope to the chest and listening for a heartbeat being a familiar one.

Using heart-lung functioning as the criterion of death served well enough until challenged in the 1960s by two major developments in medicine: (1) breakthroughs in biotechnology, which is the application of biological research and techniques to health care; and (2) advances in transplant surgery.

The Challenge Posed by Biomedical Technology

Advances in biotechnology (e.g., mechanical respirators and electronic pace-makers) made it possible to sustain respiration and heartbeat indefinitely in patients with head trauma, stroke, or other neurological injuries. This meant that, according to the traditional formulation of death, individuals who had lost all brain functions were technically still alive because they had respiration and circulation, albeit artificially maintained. Yet to many—including relatives of the permanently comatose and those who cared for them—such persons were effectively dead.

The Challenge Posed by Transplantation

In December 1967, South African surgeon Dr. Christiaan Barnard (1922–2001) successfully transplanted a heart from one human to another. In itself an extraordinary medical achievement, this first-ever heart transplant not only publicized exciting developments in transplant surgery, but also the need for hearts and other organs from newly dead bodies. High on the list of potential organ donors were artificially supported patients, that is, ones with dead brains but sustained circulation. But which of these patients qualified as organ donors? Presumably, a patient with heart-lung function was to be considered alive and, consequently, might not have life-sustaining organs removed. To do so would cause death, and thus is murder. So would ending the patient's life in order to harvest her organs. Fearing criminal or civil liability—itself part of the larger concern of medical researchers and biomedical institutions over legal liability[3]—physicians pressed for a reconsideration of the traditional heart-lung formulation of death. Beyond these legal considerations, artificially supported patients who could be declared dead offered the desirable prospect of blood-circulating organs right up to the time of removal.

WHOLE-BRAIN DEATH DEFINITION

To deal with the challenges posed by these new developments in medicine, an Ad Hoc Committee of the Harvard Medical School was formed in the 1960s. In 1968, the Committee proposed a new formulation of death, one based on brain function.

In the traditional view, if and only if heart-lung function was permanently lost might a patient be declared dead. In contrast, the Ad Hoc Committee said the permanent loss of all functions of the whole brain was enough for declaring death. In other words, patients could be declared dead when the entire brain irreversibly ceased functioning. Such a nonfunctioning brain was interpreted as exhibiting:

1. unreceptivity and unresponsivity to applied stimuli and inner need
2. lack of movement and breathing for at least one hour while being observed continuously by physicians
3. lack of reflex action, such as blinking or eye movement

For a confirmatory test of this approach, the Committee recommended the use of an electro-encephalograph (EEG), where a flat electro-encephalogram would confirm a permanently nonfunctioning brain.

A 1981 presidential commission report titled "Defining Death" reinforced this alternative formulation of death by proposing what became the Uniform Determination of Death Act (UDDA). With the UDDA, the second legal standard of death throughout the U.S. was born: irreversible cessation of all functions of the entire brain, both cerebellum and brainstem. This is called "whole brain death" or simply "brain death." (PVS patients such as Schiavo are not considered brain dead since it is only their higher brain, not their entire brain, that has irreversibly ceased functioning.)

Currently both approaches to death—heart-lung and whole-brain—are used throughout the U.S. An individual, including one artificially supported, can be declared dead who has sustained irreversible loss of either (1) circulatory and respiratory functions, or (2) all functions of the entire brain, including the brainstem.

Although generally welcomed by transplantation units and health care facilities, the new whole-brain definition of death continues to draw fire from theorists who prefer the heart-lung approach. The debate suggests that while science can determine that the heart and lungs or the brain have permanently ceased to function, medical facts alone cannot determine if a patient in such a condition is to be determined dead. That is a value judgment inevitably shaped by philosophical, ethical, religious, legal, and public policy considerations.[4]

CHALLENGES TO THE WHOLE-BRAIN
FORMULATION

Currently there are three major challenges to the whole-brain formulation of death. They are, according to the preferred formulation of death: (1) traditional heart-lung, (2) higher-brain, or (3) brainstem. (Higher-brain and brainstem represent two additional approaches to death, making—with heart-lung and whole-brain—four in all.)

Return to the Heart-Lung Formulation

One assumption of the whole-brain definition is that when irreparable brain damage is more or less total to the whole brain, both cerebral cortex and brainstem, individuals cannot possibly return to spontaneous, respirator-free body activity. This accounts for the Ad Hoc Committee's use of the term "brain-death," that is, death according to a neurological or cortical as opposed to a cardiopulmonary criterion.

However, some traditionalists reject the committee's reliance on spontaneous respiration, a brainstem function, claiming that artificially sustained life is life nonetheless. Others consider the loss of the central nervous system, even of brain function, as irrelevant to the task of defining death. Breathing and blood flow, they point out, are not subsystems that, like the growth of hair or nails, function locally and display biochemical activity for themselves. They are, rather, activities whose function extends throughout the total system and insures the preservation of other parts. This would make circulation and respiration at least as important as brain activity—perhaps more important, since brain activity depends on them. Still others contend that a distinct line between life and death cannot be drawn.

Although such criticisms of whole-brain death have been invoked over the years to revitalize the heart-lung definition, the traditional cardiopulmonary formulation is rarely used today in the U.S. as the exclusive criterion of death. Notable exceptions are found among some orthodox Jews and fundamentalist Christians who view heart-lung as the only criterion fully respectful of God-created human life and consistent with biblical teaching. It was this view that fueled the last-ditch efforts to maintain Terri Schiavo.

Adopt a Higher-Brain Formulation

Considerations of brain state certainly have expanded the definition of death. Still, the whole-brain death formulation doesn't go far enough to suit scientists and philosophers who don't see why all functions of the entire brain have to be permanently lost before death may be declared. Why not merely the permanent loss of higher functions, such as consciousness, thought, and feeling? By this standard, a patient could be declared dead with brain functions that have no role in sponsoring consciousness, such as brainstem reflexes.

If adopted, a higher-brain criterion could make the irreversible loss of functioning in the cerebral cortex the primary physiological standard for defining death, since it is the cerebral cortex wherein lies the capacity for conscious life, commonly viewed as the hallmark of personhood. Irreversible loss of the cerebral cortex means the permanent loss of the capacity for consciousness. Significantly, this higher-brain standard can be met prior to whole-brain death, which must include death of the brainstem, that part of the brain that allows spontaneous breathing and heartbeat but not consciousness. A patient in a permanent coma, then, or one who, like Schiavo, is awake but unaware, would meet the higher-brain but not the whole-brain standard of death. By the higher-brain formulation, therefore, thousands of patients currently being maintained in the U.S. could be declared dead. In contrast, they must be considered alive by either the whole-brain or the heart-lung approaches.

Consider the case of Sunny von Bulow, whose husband, Claus, was accused of trying to kill her with an overdose of insulin in 1982. The case was the basis of the movie *Reversal of Fortune.* Sunny von Bulow is still being maintained in an irreversible coma with such brain damage that, according to experts, she will never regain consciousness. Still, she can breathe on her own. Her eyes occasionally open and she shows sleep-wake sequences. So, is she alive or dead? By one interpretation—whole-brain—she's alive. By another—higher-brain—she's dead, and has been since 1982. By the same measure, Terri Schiavo died in 1990.

Adopt a Brainstem Formulation

Another view accepts the validity of declaring death on neurological grounds but contends that a permanently non-functioning brainstem, ordinarily determined by simple, low-tech, bedside tests such as checking the pupils, is always adequate for determining death. Proponents are led to this view by the fact that consciousness as well as heart and lung function depend on a functioning brainstem. This makes the brainstem-dead dead, regardless of cardiac prognosis, because they are irreversibly unconscious and apneic.[5,6]

Its supporters claim that a brainstem formulation offers advantages over both the higher-brain and whole-brain definitions. First, spontaneously breathing vegetative patients such as Schiavo would be considered alive, thus avoiding the cultural problems of the higher-brain formulation, by which such patients would be declared dead. Second, the brainstem formulation avoids common objections to whole-brain death that some patients declared "brain dead" in fact retain neuronal life above the level of the brainstem.[7]

Heart-lung, higher-brain, and brainstem formulations, all directly challenge whole-brain death. But like whole-brain, heart-lung and brainstem formulations are biological concepts, whereas higher-brain is psycho-social. It is the higher-brain formulation, therefore, that uniquely calls into question whole-brain's fundamental conception of death itself. (See chart.)

Definition of Death	Biological (Schiavo is alive)	Psycho-Social (Schiavo is dead)
Heart-lung	x	
Whole-brain	x	
Higher-brain		x
Brainstem	x	

THE BIOLOGICAL VS. PSYCHO-SOCIAL DEBATE:
ORGANISMS VS. PERSONS

According to the heart-lung, whole-brain, or brainstem definitions, individuals are dead when they have permanently lost what is essential to them as an organism—respiration and circulation, all brain activity, or simply brainstem function. By any of these formulations, then, death is strictly an organismic or a biological concept.[8] The higher-brain definition, in contrast, associates death with the irreversible loss of what is essential to an individual as a person—for example, consciousness or cognition—not just as a biological organism. This makes death a psychological and social concept.

Is the death of a human being rightly understood only biologically, as the permanent loss of functioning of an organism as a whole? Or may it also and perhaps better be understood psychologically and socially, as, for example, the permanent loss of consciousness or the capacity for consciousness? When we say that someone is dead, precisely what are we referring to—merely a biological organism that has permanently ceased to function; or something more, perhaps an entity that has permanently lost capacities uniquely human? These abstract metaphysical questions have serious clinical and moral implications. They force us to ask about the status—alive or dead—of patients who have permanently lost all brain functions and are being maintained artificially by respirators or other life support systems. Specifically, what are we to say of the estimated 40,000 PVS patients in the U.S. currently being maintained at an annual cost of billions of dollars?[9] What is morally appropriate treatment for such patients?

Death of the Organism: A Biological Perspective

The 1981 President's Commission said that the status of such patients should not alter our understanding of death as the permanent cessation of the functioning of the organism as a whole.

The Commission pointed out, first, the loss of all brain functions permanently disrupts the integrated functioning of heart, lungs, and brain. There can be no spontaneous breathing, the heart will soon stop, and the organism as a whole will die. So, although the Commission recognized whole-brain death, it didn't depart from the traditional biological or organismic understanding of death.[10]

Second, the Commission said that the many thousands of PVS patients are alive because even though they are permanently unaware they still exhibit integrated functioning of brain, heart, and lungs. So long as there is integrated functioning of the circulatory, respiratory, and central nervous system, then, the "organism as a whole" is alive. But the Commission emphasized that these cases of "partial brain impairment" (such as Schiavo) must be distinguished from cases of "complete and irreversible loss of brain function." Specifically, it said:

> The President's Commission...regards the cessation of the vital functions of the entire brain—and not merely portions thereof, such as those responsible for the cognitive functioning—as the only proper

neurological basis for declaring death. This conclusion accords with the overwhelming consensus of medical and legal experts and the Public.

Today the consensus may not be as "overwhelming" as it was a quarter-century ago but it still stands, supported by the traditional understanding of death as the permanent cessation of the functioning of the organism as a whole. For heart-lung, whole-brain, and brainstem theorists, then, PVS patients such as Terri Schiavo are still alive since they exhibit integrated functioning of the most important organic subsystems, such as temperature regulation, spontaneous heartbeat, and normal blood pressure.

To higher-brain theorists, however, these patients are dead. They have permanently ceased to function as persons. Biologically they may be alive, but socially and psychologically, they're not.

Death of the Person: A Psycho-Social Perspective

Despite its widespread endorsement, a growing number of theorists object to the whole-brain standard—not because it goes too far in defining death, as some traditionalists claim, but because it doesn't go far enough.

Higher-brain enthusiasts say that whatever makes us uniquely human, such as consciousness and cognition, is what matters in determining human death. Without awareness, without being able to think, reason, or remember, patients such as Terri Schiavo or Sunny von Bulow can't ever function as persons. They're dead.

By this account, then, the whole-brain standard of death may adequately capture the death of non-human animals, but not a human death. Human beings are dead, say higher-brain theorists, when they are no longer persons. And that means when there is irreversible loss of higher brain functions. Without higher brain functions, there can be no integration of the mind and body and, thus, no basis for asserting that human life is present. By this standard, Schiavo was a costly tempest in a teapot, since the subject was long since dead. The same can be said of the many similar patients currently being maintained at considerable cost.

It's worth noting that not all higher-brain theorists are agreed on what it is that is essential to us as persons—what, metaphysically speaking, is necessary for a human being to be a person. This is why they sometimes employ the purposely ambiguous term "higher brain function." It's "a way to make clear that the key philosophical issue is which of the many brain functions are really important," says bioethicist Robert Veatch.[11] So, this makes the key question: What exactly is it that has lost life or ceased to be when we say that someone like you or me is dead?[12] That question starkly contrasts with the procedural one that ordinarily monopolizes cases such as Schiavo, namely: "What does the patient want and who is entitled to say?"

Although the higher-brain school of thought has attracted a considerable following, it has also attracted critics of its psycho-social, person-based perspective of death.

Problems with the Person-Based View

Philosopher David DeGrazia has identified what he calls some "irresolvable tensions" with the person-based, higher-brain concept of human death.[13]

First of all, says DeGrazia, human beings undoubtedly are organisms as well as persons, which means that biological death still applies to humans. What, then, are we to make of permanently unconscious patients? Are they dead as persons but alive as organisms? Doesn't the person-based, higher-brain view imply two deaths for a single human being: one of the person and a later of the organism? "This is somewhat odd," DeGrazia writes, "since we are accustomed to believing that there is just one death associated with every human being."

Another conceptual problem relates to the meaning of "personhood." Because philosophers are not agreed on what constitutes personhood, any higher-brain standard that relies on a concept of it will prove controversial. More troublesome, the unsettled nature of personhood has grave, practical implications, as evident in DeGrazia's most serious objection to the higher-brain standard: the "slippery slope" upon which he sees the person-perspective teetering.

DeGrazia fears that defining death as loss of personhood invites an expansion of those humans to be counted as dead, since personhood is generally thought to require more than consciousness or the capacity for consciousness. Indeed, today's bioethicists generally associate "person" with rational attributes or sentience. Whatever the character(s) of a person, presumably conscious individuals who lacked it (or them) are to be considered dead. Among these patients certainly would be ones like Schiavo, but probably also: disabled adults and children, including Parkinson's and Alzheimer's patients; the mentally ill and retarded; and the frail elderly.

The Person-Based Reply

For their part, person-based, higher-brain theorists say that critics like DeGrazia miss the point.

When we permanently lose consciousness, we lose the possibility of any meaningful existence, including any meaningful proposed candidate of personhood. We have no self-awareness, for example, or sense of personal identity—no sense of a self that persists from one moment to the next. We can't think, evaluate, or choose. We have no social existence. We can't speak, think, feel, work, or play. We can't befriend or love. "What possible meaning and value can life have under such circumstances?" person-based theorists ask. Besides, as Veatch points out, even if there are living human beings who don't satisfy the various concepts of personhood, "as long as the law is only discussing whether someone is a living individual, the debate over personhood [and personal identity] is irrelevant."[14]

Higher-brain theorists respond further that it is only from a biological or organismic perspective that an individual appears to die twice. There is, in fact, only one death, regardless of whatever biological or minor brain functions might be present. Terri Schiavo didn't die twice, she died once–not on March 25, 2005, but 15 years earlier when she incurred catastrophic brain damage. Sunny von

Bulow will not have died twice. She died back in 1982. What is being maintained in a Manhattan hospital is a breathing cadaver, albeit a fabulously wealthy one. To talk about "two deaths," then, is to beg the question, which is simply whether the higher-brain standard is preferable to the whole-brain standard. And since an uncovered whole-brain standard always reveals higher-brain functions such as self-awareness or rationality, then why not define death by reference to the higher-brain standard?

As for potential abuses, Veatch, for one, thinks that it is the whole-brain formulation of death that stands on the slippery slope, not the higher-brain. After all, he says, for no good reason whole-brain effectively draws "a sharp line between the top of the spinal cord and the base of the brain (i.e., the bottom of the brain stem)," thereby discounting the significance of any spinal reflexes. But if spinal reflexes can be ignored in determining death, then why can't some brainstem reflexes as well? Why can't the wincing and tearing of patients like Schiavo, for example? The typical reply is that brainstem reflexes are more integrative of bodily function, and, so long as the central nervous system can retain the capacity for integration, a person is alive. But Veatch doubts that brainstem reflexes are more integrative of bodily function than spinal reflexes. "Whatever principle could be used to exclude the spinal reflexes," he writes, "surely can exclude some brain stem reflexes as well."

By contrast, Veatch insists that defenders of the higher-brain formulation, like himself, in fact are avoiding the slipperiness by relying on

> classical Judeo-Christian notions that the human is essentially the integration of the mind and body and that the existence of one without the other is not sufficient to constitute a living human being. Such a principle provides a bright line that would clearly distinguish the total and irreversible loss of consciousness from serious but not total mental impairments.[15]

Other defenders of the higher-brain, person-based position have taken a less technical, more pragmatic approach to the whole-brain/higher-brain debate. One, philosopher Martin Benjamin, simply asks which conception of the human individual makes more sense? He believes there are powerful practical reasons for understanding human beings as persons, not merely as biological organisms. For one thing, such a view jibes with what really matters to us about human life and death: opportunities for acting and enjoying. Death makes all of this experience impossible; that's why it's a great loss.

Benjamin is also troubled by the fact that the whole-brain formulation effectively leaves patients who are in need of new hearts and livers waiting for the organs of PVS patients until the latter meet the UDDA. But by then their hearts and livers may no longer be suitable for transplantation. The same issue arises with the estimated 1,000 to 2,000 babies born annually in the U.S. with anencephaly, the total or near total absence of the cerebral hemisphere.[16] Anencephalic infants who aren't stillborn generally don't live longer than a few weeks. In some cases their kidneys and hearts, though undeveloped, could be transplanted to other infants who might die without them. For the transplants to have a reasonable chance of success, however, they need to be taken from these infants before they meet the criteria of whole-brain death. But even if the parents of the anencephalic infant agrees to the transplant, the law does not permit this sort of organ donation.

Beyond the matter of transplants, higher-brain theorists such as Benjamin hope that a shift from mainly a biological to a psycho-sociological conception of death may help settle an array of bioethical issues, including abortion, embryo and stem cell research, euthanasia, and assisted suicide.[17] But critics worry about the implications. Imagine a society, they suggest, where adult human non-persons— perhaps Parkinson's patients or the mentally retarded—could be used in experimental research.

LINGERING QUESTIONS ABOUT BRAIN-DEATH

Besides inviting a spirited response from higher-brain theorists, the current whole-brain formulation of death continues to be criticized for being conceptually confusing and even harmful. Adding to the critical mix are the voices of those who say that any biologically based definition fails to understand that death is not an event but a process. Such are among the concerns that today swirl around brain-death.

Definition or Permission?

The "Report of the Harvard Committee to Examine the Definition of Brain Death"—the official subtitle of the Harvard Committee's 1968 report implies— that the committee was proposing an alternative definition of death. In the eyes of its supporters and many of its detractors, it did precisely that. For them the only issue involves the relative breadth of that definition. But amidst the critics is another school of thought, one that views the report as offering not a necessary new definition of death but criteria for permitting death to occur unopposed.

The concern of the Harvard Committee, it should be remembered, was plainly physiological, specifically with (1) the irreversible loss of reflex activity mediated through the brain or spinal cord, with (2) electrical activity in the cerebral neocortex, and/or with (3) cerebral blood flow. On the basis of medical facts—such as reflex activity and cerebral blood flow—the Committee advocated whole-brain criteria for determining death. Because of its emphasis on organic integration as defining life, whole-brain enthusiasts read in the criteria a new definition of death, "brain death." On the other hand, Committee reference to consciousness, personality, or mental activity permitted others to read a higher-brain definition in the criteria. By conflating criteria and definition, the Committee set the stage for conceptual confusion.[18]

The problem is that a definition of death cannot be derived from medical facts alone, as evidenced by the whole-brain/higher-brain dispute. Each side, for example, generally agrees on the medical facts in a PVS case, but dispute the meaning of these facts—how they're best interpreted. For psycho-social reasons, higher-brain theorists believe that the medical facts determine that the patient is dead. For biological reasons whole-brain theorists believe that the patient is still alive. These opposed viewpoints leave little doubt that a definition of death is, at base, a philosophical (and legal) issue, not a medical one.

Now, if the medical facts in these cases invite interpretation, who is to say that the interpretation must necessarily favor one or the other, whole-brain or higher-brain orientations? Perhaps the facts are best interpreted strictly as criteria that do not define death but permit it to take place. If so, then what the Harvard Committee proposed, unintentionally perhaps, was not a set of conditions for determining death but for allowing it to occur. By this account, the Committee and, later the President's Commission, wasn't addressing the question of whether patients with irreversible loss of the entire brain are dead but rather how such patients should be dealt with. They were really saying—or should be viewed as saying—not that such patients are dead, but that they may be allowed to die, by turning off a respirator, for example.

The difference between definition and permission in these matters is morally important, for once patients are declared dead—as in "brain dead"—then they are no longer persons with certain moral and legal rights. They're corpses. And as corpses they can be treated, in the words of philosopher Hans Jonas, however "law or custom or the deceased's will or next of kin permit and sundry interests urge doing with a corpse." Once assured we're dealing with a corpse, for example, what's to stop us from maintaining the body in an artificially animated state as a source for life-fresh organs—as a "plant for manufacturing hormones or other biochemical compounds. . .a self-replenishing blood bank?"[19]

Jonas happens to believe that a patient with irreversible loss of the entire brain is nonetheless a patient—"'an organism as a whole minus' the brain, maintained in some partial state of life so long as the respirator and other artifices are at work." Therefore, for him the question is not "Is the patient dead?" but "How should the patient be dealt with?" This latter moral question is basically asking: "Are we justified, let alone obligated, in artificially supporting the life of a brainless body?" No, say Jonas and others like him, while whole-brain and higher-brain enthusiasts treat the question as moot, since in their views the patient is already dead.

Help or Harm?

Although Hans Jonas rejected the Harvard criteria as a definition of death, he at least viewed the criteria as establishing needed ground rules in our modern, high-tech era for withdrawing life support. Others have been less charitable.

As early as the 1970s and 1980s, some critics were calling the Harvard criteria unnecessary and harmful. One of them, physician/bioethicist Norman Fost, recently revisited the issue. He has concluded that events over the last three decades prove that the new definition has failed its main original social purposes of (1) ending medically worthless treatment and (2) improving organ supply. Fost says:

Overtreatment—the continuation of life-sustaining treatment on patients who have no reasonable prospects for meaningful survival and often no clear interest in or desire for such treatment—seems far more widespread today than in 1968, when the redefinition was proposed as the solution to that problem...[and] organ supply lags further and further behind demand.[20]

Supporting Fost's second point: Currently, of the approximately 75,000 people on waiting lists for organ transplantations, less than a third will receive the needed organ. Nationwide, an average of five people a day die awaiting liver transplants alone.[21] Compounding things, according to Fost, the statutes have made it very difficult to develop sensible, coherent policies and practices on withholding and withdrawing life support from a wide range of patients as well as to have a more rational policy of organ procurement involving a much broader population of patients than those who are "brain dead." Consider, for example, non-heart-beating cadavers (NHBCs).

Non-Heart-Beating Cadavers   Brain criteria are used in most organ procurement centers. Still, many centers will remove organs from patients declared dead by traditional heart-lung criteria.[22] This practice, done with appropriate patient consent (e.g., do not resuscitate or DNR orders), makes for a quick pronouncement of death and a rapid, damage-minimizing removal of organs from dead bodies. But in some cases, this procedure has been refined to a controversial degree.

For example, under the so-called Pittsburgh protocol, in place at the University of Pittsburgh Medical Center since 1992, a consenting life-support patient is taken to the operating room and disconnected from life support, leading usually to cardiac arrest.[23] Since the patient has executed a valid DNR order, no attempt to resuscitate him is made. After the heart stops functioning for two minutes death is declared, despite any brain functions, on the basis of "irreversible cessation of circulatory and respiratory functions."[24] The body can then be artificially supported to insure fresh organs.

Alexander Capron, a professor of law and medicine, as well as the chief theorist in the President's Commission, views the Pittsburgh protocol as a flat-out contradiction of the UDDA. He says, "The failure to attempt to restore circulatory and respiratory functions in these patients prevents lawfully declaring that death has occurred because irreversibility must mean more than simply 'we choose not to reverse, although we might have succeeded.'"[25]

Does the Pittsburgh protocol violate the sacrosanct "dead-donor-rule," the principle that prohibits the removal of vital organs from donors prior to their death? Or does it not, since NHBCs are dead according to the whole-brain definition? Currently a patient may be determined dead by one standard but alive by the other. Reason enough, according to some theorists, for single standard of death,

holding that irreversible cessation of all function of the entire brain is the death of the person and that one can know that indirectly by circulatory cessation or directly by examination of the brain and its functioning. Then the error would be obvious for those who wrongly believe that cessation of spontaneous heartbeat for 2 minutes allows them to declare the person dead and to place the body on artificially supported circulation.[26]

Event or Process?

Any biologically based definition of death views death as an event in which the biological organism permanently ceases to function. It is further assumed that a single criterion—heart-lung, entire brain, and brainstem—demarcates the moment of death.

But some bioethicists believe that it may be impossible to pinpoint a single criterion of human death because death (or dying) in our high-tech medical environment is less an event than a process that defies demarcation by a single point. At various points along the way, capacities—respiratory, hormonal, and cardiac—are compromised and must be supported. Does it make sense, then, to say that the organism died at some specific point in this process? Isn't it more reasonable to say that "the organism was fully alive before the chain of events began, is fully dead by the end of the chain of events, and is neither during the process."[27]

Still, there are important questions that demand specificity about when the organism actually died. When can life support be withdrawn, organs be harvested, or the body be cremated? In 2003, the Michigan State Court of Appeals upheld a 2001 ruling allowing a divorce for a woman comatose since a 1994 auto accident. The woman had filed for divorce several times but had not followed through. Friends said that the woman, who had a $1.5 million dollar estate, planned to file again but was prevented by the accident. After she was hospitalized, her brother and legal guardian pressed the case. In the court's eyes, obviously, the woman was alive, that is, she hadn't reached that point that marks the moment of death. Absent this assumption, how would the court possibly decide such a case?

CONCLUSIONS

Although the whole-brain definition is widely endorsed in the U.S., it isn't surprising that disagreement continues about both a single definition and criterion. With conceptual issues, death no exception, much depends on the observer.

As we will see in the chapters ahead, our understanding of death, including our attitudes and feelings towards it, reflect our basic beliefs about life itself, including our nature and destiny. On these matters people differ, even people of similar backgrounds.

Recall, again, the Schiavo case, where people of strong religious faith, even within the same religion, were divided. For some of them, Terri Schiavo's life had value and dignity regardless of her condition. She was a person, albeit a vegetative one. Since she had biological vitality, her life had sanctity. For others of equal faith, Terri Schiavo's life had passed into mere existence. For them it wasn't biological life that mattered, but its quality. True, they didn't say she was a non-person, at least not publicly, but they obviously were mostly concerned with her status as a person, as were the majority of Americans, according to polls.

As advanced medical technology increasingly blurs the distinction between living and merely existing, the person-based approach to death will continue to bedevil us. To ignore quality of life seems wildly unrealistic, even cruel and immoral. But the same might be said of labeling Grandma a "non-person" because she has Alzheimer's disease.

For its part, the prevailing whole-brain formulation of death is not conceptually coherent. The Pittsburgh protocol, for example, shows that a patient may be determined dead by one standard (brain) but alive by the other (heart-lung). No wonder bioethicists are concerned about potential violation of the dead-donor rule, as well as the cornerstone principle of medical ethics, "Do no harm," as both apply to living patients who are potential organ donors.

It is true that, aggregately, cases covered by a Pittsburgh-like protocol are rare, overwhelmingly outnumbered by deaths not requiring scientifically precise assays. Indeed, that the practice goes on at all may suggest that the whole-brain formulation has succeeded in an initial goal of the Harvard Committee: providing physicians legal protection they otherwise would lack, and without which there would be fewer transplantations. Still, prior to a brain-death statute, several states, notably Wisconsin, were quietly and successfully procuring organs from patients who were not brain dead by prevailing standards. Furthermore, it isn't by any means certain that the statute, a new definition of death, has significantly affected organ procurement.[28]

Beyond expediting transplantations and providing physicians legal protections, the new whole-brain statute supposedly was needed to facilitate discontinuation of life support. There, too, the record is uneven. Brain-dead patients sometimes have been maintained at the family's insistence. Also, in some jurisdictions the physician may declare death when the brain is dead but is not required to. This seemingly would give the physician, perhaps together with the family, the legal discretion to declare death, thereby leading not only to conflicting decisions in medically identical cases but possibly to a prolongation of suffering. Then there are cases in which cultural considerations have been ignored once the brain death has been determined. In 1994, for example, two Japanese students who had been shot were declared brain dead under California law, notwithstanding that their parents lived in Japan, where brain criteria for death pronouncement are not recognized.[29]

The failure to reach consensus about death has led some theorists to back a public policy that would implicitly acknowledge multiple, valid definitions of death. From these, patients or their legal surrogates could choose according to their own values and philosophies. New Jersey, for example, operates under a whole-brain formulation of death but permits patients for religious reasons to choose heart-lung criteria. Some say that offering a menu of options—heart-lung, whole-brain, higher-brain—would maximize personal freedom, square with the nature and ideals of a democratic and pluralistic society, and expedite organ transplants by decriminalizing cases that today are considered killing, as with PVS patients and anencephalic newborns.

Others see only confusion and controversy in such a "cafeteria" plan. They doubt that the general public would grasp, let alone embrace, the validity of multiple meanings of death. Unacceptable to the many who view death as a profoundly spiritual event would be the implicit secular notion of reducing its definition to "just another" choice. Then there are the practical matters raised by conscientious choice, including insurance coverage and impact on heath care professionals who may consider the option selected inappropriate.

Such concerns have brought some theorists to feel that, perhaps, legal and social issues are best viewed as separate and distinct points in the process of dying that allow, even require, different answers. Accordingly, they propose "decoupling" or separating such matters from a determination of death. For example, life support might be withdrawn when higher brain function is permanently lost, whereas organs might be removed when the entire brain ceases to function. Neither decision, however, applies a single criterion of death justified by some definition of death. Circumstance rules: the best use of resources, for example, in the case of withdrawing life support; the greatest number or organs appropriately harvestable, in the case of organ removal. While such a position avoids the problems of multiple definitions, it may raise another as potentially divisive: voiding the dead-donor rule. In any event, decoupling theorists strongly oppose the conscientious choice model, generally preferring the current whole-brain formulation as a default position to their own.

Defining and establishing criteria of death clearly remain problematic, inevitably inviting different approaches and defenses. Ultimately, it may be enough to accept death as "the permanent and irreversible cessation of the relevant aspects of life, where different accounts select different aspects as relevant."[30]

REFERENCES

1. *Smith v. Smith*, 229 Arkansas 579, 317 S.W., 2d 275, 1958.
2. Ned Block, Owen Flanagan, and Guven Guzeldere, eds., *The Nature of Consciousness: Philosophical Debates,* Cambridge, MA: MIT Press, 1997, p. 488.
3. Tina M. L. Stevens, *Bioethics in America: Origins and Cultural Politics,* Baltimore:Johns Hopkins Press, 2003.
4. Robert M. Veatch, "The Conscience Clause," in *The Definition of Death: Contemporary Controversies,* Stuart Youngner, Robert M. Arnold, and Renie Schapiro, eds., Baltimore: Johns Hopkins University Press, 1999, p. 140.
5. Fred Plum, "Clinical Standards and Technological Confirmatory Tests in Diagnosing Brain Death," in *The Definition of Death,* pp. 34–69.
6. Chris Pallis, "On the Brainstem Criterion of Death," in *The Definition of Death: Contemporary Controversies,* Stuart Youngner and others, eds., Baltimore: Johns Hopkins University Press, 1999, pp. 93–100.
7. Ibid., p. 95.
8. David DeGrazia, "Biology, Consciousness, and the Definition of Death," *Report from the Institute of Philosophy & Public Policy.* Retrieved March 2, 2005, from http://www.puaf.umd.edu/IPPP/winter98biology_consciousness.htm.
9. Maura Dolan, "Out of a Coma, Into a Twilight," *Los Angeles Times,* January 2, 2001, p. A1.

10. "Defining Death," *U.S. President's Commission for the Study of Ethical Problems in Medicine and Biomedical and Behavioral Research,* Washington Government Printing Office, 1981, Ch 1.

11. Veatch, "The Impending Collapse of the Whole-Brain Definition of Death," in Tom Beauchamp and Robert M. Veatch, *Ethical Issues in Death and Dying,* 2nd ed., Upper Saddle River, N.J.: Prentice Hall, 1996, p. 40.

12. Martin Benjamin, "Pragmatism and the Determination of Death," in Thomas A. Mappes and David DeGrazia, *Biomedical Ethics,* 5th ed., New York: McGraw-Hill, 2001, pp. 316–324.

13. DeGrazia.

14. Veatch, "The Impending Collapse of the Whole-Brain Definition of Death," in Tom Beauchamp and Robert M. Veatch, *Ethical Issues in Death and Dying,* 2nd ed., Upper Saddle River, N.J.: Prentice Hall, 1996, p. 41.

15. Ibid., p. 42.

16. Thomas Mappes and David DeGrazia, *Biomedical Ethics,* 5th ed., New York: McGraw-Hill, 2001, p. 692.

17. Benjamin. p. 324.

18. Martin S. Pernick, "Brain Death in a Cultural Context," in *The Definition of Death: Contemporary Controversies,* Stuart Youngner and others, eds., Baltimore: Johns Hopkins Press, 1999, pp. 3–33.

19. Hans Jonas, "Against the Stream Comments on the Definition and Redefinition of Death," in Tom Beauchamp and Robert M. Veatch, *Ethical Issues in Death and Dying,* 2nd ed., Upper Saddle River, N.J.: Prentice Hall, 1966, pp. 23–37.

20. Norman Fost, "The Unimportance of Death," in *The Definition of Death: Contemporary Controversies,* Stuart Youngner and others, eds., Baltimore: Johns Hopkins Press, 1999, pp. 161–177.

21. Hugo Martin, "Home from the War in Iraq, Marine Faces the Fight of His Life," *Los Angeles Times,* January 29, 2005, p. B6.

22. Stuart Youngner, Robert M. Arnold, and Renie Schapiro, eds., *The Definition of Death,* Baltimore: Johns Hopkins University Press, 1999, p. xiv.

23. Alexander Morgan Capron, "The Bifurcated Legal Standard for Determining Death," in *The Definition of Death: Contemporary Controversies,* Stuart Youngner and others, eds., Baltimore: Johns Hopkins Press, pp. 117–136.

24. Fost, p. 173.

25. Capron, p. 132.

26. Joanne Lynn, M.D., and Ronald Cranford, M.D., "The Persisting Perplexities in the Determination of Death," in *The Definition of Death: Contemporary Controversies,* Stuart Youngner and others, eds., Baltimore: Johns Hopkins Press, 1999, pp. 101–116.

27. Baruch A. Brody, "How Much of the Brain Must Be Dead?," in *The Definition of Death: Contemporary Controversies,* Stuart Youngner and others, eds., Baltimore: Johns Hopkins Press, 1999, p. 79.

28. Fost, p. 168.

29. Veatch, "The Conscience Clause," p. 138.

30. John Martin Fischer, ed., *The Meaning of Death,* Stanford: Stanford University Press, 1993, p. 8.

2

Death in the West

Doing research in a small Wisconsin town over 30 years ago, Michael Lessy discovered a trove of black and white photographs dating from the 1890s. Lessy assembled them in a book titled *Wisconsin Death Trip*, published in 1973 and made into a film in 1999.

A WISCONSIN DEATH TRIP

The photographs Lessy unearthed revealed a horrifying portrait of Black River Falls, a midwestern town collapsing with the U.S. economy of the day. But they revealed something else: a picture of death and dying that by today's standards is at once enviable and shocking.

On a recent National Public Radio program, Lessy described death and dying in small town America in the late nineteenth and early twentieth centuries:

> They died at home. The corpse was photographed. And often the photograph was placed in the family album in the parlor, so that when people came to visit, they would often go through the family album and use that as an occasion to talk about the passing of that person...One could choreograph the end. One could arrange to say the proper goodbyes, be given the sacraments, be surrounded by your family. You could ask to be forgiven. And they could slip away.[1]

Significantly in this depiction is where one died (*at home*), how (*surrounded by family*), and who was in charge (*the dying*).

Today, by contrast, a "Wisconsin death trip" would reveal a starkly different portrait. Dying in America now occurs mainly—75%–85% of the time—in institutions. There, death and the dying can be kept out of sight, as if it is something unnatural to be ashamed of. If we don't want to, we needn't be bothered by it. We have professionals and their machinery to tend to the tough and dirty business of dying. Even if we wish to be near our dying loved ones, medical stuff can get between us: tubes, wires, carts, machines, personnel. Of course, we'd all prefer it otherwise. Ideally, we'd like the death of the past: at home, in our own beds, surrounded by family and friends. But we're not naïve. We know that today such a death is rare. What awaits us, in all likelihood, is the death in a nursing home or other skilled-care facility after an extensive and expensive illness. We know, too, that more than once we'll likely be reminded that our dying is a drain on the resources of our family and the larger society.

At the dawn of the new millennium, we find ourselves grappling with the effects of a great change in traditional ideas and feelings about death that occurred in the twentieth century. Once tame and familiar, death has become alarmingly strange.

The story of this cultural transformation in attitude toward death is as long and complicated as the unfolding of Western civilization itself. It involves a revolution in feeling that interplays with related revolutions in ideas, politics, industry, socioeconomic conditions, and demography.[2] No one has told this compelling tale more robustly (in *The Hour of Our Death*) or more succinctly (in *Western Attitudes Toward Death*) than historiagrapher Philippe Aries (1914–1984). The powerful theme of his narrative is that the ideas and attitudes of our ancestors exist in our own time as active philosophies of death (and, thus, of life). To trace the ancestral roots of our fear of death, then, is to understand the fears and uncertainties of the present.

For his monumental study of the changing attitudes toward death in Western civilization over two millennia, Aries explored large urban cemeteries, surveyed ancient funerary practices, pored over wills and notarian records, investigated literary and archaeological sources, and studied liturgical services. These artifacts largely form the basis for the picture he draws of changes in Western attitudes toward death over the centuries.

Aries's story of death in the West, from the Middle Ages to the mid-twentieth century, unfolds in epochs, characterized according to each age's attitude toward death. Here his taxonomy has been conflated to two major periods: premodern (up to 1900) and modern (1900–1975). A third period, postmodern (1975 to present), has been added to draw attention to significant, ongoing changes in our own time, such as the institutionalized and technologized death. Our historical overview of philosophical thinking about death and dying will depart in other ways from the course Aries charts, though ever mindful of his guidance through this labyrinthine subject.

PREMODERN ATTITUDE (TO 1900):
DEATH VISIBLE AND TAMED

For a long time—nearly 2,000 years, according to Aries—death was viewed as the familiar destiny of the human race. In this sense, it was "visible." This is not to say that death engendered no fear, but rather that there were distinct ways prescribed by custom, religion, or philosophy to channel or direct the fear. In a word, death was "tamed," which it generally remained up to the twentieth century. Still, despite this consistent depiction of death, interesting and noteworthy features distinguish ages within this long stretch of time.

Early Middle Ages (500–1000): Death as Destiny

During the chaotic first half-century following the fall of the Roman Empire (taken as 476 CE), death was familiar and near. Viewed with a sentiment somewhere between passive resignation and mystical trust, death was awareness of a destiny of all life. It was something "as banal as seasonal holidays." And as with them, personal feelings found expression largely in community ritual and religious ceremony. This "household sort of death" Aries calls a "tamed" death, to contrast it with what death became in modern times: "wild," that is, frightening and unnatural.[3]

Muted in this picture, however, is the fear introduced through the doctrines of the early Christian Church, which, with the disappearance of the Roman Empire, had become the most powerful organization of the time. Embracing most Western Europeans, the Church offered to the spiritual lives of people what the feudal and manorial system offered to their political and economic lives: unity, solidarity, security.[4] In a time of pervasive unrest and unhappiness, even shame and guilt, the medieval Church gave assurance and the hope of a better life, albeit posthumously. To those who followed its doctrine and ritual, it promised eternal bliss. But to those who didn't, it threatened eternal damnation.

Central to the consolidation of the Church's power and the codification of its theology was St. Augustine (354–430). The North African bishop and student of the *Bible* and Plato was so profound a conceptualizer of Christianity that at the Reformation in the sixteenth century both Protestants and Catholics appealed his authority. It's hardly an exaggeration, then, to say that to understand Augustine is to understand how people in the West largely felt about death throughout most of the Middle Ages—why they could feel hope and joy, but also fear and anxiety.

St. Augustine   In his youth, Augustine was a Neoplatonist. At the time, Neoplatonism was a brand of philosophy associated with Plato (427–348 BCE) that emphasized the spiritual and ethical, even the mystical. Augustine was particularly drawn to the thought of the first and most original of the Neoplatonists, the Roman philosopher Plotinus (205–269). Indeed, upon reading his treatises (*Enneads*), Augustine remarked that the pagan would have had to change "only a few words" to be a Christian.[5]

Neoplatonism   Fundamental to Neoplatonism was the metaphysical belief that Ideas are the only reality; that ultimate reality is essentially spiritual and not knowable in true form.

To gain a sense of what this means, consider that abstractions such as beauty or courage can only be appreciated in their particular manifestations, as a beautiful picture, for instance, or a courageous person. So, too, with ultimate reality, which Neoplatonists variously termed Good, Pure Idea, or God. Neoplatonism taught that, although we can never know Good on earth, by living a life of contemplation and true wisdom we can approach an understanding of it and thereby prepare ourselves to enter the City of Good upon our death and there contemplate true reality.[6] This hope for life after death, even if impersonal, was tremendously consoling in very hard times.

Augustine warmed to the teachings of Neoplatonism, especially:

- an immaterial reality of which physical reality was merely a lower level
- a spiritual human nature that allowed human beings to know and relate to God, by shunning the physical world, for example
- the notion of evil as the absence of good
- the promise of salvation for a life properly lived
- the end of history as the final separation of good and evil, or what Augustine termed the City of God and the City of Satan

Upon all these Neoplatonic beliefs, Augustine staged doctrine for the early Roman Catholic Church and for Christianity, in general, in his great work, *The City of God* (413).

Christian Doctrine   Augustine, nevertheless, altered Plotinus's metaphysics to fit Christian doctrine. Two of his changes bear on death.

First, Augustine substituted a personal for an impersonal immortality. In personal immortality, the individual is thought to survive death as a discrete personality with consciousness intact. In impersonal immortality, the individual supposedly merges into an impersonal (or suprapersonal) oneness with ultimate reality. Personal immortality is associated with the major Western religions: Judaism, Christianity, and Islam. Impersonal immortality is associated with Eastern religious philosophies such as Buddhism and Hinduism.

Second, Augustine rejected Plotinus's prescription for salvation as intellectual activity and contemplation. In other words, he didn't believe that developing moral and intellectual virtues was the way to reunion with God. For Augustine the royal road to salvation passed through the Christian Church. He taught that human beings, as descendants of Adam, were afflicted with his moral disease of pride. From that inherited flaw there was only one escape: "the grace of the Savior Christ, our God and Lord." Since the infallible Christian Church was established to represent God on earth, the Scriptures and the authority of the church were the main source of all knowledge, not the material world.

In this way, then, Augustine set in place the building blocks for the great system of medieval thought called Scholasticism. Scholars generally agree with the following assessment of this schools of philosophy taught by academics at universities between approximately 1100 and 1500:

[Scholasticism] made of the world an allegory, each symbol of which could be interpreted in religious terms. It denied the value of curiosity and of any study of phenomena of the world, since the motherlode of all knowledge lay in the Scriptures. The method of acquiring new knowledge was logic, the use of word and thought rather than investigation.[7]

As for death, Scholasticism adopted Augustine's carrot-and-stick approach to explaining this greatest of all mysteries, promising reward and threatening penalty.

The Fear of Death   To be sure, the Church's theological orientation away from the miseries of the present life to the joys of the life to come lent profound reassurance to largely uncertain and unsatisfying lives. Both descriptive and prescriptive, the early Christian doctrine told people who and what they were and how they should live. It also provided answers to some of life's greatest mysteries. Thus:

- evil was the absence of good
- evil and suffering existed because of the human's misuse of free will
- God gave humans free will and with it the potential for evil in order to bring good from evil and, ultimately, to show mercy

But the most extraordinary of Augustine's explanations was death as a penalty for sin. As he writes in the *Enchiridion* (*handbook*):

> ...there is one form of punishment peculiar to man—the death of the body. God had threatened him with this punishment of death if he should sin, leaving him indeed to the freedom of his own will, but yet commanding his obedience under pain of death; and He placed him amid the happiness of Eden.(pp. 31–32)... Thence, after his sin, he was driven into exile, and by his sin the whole race of which he was the root was corrupted in him, and thereby subjected to the penalty of death...[God] judged it better to bring good out of evil, than not to permit any evil to exist. And if He had determined that in the case of men, as in the case of the fallen angels, there should be no restoration to happiness...would it not have been just...? Certainly so God would have done, had He been only just and not also merciful, and had He not designed that His unmerited mercy should shine forth the more brightly in contrast with the unworthiness of its objects.[8]

Of the greatest mystery, then, Augustine was teaching that, though death was the familiar and well-deserved destiny of all, it didn't mean annihilation or nothingness. There was life after death.

With that hope—with all eyes turned to conscious afterlife—death took on meaning and purpose as a potential portal to eternal bliss, and was thus tamed.

Still, the philosophy of living only for the hereafter had a fearsome shadow side. As Adam's offspring, Augustine taught, all humans were marred by "original sin" and stood not only "in the penalty of death" but of "damnation." To avoid such a fate, Augustine and the Church urged mortification of the flesh. This meant—and for many still means—that failing sufficiently to renounce world, flesh, and devil—that is, scrupulously to obey the will of God as mediated through Church doctrine—one could pass through the door of death to dwell in bottomless perdition. Regardless of how good people were or appeared to be, they never knew for sure what awaited them: hell or heaven. In a world where the past offered no clue to the future, what else must life have been if not "desperately hazardous, full of snares. . .irrational"?[9]

It is, then, within this larger, more fearsome context of saving one's immortal soul from eternal damnation that Aries's "death visible and tamed" must be understood in the early Middle Ages. This context also helps one appreciate the significance of the change in death attitudes that occurred in the later Middle Ages.

Later Middle Ages (1000–1400): Death of Self

Several historical developments help explain the slow but inevitable evolution of death from tame to wild. One of the most significant occurred between 1000 and 1400 when a more personal feeling about death began to emerge. Yes, everything died. But that abstraction could no longer contain the individual's awareness that it was he or she who must die. Death was universal destiny, but also specific biography.[10]

This emerging awareness of personal mortality was part of a larger shift in the manner in which people thought about their surroundings and affairs. They were basically more curious about the natural world, more drawn to the good things of life. They had a sense of self and personal freedom. This new worldliness, materialism, and individuality of the later Middle Ages helped make death less abstract and more concrete. Death was less something that happened to everyone than to oneself. It was, thus, less natural and acceptable, more unnatural and unwelcome. Of course, the religious orientation of the early Middle Ages was still formidable. At the same time, it was beginning to shift, and with that the process of secularization, whereby the realm and influence of the sacred progressively weakens, had commenced.

The many events and forces behind this embryonic secularization, which brought profound changes in beliefs about life and death, are too many but to mention. Certainly the Crusades, which introduced new ways of living, were among them. So was the rise of cities, which increased freedom and mobility and introduced a new class of profit-minded "entrepreneurs." Also playing a big part in the flowering curiosity about the world were the medieval universities. There, in Paris for example, ideas that threatened the religious, scholastic view of the world were fiercely debated.

One debate is worth noting. The "battle of the universals," as it's called, represents a shift in orientation from heaven to the world, from the theological to the scientific. Its influence on attitudes toward death can still be seen today.

Battle of the Universals   Plotinus taught that in the hierarchy of being nature is a progression through eternal exemplars to physical objects. This meant that individual particular things that we see, for example, are images or reflections of their eternal archetypes, which are known by reason. As an upshot, objects of sense perception are less real than objects of reason. A particular tree, for example, is less real than the idea-tree; a particular human being is less real than the idea-human being. Again, whereas the words "Plato," "Plotinus," and "Augustine" name particular men experienced in sense perception, the word "man," and similar general terms, name universals, which are known by reason.

The battle of universals was about whether universals were really real or not. Scholastics termed *realists* said they were, that particulars (e.g., the individual man Plato) were, indeed, less real than universals (e.g., "man"). Opposing this orthodox, religious view of the realists were the *nominalists,* who held that the idea or universal (e.g., the idea-tree or the idea-human being) was only a generalization or name created by the mind after experience with the particular objects (e.g., individual trees or human beings).

To us, such a debate must seem achingly arcane, as some of ours probably will appear to future generations. But back then nothing less than the integrity of Christian doctrines hung in the balance. Consider that the view of particulars being less real than universals meshed with a variety of orthodox teachings, including:

- the insubstantial nature of this world compared with the next (which is fixed and eternal)
- how all of us share the sin of (the universal man) Adam
- how theological truths can be known (because the knowable world is a reflection of the divine Mind)

Furthermore, if, as the nominalists claimed, the only reality lay in particular things and universals were merely names or mental constructs for them, then reality lay in the actual phenomena of the world. That, in turn, would directly challenge Church teaching by making the study of the world and the means of knowing it respectable. Augustine, remember, had subordinated knowledge of the world to Church-guided reason as the path to true reality, God. Now realists were standing that view on its head.

Ultimately, nominalism won out, but not before a "middle position" termed conceptualism had its day. Developed by Peter Abelard (1079–1142) and adopted by St. Thomas Aquinas (1225–1274), the *conceptualists* rejected both the realists' claim that universals were wholly independent objects and the nominalists' denial of that claim. Instead, they proposed a sort of compromise. They said that universals were not real in the sense of an actual thing but were real in the metaphysical sense of existing prior to particular things as Ideas in the mind of God. Thus, the reason that all individual human beings are alike or all trees are alike is that they reflect eternal patterns that exist in God's mind as Ideas. In addition, when the human mind thinks universals—that is, abstracts common properties from individual things—it shares in some way in the divine intellect.

But conceptualism had a grave implication. It was really saying that God could not have made things other than they are because He was following the eternal patterns in His mind. This amounted to claiming that the conceptualistic synthesis of theology and philosophy, faith and reason, ingeniously worked out by Aquinas and presented in his prodigious *Summa Theologica,* implied not an omnipotent but a limited God. That notion—a God whose will is limited by reason—turned William of Ockham (1285–1349), for one, away from conceptualism and back to nominalism. All things, Ockham claimed, are as they are simply because God chose to make them that way and not because they reflect Ideas in God's Mind. In the language of the debate: Universals only exist in the *human* mind.

The Separation of Faith/Religion and Reason/Philosophy   With Ockham's claim that things could be other than they are had God so willed it, the medieval view of the world as allegory embedded with religious symbolism basically was inverted. After all, correctly forming and using universals supposedly provided a window to the reality beyond. Since the world reflected the divine Mind, studying it illuminated theological truth. Now Ockham's nominalism was effectively ruling out any empirical *or* rational way to religious truth, leaving revelation as the sole source. Also, now there were essentially two kinds of truth: one accessible through philosophy or science that is a product of human reason; another received through revelation that is a matter of faith. This not only made theological and philosophical truth independent and not derivable from each other, but potentially contradictory.[11] The doctrine of personal immortality, for example, might be false philosophically speaking but true theologically.

While Ockham didn't go so far as to separate faith and reason, he nevertheless set the stage for thinking about the facts of experience in a scientific rather than religious way. This trend quickened with the recovery of all the works of Aristotle, whose emphasis on comprehensive worldly knowledge challenged Neoplatonic mysticism and further disrupted Scholasticism. Drawn to the study of the world for its finite truth, Ockham formulated the famous formula that bears his name. *Ockham's razor* states: "What can be explained on fewer principles is explained needlessly by more." (Thus, nominalism more simply accounted for universals than realism or conceptualism.) This test of economy guided the search for scientific knowledge in subsequent centuries by preferring the simpler account of natural occurrence than could be derived from earlier occult explanations of nature.[12] Regarding death, this meant that since it could be accounted for as a natural event, death didn't require a supernatural explanation. Perhaps not. But absent that explanation, how would people fit death into life, emotionally?

The Fear of Death   In the later Middle Ages, then, events inside and outside the universities were turning eyes away from the soul's destiny after death to life here and now. As study of the world became more respectable, so did fondness for what it had to offer. Though still influential, the medieval Church's depiction of human life and destiny, once taken on faith, was now being tested. Supernatural explanations for death strained to meet challenges posed by facts, reason, and a new scientific way of thinking. Forced to compete with more secular interests and material attachments, the earlier strict theological orientation away from the world toward heaven didn't seem as appealing. Neither did death as a passage to a better life. To die *might* promise salvation, but it *certainly* meant separation and severance from things.

Its supernatural moorings weakened, death made less sense. Its relationship with collective destiny enfeebled, death seemed less a wholly natural part of life than a rupture from daily living and rational society. Of this psychological shift Aries writes:

> In the mirror of his own death, each would discover the secret of his individuality. And this relationship—which Greco-Roman antiquity... had glimpsed briefly and had then lost—has from that time on never ceased to make an impression on our Western civilization. With little difficulty the man of traditional societies, the man of the first Middle Ages...became resigned to the idea that we are all mortal. Since the Early Middle Ages Western man has come to see himself in his own death. He has discovered *la mort de soi*—one's own death.[13]

So, as the relationship between death and individual biography strengthened, death slowly turned less familiar and near, more frightening and obsessive. And with that, says Aries, came a new challenge: How to channel the fear of death?

The two periods immediately following the Middle Ages offered different answers to that challenge. Thinkers of the Enlightenment generally chose to deal with the fact of one's own death rationally, whereas those of the Romantic age typically dealt with it sentimentally. Though opposed, both responses were secular, a trend that would accelerate with the approach of the modern age.

The Age of Enlightenment (1650–1750): Fear Checked by Reason

Approximately between 1650–1750, the period termed the Age of Enlightenment saw a revival of classical values, notably reason. Rediscovering the ancient Greek ideal of reason as a ruling principle of life, neoclassical thinkers scrutinized previously accepted doctrines and traditions, and confidently professed that the proper use of the mind was the secret of progress and perfection. Reason, for example, could lead to an understanding and control of physical nature, including the human body. The philosophical basis for this belief was established earlier by the French philosopher René Descartes (1596–1650), who proposed that the world and every body in it was a machine.

However, the Enlightenment's faith in reason was not limited to physical nature and the body. It extended to all the social sciences. From politics to economics to ethics, law or design was thought to operate in every area of human life. In addition, the intellect could discover it. All it had to do was follow the pattern for discovery set by the mathematician and scientist Isaac Newton (1642–1727). And that's exactly what the great intellects of the age did. Chief among them were:

- *Adam Smith and Economic Law:* The Scottish political economist and moralist Adam Smith (1723–1790) saw a "natural law" operating in economic affairs. The law of supply and demand, if permitted to operate, would structure economies to run with machine-like efficiency and precision, according to Smith's *The Wealth of Nations* (1776).

- *John Locke and Political Law:* Just as Newton envisioned a single principle holding all of the objects of the universe together, so the English philosopher John Locke (1642–1727) pictured a "law of nature" operating in political affairs. According to this political law, human beings have certain basic rights, among them: life, liberty, and property. It was this declaration of natural rights that provided a rallying cry for the revolutionary political developments in America and elsewhere in the Western world. But the scope of natural rights theory was to extend well beyond political philosophy. From it has been staged all civil rights movements, including patient rights. Ironically, one of those rights Locke opposed: the right to physician-assisted suicide.

- *Immanuel Kant and Moral Law:* Even in ethics, laws of reason supposedly operated. Thus, according to the German philosopher Immanuel Kant (1724–1804), reason without recourse to experience could discover moral certainty. In the *Foundations of the Metaphysics of Morals* (1784), which contains his ethical theory based on the good will, Kant asserted that moral laws, like the laws of physics, imply absolute necessity. Commandments like "Thou shalt not kill" or "Thou shalt not lie," if they're to have moral status, must extend to all rational creatures everywhere at all times. They must be absolute and universal. Their ground must be found in pure reason, not in experience. Reason tells us what to do—what principles of action are objectively required. Reason tells us what principles of action have the force of a "categorical imperative" or unconditional moral duty. So thinking, Kant was led to universal prohibitions of actions such as lying, stealing, murdering, and suicide. In other words, it is against the moral law of *reason* to lie, steal, murder, or take one's own life.

The Fear of Death   Corollary to the Enlightenment's faith in reason to discover immutable truth in all human affairs was the conviction that the human passions should be subject to rational control. Reason could and should control emotions.

The Dutch philosopher Baruch Spinoza (1632–1677), for example, sought to harness human emotion through mathematical reason. He even presented ethics in the form of Euclidean geometry (*Ethica,* 1677). Human actions he likened to "lines, planes, and bodies." Human behavior he understood as any other natural phenomenon, that is, by reference to causes and effects. Although conduct was determined by prior causes, Spinoza thought that human beings could still control their attitudes to determined events. This made an emotion such as fear a subjective problem that could be overcome by reason.[14]

How, then, were rational persons to face death? Simply by not expressing, acting, or dwelling on it. Rational individuals subjected the fear of death to the rule of reason and common sense. In a word, they suppressed their fear of death.

Suppression, in which one decides not to express a feeling or act on a desire,[15] is one of many mechanisms we have for trying to reduce anxiety, according to Freudian theory. But it isn't the most mature one. That distinction Freud ascribed to "sublimation," the unconscious process of channeling primitive emotional energy (e.g., energy associated with sex or aggression) to creative or social purposes.[16]

Although suppression retained potency throughout the nineteenth century,[17] it is sublimation that better captures how that period, termed Romanticism, tended to channel the fear of death.

Romanticism (l750–1850): Fear Sublimated in the Death of Others

The early successes of science in answering many of life's mysteries rolled on throughout the nineteenth century. A clearer understanding of the atom as the basic building block of matter, the evolution of life forms as the result of a struggle of species survival across vast reaches of time, intelligence as complex circuitry and the mind as an equally complex series of chemical reactions, all were conspiring to reduce the most important processes of life to simple mechanisms.

The German philosopher and economist Karl Marx (1818–1883) represented the sociological counterpart of this emerging materialistic paradigm. Marx reduced human nature to social beings. We are, he said, no more and no less than the sum total of our social relations. Like the great Enlightenment thinkers who looked for laws operating in nature and human affairs, Marx, too, believed that there were discoverable universal laws operating behind historical change. Writing with the German socialist theorist Friedrich Engels (1820–1895) in the *Communist Manifesto* (1848), Marx attempted to show why these laws are economic in nature.

As more and more the tools of science helped provide a naturalistic account of things, supernatural explanations looked increasingly obsolete. And yet, this unstoppable drift toward demystifying the world and the human's place in it did not advance without Romantic resistance.

Although an elusive term, Romanticism has been described as, fundamentally, "a state of mind or particular outlook on life, in which the human emotions and the human imagination act upon facts, either accepting them or leaving them alone, since the romanticist is interested chiefly in considering things as they would like them to be rather than as they are."[18]

While rejecting the Enlightenment belief in inherent law, order, and pattern, the Romantics still laid great stress on the individual. But they viewed the individual more a creature of *feeling* than of reason. Where the thinkers of the Enlightenment were led by reason in their pursuit of truth and knowledge, the Romantics trusted emotions and intuitions as ultimately more reliable guides. Indeed, fundamental to the Romantic manifesto was the belief that human reason had frontiers that only intuition, derived from God via Nature, could transcend.[19] Sometimes vaulting reason's limits was put into the context of religious faith. More often, though, the task of uncovering the more meaningful reality fell to the Romantic artists. Their intense expression of feeling, it was thought, was in touch with the deeper significance of life. (This explains the affection of many Romantics for Kant's notion of a deeper, unseen reality underlying the world, which itself conforms to categories of the mind, rather than the mind having to conform its categories to the world.)

Students of Romanticism typically refer to the age as "sentimental." By this, they mean that emotion was valued and expressed for its own sake, often excessively. The painting, poetry, literature, and architecture of the age certainly support this ascription. But so does the Romantic attitude toward death, which veered toward the immoderate and excessive. "Passion without limit or reason" is how Aries puts it,[20] in contrast to the Enlightenment's measured and controlled sentiment.

Scholars remind us that the Romantics thought too much of life and of the individual to practice the stoical self-restraint of the neoclassicists in the face of death. More commonly, the cruel finality of death would leave them overwhelmed by sadness and melancholy, even terror. It was not unusual, then, for the Romantic artist to "dwell upon the moment of death, upon the agony of the parting soul and body."[21] But this wasn't done out of traditional religious conviction that death was the door to eternal life. Few if any of the great Romantics, in fact, held orthodox religious belief, hewing instead toward a mysticism that equated Nature with God.[22]

The Fear of Death   Despite a distaste for both traditional religious teaching and neoclassical intellectualizing, the Romantic was anything but comfortable with the idea that death put an end to living. As scholars George Anderson and Robert Warnock remind us:

> The fears of the unknown—a basic human weakness, of the possible life after death, of the "undiscovered country," "the road that cannot be retraced," plague him and attract him at once and at the same time. His undiscovered country he peoples with supernatural beings of the most varied kinds, which give him an excellent opportunity to express his often grotesque fancy—angels and archangels, principalities and powers, trolls and demons, ghosts and spooks, fairies and monsters, demon-lovers and fays, warlocks and witches, and the Arch-Fiend himself. Crime and violence are constant romantic associates of Death. Anything, in other words, which can engender the atmosphere of terror is fuel for the romanticist's furnace.[23]

This Romantic tendency to instill death with dramatic value and symbolism enjoyed unfettered expression in the ubiquity of death. "Funeral processions, mourning clothes, the spread of cemeteries and of their surface area, visits and pilgrimages to tombs, cult of memory"—death appeared omnipresent in the nineteenth century.[24] Did this mean a newfound comfort with death? Not really. Aries sees it more as a weakening of the deeply rooted old familiarities. As he says:

> Death was no longer familiar and tame, as in traditional societies, but neither was it absolutely wild. It had become moving and beautiful like nature, like the immensity of nature, the sea or the moors. The compromise of beauty was the last obstacle invented to channel an immoderate emotion that had swept away the old barriers.[25]

Significantly, these new perceptions and the immoderate feelings they provoked were not directed strictly toward the self but its extensions, such as family members, friends, and lovers.[26] The new felt apprehension, then, was sublimated in emotion concentrated in "death of the other," in the manner of the ancient Sumerian king, grief stricken by the death of his beloved friend in *The Epic of Gilgamesh* (2750–2500 BCE).

By the end of the nineteenth century, sublimation was taking a related form: protecting the dying from the imminence of their own deaths. Thus, Ivan Ilyich, systematically protected and emotionally isolated from the truth of his fatal condition by intellectualizing family, friends, and physician. This false protection modern psychologists might term "pseudo-denial." Moralist Leo Tolstoy (1828–1910) bluntly calls it "the lie"[27] in which Ilyich is expected to participate. Tolstoy was prescient. A century later, philosopher Sissela Bok would call our attention to the choices physicians face in communicating with the gravely ill, and how often they choose to lie.[28]

On the threshold of the modern age, then, death was becoming too fearsome to acknowledge. Family, friends, physicians, all provided—were expected to provide—a "constant tranquillization about death," as much for themselves as for the dying. And even when death finally came, the public tranquility was not to be upset, its carefreeness not disturbed.[29] All were signs unmistakable that the pre-modern era was at an end. Death, for the longest time familiar and tame, was becoming invisible and wild.

THE MODERN AGE (1900–1975): DEATH INVISIBLE AND WILD

The fear and denial of death emerging at the end of the nineteenth century solidified with certain convulsive events and wrenching socio-cultural changes of the twentieth century. Some of these developments that made it difficult to accept death were:

- the loss of religious certainties and myths, leaving death disconnected from transcendent meaning and purpose
- the continued weakening of the centuries-old clerical control of dying, contributing to the further secularization of death and the loss of its spiritual significance and uniqueness
- the fading of agrarian America and the extended family, taking with them opportunities to experience aging and death as natural phenomena
- the rising affluence, with overweening attachment to material things, leading to a systematic "interdiction of death in order to preserve happiness"[30]

These and other changes—e.g., the change from an industry- to an information-oriented society, the growth of higher education, the increasing secularist population—constituted the "modernization of America," considered here to be the period in the twentieth century up to 1975. But one feature more than any other defined this modern society and distinguished it from traditional societies: the dominance of science.

With facts about the natural world its content, and controlled experiment its method, science gave rise to a view of the world opposed to the traditional or religious vision. This conceptual shift largely explains how death, for so long familiar and tamed, became invisible and wild.

Scientific vs. Traditional Worldview

A worldview (or weltanschauung) is a comprehensive conception of the world from a particular standpoint. Often unconscious but generally coherent, a worldview consists of beliefs about how the world operates. It allows us to interpret and form opinions about human nature and destiny, about self and others, about society and morality, truth and meaning. A worldview is a kind of map of reality.

Philosopher of religion Huston Smith contrasts the competing scientific and traditional worldviews as follows:

1. In the traditional, religious view spirit is fundamental and matter derivative ...The scientific world...turns spirit into tiny rivulets on a single planet in a desert approximately fifteen billion light-years across.

2. In the religious worldview human beings are the less who have derived from the more...They are creatures of their Creator, or (stated philosophically) emanations from the One that contains every perfection...Science reverses this etiology, positioning humanity as the more that has derived from the less. From a universe that was devoid of sentience at its start, life eventually emerged, and from its simplest form has advanced to the elevated stature that we human beings now enjoy. Nothing in science's universe is more intelligent than we are.

3. The traditional worldview points toward a happy ending [e.g., heaven in Western religions or Nirvana in Buddhism and Hinduism; also: the coming of the Messiah in Judaism, the Second Coming of Christ in Christianity, the coming of al-Mahdi in Islam]; the scientific worldview does not...[In the scientific worldview] death is the grim reaper of individual lives, and whether things as a whole will end in a freeze or a fry, with a bang or a whimper (or keep cranking out more insentient matter in an expanding universe) is anybody's guess....

4. Having been intentionally created by omnipotent Perfection—or...flowing as it does from that Perfection "like a fountain ever on," in Plotinus's wording— the traditional world is meaningful throughout. In the scientific worldview, meaning is only skin-deep, "skin" here signifying biological organisms on a single speck in the sidereal universe.

5. Finally, in the traditional worldview people feel at home. They belong to their world, for they are made of the same spiritually sentient stuff that the world is made of.... Nothing like this sense of belonging can be derived from the scientific worldview.[31]

Consistent with Smith's depiction of the scientific worldview was the great appeal of modernizaton: the promise of infinite progress through science and technology, embracing the conquest of disease and the indefinite extension of life. And corollary to this promise was a view of death as unnatural, an enemy to be contained and ultimately defeated.

Since World War II, and especially in the last quarter century, the United States and the world as a whole have been treated to many dramatic examples of the limitations of science and technology to control nature and minimize uncertainty. Among them are the failures: to cure cancer and AIDS, to ward off acts of terrorism, to prevent breakdowns in vital services, to banish poverty and hunger, to stop assaults on the natural environment and avoid natural disasters, such as Asia's deadly tsunami in 2004 or the U.S. Gulf Coast's Hurricane Katrina and Pakistan's earthquake in 2005. All have contributed to a growing disillusionment and cynicism toward the Enlightenment credo of infinite progress through science and technology. This doesn't mean that we've abandoned science or its method of getting at truth. We're still inclined to equate "genuine" with "scientific" knowledge. And, as Smith notes, that equation has put the realm of faith, meaning, and values on the defensive,[32] with serious implications for death and dying in the present, postmodern age.

POSTMODERN AGE (1975–PRESENT): DEATH OPEN AND AVAILABLE

As the name suggests, postmodernism expresses the pervasive view that modernity, beginning with the Enlightenment in this context, has ended and the postmodern age has begun. Precisely when the postmodern era started is a matter of disagreement, with philosophers generally preferring the early 1970s. Its date of birth is far less important than its rejection of two mainstays of modernism: faith in reason to attain truth, and confidence in the inevitability of progress. The upshot is widespread uncertainty and skepticism. This makes postmodernism a crisis of epistemology.

In the postmodern age settled convictions about knowledge, belief, and values are routinely challenged or rejected as subjective and variable. Ideologies and philosophies often are reduced to power plays and masks for political and social agendas. Religious and moral beliefs, though different and sometimes opposed, are considered equally valid. None has any more truth or meaning than given it by its believers. The recorded past is not what happened, but what someone says happened. This makes history a construction of, by, and for the "winners," usually white European males. In the postmodern age, in brief, our existence is unplugged. It's disconnected from the existential power source of enduring values and binding truths. For better or worse, such is the cultural environment in which we live today, and die.

What is death and dying generally like in the postmodern age? The short answer is: a solitary affair, as we suggested at the beginning of this chapter.

"Dying," writes nurse and social scientist Jeanne Quint Benoliel, "increasingly has become an individualized experience without the communal rituals that sustained individuals and families in years gone by."[33]

Recall, in contrast, the Lessy description that we began with. Not likely to be enacted in the modern hospital is the traditional ceremony of the dying presiding over a gathering of relatives and friends. More often, physicians, nurses, and technicians will have all the leading roles. Family and, astonishingly, the dying will comprise the support cast. Medical professionals, not Nature or God, even will determine when death comes, and how.[34,35] Medical matters will take priority, not emotional or spiritual ones. Life-prolonging goals and overly aggressive treatment often will be the dominant themes, both intended more for the family's benefit than the patient's.[36] Aries coined a term for this familiar kind of dying today: "medicalized death." Dr. Sherwin Nuland calls it "technological hubris" (in his 1984 award-winning *How We Die: Reflections on Life's Final Chapter*).

In the postmodern age, then, medicalized death is largely a technical phenomenon, "a starkly unnatural event,"[37] almost a failure of medical technology. It seems to have less to do with the dying than the living. For the living, the medicalized death succeeds as an instrument of death avoidance. It supports the illusion of ultimate victory over death by technology and if victory is not possible, it assures us a "good death." And what is the "good death" in the postmodern age?

Lessy, for one, thinks the "good death" today is probably one that is relatively painless and not too ugly, in contrast to the recent past: at home, choreographed, and personal. The cultural focus today tends to be more on how we die than on death itself. It's the dying that seems to frighten us—the suffering, the deterioration, the helplessness, the dependency. "We want control," Lessy believes, "whether it's through a morphine drip or through a combination of sedative and asphyxia. We want to be able to say now and not later, in this fashion, and not in any other fashion, certainly no pain. And, could we keep the bills down if possible?"[38] Philosopher Sissela Bok agrees, writing:

> The growing fear, if it is not of the moment of dying nor of being dead, is of all that which now precedes dying for so many: the possibility of prolonged pain, the increasing weakness, the uncertainty, the loss of powers and chance of senility, the sense of being a burden. This fear is further nourished by the loss of trust in health professionals. In part, the loss of trust results from the abuses which have been exposed—the Medicaid scandals, the old-age home profiteering, the commercial exploitation of those who seek remedies for their ailments; in part also because of the deceptive practices patients suspect, having seen how friends and relatives were kept in the dark; in part, finally, because of the sheer numbers of persons, often strangers, participating in the care of any one patient. Trust which might have gone to a doctor long known to the patient goes less easily to a team of strangers, no matter how expert or well-meaning.[39]

Sociologist Jeanne Guillemin distills the contemporary attitude toward death and dying. She says simply: "We want it never to happen, to be a non-experience, or an event that cannot threaten our dignity."[40]

And yet, we are confronting death today with surprising candor. We buy pre-need burial plots. We debate the merits and perils of euthanasia and physician-assisted suicide. We talk of the emotional "stages of dying." We execute directives for end-of-life treatment. We make formal studies of death and dying. We consult books, tapes, and services on dying, death, and bereavement. We call upon hospice to insure a death with care and comfort. In a word, we *plan* for death.

So, what should we make of this new "openness and availability" with regard to death?[41] Does it point to a new maturity, honesty, and courage? Or is it, perhaps, masking a new kind of fear?

The Fear of Death

It's not easy to interpret our rational planning for death given the speed at which attitudes change today. But Guillemin, for one, sees in the postmodern age a paradox. Fearful denial of death runs parallel with rational planning for it. She writes:

> . . .death is far from tamed; it is now newly wild and familiar. The current discussion of how to die gives evidence of terrible fears that those final circumstances are beyond one's control. In a culture that prizes individual autonomy, there is no more degrading scenario than the gradual diminution of physical and mental powers, the prolonged and painful helplessness, with mental lapses preceding and even obscuring the experience of dying. American anxiety about dying centers on how the individual can avoid dependence.[42]

So, the fear is still there, according to Guillemin; it's just different. It's the fear of dependency, the loss of control. And feeding that postmodern fear is the specter of where and how we are likely to die: in a hospital, perhaps "experiencing what it means to be 'worked on' by reams of strangers, to be coded for resuscitation (or not), to lie among others near death or already dead, to be dependent on and surrounded by wires and machines."[43]

In the postmodern age, then, death may be "invisible" for occurring out of our sight, but it is not out of our minds. Rather than easing fear and anxiety, the place where we are most likely to die, the hospital, appears to be intensifying it. If so, then in the postmodern age the discernible rational planning for the "good death" seems less a mature confrontation with individual mortality than a desperate channeling of the fear of dying into devising ways and means of controlling the fearsome circumstances of our end, and thereby securing a "dignified" death. The problem, of course, is that there's nothing dignified about dying.[44]

CONCLUSIONS

Aries's 2,000 year panoramic survey of cultural attitudes toward death in Western civilization shows a movement from the "tame and familiar" (approximately up to

1900) to the "wild and invisible" (1900–1975). A consideration of the postmodern age, approximately from 1975 to the present, suggests still another shift in attitudes that has been termed "open and available."[45]

From studies such as Aries's it's tempting to infer that we learn to fear death, more or less, according to the cues given us by our socio-cultural environment. Certainly language, art, religious and funerary rituals, and other public symbols— together with early childhood influences—not only show but shape feelings about death.

However, while acknowledging the influence of culture and childhood experience, most psychologists today probably would say that the fear of death is less the product of nurture than nature; that it is natural not acquired, and thus a fear that no one entirely escapes.

Some prominent thinkers would go further, arguing that death fear is a distinguishing feature of a human being and, curiously, that that fear, if we permit it to, humanizes us. Conversely, if we shrink from the fear of death, we shrink our responses to everything else in life. Are they right? Is death fear and anxiety inherent in human beings; and, if so, is that something we can and should control? It is to such concerns that the further pursuit of the nature of death now takes us.

REFERENCES

1. "Death & Society" (transcript), *The End of Life*, National Public Radio, January 25, 1998. Retrieved January 29, 2005, from http://www.npr.org/programs/death/980125.death.html.

2. Philippe Aries, *The Hour of Our Death*, New York: Oxford University Press, 1981, p. 609.

3. Philippe Aries, *Western Attitudes Toward Death*, Baltimore: Johns Hopkins University Press, 1974, p. 14.

4. Neal Cross, Leslie Dae Lindou, and Robert C. Lamm, *The Search for Personal Freedom*, 3rd ed., vol. one, Dubuque: Wm C. Brown Company Publishers, 1968, Ch. 14.

5. W. T. Jones, *Kant to Wittgenstein and Satrre*, New York: Harcourt, Brace & World, Inc., 1969, p. 120.

6. Cross and others, Ch. 14.

7. Ibid., p. 283.

8. Saint Augustine, *Enchiridion on Faith, Hope, and Love*, J. B. Shaw, trans., Washington: Regnery Publishing, Inc., Gateway Edition, 1996, pp. 33–34.

9. Jones, p. 120.

10. Aries, 1981, p. 609.

11. Samuel Stumpf, *Philosophy: History & Problems*, 3rd ed. New York: McGraw-Hill Book Company, 1983, p. 191.

12. Jones, p. 323.

13. Aries, 1974, pp. 52–53.

14. Benedict de Spinoza, "Treatise on the Correction of the Understanding," in *Spinoza's Ethics,* London: Everyman edition, 1910.

15. James C. Coleman and Constance L. Hammen, *Contemporary Psychology and Effective Behavior*, Glenview, IL: Scott, Foresman and Company, 1974, p. 140.

16. James McConnel, *Understanding Human Behavior*, 2nd ed., New York: Holt, Rinehart and Winston, 1977, p. 499.

17. Alan W. Friedman, "Modern Attitudes Toward Death," in *Death and the Quest for Meaning*, Stephen Strack, ed., Northvale, NJ: Jason Aronson, Inc., 1997, p. 119.

18. George Anderson and Robert Warnock, *The World in Literature*, vol. 2, bk. three, Glenview, Ill: Scott, Foresman and Company, 1976, p. 269.

19. Ibid., p. 270.

20. Aries, 1981, p. 609.

21. Anderson and Warnock, p. 271.

22. Ibid., p. 276.

23. Ibid., p. 271.

24. Aries, 1974, p. 106.

25. Aries, 1981, pp. 102–103.

26. Ibid., p. 608.

27. Leo Tolstoy, *The Death of Ivan Ilyich,* New York: Bantam Books, 1981, pp. 102–103.

28. Sissela Bok, *Lying: Moral Choice in Public and Private Life,* New York: Vintage Books, 1979, p. 234.

29. Martin Heidegger, *Being and Time*, trans. John Macquarrie and Edward Robinson, San Francisco: Harper & Row, Publishers, 1962, p. 298.

30. Aries, 1974, p. 94.

31. Huston Smith, *Why Religion Matters*, San Francisco: Harper San Francisco, 2001, pp. 34–38.

32. Ibid., p. 100.

33. Jeanne Quint Benoliel, "Death, Technology, and Gender in Postmodern American Society," in *Death and the Quest for Meaning*, Stephen Strack, ed., p. 44.

34. Benoliel, p. 40.

35. Linda Belkin, *First, Do No Harm*, New York: Simon & Schuster, 1993.

36. D. W. Moller, *On Death Without Dignity: The Human Impact of Technological Dying*, Amityville, NY: Maywood, 1990.

37. Jack McKue, "The Naturalness of Dying," *JAMA*, April 5, 1995, p. 1042.

38. "Death & Society"(transcript), *The End of Life*, National Public Radio.

39. Bok, p. 245.

40. Jeanne Guillemin, "Planning To Die," *Society*, July/August, 1992, p. 30.

41. Friedman, p. 130.

42. Guillemin, p. 31.

43. Guillemin, p. 32.

44. Paul Ramsey and Margaret A. Farley, *The Patient as Person. Second Edition: Exploration in Medical Ethics*, New Haven: Yale University Press, 2002.

45. Friedman, pp. 125–130.

3

The Consciousness of Death

I n the spring of 2004, in the midst of a major investigation into the U.S. Army's prison system at Abu Ghraib in Iraq, the world watched in horror a video that appeared on a website linked to the Islamist terrorist group, Al Qaeda.

THE BEHEADING OF NICHOLAS BERG
AND THE IMMINENCE OF DEATH

The tape showed a man, later identified as 26-year-old Pennsylvanian Nicholas Berg, sitting in an orange jumpsuit in front of five armed and hooded men. After one of the men read a statement, Berg was pushed to the floor. He was then heard screaming as his throat was cut. The grizzly deed done, one of the captors then held up Berg's severed head.

We can only wonder whether Nicholas Berg knew he was about to die. If he did, what passed through his mind? Maybe he was too scared to think. On the other hand, perhaps he had some last minute thoughts, some regrets, as a character did in a story by Fyodor Dostoyevsky (1821–1881). Also strong and healthy and about to be executed in the prime of life, the man had only five minutes to live, though to him they seemed an eternity. He set aside two minutes to take leave of his comrades, another two to think final thoughts, and one to look about him for the last time. Nothing was as dreadful as the continual thought: "What if I were not to die! What if I could go back to life—what eternity! And it would all be mine! I would turn every minute into an age; I would lose nothing. I would count every minute as it passed, I would not waste one!" The idea was so disturbing that he wished to be shot quickly.[1]

No one knows, of course, whether Nicholas Berg shared the sentiment of Dostoyevsky's condemned man. What we do know is that, like nothing else, the imminence of death can concentrate the mind. That's why Socrates urged a deathlike state in life, a widely embraced view, according to Stephen Levine. In his

A Year To Live: How To Live This Year As If It Were Your Last (1998), the counselor to the terminally ill notes that most cultures and spiritual traditions support the Socratic view that preparing for death throughout life is an act of wisdom. But not everyone concurs. Rather than rehearse the inevitability of death, a competing school of thought prefers to pay death little if any concern. Still, both traditions agree that it is important to defeat death fear and denial.

In the next chapter, we'll look at these two approaches to death, one that practices dying, the other not. Here it's important to state a shared assumption that easily can pass unexamined. Although they disagree about how to do it, both traditions assume that fear and denial of death are conquerable. In other words, whether we're to give our death much or little concern, freedom from denial, fear, and anxiety about our mortality is at least possible. Is it? Or is death apprehension always with us, as some students of human existence claim?

In this chapter, we sample the views of several such thinkers. While we focus on the suggestive thought of philosophers Soren Kierkegaard and Martin Heidegger, we'll see how others, including Ernest Becker and Otto Rank, have addressed the consciousness of death in similar ways.

We begin with a related matter: the widespread belief that the fear of death has an instinctual or natural basis, as opposed to a socio-cultural one.

THE INSTINCTUAL BASIS OF THE FEAR OF DEATH

In 1974, the year that Philippe Aries's *Western Attitudes Toward Death* was offering a brief social history of the fear of death, Ernest Becker was winning the Pulitzer Prize for *The Denial of Death,* a psycho-social examination of death fear and denial. In that work, the short-lived, cultural anthropologist assembled biological and psychoanalytical arguments for supporting the position that the fear of death is, in the main, instinctual. But beyond that, Becker recognized that this modern clinical picture of the fear of death corresponded almost exactly to Soren Kierkegaard's understanding of human nature. Indeed, Becker compared the Danish philosopher's stature in psychology to Freud's. Why this regard for Kierkegaard? We'll find out presently. But first, let's review the two categories of arguments—from biology and psychoanalysis—that Becker found compelling for treating the fear of death as instinctual.

The Argument from Biology

The argument from biology for saying that death fear is instinctual begins with the observation that, in order to survive, all animals need to be protected from both other animals and nature by fear-responses. Rather than disappearing in humans, these fear-responses were actually heightened because of human vulnerability. In the Darwinian struggle for survival, only the most fearful individuals—those most realistic about their position in nature—survived to pass on to their offspring "a realism of high survival value." The result, says Becker, was "the emergence of man as we know him: a hyper anxious animal who constantly invents reasons for anxiety, even where there are none."[2]

So viewed as a biological problem, the fear of death is basic to the instinct of self-preservation. Without it, we couldn't survive. This doesn't mean, however, that we are always conscious of this fear. We have ways to put it out of our minds in order to function normally. So, although the fear of death is ever-present on the unconscious level, we are generally unmindful of it in our conscious lives.

While Becker respected the argument from biology and evolution, he held in higher regard the argument from psychoanalysis.

The Argument from Psychoanalysis

In accounting for the universal dread of death, psychiatrist Elisabeth Kubler-Ross suggests that we keep in mind two basic psychoanalytical teachings—she calls them "fundamental facts"—that pertain to the unconscious mind. In the unconscious: (1) our own death is never possible, and (2) a wish is a deed. Both require some understanding of the unconscious mind.

The Unconscious Mind and Death   According to psychoanalytic theory, the unconscious is that vast portion of the mind—much larger than the conscious mind—that stores thoughts and feelings that we aren't directly or fully aware of, especially ones that arouse anxiety. Although we aren't aware of the content of the unconscious mind, experts think that it can affect our dreams and fantasies, even our thoughts and actions. Unlike the choice-making conscious mind, the unconscious—the mind that does not know—is not a logical or analytical faculty. It can't make temporal connections or sort out causes and effects.

Suppose that I wish that someone were dead, and a short time afterward the individual dies. Now, I know consciously that I didn't kill the person, but my unconsciousness does not. The unconscious mind does not discriminate between wish and deed. So, according to the psychoanalytic model of human nature, to my unconscious mind I killed the person I wished dead. Since I'm a cognitively mature adult, this confusion between wish and deed doesn't pose a problem since I can sort things out. But a child is different. The young, cognitively under-developed child is unable to make the wish-deed distinction. This is why a two-year-old who angrily wishes Mom or Dad dead can feel responsible for the actual death of the parent, even if the wish and death are widely separated in time.

Magical thinking—the name for this wish-deed confusion—isn't confined to childhood. The adult mind is also susceptible to this self-deception, especially in coping with the crisis of death. In her 2005 award-winning book *The Year of Magical Thinking,* Joan Didion writes achingly of the year in which her life fell apart with the sudden death of her husband, author John Gregory Dunne (1932–2004), and the grave illness of her daughter, who died in 2005 after the author completed her book. Struggling with profound grief, Didion shares many wishful episodes of feeling omnipotent. She compares them to "the way children think," as if her "thought or wishes had the power to reverse the narrative, to change the outcome."

In one scene from her chronicle, Didion is cleaning out Dunne's closet when suddenly she is frozen by the following thought:

> I couldn't give away the rest of his shoes. I stood there for a moment, then realized why: he would need shoes if he was to return. The recognition of this thought by no means eradicated the thought. I have still not tried to determine (say, by giving away the shoes) if the thought has lost its power.[3]

As most adults would, Didion comes to recognize her magical thinking as delusional. Thought, wishes, and language cannot make things the way they were.

But the magical thinking child doesn't yet understand her limitations. Consequently, when her desires are frustrated, she is apt to direct hostile and destructive feelings toward parents and other authority figures. And since no child escapes pain and frustration during the socialization process, no child escapes forming hostile death wishes toward his socializers, according to psychoanalytic theory.

The confusion of magical thinking and omnipotence, psychoanalysts believe, is the main cause of guilt and helplessness in the child. It also accounts for the fear of death, because, as Kubler-Ross says, in the unconscious "...death in itself is associated with a bad act, a frightening happening, something that in itself calls for retribution and punishment." A psychological law of talion—"an eye for an eye, a tooth for a tooth"—effectively threatens the child with punishment for malevolent feelings. "I am responsible for the death I wished; I will have to die in return."[4]

Whether or not we successfully repress the fear—that is, carefully and systematically learn to ignore the idea of our own death and absorb it in life-affirming and expanding activities—depends largely upon how we develop socially. The child who is well-loved and develops strong feelings of security and adequacy is thought capable of retaining in the unconscious something of this infantile omnipotence. This, in turn, helps her later in handling the fear and anxiety of death. In fact, it is thought that this persistent inner feeling of invulnerability, this "inner sustenance," enables the majority of people to remain relatively untroubled by the certainty of their own deaths, even when in harm's way. (An aviation psychologist during World War II, Herman Feifel found that the most successful pilots were "those who felt they could not die").[5] Emotionally deprived children, by contrast, will find it far more difficult to isolate the possibility of death from themselves. Therefore, they may have more fear and anxiety about death.

It's tempting to frame the nature-nurture debate in mutually exclusive terms, as one or the other but not both. But, perhaps, our fear of death reflects *both* instinctual (i.e., biological and psychoanalytical) *and* environmental influences (i.e., socio-cultural and early childhood experiences). And even if both together better explain than either alone does, they still do not account for all the possible influences on our fear of death. Whether nature or nurture—the inner psycho-dynamic environment or the outer social environment—we're still talking factors outside the individual's sphere of influence.

However, what about our own role in how we relate to our own death? Each of us, after all, uniquely processes not only our particular developmental experiences but also the certainty, itself, that we will die. As far as we know, we are the only animal that is aware of its mortality. We alone can grasp the concept of a future, and with it an inevitable death. At some point, if we are "normal," it dawns on us: *I will die.* What do we make of that fact? How do we process the consciousness of the certainty of our own dying?

The way we relate to our mortality is for many modern writers and thinkers the starting point for philosophical thinking about death. It is, indeed, a chief concern of existentialism, a philosophy that emerged in the twentieth century with broad appeal to many distinguished philosophers, psychologists, and writers who shared a common interest in "extreme situations," including the fear and anxiety of death.[6]

EXISTENTIAL THOUGHT AND THE FEAR OF DEATH

During World War II as a French Resistance fighter, Jean Paul Sartre formulated the basic claims of atheistic existentialism. At its core is the statement that the universe has no intrinsic meaning or purpose. According to this view and contrary to much religious teaching, the universe is neither being guided by divine intelligence nor progressing purposively. In such a universe, not only does life itself have no inherent purpose or meaning but human beings have no fixed nature or ultimate destination. This puts existentialism at odds with the traditional Western view of human beings as distinguished by some unique feature such as reason, will, or intellect, not to mention divine likeness.

Furthermore, finding ourselves in a non-purposive universe, living non-purposive lives, we are completely free to choose and act. This makes us totally responsible for our lives. The whole of our existence and conduct rests squarely on us. We alone are accountable for our nature and goals. We are thus left, in Sartre's famous words, "condemned to be free." That realization—that we have no one to blame but ourselves—is for Sartre the basis for our feelings of despair, guilt, and isolation. It also gives rise to unease and distress about death. Specifically we fear that death will come before we have lived a meaningful life. This is the existential fear of Ivan Ilyich.

But existentialists talk about another kind of fear, one that also gripped Ivan Ilyich—the fear of nonexistence. Since this stubborn fear of annihilation or nothingness does not lend itself easily to protective barriers, it is very hard to conquer.

For a penetrating, philosophical look at the fear of nonexistence, we can hardly do better than to sample the thought and writings of two philosophers that influenced Sartre—one religious, the other not—Soren Kierkegaard and Martin Heidegger.

KIERKEGAARD

Kierkegaard's contributions to our appreciation of the fear and the consciousness of death resides in his interest in the nature of being and existence (termed *ontology,* which is a branch of metaphysics). For the melancholy Dane and progenitor of modern existentialism, to understand our true nature we must see ourselves as a union of opposites.

Human Nature as a Union of Opposites

On one hand, like all animals, we are finite, which shows the biological part of our nature. On the other hand, we, uniquely, have awareness of this fact, which shows our spiritual nature and is our differentiating characteristic. For Kierkegaard, then, we are animals with self-awareness. To be human is to know we will die.

Many others have shared Kierkegaard's basic view that we are a union of opposites. The existential theologian Paul Tillich (1886–1965), for example, called it "finite freedom," whereas the theologian Reinhold Niebuhr (1892–1971) preferred "nature" and "spirit." In *The Heart of Man* the neo-Freudian Erich Fromm (1900–1980) identified the essence of a human being as contradiction of animal, on the one hand, and active intelligence, on the other. Rollo May (1909–1994) spoke of the "human dilemma" as "the capacity of man to view himself as object and as subject." In *Psychology and the Human Dilemma,* the existential psychoanalyst writes:

> It is not simply that man must learn to live with the paradox—the human being has *always* lived in this paradox or dilemma, from the time that he first became aware of the fact that *he* was the one who would die and coined a word for his own death. Illness, limitations of all sorts, and every aspect of our biological state. . .are aspects of the deterministic side of this dilemma—man is like the grass of the field, it withereth. The awareness of this, and the acting on this awareness, is the genius of man the subject.[7]

A comparable expression of human uniqueness comes from death expert Feifel:

> Throughout man's history, the idea of death has posed the eternal mystery which is the core of our religious and philosophical systems of thought. And it is quite possible that this idea is also the prototype of human anxiety. Insecurity may well be a symbol of death. Any loss may represent total loss. One of man's most distinguishing characteristics, in contrast to other species, is his capacity to grasp the concept of a future—an inevitable death. In chemistry and physics, a "fact" is always determined by events which have preceded it; in human beings, present behavior is dependent not only on the past but even more potently, perhaps, by orientations toward *future* events. When we stop to consider the matter, the notion of the uniqueness and individuality of each one of us gathers full meaning only in realizing that we are finite. And it is in this same encounter with death that each of us discovers his hunger for immortality.[8]

Then there is the eminent mythologist and writer on religion Joseph Campbell (1904–1987), who writes in his popular *Myths to Live By:*

> If a differentiating feature is to be named, separating human from animal psychology, it is surely this subordination in the human sphere of even

economics to mythology. And if one should ask why or how any such unsubstantial impulse ever should have become dominant in the ordering of physical life the answer is that in this wonderful human brain of ours has dawned a realization unknown to the other primates. It is that of the individual, conscious of himself, and aware that he, and all that he cares for, will one day die.[9]

But amidst this constellation of like thought, Otto Rank merits special attention, since his view paralleled Kierkegaard's.

Briefly, for Rank we humans are part animal: controlled, driven, and limited by biological forces and urges. However, we are also part spiritual, as shown in our rationality, ethical activity, creation of goals and meaning, and religious consciousness. In contrast to Freud, for whom narcissism was the human's motivational mainspring, Rank saw humans as driven by a need for cosmic significance—a need to transcend their finiteness and attain some kind of immortality. We have a need to feel that life matters, that we are both special *and* a part of something larger and more encompassing. Traditionally, this need to feel "heroic" was met by religion. But with the fraying of traditional religious belief in the twentieth century, the human need for transcendence became problematic. Finding a solution to the question of immortality thus loomed large for Rank. In fact, he considered it one of our most important developmental tasks, a view anticipated by Kierkegaard as "the predicament of the existing individual."

"The Predicament of the Existing Individual"

According to Kierkegaard the awareness of our own mortality is the price we pay for being a self-conscious animal, for being human. It also gives rise to what he termed "the predicament of the existing individual."

Kierkegaard says that "the predicament of the existing individual" arises from our being a "synthesis of the temporal and the eternal situated in existence."[10] In other words, we live between time and eternity. We are finite but crave to be infinite. Kierkegaard also terms this "a synthesis of the soulish and the bodily," by which he means a union of a sense of self and a body.

This sense of self—call it "spirit" or "soul"—is uniquely human. Lacking such a symbolic inner identity, other animals don't experience the anxiety or dread that we self-aware humans do. We know we will die, they don't. They're innocent, whereas we worry and fear. Dread or anxiety is the inevitable price we pay for our self-awareness. It is our existential situation. We "cannot live heedless of [our] fate, nor can [we] take sure control over that fate and triumph over it by being outside the human condition."[11] That's our predicament. We live, as it were, within the "gap" between the opposites, variously termed: nature and spirit, the finite and the free, the temporal and the eternal. Where, then, does this leave us finite, temporal beings, who aspire to be infinite and eternal? Intensely conflicted, according to Kierkegaard. The resulting anxiety and dread he terms, epigrammatically, "the dizziness of freedom."

"The Dizziness of Freedom"

Decades before Freud formalized various ways we use to ward off psychic harm and threat—so-called defense mechanisms, such as denial—Kierkegaard recognized their presence in how we relate to the ever-present dread of our own mortality.

In life, in making decisions, we can live "authentically" or "inauthentically," to use the terminology of later existentialists such as Sartre. We live authentically, according to Kierkegaard, when we face the anxiety of human existence, and allow it to propel us to greater self-awareness, growth, and responsible action; to deeper, more meaningful and moral relations with others; and ultimately to a relationship with the Infinite, the Divine, or God.

By this account, anxiety is not necessarily limiting and diminishing, but potentially liberating and enlarging. It can be the way to unlimited possibility, what Kierkegaard cryptically terms "the reality of freedom as possibility anterior to possibility."[12] Interpreting, existentialism scholar Walter Kaufmann (1921–1980) writes: "[T]he self is essentially intangible and must be understood in terms of possibilities, dread and decisions. When I behold my possibilities, I experience the dread which is 'the dizziness of freedom,' and my choice is made in fear and trembling."[13] It is this "dizziness of freedom," according to Kierkegaard, that triggers a dialectical process—a forced change through the conflict of opposing forces—that provides the ongoing, growing element that constitutes our true existence. This dialectical process whereby we reconcile the opposed elements of our nature largely governs our relationship to the world and other people. It determines whether we arrive at the experience of unity and oneness with them, or disunity and separation.

The resulting dread or anxiety from the freedom and, ironically, the *necessity* of having to choose—the "dizziness of freedom"—is basic to what being human means. But we often shrink from the dread, as when we deny the truth of our human condition—the truth that we are finite, temporal beings aspiring to be infinite and eternal. The result is neurotic anxiety or what Kierkegaard calls "shut-upness."

"Shut-upness"

Neurotic anxiety is basically being afraid without knowing why. In contrast to realistic anxiety, where the danger is known, in neurotic anxiety the danger is unknown, yet to be discovered. In the state Kierkegaard terms shut-upness, we are neurotically anxious. The undiscovered danger is our own mortality, which we are running from in terror. The faster we run, the more we deny, and the more neurotically anxious we get and inauthentically we live.

There are many ways that we are socialized to "shut-up," that is, to become neurotically anxious by denying death. Starting early in life we internalize the seemingly all-powerful, death defying qualities of our parents. We borrow from them a sense of immortality. Later we immerse ourselves in the business of life—raising families, doing jobs, developing talents, practicing religions. Outwardly worthy, these projects may, though not necessarily, anesthetize us to death by providing an ersatz immortality. They can make us feel immortal because they survive us. Some scholars say that this can happen when we strongly identify with a larger, "world historical process." In other words, we derive our sense of self-worth and significance largely from what we do. Since the project or cause outlives us, we live on through it. Also, since it is larger than any single individual, our death is nothing special, just one among others.[14]

Notice that such thinking tends to intellectualize death. It transforms one's death, which is always particular and personal, into something general and impersonal. It makes death a universal occurrence, a shared destiny, an event that befalls all forms of life. Death is that, of course. But it's also biographical. Death doesn't just happen to anyone; it happens to a particular person, to me.

Intellectualizing death appears to "tame" it, to recall Aries's term. But that's a self-delusion, and a dangerous one at that. For Kierkegaard, this self-delusion consists specifically in thinking that human existence involves objective thinking, whereas it involves subjective thinking. Unless confronted on the subjective level, death is not tamed but denied.

Once we deny death, we set ourselves up for neurotic-anxiety that can interfere with living and block us from developing our potential, including wholesome relationships. Cut off from what makes us human, we are "shut-up." For Kierkegaard, then there is a tight connection between "shut-upness" and how we think about our life and death, whether objectively or subjectively.

Objective vs. Subjective Thinking

According to philosopher Robert Solomon, objective thought is always externalized. This means that it is directed away from one's own existence toward something else. At times, this is appropriate, as in doing mathematics or science, where objective thought yields objective truth. Objective truth is truth for anyone.

But there's also subjective truth. Subjective truth is personal. It is not truth for anyone but truth for an individual. It is attainable not through objective but subjective thought. In contrast to externalized objective thought, subjective thought is internalized. It's characterized by reflective inwardness.[15] When we turn inward, according to Kierkegaard, we are reminded that we are finite and temporal and must face the prospect of our own death.

What Kierkegaard terms "shut-upness," then, is denying death by only objectively thinking about it. An example of this is when we show no more concern for our own death than for the death of others. In so doing we reduce death to something like a mathematical or scientific truth.

Consider, as an example, the intellectual denial of a patient when asked how he *feels* about having terminal cancer. Instead of expressing what he *feels,* he says what he *thinks.* "Lots of people get cancer," he points out. "I'm no different than anyone else. Everyone has to die of something." Yes, death certainly has this objective status. But it's also profoundly personal. That's what Kierkegaard is driving at and the patient is avoiding. Kierkegaard urges us to turn inward. He is saying: "Be concerned about your own death. Don't deny it by objectivizing it." For Kierkegaard facing death in subjective thought is the hallmark of the mature personality.

As another example of denying death through objective thought, recall the aforementioned world-historical living, as with the career-driven Ivan Ilyich. Although Kierkegaard never linked living for a cause, job, or project with fear of dying, others have.[16,17] The idea is that the obsessive endeavor symbolizes social immortality. At the same time, it turns our thought outward in the direction of the obsessive project. Thus, whatever the all-consuming pursuit—his legal career for Ilyich—it keeps us from thinking *subjectively* about our own biological death by conferring a sense of (social) immortality. In this way, it allows us to deny death, to run from what Becker terms: "the terror to have emerged from nothing, to have a name, consciousness of self, deep inner feelings, an excruciating inner yearning for life and self-expression—and with all this yet to die."[18]

Psychoanalyst Rank, writer Tolstoy, and philosopher Kierkegaard would agree with anthropologist Becker. All say that, confronted by the overwhelming terror of death, we strive to keep it unconscious. This includes erecting elaborate systems of "heroic projects" or "world-historical" living for transcending death. All of this "character armor" allows us to feel safe and in control, a necessary delusion, perhaps, but nonetheless a basic dishonesty about our whole situation. (Becker further believed that, driven to deny our mortality and achieve a heroic status, we collectively create surplus evil, such as warfare, ethnic cleansing, and genocide. In this view, he is hardly alone.)[19,20,21]

Relation with the Infinite

Like Socrates, both Kierkegaard and Becker endorse "death rehearsal" as an antidote to the delusion of immortality. Cultivating awareness of our death, they agree, leads to disillusionment.

For Kierkegaard practicing to die means being taught by it. Only by facing our death are we led to the faith necessary to express in existence whatever is essentially human, including the infinite and eternal, and thereby have our "anxiety transformed into joy." As he writes in his journals:

> Only by an infinite relationship to God [can] doubt be calmed, only by an infinitely free relationship to God [can] anxiety be transformed into joy. [A man] is in an infinite relationship to God when he recognizes that God is always in the right, in an infinitely free relationship to God when he recognizes that he himself is always in the wrong. In this way, therefore, doubt is checked, for the movement of doubt consists precisely in the fact that at one instance he might be in the right, at another in the wrong, to a certain degree in the right, to a certain degree in the wrong...So whenever doubt would...teach him that he suffers too much, that he is tried beyond his powers, he thereupon forgets the finite in the infinite thought that he is always in the wrong. Whenever the affliction of doubt would make him sad, he thereupon raises himself above the finite into the infinite; for the thought that he is always in the wrong is the wing whereby he soars above finitude, it is the longing wherewith he seeks God, it is the love wherein he finds God.[22]

Psychologically, then, the fear of death is for Kierkegaard the catalyst of growth. Ontologically, it is the way we actualize our essential self. And theologically, it is a means to a personal relationship with God. To understand this nexus of psychology, ontology, and theology requires a thorough study of Kierkegaard. Absent that here, let's settle on the following distillate, which we'll relate to Ivan Ilyich:

> For Kierkegaard, consciousness of death really matters. It is vital because it creates the necessary anxiety for propelling us up a hierarchy of being or consciousness itself—from the sensory and unreflective to the reflective and moral, ultimately to the religious, where selfhood and "true existence" are achieved through a relation with the infinite.

Ivan Ilyich models this process. Having lived a thoroughly self-centered and unreflective life, he becomes thoughtful and *moral* in the throes of a fatal illness. This occurs precisely when he stops thinking about himself and grieves for his child and wife. "He felt sorry for them," Tolstoy tells us, "he had to do something to keep from hurting them." This concern for the other unsettles his self-absorption. He is suddenly thinking less about himself, more about them; less in terms of "my death," more in terms of their welfare. He feels responsible for them. From this unfamiliar moral highground of empathy, care, and love, Ivan Ilyich leaps or is transported to a relation with the infinite. He discovers a spiritual place of no suffering either for him or them. Thus, in one of the story's most moving passages, Tolstoy writes of Ilyich's epiphany:

> He searched for his accustomed fear of death and could not find it. Where was death? What death? There was no fear because there was no death. Instead of death there was light. "So that's it!" he exclaimed. "What bliss!"

The face-to-face encounter with the other, it seems, allowed Ivan Ilyich to face his own death and put his life in perspective.

Crucial to this metamorphosis is the courage to engage the anxiety of death and move through it. That's Tolstoy's point, and Kierkegaard's. This means that running from death—blocking consciousness of it—is really running from oneself. It is self-alienating. Embracing the anxiety, on the other hand, triggers the dialectical process by which we ultimately attain self-realization through a faith relationship with God. For Kierkegaard this relationship is the highest level of consciousness, choice, and living for a finite and temporal being aspiring to be infinite and eternal. It is Kierkegaard's answer to Rank's question of immortality.

Fundamental to this development is a relation with others. For Kierkegaard and Tolstoy, even more so later for philosopher Emmanuel Levinas (1906–1995), this means hearing the ethical call of others and responding with love. In caring for the other, we care for ourselves. Their pain and suffering, like our own, is inherent in mortality. Facing them allows us to face our own death and become fully human.

HEIDEGGER

Kierkegaard's *Concluding Unscientific Postscript* contains, perhaps, existentialism's central statement of how human beings relate to death.[23] Heidegger's single chapter of *Being and Time*,[24] on the other hand, accounts for why existentialism is widely associated with death.[25]

Unlike Kierkegaard, the hermit-like Heidegger did not enjoy the luxury of religious faith, preferring instead, from his days as a student, Nietzsche's dictum "God is dead."[26] Nor did he feature the role of the other in helping one face one's own death, as both Kierkegaard and Tolstoy seem to have done. For Heidegger, we face death alone.

Central to understanding Heidegger on death is what this most abstruse of philosophers views as uniquely human: awareness of one's being (and, indeed, of Being itself).

Awareness of One's Being

For Heidegger, to be aware of one's being means more than awareness of the naked *fact* of one's existence. In that sense tools, objects, and other such things have a kind of being—they exist. But a human being isn't a chair or a hammer. Heidegger says that unlike such things a human being "always has to be (i.e., realize) his being as his own." This means that only human beings are aware of themselves with a future, with possibility. In this respect metaphors such as "project" or "work in progress" apply. Human beings uniquely are aware of themselves as in the process of becoming something of their own making. Success at this "project" of self-creation depends entirely on one's own choices among the possibilities one faces. And it's in the awareness of choice and possibility—and of ultimately succeeding or failing—that one becomes fully conscious of one's own being (and of being itself).

Heidegger didn't believe, however, that we are completely free in our choice making. Each of us is born to particular parents, at a particular time and place. Over these and many other life circumstances we have no influence. We are, as it were, willy-nilly "thrown into the world." In our "thrownness," this "basic perilousness of our existence," we are driven by the anxiety and dread of realizing that all our ambitious projects—including the realization of self—will end in death.

"Thrownness" and "Angst"

For Heidegger, death is the most distinctive instance of "thrownness."[27] It not only limits all possibilities, it ends them. Death means we are finite. But our finitude isn't merely biological (as a member of a species) or psychological (as an individual). It is part of our being because death is always with us. We are finite because our being is penetrated with non-being or nothingness. This mind-boggling notion can only be comprehended in the mood of anxiety that Heidegger terms "angst."

In English, we associate "angst" with deep insecurity or intense emotional strife. Kierkegaard used it to refer to the fear of failing in one's responsibilities to God. For Heidegger angst is an ever-present condition of being that reveals its finite nature. More descriptive of anxiety than was Kierkegaard, Heidegger (in *Concept of Dread*) contrasts this kind of anxiety with fear, which always has an object (e.g., the feared *storm, exam, robber*). Angst, by contrast, refers to nothing in particular, which is precisely the point. Call it what you will—nothing, negation, the "not"—non-being penetrates the core of our existence, and angst reveals this. Angst shows the "worm at the core." By disclosing the threatening temporality of the world, angst brings us haphazardly-thrown-into-the-world creatures face to face with our own finitude, with nothingness, with the fact that we are "beings-towards-death."

"Being-Towards-Death"

The "death" of Heidegger's "being-towards- (or unto) death" is not the biological termination that awaits us all at some indefinite time in the future. Rather, it is the ever-present certainty of the uncertainty of our existence. We always live with death, with the possibility of our own death. At any moment we can die. Maybe death has nothing to do with us now, but it is always with us nonetheless. And this awareness of our tenuous and tentative state of being interpenetrates our entire life experience. In other words, "It is precisely Nothingness that makes itself present and felt as the object of our dread."[28]

At the same time, death is what gives life its existential urgency. It allows us to understand our existence, to measure ourselves in the light of finite possibilities, to make choices and take responsibility for them. Only by taking death into ourselves, then, is an authentic existence possible for us. Although this may be terrifying, it is also liberating, according to Heidegger. It opens us to projects and possibilities that otherwise might be swamped by life's petty concerns.

Accepting the imminence of our death may be liberating, but it isn't easy. It is something that must be won or achieved. For Heidegger, we must *become* mortal.[29] Failing that—forgetting that death is one's own most possibility—we alienate ourselves from future possibilities and slip into the condition of "freedom-towards-death" or "resoluteness." Heidegger calls this loss of one's authentic character "fallenness," a concept similar to Kierkegaard's "shut-upness."

"Fallenness"

"Fallenness" or inauthentic existence occurs when we so lose ourselves in present activities and concerns that we block out thought of our death and anxiety. Idle chatter, juicy gossip, vain curiosity, vapid conversation, pointless activities, all function to divert and distract us from anticipating our death and, thus, from affirming ourselves. They are ways that death is denied, and therefore oneself as well.

The drift into inauthentic existence or fallenness can be subtly camouflaged in social custom. Like Ivan Ilyich I can live as I'm supposed to but not as I should. I can follow a social script instead of living my own life. For Heidegger this is precisely the human tendency: to collapse to social pressure and escape from oneself by finding refuge in what he calls the "every-day-state-of-mind."

This every-day-state-of-mind is an impersonal identity, represented linguistically by the "one." Thus, "one" does, says, or thinks this or that, never "I." In this inauthentic "public self," it is the "one" who is responsible for what happens to me since it is the "one" who has taken over all my decisions. Of course, that means there is no "one" in particular who is answerable for anything, certainly not the "I." That's the beauty of it. The "one" takes the "I" completely off the hook, especially regarding death.

The "I" doesn't have to face death because it is always "one," not "I," who dies. The "one" thereby allows the "I" to talk about death, seemingly free from anxiety, while, in fact, being anxious about it. As Heidegger puts it: "One *knows* about the certainty of death, and yet 'is' not authentically certain of one's own."[30] In this way, the public and impersonal "one" (and the "they") permits the "I" to "flee in the face of death," rather than to live in its light.

"Fleeing in the Face of Death" vs. "Living in the Light of Death"

"Fallenness" is especially evident in "fleeing in the face of death." Fleeing in the face of death, says Heidegger, means "giving new explanations for it, understanding it inauthentically, concealing it."[31] Recall our hypothetical cancer patient who objectivizes and externalizes death by treating it as something that befalls everyone in general but no one in particular. This gives him emotional cover. It allows him to retreat from death, to disown it, to delude himself. Such self-deceits always miss the fact that death in each case is mine, and therefore to conceive of it as a possibility is to conceive of it as *my* possibility.[32] Death doesn't just happen; it happens to me. "I die," not "one must die."

Opposed to living inauthentically by "fleeing in the face of death" is living authentically in "the light of death." Living in the light of death is accepting death, realistically and fully. Once we do, then death doesn't just happen to us as a random, cruel, meaningless destruction of our best laid plans.[33]

When we flee in the face of death, we treat death as an event, whereas when we live in its light, we treat death as an existential phenomenon. The distinction between death as an event and as an existential phenomenon is another important aspect of Heidegger's take on death, as well as Tolstoy's in *Ilyich*.

Death as an Event

Treating death as an event means making it an abstract, ordinary occurrence that happens to someone else, never to oneself. Psychologically, it's a convenient way to avoid confronting one's own death. Heidegger believed, again, that public language both reflects and encourages the tendency to avoid death by treating it as an event.

Consider that throughout his ordeal Ivan Ilyich's family and friends variously downplay, deny, lie about, or coldly tolerate his condition. This idle, ambiguous death talk is the language of Heidegger's inauthentic, "public self." It is the linguistic custom employed to keep death at bay by treating it as an impersonal event. As Heidegger writes:

> In the publicness with which we are with one another in our everyday manner, death is "known" as a mishap which is constantly occurring—as a "case of death." Someone or other "dies," be he neighbour or stranger. People who are no acquaintances of ours are dying: daily and hourly. "Death" is encountered as a well-known event occurring within-the-world. As such it remains in the inconspicuousness characteristic of what

is encountered in an everyday fashion. The "they" has already stowed away an interpretation for this event. It talks of it in a "fugitive" manner, either expressly or else in a way which is mostly inhibited, as if to say, "One of these days one will die too, in the end; but right now it has nothing to do with us."

In other words, in death talk expressions like "one dies" makes death something indefinite that will eventually come but is of no present threat. In this way:

The expression "one dies" spreads abroad the opinion that what gets reached, as it were by death, is the "they." In [the] public way of interpreting, it is said that "one dies" because everyone else and oneself can talk himself into saying that "in no case is it I myself", for this "one" is the "nobody."[34]

Tolstoy makes the same point more simply when he writes of Ilyich's acquaintances: "'Well, isn't that something—he's dead, but I'm not,' was what each of them thought or felt."[35]

Ilyich's friends have a false security about death. That's Heidegger's point. The public way of interpreting death as an event always creates a false certainty about it. Trite expressions such as "one dies" or "everyone dies" or "death is a natural part of life" allow us at once to admit the certainty of death intellectually and avoid facing it emotionally. But all this accomplishes, says Heidegger, is to "weaken that certainty by covering up dying still more...to alleviate [our] own thrownness into death."[36] In other words, all the death circumlocution merely feeds the temptation to cover up from oneself the inevitability of one's own death. As a result:

Dying, which is essentially mine in such a way that no one can be my representative, is perverted into an event of public occurrence, which the "they" encounters. In the way of talking which we have characterized, death is spoken of as a "case" which is constantly occurring. Death gets passed off as always something "actual"; its character as a possibility gets concealed...[37]

Ultimately, this evasive concealment of death so dominates our interactions that "...[t]he 'neighbours' often still keep talking the 'dying person' into the belief that he will escape death and soon return to the tranquillized everydayness of the world of his concerns."[38]

Such "solicitude," says Heidegger, is meant to console. It doesn't, of course. In Ilyich's case, it leaves him emotionally isolated and desperately confused. Expected to be indifferently tranquil to the fact that "one dies," Ilyich is not permitted the courage for anxiety in the face of death.[39] That's what Heidegger would say is alienating him from his distinctive potential for being and, thereby, preventing him from triumphing over death. And supporting this self-alienation is the "everyday-state-of-mind" that holds up death as an event that happens to "one"—"One" dies—as opposed to a phenomenon to be understood existentially—"I" die.

Death as an Existential Phenomenon

The Renaissance poet John Donne (1572–1631), who often wrote and preached on death and mortality, memorably says:

> Perchance he for whom this bell tolls, may be so ill, as that he knows not it tolls for him; and perchance I may think myself so much better than I am, as that they who are about me...may have caused it to toll for me...and therefore never send to know for whom the bells tolls; it tolls for thee ("Meditation XVII").

Heidegger puts the same point philosophically: "Dying is not an event; it is a phenomenon to be understood existentially...By its very essence, death is in every case mine, in so far as it 'is' at all."[40] This is basically what Ivan Ilyich is grappling with.

Up against all of his death denying objective thinking about death as an abstract event, Ilyich must now place the fact that it is he who is dying. How to reconcile the hypothetical, death-avoiding "*Everyone* must die" with the real, death facing "It is *I* who am dying"? Here's Tolstoy's account of Ilyich's dilemma:

> The syllogism he [Ivan] had learned from Kiesewetter's logic—"Caius is a man, men are mortal, therefore Caius is mortal"—had always seemed to him correct as applied to Caius, but by no means to himself. That man Caius represented man in the abstract, and so the reasoning was perfectly sound; but he was not Caius, not an abstract man; he had always been a creature quite, quite distinct from all the others...
>
> Caius really was mortal, and it was only right that he should die, but for him...Ivan Ilyich, with all his thoughts and feelings, it was something else again. And it simply was not possible that he should have to die....
>
> "If I were destined to die like Caius, I would have known it; an inner voice would have told me. But I was never aware of any such thing and I and all my friends—we knew our situation was quite different from Caius's. Yet now look what's happened! It can't be. It just can't be, and yet it is. How is it possible? How is one to understand it?"
>
> He could not understand it and tried to dismiss the thought as false, unsound, and morbid, to force it out of his mind with other thoughts that were sound and healthy. But the thought—not just the thought but, it seemed, the reality itself—kept coming back and confronting him.[41]

In this touching scene, Ivan Ilyich is struggling to absorb what is for Heidegger a great truth: The totality of our being must be understood in the light of death. Only then, by fully accepting his mortality, can Ivan Ilyich transform death and discover understanding and forgiveness. Only when "touched by the interior angel of death" can he finally cease to be Heidegger's "impersonal and social"[42] and, thus, be free to be himself.

In death, Tolstoy tells us, there was "greater beauty—above all...greater significance" expressed in Ivan Ilyich's face than in life. "His expression," Tostoy notes, "implied that what needed to be done had been done properly." At the same time, there was in the expression of the dead man "a reproach or reminder to the living." That warning concerns the critical importance of fully accepting one's own death. In Heidegger's words, Ivan Ilyich is a cautionary tale about how "one fails to recognize this when one interposes the expedient of making the dying of Others a substitute theme for the analysis of [one's own death]."[43]

CONCLUSIONS

Scholar Ronald Blythe properly describes Ivan Ilyich's death as "one of the most self-identifying deaths in all literature; his death in life, his death as transient flesh, they are still visibly exact reflections of our deathliness."[44] Blythe goes on to quote a contemporary of Heidegger, the Belgian poet and playwright Maurice Maeterlinck (1862–1949), who himself often decried the scant attention people give their own deaths:

> We deliver death into the dim hands of instinct and we grant it not one hour of our intelligence. Is it surprising that the idea of death, which should be the most perfect and most luminous, remains the flimsiest of our ideas and the only one that is backward? How should we know the one power we never look in the face? To fathom its abysses we wait until the most enfeebled, the most disordered moments of our life arrive.[45]

Certainly, this is true of Ivan Ilyich, and it's probably why Heidegger considered Tolstoy's powerful story so reflective of our own deathliness. For Heidegger, as well as Kierkegaard and many other philosophers, artists, and psychologists, refusing to face death is "the most certain way of shrinking our responses to everything else."[46]

But Heidegger, at least, is saying something more controversial and disputable: Although facing death is a precondition for a fuller understanding of life, even acceptance of our mortality does not quell death anxiety. In other words, to the question "How does each of us live in the face of our own death?" Heidegger is responding: "always with anxiety"—*always*.

Over 2,000 years ago the Greek philosopher Epicurus (341–270 BCE) offered an opposed view. As to the consciousness of death—the practical matter of living after (or while) looking into the abyss and seeing the annihilation or nothingness that awaits us—Epicurus said that we have no reason for fear or anxiety. Despite our feelings to the contrary, he assures us that death is nothing, since while we are alive, we are free of death and when death comes we won't be alive. To which Kierkegaard might reply: "So much objectivizing of death," and Heidegger, "Sheer intellectualizing as an event what can only be understood existentially." Still other philosophers would remind us that annihilation does not still death's mystery. "What, after all," they would ask, "is more unknown than nothingness?"[47]

Still, Epicurus's famous aphorism nags: "When I am, death is not; and when death is, I am not." *Is he right? Is fear and anxiety concerning death irrational? Can we rid ourselves of them? Should we, as Epicurus believed, in order to get the most out of life?* As we'll see in the next and final chapter on the nature of death, the Epicurean position poses a direct challenge to any viewpoint that insists that death anxiety is unconquerable.

REFERENCES

1. Fyodor Dostoyevsky, *The Idiot,* New York: Modern Library, 1935.
2. Ernest Becker, *The Fear of Death,* New York: First Press Perspectives, 1997, p. 17.
3. Joan Didion, *The Year of Magical Thinking,* New York: Alfred A. Knopf, 2005, p. 37.
4. Elisabeh Kubler-Ross, *On Death and Dying,* New York: Simon and Schuster, Touchstone, 1997, pp. 16–17.
5. Elaine Woo, "Herman Feifel, 87: Pioneer in Studies of Death," *Los Angeles Times,* January 24, 2003, p. B15.
6. Walter Kaufmann, "Existentialism and Death," in *The Meaning of Death,* Herbert Feifel, ed., New York: McGraw-Hill Paperback Edition, 1959, pp. 39–63.
7. Rollo May, *Psychology and the Human Dilemma,* New York: Van Nostrand Reinhold Company, 1967, p. 20.
8. Herman Feifel, *The Meaning of Death,* New York: McGraw-Hill Book Company, 1959, pp. xi–xii.
9. Joseph Campbell, *Myths To Live By,* New York: Viking, 1972, p. 22.
10. Soren Kierkegaard, *Concluding Unscientific Postscript to the Philosophical Fragments,* D.F. Swenson, trans., Princeton, NJ: Princeton University Press, 1941, p. 267.
11. ———, *The Concept of Dread,* Walter Lowrie, trans., Princeton, NJ: Princeton University Press, 1957, p. 40.
12. ———, *Concluding Unscientific Postscript,* p. 38.
13. Walter Kaufmann, *Existentialism from Dostoyevsky to Sartre,* New York: Meridian, 1989, p. 17.
14. Michael Slote, "Existentialism and the Fear of Dying," in *Language, Metaphysics, and Death,* John Donnelly, ed., New York: Fordham University Press, 1978, p. 70.
15. Robert C. Solomon, "Kierkegaard and 'Subjective Truth,'" *Philosophy Today,* Fall, 1977, pp. 202–215.
16. Slote, p. 71.
17. Ibid., pp. 72–73.
18. Becker, p. 87.
19. R. W. Firestone, "The Origins of Ethnic Strife," *Mind & Human Interaction,* vol. 7, no. 4, 1996, pp. 167–191.
20. Max Horkheimer and Theodor Adorno, *Dialectic of Enlightenment: Philosophical Fragments,* E. Jephcott, trans., Stanford, CA: Stanford University Press, 2002, p. 11.
21. James Baldwin, "Letter from a Region in my Mind," in *The Fire Next Time,* New York: Vintage, 1992.
22. Soren Kierkegaard, *The Journals of Kierkegaard,* Alexander Dru, trans., London: Collins, 1958, p. 54.
23. Slote, p. 69.
24. Martin Heidegger, *Being and Time,* John Macquarrie and Edward Robinson, trans., New York: Harper & Row, Publishers, 1962, pp. 274–311.

25. Kaufmann, "Existentialism and Death," p. 39.

26. Felix Marti-Ibanez, *Tales of Philosophy,* New York: Dell Publishing/Laurel Edition, 1969, p. 309.

27. Ninian Smart, "Philosophical Concepts of Death," in *Man's Concern with Death,* Arnold Toynbee and others, eds., New York: McGraw-Hill Book Company, 1968, pp. 25–35.

28. William Barrett, *Irrational Man: A Study in Existential Philosophy,* New York: Anchor Books, 1962, p. 226.

29. Simon Critchley, *Very Little…Almost Nothing—Death, Philosophy, Literature,* New York: Routledge, 1997, p. 68.

30. Heidegger, p. 302.

31. Heidegger, p. 298.

32. Critchley, p. 74.

33. Smart, p. 34.

34. Heidegger, p. 297.

35. Leo Tolstoy, *The Death of Ivan Ilyich,* New York: Bantam Books, 1981, p. 37.

36. Heidegger, pp. 299–300.

37. Ibid., p. 297.

38. Ibid.

39. Ibid., p. 298.

40. Ibid., p. 284.

41. Tolstoy, pp. 93–94.

42. Barrett, p. 225.

43. Heidegger, p. 284.

44. Tolstoy, p. 16.

45. Ibid., p. 16.

46. Ibid., p. 14.

47. Emmanuel Levinas, *God, Death, and Time,* trans. Bettina Bergo, Stanford, CA: Stanford University Press, 2000.

4

The Evil of Death

In Samuel Beckett's play *Waiting for Godot,* two characters pitifully sit around, idly passing time and waiting. What they're waiting for is hope, often constructed as death.

WAITING FOR GODOT

The limitations imposed by multiple strokes a constant presence, Elisabeth Kubler-Ross was quoted as saying not long before her death in 2004, "I called God every name in the book, in every language." Finally over her anger and depression, the highly regarded authority on death said that she welcomed death.[1]

If death can bring a merciful end to the pain and suffering of disease, it can also relieve the tedium and boredom of life. A handful of years before his recent death, psychiatrist and best-selling author M. Scott Peck (1936–2005) recalled once telling an audience, "We get to die," adding: "I don't know about you, but I'm getting a bit tired. Not so tired that I'm ready to call it quits, but if I thought I'd have to wade through this crap for another three or four hundred years, I would cash in my chips sooner rather than later."[2]

If the end of suffering and tedium aren't enough to recommend death, how about the certain knowledge that, even if we're not going to a better place, then at least we're not leaving much behind? The Roman emperor-philosopher Marcus Aurelius (121–180), plagued throughout his reign with constant wars, allowed the following cynicism to curl his ordinarily stoic upper lip:

> There is no man so fortunate that there shall not be by him when he is dying some who are pleased with what is going to happen. Suppose that he was a good and wise man, will there not be at last some one to say to himself, Let us at last breathe freely being relieved from this schoolmaster? It is true that he was harsh to none of us, but I perceive that he tacitly condemns us—this is what is said of a good man. But in our own case

how many other things are there for which there are many who wish to get rid of us. Thou wilt consider this then when thou art dying, and thou wilt depart more contentedly by reflecting thus: I am going away from such a life, in which even my associates in behalf of whom I have striven so much, prayed, and cared, themselves wish me to depart, hoping perchance to get some little advantage by it. Why then should a man cling to a longer stay here?[3]

Such are among the many testimonies, new and old, to the belief that death is not always a bad thing for the individual who dies. One's life circumstances may, indeed, leave one impatiently waiting for Godot.

Still, to say that death is sometimes not bad is one thing. To say that death can *never* be bad for the individual who dies is quite another. And yet many philosophers say just that.

Those who make this claim don't deny that death can occasion suffering for *others,* and so be viewed as bad for persons. They would also agree that death can be considered bad because of a possible conscious afterlife of more pain and suffering. And they'd readily admit that a long, hard dying surely can be considered bad. So what do they mean?

They are talking about death as annihilation. Death as annihilation means death as a permanent end to consciousness or an "experiential blank." If death is nothingness, the question then is: "How exactly can death itself (*nothingness*) be bad *for the individual who dies*?"[4] In philosophy, this question is sometimes termed the problem of the evil of death. It's in response to the problem of evil that many philosophers say that death can never be bad for the individual who dies. As you might expect, not everyone agrees. Modern philosophers, as we're about to see, have been especially skeptical of this viewpoint.

THE PROBLEM OF THE EVIL OF DEATH

Traditionally philosophers have furnished arguments intended to show that death is not or cannot be bad for those who die. These arguments derive from one advanced in the ancient world by Epicurus. By the same token, the opposed position—that death is or can be bad for the individual who dies—typically proceeds from an attack on the Epicurean argument.

Death as Not Bad: The Epicurean Argument

Epicurus, who taught philosophy as a way to live, apparently believed that fear was a great evil that afflicted humankind, specifically fear of the gods (superstition) and fear of death. Using what resembles modern cognitive therapy, Epicurus urged his followers to recognize their dark, negative assumptions about these twin fears, and to dispute them using logic and evidence. Getting rid of these two sources of all human misery was the ultimate goal of his considerable speculations about the universe, as recorded in *De Rerum Natura (On the Nature of Things),* a famous philosophical poem by the Roman poet Lucretius (99–55 BCE). Lucretius is credited with preserving and popularizing the thought of Epicurus and his philosophically kindred predecessor, the atomist Democritus (460–370 BCE).

Basically, Epicurus is thought to have used two assumptions—that nothing comes from nothing and that nothing exists except atoms moving in void—to support a materialistic psychology that conceived of the soul (taken as reason) as composed of atoms. This made death not a sensation but merely a natural dispersion of the particular combination of atoms that comprise a human soul. If death lacks sensation, it means the absence of pain for the one who dies, and therefore cannot be bad for him.[5] Thus, Epicurus proclaims in his famous "Letter to Menoeceus": "Death is nothing to us, for that which is dissolved is without sensation; and that which lacks sensation is nothing to us."[6] Expressed succinctly by philosopher Stephen Rosenbaum, the argument is roughly that:

> since (a) something can be bad for a person only if the person can be affected by it; (b) a person cannot be affected by something after the person ceases to be; and (c) a person's being dead occurs after the person ceases to be; therefore, a person's being dead cannot be bad for the person.[7]

A contemporary Epicurean with respect to death, Rosenbaum carefully distinguishes between what Epicurus is saying and not.

While Epicurus is saying that being dead is not bad for a person, he is not asserting that the *process* of one's dying is not bad for one. Dying, after all, often involves pain and suffering, which are presumptively bad. Nor is Epicurus asserting that the *prospect* of one's dying or death isn't bad for one, since he uses death as not being bad to argue that the prospect of one's death should not disturb one.[8] Additionally, there is nothing in the Epicurean argument that is inconsistent with the facts that a person's death can occur prematurely or that one prefers life to death.

Mindful of these clarifications, when we inspect Epicurus's argument we see that it relies for its force on two key assumptions. One is termed the experience requirement, the other the existence requirement.[9]

The Experience Requirement   The experience requirement relates to the nature of harm and the nature of death. It can be stated syllogistically as follows:

> *Regarding harm*: A harm to a human being is something that is bad for the person. But for something to be bad for a person, it must be experienced by that person.
>
> *Regarding death*: Death is annihilation or an experiential blank.
>
> *Combining harm and death*: Since something bad for a person must be experienced by that person and since death is an experiential blank, then death cannot be bad for a person.

The Existence Requirement   The existence requirement deals with the nature of personal experience, specifically with who can be the subject of harms or bad things, as well as with what it means to be dead. Argumentatively, it can be stated as follows:

Regarding subjects of misfortunes: A person can be the subject of harm (a bad thing) only if he or she exists at the time the harm (or bad thing) occurs.

Regarding being dead: When death occurs, that is, when someone is dead, there is no longer a subject to whom any harm (or bad thing) can be ascribed.

Combining subjects of misfortunes and being dead: Since a person must exist to be the subject of harm and a person who dies does not exist, death cannot be a harm (that is, a bad thing) for the one who dies.

The Epicurean position depends on the acceptance of both the experience and existence requirements to establish that death cannot be a bad thing for one who dies. Any counter arguments, therefore, must discredit these considerations by showing that a person can be harmed without ever experiencing the harm and that a person who doesn't exist can be harmed.

Death as Bad: Deprivation Theory

In 1970, philosopher Thomas Nagel published an essay titled "Death," in which he argued, against the Epicurean view, that death is bad for the one who dies, even if there is no conscious survival of death.[10] Taken as an irreversible end of life, death is an evil, Nagel said, not because being dead or nonexistent or unconscious is objectionable, but because of the desirability of what it deprives us of.

According to this so-called deprivation theory of death's badness, death deprives us of all the possibilities of continued life, or, simply, the goods of life. "If there is no limit to the amount of life that it would be good to have," Nagel writes, "then it may be that a bad end is in store for all of us." Contemporary critiques of the Epicurean viewpoint generally develop some version of deprivation theory.

Though generally friendly to Nagel's view, some philosophers still ask: "If death always limits the possibilities of *good* that one could have experienced had her life continued, aren't there possibilities of *bad* imaginable?" As Jeff McMahan points out:

Simply to point out that there is an imaginable possible future life that a person might have had if he had not died seems insufficient to show that he met with a bad end. For we can also imagine possible future lives that the person might have had which would not have been worth living, relative to which his death could be judged not to be bad, or even to be good.[11]

McMahan does believe that death can be a deprivation but only if, on balance, the life lost would have been worth living. In other words, any determination of the badness of the death depends on what's lost. What exactly has the one who dies been deprived of? To what degree did the individual desire these goods? How closely did she identify with them? Until questions like these are answered, McMahan would reserve judging whether a particular death was or was not bad for the one who died.

Although this qualified deprivation theory may be preferable to the unqual-ified version, *any* deprivation theory still must show how something can be bad for a person even though she never experiences it as unpleasant. After all, if death is an experiential blank but is nonetheless bad for the one who dies, this implies that something that isn't experienced as unpleasant can still be bad for that person. How is that possible? Surely, what we don't know can't hurt us—or can it?

How What We Don't Know *Can* Hurt Us   Some things that are bad for us we experience as unpleasant, pain for instance. But that's not the whole of it, according to deprivationists. They believe that we can be harmed without ever being aware of it. Nagel and some other philosophers—Joel Feinberg (1926–2004) among them—have adduced various scenarios to show this.

Imagine, Nagel suggests, an intelligent man reduced to the state of a contented infant as the result of a brain injury.[12] Although all of his needs can be satisfied by a custodian, most people probably would agree that this development is a severe misfortune for the man, not because a contented infant is unfortunate, but because an intelligent adult has been reduced to a state of infancy. We pity such a person, even though the person doesn't mind his condition. We feel sorry for him, acknowledging that what he once was no longer exists. Even though, like a dead person, he hasn't a clue about his condition, we're still moved by it. In brief, we call it a great misfortune for *him,* albeit one that he isn't even aware of.

Deprivationists like Nagel are pointing out that we generally ascribe fortune and misfortune, good and evil, to a person only because of the person's capacity to enjoy and suffer. This is an error, they believe. They say that we can have experiences without "ordinary spatial and temporal boundaries." We can be the subjects of good and evil in relational ways, as with the man in the example. The tragedy of an intelligent adult reduced to the state of an infant is the pitiful gap between what is and what could be (or could have been). For Nagel this shows that something can be bad for us without being positively unpleasant to us. Like the intelligent adult who has disappeared, some evils consist merely in the deprivation or absence of goods.[13] The betrayal by a friend, the loss of a repu-tation, the cheating of a spouse, some things that are bad for us may not— perhaps never—be experienced by us.

Death, say deprivationists, is just such an evil. Exactly as in the case of the intelligent adult reduced to infancy, death represents a contrast between reality and possible alternatives, including unfulfilled hopes and unrealized dreams. If the intelligent adult who is reduced to a creature for whom "happiness consists of a full stomach and a dry diaper"[14] can properly be termed the subject of a misfortune, so can one who dies. After all, if one can be harmed without ever being aware of it— such as even by less dramatic acts of loss, betrayal, deception, ridicule—then in theory being dead is no barrier to being harmed.

But even if it is plausible to be harmed without ever experiencing the harm, isn't it so because one *could* experience it? So long as one is alive, there is the possibility, even if remote, of discovering, say, the betrayal or slander, and, as a result, being made miserable. Indeed, all the examples to demonstrate how one can be harmed without ever knowing it involve *living* persons, not dead ones—even

Nagel's brain-damaged adult who, although perhaps psychologically dead, is not dead biologically.

In wondering how death can be *both* an experiential blank that occurs after one exists *and* a harm to the individual who dies, critics of deprivation theory are now asking, "Who exactly is the subject of this harm?" In other words, even if deprivationists have answered satisfactorily the "selfless unexperienced deprivation of good"[15] objection, critics aren't entirely satisfied. Never mind *what* the deprivation consists in, they say, *who* is it that is being deprived?

How the Dead Can Be Harmed   Philosopher John Martin Fischer, for one, believes that even though the examples may not decisively show how misfortune can be ascribed to the dead, they do point up how a subject can suffer something "independent of either actual *or possible* experience."[16]

To see what Fischer means, consider some real-life cases. Imagine, for instance, the adultery that goes undiscovered by the betrayed spouse. Granted, its discovery would make the betrayed spouse miserable, but is that what makes the cheating bad? Or is there something about adultery, itself, that makes the spouse unhappy when discovered? If there is, then even if undiscovered, adultery is bad for the spouse. Again, is having your reputation ruined by someone's spreading malicious lies only bad when you suffer the consequences of it? Or is your good name's besmirchment a bad thing even if you never learn of it? Similar analyses can be applied to death, as with Nagel's man reduced to infancy. Is this a misfortune only because on some level the man might know of his deplorable state, or because his state is deplorable though he never knows it?

Even if such examples don't decisively show how harm can be ascribed to a nonexistent subject, they do the next best thing, say deprivation theorists such as Fischer: They make it plausible that something can be bad for a subject even though that subject cannot possibly experience it. And that, in turn, makes it reasonable, though not necessary, to reject the existence requirement of the Epicurean argument and save the deprivation theory. Moreover, even if the existence requirement is not met, Fischer and others take heart. They believe that if such examples make it reasonable to believe that whether or not an individual experiences something as bad is irrelevant to its badness, then it is equally reasonable to think that "death (although an evil) is interestingly different from 'standard' evils or harms in that it is impossible to experience it as bad (and the existence requirement is not met)."[17]

Let's give deprivation theory its due and grant that death, though an experiential blank, is a bad thing for one who dies because of the goods the individual is deprived of. Why is it, then, that we ordinarily don't consider prenatal nonexistence, also an experiential blank, a bad thing for the same reason? Death, after all, is presumed bad for one who dies because it means less life than continued existence. On the assumption that more existence is better than less existence, can't the same be said of prenatal nonexistence? Say, for example, you were born earlier than you were but would die on the same date. Since you would have more life, you seemingly would be deprived of the goods of life by being born later. So, isn't prenatal nonexistence a deprivation in the same way that posthumous nonexistence is? And yet, we ordinarily don't view prenatal non-existence as deprivation and a bad thing. How to explain the intuitively asymmetric attitudes toward prenatal and posthumous nonexistence?

THE RATIONALITY OF DEATH

For Epicurus there wasn't, in fact, any way to rationalize the asymmetry in our attitudes toward prenatal and posthumous nonexistence. He argued by analogy that rational persons ought to be indifferent to death as they are indifferent to prenatal existence. Thus:

> . . . We felt no distress, when the Poeni [Phoenicians] from all sides came together to do battle, and all things shaken by war's troublous uproar shuddered and quaked beneath high heaven, and mortal men were in doubt which of the two people it should be to whose empire all must fall by sea and land alike. [T]hus when we shall be no more, when there shall have been a separation of body and soul, out of both of which we are each formed into a single being, to us, you may be sure, who then shall be no more, nothing whatever can happen and excite sensation, not if earth shall be mingled with sea and sea with heaven . . . [Y]ou may be sure that we have nothing to fear after death. . .he who exists not, cannot become miserable, and . . . it matters not a whit whether he has been born into life at any other time, when immortal death has taken away his mortal life.[18]

Epicurus's point, by way of Lucretius, is that rationality dictates that we take the same attitude toward posthumous nonexistence as to prenatal nonexistence. Since we don't associate the latter (prenatal) with anything bad, it doesn't make sense to associate the former (posthumous) with anything bad either. From which it follows—since presumably it is rational to fear only that which is harmful to us—that it is irrational to fear death. The Epicurean point is poignantly captured by a disconsolate Mark Twain in his memoirs, dictated in the last years of his life after the deaths of several family members:

> Annihilation has no terrors for me, because I have already tried it before I was born—a hundred million years—and I have suffered more in an hour, in this life, than I remember to have suffered in the whole hundred million years put together. There was a peace, a serenity, an absence of all sense of responsibility, an absence of worry, an absence of care, grief, perplexity; and the presence of a deep content and unbroken satisfaction in that hundred million years of holiday which I look back upon with a tender longing and with a grateful desire to resume when the opportunity comes.[19]

The Epicurean argument from prenatal nonexistence presents a hurdle for deprivation theorists, who believe that death is a bad thing for a person. If, as

Epicurus and Twain suggest, it's appropriate to take symmetric attitudes toward past and future bads that aren't experienced as bad by the person, then this puts deprivationists on the horns of a dilemma. Either (1) we need to rethink our attitudes toward prenatal existence (which means admitting it may be a bad thing); or (2) death may not be a bad thing.[20] Since deprivationists can't logically endorse 2, they attack 1.

Is It Irrational to Fear Death?

Deprivationists typically say that the Epicurean-supported principle that would logically compel us to take symmetric attitudes toward past and future bads is as false as the Epicurean experience and existence requirements. One way of demonstrating this, they believe, is, again, through imaginative examples. This time the examples involve our *consistently* asymmetric attitudes toward past and future experienced bads and goods.

Philosopher Derek Parfit obliges with a scenario that finds him awakened in a hospital bed to learn that either (1) he is the patient who has already suffered through a ten-hour operation the day before or (2) the one who will undergo a short operation later that day. He writes: "I ask the nurse to find out which is true. While she is away, it is clear to me, which I prefer to be true. If I learn that the first is true, I shall be greatly relieved."[21] Brueckner and Fischer similarly ask you to imagine being in a hospital to test a new drug that induces pleasure for an hour followed by amnesia. You awaken to learn that either you tried the drug the day before and had an hour of pleasure or will try it the next day and experience an hour of pleasure. "When [the nurse] checks on your status," they write, "it is clear that you prefer to have the pleasure tomorrow."

Such examples are intended to show deep-seated, temporal asymmetries in our attitudes toward "experienced goods" and "experienced bads." We seem to be indifferent to past goods and bads, whereas we look forward to future goods and fear future bads. While deprivation theorists don't necessarily defend the rationality of these kinds of asymmetries, they don't think it's unreasonable to hold them. Indeed, understanding our natural bias to the future, they say, helps explain our asymmetric attitudes toward prenatal and posthumous nonexistence. Brueckner and Fischer explain:

> Death is a bad insofar as it is a deprivation of the good things in life (some of which, let us suppose, are "experienced as good" by the individual). If death occurs in the future, then it is a deprivation of something to which we look forward and about which we care—*future* experienced goods. But prenatal nonexistence is a deprivation of past experienced goods, goods to which we are indifferent. Death deprives us of something we care about, whereas prenatal nonexistence deprives us of something to which we are indifferent.[22]

By this account, the fear of death may be rational.

But even if death fear is fitting or appropriate, is an individual rational by being led by this fear?

Is It Rational to Be Led by the Fear of Death?

Philosopher Jeffrie Murphy, for one, thinks not. Murphy attempts to show why by drawing a parallel between fearing death, a nonmoral problem, and moral feelings of guilt.[23]

Feeling guilt for wrongdoing is normal and natural. But a person may be rational or irrational in feeling the guilt. Rational guilt is fitting, appropriate, and useful. It often leads to apology, reparation, resolution, and character improvement. Irrational guilt, by contrast, is obsessive and unrelenting. It can dominate, incapacitate, and even destroy an individual. In a like manner, while the fear of death is rational, a person may not be rational in fearing it.

But when exactly is our fear of death *rational?* When is it fitting, appropriate, and useful; when not? Murphy thinks that only an adequate understanding of death can provide an answer to this question. This leads him to the role of projects and prudence in self-definition.

Projects and Prudence Death brings an end to "projects" or opportunities for achieving personal, professional, social, or moral goals. This is why deprivationists consider death bad for the one who dies. The projects irreversibly interrupted could be anything by means of which we define ourselves—raising a family, expressing love, advancing a cause, doing art, improving character, making amends. Whatever they might be, death puts an end to these "goods of life." Death means no more chances. So, we need to make the most of the uncertain amount of time we have. We want to make the right choices for the right reasons. Having a prudent fear of death helps us do this.

Recall once again the torment of Ivan Ilyich, the man who discarded opportunities to follow his brighter impulses and, thereby, to live a different and better life from the one he chose. If Ilyich had had a prudent fear of death, he'd likely have avoided the lapses and mistakes that haunt him on his deathbed and make his dying unbearable. Again, if Dostoyevsky's prisoner (recall from Chapter 3) had cultivated a more prudent fear of death, he might not regret having taken life for granted. And afterwards, having gained a last minute reprieve, he might have lived with a greater appreciation of life. Instead, he admits to having wasted many minutes.

Real life examples are no less instructive of a prudent fear of death.

Consider Lee Atwater (1951–1991), the Republican consultant with a notorious reputation for doing whatever it took to destroy the reputations of opponents. Shortly before his death of an inoperable brain tumor, Atwater converted to Catholicism and issued several public apologies to individuals he had attacked. In one he wrote: "My illness has taught me something about the nature of humanity, love, brotherhood, and relationships that I never understood, and probably never would have. So, from that standpoint, there is some truth and good in everything."[24] Perhaps Atwater would have come to this realization sooner had he prudently feared death earlier.

Such examples teach that a prudent fear of death is impetus to the examined life. In this sense, a prudent fear of death can be considered rational, and even desirable.

An imprudent fear of death, by contrast, blocks self-examination. It keeps us from being diligent about the kind of lives we're living. It interferes with the conception, clarification, and completion of our life-projects by fostering the illusion of having infinite time to do what we want to do. Because imprudent fear goes against self-interest, it's irrational.

In the months before his death baseball great Mickey Mantle (1931–1995) publicly confessed to many years of carousing and drinking that harmed his health, marriage, and family. Driving Mantle's reckless lifestyle was the fear that, like his father and grandfather, he too would die a young man. In a widely broadcast press conference shortly before he died, Mantle courageously said that he was no role model. Perhaps it was an *imprudent* fear of death that had kept Mickey Mantle unmindful of the life he was living.

What can be said of people whose fear of death may be imprudent and irrational? Certainly not that they are bad people. None of us can fully control our feelings about death. On the other hand, such feelings ordinarily are remediable. As Murphy reminds us: "The irrational fear of death, if it pervades the life of a person, becomes a kind of neurosis; and normally the proper response to a fearful neurotic is not blame but is rather a suggestion that he seek therapeutic help in extinguishing his fears."[25] People with imprudent, irrational fear of death need help, not blame.

It's worth emphasizing that a prudent, rational fear of death can keep one, not clinging to life, but locked into it, sometimes right up to the end. Consider the death of the American writer Henry David Thoreau (1817–1862). In the throes of a deadly illness, though one which never deadened his cheerfulness, Thoreau was offered this true-but-trite consolation that would have tickled Heidegger: "Well, Mr. Thoreau, we must all go." Whereupon the author of *Walden* reminded his well-intentioned friend: "When I was a very little boy I learned that I must die, and I set that down, so, of course, I am not disappointed now. Death is as near to you as it is to me." A few days before his death Thoreau was asked by a curious visitor, "You seem so near the brink of the dark river that I almost wonder how the opposite shore may appear to you." Thoreau responded. "One world at a time."[26]

CONCLUSIONS

In his prominent work *The Seven Storey Mountain* (1948), the monk and religious writer Thomas Merton (1915–1968) writes: "Death is someone you see very clearly with eyes in the center of your heart: eyes that see not by reacting to light, but by reacting to a kind of a chill from within the marrow of your own life."[27] For someone like Heidegger, as we saw in Chapter 3, there's no escaping that chill, no fire hot enough to drive it from the marrow of our life. Even in resolute acceptance, Heidegger finds death anxiety.

But aren't the deaths of Socrates, Thoreau, and many others powerful counter instances to this belief? Don't they leave us questioning whether, even in resolute acceptance of death, there still must be anxiety?[28]

The Epicureans and Stoics thought that we needn't remain slaves to death fear and anxiety. Writing in the sixteenth century Montaigne, similarly, called the premeditation of death "the premeditation of freedom," adding: "He who has learned to die has unlearned to be a slave."[29] And most philosophers today probably would second the sentiment of Sissela Bok: "To stick one's head in the sand hampers freedom—freedom to consider one's life as a whole, with a beginning, a duration, and an end."[30] The traditional, philosophical view, then, is that if death destroys us, the idea of death saves us. Philosophical thinking about death is fundamental to becoming human.

Still, how far to go to extinguish our fear and denial of death? Like the Epicureans and Stoics, Montaigne believed that the way to live free of death anxiety is to make death companionable. Spinoza, by contrast, while acknowledging the importance of facing the inevitability of death, shared the Enlightenment bias of not thinking about it at all. Kierkegaard, Tolstoy, and others faced down death in a face-to-face encounter with the other. In facing the other, they appear to say, we become fully human. In the view of Heidegger, by contrast, it is facing our own death that is fundamental to becoming human.

So, within the tradition that teaches that through rational understanding we can liberate ourselves from the potentially enslaving fear of death, there's disagreement about how best to desensitize ourselves to that fear. There's also disagreement about which is more basic to becoming human—facing one's own death or facing the other. But—and this is the key point—there seems no disagreement about the connection between facing death (and ultimately accepting it) and personal autonomy.

To the degree that we can approach the fact of our own mortality, and successfully integrate it into our lives, we are more or less free. The reason, it's worth repeating, is that entertaining thoughts of our mortality helps us live more consciously and thus avoid living the unexamined, counterfeit life of an Ivan Ilyich. In concentrating the mind, death helps us to live as we should, not merely as we are supposed to, so that when our time comes to die, we depart, not without regrets necessarily, but with the right ones.

REFERENCES

1. "Death: Elisabeth Kubler-Ross," *The (Ventura) Star,* April 25, 1998, p. C3.

2. M. Scott Peck, M.D., *Denial of the Soul,* New York: Harmony Books, 1997, p. 108.

3. Marcus Antoninus Aurelius, *The Meditations of Marcus Aurelius Antoninus,* bk. X, in *The Stoic and Epicurean Philosophers,* W. J. Oates, ed., New York: Random House, 1940, pp. 569–570.

4. John Martin Fischer, ed., *The Meaning of Death,* Stanford: Stanford University Press, 1993, p. 15.

5. Epicurus, "Letter to Menoeceus," Cyril Bailey, trans., in *The Stoic and Epicurean Philosophers,* pp. 30–31.

6. Ibid., pp. 30–33.

7. Stephen Rosenbaum, "Epicurus and Annihilation," in Fischer, pp. 291–304.

8. Epicurus, "Letter to Menoeceus," p. 30.

9. Fischer, p. 16.

10. Thomas Nagel, *Mortal Questions,* Cambridge: Cambridge University Press, 1979, pp. 1–10.

11. Jeff McMahan, "Death and the Value of Life," in Fischer, pp. 223–266.

12. Nagel, p. 5.

13. Ibid., p. 6.

14. Ibid., p. 7.

15. John Donnelly, ed., *Language, Metaphysics, and Death,* New York: Fordham University, 1978, p. 3.

16. Fischer, p. 21.

17. Ibid., p. 22.

18. Lucretius, *On the Nature of Things–De Rerum Natura,* H. A. J. Munro, trans., in *The Stoic and Epicurean Philosophers,* Bk. III, p. 131.

19. Mark Twain, *The Autobiography of Mark Twain,* Charles Neider, ed., New York: HarperPerennial, 1990, pp. 326–327.

20. Anthony L. Brueckner and John Martin Fischer, "Why Is Death Bad?" in Fischer, p. 227.

21. Ibid.

22. Ibid., p. 228.

23. Jeffrie G. Murphy, "Rationality and the Fear of Death," in Fischer, pp. 41–58.

24. Tom Turnipseed, "What Lee Atwater Learned And Lessons For His Protégés," *The Washington Post,* April 16, 1991, p. A19.

25. Murphy, p. 56.

26. Claudia Melnik, "Brave and 'Conscious' Deaths," *The Natural Death Handbook,* 1993 ed., Ch. 2. Retrieved May 20, 2005, from http//www.globalideasbank.org/natdeath/ndh2.html.

27. Thomas Merton, *The Seven Storey Mountain,* New York: Harcourt Brace & Company/A. Harvest Book, 1998, p. 107.

28. Walter Kaufmann, "Existentialism and Death," in *The Meaning of Death,* Herman Feifel, ed., McGraw-Hill Paperback Edition, 1959, p. 50.

29. Michele de Montaigne, "That To Philosophize Is To Learn To Die," in *The Essays of Montaigne,* E. J. Trechmann, trans., London: Oxford University Press, 1927, p. 81.

30. Sissela Bok, *Lying: Moral Choice in Public and Private Life,* New York: Vintage Books, 1979, p. 243.

PART II

Survival of Death

Introduction: *A Death in the Family*

In his autobiographical novel *A Death in the Family* (Pulitzer Prize, 1957), James Agee (1909–1955) poetically portrays the impact of a man's shattering death on his wife and family.

In an early scene—the family huddled at home trying to absorb the news that Jay Follet has just been killed in an auto accident—Mary, Jay's wife, feels the presence of her husband in the house. When she senses it move to the children's room, she follows it and feels its presence throughout the room "as if she has opened a furnace door." Overcome, the devoutly religious woman falls to her knees and whispers to her husband, who did not share her faith:

> "Jay. My dear. My dear one. You're all right now, darling. You're not troubled any more, are you, my darling? Not any more. Not ever any more, dearest. I can feel how it is with you. I know, my dearest. It's terrible to go. You don't want to. Of *course* you don't. But you've got to. And you know they're going to be all right. Everything is going to be all right, my darling. God take you. God keep you, my own beloved. God make His light to shine upon you."[1]

But even these tender words, Mary senses, can't hold her husband, and his presence begins to fade. And then "he was gone entirely from the room, from the house, and from this world."

As children of the Enlightenment, many of us might say that Mary Follet was exhibiting shock, a familiar response to a sudden crisis. Numbed by the news of her husband's tragic death, Mary could only begin to deal with it by reinventing his essence.[2] What she senses as her husband's presence, science whispers, is actually a

83

projection of her own grief riven mind as it shudders to say goodbye. And, to ice our case, we could point to outstanding textual examples throughout Agee's poignant tale of psychiatrist Kubler-Ross's well-known, five-stage model of emotional response to death: denial, anger, bargaining, depression, and acceptance.[3]

But such a glib analysis likely would elicit disdain from countless millions of people who, like Mary, believe that death is not the end of life; that what we *really* are, our spiritual essence, survives death; that there awaits us an afterlife; and that the world to come will be a good place with a loving God. Mary and Jay will be reunited.

Such is the view, evidently, of most Americans. According to a 1998 international religion survey, we are among the least likely to harbor any doubts about life after death. A more recent study, conducted in 2003 by Barna Research Group, shows an overwhelming majority of us believe that heaven (76%) and hell (71%) exist.[4] To such "true believers" a strictly psychological account of Mary's experience not only explains the phenomenon but explains away any possible supernatural basis for it. Mary's profoundly spiritual experience, in short, is reduced to run-of-the-mill religious denial.

"Survival of Death," Part Two of philosophical thinking about death and dying, takes up three issues suggested by the experience of Mary Follet and by popular belief. The first, to be considered in Chapter 5, deals with the traditional view that human beings are essentially spiritual and that the spiritual part, often termed the "soul," survives death and may even be immortal. While survivalist belief crosses cultures and spans generations, views about the nature of postmortem life vary widely. As we'll see, in Chapter 6, the Christian depiction of afterlife espoused by Mary and most Americans is only one of many survival hypotheses. Are some more credible than others? Are there compelling reasons to believe in *any* of them, or are they all the appendices of our primitive past? That we will discuss in Chapter 7.

REFERENCES

1. James Agee, *A Death in the Family,* New York: Bantam Books, 1969, pp. 181–182.
2. Mary Jane Moffat, *In the Midst of Winter,* New York: Vinage Books, 1992, p. 212.
3. Elisabeth Kubler-Ross, *On Death and Dying,* New York: Simon and Schuster, Touchstone Edition, 1997.
4. Connie K. Kang, "Next Stop, the Pearly Gates," *Los Angeles Times,* October 24, 2003, p. A18.

5

The Self and Its Relation to Death

The terminally ill patient recognizes Becker's paradox that humans are aware of finitude yet have a sense of transcendence." It is this paradox, writes gerontologist Kenneth Doka in *Death and Spirituality,* that underlies several spiritual needs of dying persons. Among these are "transcendental" needs. "We seek assurance," says Doka "that our life, or what we have left, will continue."[1]

There are a number of ways we find assurance of ongoing life after death. One of the oldest and most enduring, of course, is through our progeny. However, we can also live on in the esteem and gratitude of future generations for our works and accomplishments. And then there are those of us who reconcile ourselves to death through the ongoing life of a larger group of which our life was a significant part, such as a service or a professional organization.

Beyond these worldly versions of defeating death—apart from the ordinary symbolic, creative, and social assurances of ongoing life—many of us look forward to a postmortem transition to another form of being or consciousness. We're like Mary Follet: We believe in personal survival of bodily death. This belief implies that we are more than our physical, material bodies; that there is within each of us something immaterial or spiritual. Call it what you will—"soul," "mind," "inner self"—it is this essential spiritual entity that can survive the death of the body. For the great many, it is this belief—that they will survive death as individual personalities, and even attain immortality—that constitutes the great reassurance of life beyond the grave.

Central to this optimistic belief in personal postmortem survival, the view that humans have a dual nature appears in the teachings of the world's major religions and has been espoused by some of the most distinguished Western philosophers. In the modern age, this view has been generally criticized as a mischaracterization of human nature.

If it is that, then the philosophical basis for posthumous survival is fatally flawed. Reason enough, then, to launch this second part of philosophical thinking about death and dying with an examination of the dualistic view of human nature.

DUALISTIC VIEW OF HUMAN NATURE

The view that a human is composed of two kinds of things—the material body and the immaterial soul or mind—is a fundamental teaching of Judaism, Christianity, and Islam. But it can also be found in Hinduism. Even Buddhism, which does not distinguish between body and soul the same way Western religions generally do, accepts the belief that the essence of a person is reborn into a new body after death.

In Western philosophy, the most famous exponents of the dualistic view of human nature were Plato and Descartes. Both held the radical view that a human being is, essentially, a mind.

Plato

It is to Pythagoras, the sixth century BCE philosopher/mathematician, that we must first turn to find the inspiration of Plato's conception of the soul.

Pythagoras conceived of the soul as not only immortal but also eternal. In other words, not only is the soul imperishable, it exists before it comes to be embodied and will continue to exist forever after its final disembodiment. Pythagoras also subscribed to the doctrine of transmigration of the soul, or reincarnation. According to this doctrine, which appeared simultaneously in Greek life and in India, the immortal but fallen soul passes through a cycle of births, its various guises determined by the kind of life of its previous existence.[2] In its various incarnations the soul undergoes a process of atonement and purification. If successful, it returns to its divine origins. If not, the cycle of birth and death continues until the soul achieves liberation. Pythagoras believed that interference with this process, by suicide for example, violates divine law.[3]

In its time, the Pythagorean was a small minority view, as was the Epicurean belief that the soul, at death, is annihilated. Far more popular was the belief that each soul comes into existence with the body whose death it survives.[4] Still, despite its limited appeal, the Pythagorean notion of an immortal and imprisoned soul significantly influenced the ideas of possibly the greatest philosopher of all time, Plato.

The Soul's Existence

Plato is considered the first philosopher who attempted to prove the existence of *psyche* (Greek for soul), with connotations akin to "mind" or "inner self." Plato's argument for the existence of a soul, mind, or inner self derives from his distinction between two realms. One is the world of imperfect, changing physical objects that we experience with our senses; the other is a world of perfect, unchanging ideas that we know with our minds. Earlier, in Chapter 2, we saw this metaphysical view in the thought of the Neoplatonist Plotinus and St. Augustine. Here we are relating it to the existence of the soul and belief in immortality.

Pre-Existence: A Pre-Life as Necessitated by Knowledge of Forms   In his great monument to death, titled *Phaedo,* Plato has Socrates explain the soul's existence with examples from geometry. In geometry, the mind can discover unchanging truths about ideally *perfect* lines, squares, circles, and other figures without ever having seen such figures. How can this be? Plato's explanation is that the mind must contain an idea of a perfect circle and a perfect square and a perfect triangle. It is based on knowing these ideal, invisible objects that we are able to recognize their visible representations or replicas.

But it's not only geometric figures that remind us of ideal objects. According to Plato, all the innumerable imperfect things that we experience in our lives also remind us of their ideals. Our mind can contemplate perfect beauty or perfect goodness, for example, something our senses never experience. It was Plato's contention that it is this knowledge of perfect beauty or perfect goodness that enables us to recognize things that are only imperfectly beautiful and imperfectly good. The same can be said of every particular instance of a class of things. The many roses we see, cats we pet, human beings we meet—all are shadows of what we think of, indeed what we *know,* as a perfect or ideal rose, cat, or human being.

Plato called ideals or perfections Forms, and believed that the sensible things in our experience remind us of their Forms. But how is it possible that we have knowledge of these Forms? How is all learning actually recollection? These Forms are non-sensible; they don't exist in the visible world; we can't have sense experience of them. And yet, must we not have experienced them *somewhere* to be able to recall them? To Plato all of this suggested the existence of a pre-life. Accordingly,

> . . .[our] souls existed previously, before they were in the form of man—without bodies and must have had intelligence. . . if, as we are always repeating, there is an absolute beauty and goodness, and essence in general, and to this, which is now discovered to be a previous condition of our being, we refer all our sensations, and with this compare them—assuming this to have a prior existence, then our souls must have had a prior existence. . . .[5]

Nevertheless, even if souls exist in a pre-life, what about afterlife? In another part of *Phaedo,* Plato has Socrates demonstrate that the existence of a pre-life necessitates an afterlife from what he terms the "law of opposites."

Law of Opposites: An Afterlife as Necessitated by a Pre-Life   The relevant passage opens with Socrates asking Cebes, one of the speakers in *Phaedo,* "Are not all things which have opposites generated out of their opposites?" Socrates explains that he means such things as good and evil, just and unjust, and various processes that equally involve a passing into and out of one another, such as cooling and heating. Socrates then extends this notion of opposites generated out of their opposites to life and death.

S: Then suppose that you analyze life and death to me in the same manner. Is not death opposed to life?

C: Yes.

S: And they are generated from the other?

C: Yes.

S: What is generated from life?

C: Death is.

S: And what from death?

C: I can only say in answer—life.

S: Then the living, whether things or persons, Cebes, are generated from the dead?

C: That is clear. . . .

S: Then the inference is that our souls are in the world below?

C: That is true.

S: And one of the two processes or generations is visible—for surely the act of dying is visible?

C: Surely. . . .

S: And may not the other be inferred as the complement of nature, who is not to be supposed to go on one leg only? And if not, a corresponding process of generation in death must also be assigned to her?

C: Certainly.

S: And what is that process?

C: Revival.

S: And revival, if there be such a thing, is the birth of the dead into the world of the living?

C: Quite true.

S: Then there is a new way in which we arrive at the inference that the living come from the dead, just as the dead come from the living; and if this is true, then the souls of the dead must be in some place out of which they come again. And this, as I think, has been satisfactorily proved.

C: Yes, Socrates. . . all this seems to flow necessarily out of our previous admissions.[6]

Taken together, the existence of a pre-life and, by the law of opposites, the existence of an afterlife constitutes one proof for the soul's existence. By "existence" Plato means both eternal and immortal. Each soul exists outside time, being without beginning or end. In other words, it exists before it ever comes to be embodied, and it will exist after it becomes permanently disembodied.

As a further demonstration of the soul's immortality, Plato submitted the soul's immaterial nature.

Immaterial Nature of the Soul: The Soul as Simple and Therefore Indissoluble
According to Plato, the body and soul are different in the following way. Briefly, the body, as a composite or compound, is perishable. By contrast, the soul, as simple or uncompounded, is not subject to change. In its permanence, then, the soul resembles the unchanging Forms or absolutes. Like them, the soul is indissoluble. As Plato has Socrates say, again in *Phaedo*:

> ...the soul is in the very likeness of the divine, and immortal, and intelligible, and uniform, and indissoluble, and unchangeable; and the body is the very likeness of the human, and mortal and unintelligible, and multiform, and dissoluble, and changeable.[7]

This being the case, then the body is "liable to speedy dissolution," whereas the soul is "almost or altogether indissoluble."

As a historical note, this particular metaphysical argument for the soul's immortality was later adopted by Roman Catholicism, as captured in the following words of the French Catholic philosopher Jacques Maritain (1882–1973):

> A spiritual soul cannot be corrupted, since it possesses no matter; it cannot be disintegrated, since it has no substantial parts; it cannot lose its individual unity, since it is self-subsisting, nor its internal energy, since it contains within itself all the sources of its energies. The human soul cannot die. Once it exists, it cannot disappear; it will necessarily exist forever, endure without end.[8]

More generally, the Platonic body-soul distinction, together with its full metaphysical implications, was adopted by early Christianity as a theological doctrine and given the status of a self-evident truth, until reformulated by the French philosopher Rene Descartes in the seventeenth century.

Descartes

Considered the first of the modern European philosophers, Descartes was struck by what he considered the errors of past philosophers and determined to construct a system of philosophy that would withstand the tests of reason. The so-called founder of modern philosophy saw his model in the method and certainty of mathematics.

Consider that geometry and algebra yield complex truths from simple truths, ones that are so clear and distinct that they cannot be doubted. Impressed, Descartes sought the same kind of certainty as the departure point of his philosophy. He was after, in short, a truth so "clearly and distinctly perceived" that it could not be doubted. This he discovered in his own existence as a thinking being. Thus, while he could doubt everything, even to considering life a dream, he could not doubt the truth that "I think, therefore I am." And so, using the "*cogito*" (Latin for "I think") as his first principle, Descartes came to conclude that a human being was essentially a "thing which thinks," and that "soul" means a "thinking being."[9]

For Descartes a "thinking being" or "soul" was simple and immaterial, in contrast to a body, which was a composite with extension. Each, however, was a substance. This meant that his body and mind (or soul) required nothing but itself to exist. In other words, his corporeal substance, body, and his spiritual substance, mind, were independent of each other. Each could be understood without reference to the other. But, as essentially a spiritual substance or "thinking being," he—or more properly his mind (or soul)—could exist apart from his body. The same could be said of any other human being.

According to the Cartesian view, then, not only can we conceive of ourselves as existing without a body, but since we can, we are not purely physical things. Furthermore, since we cannot conceive of ourselves without thinking, it is mind, not body, that defines us. Earlier Plato proclaimed the same superior status of the soul, writing in probably the last of his dialogues, *Laws*: "What gives each one of us his being is nothing else but his soul; whereas the body is no more than a shadow that keeps us company." Two millennia later, Descartes agreed that "it is well said of the deceased that the corpse is only a ghost" (Plato, *Laws,* lines 969a–b).

So, for both Plato and Descartes, we are essentially immaterial, conscious beings who can exist without our material, unconscious bodies. And it is exactly this kind of extreme dualism that provides a necessary philosophical basis for the belief that the inner self, soul, or mind can exist apart from the body; and, therefore, that individual personality survives death, and is even immortal. If dual-substance theory doesn't add up, then the *philosophical* foundation for all survival hypotheses collapses.[10]

THE MIND-BODY PROBLEM

Descartes' dual-substance theory presumed that mind and body are causally connected so that mental events can cause physical events and vice versa. This dualistic interactionism, as it is called, raises several questions that, collectively, philosophers term the mind-body problem. The central issue in the mind-body problem is how the mind and body, which are distinct and separate, interact.

If, as Descartes claimed, mind (i.e., consciousness) and body (understood here as the brain) are two different substances, how do they interact? Mind, after all, presumably is immaterial while body or brain is material. How can something that is immaterial interact with something that is material? For example, when you *will* to raise your hand, how exactly does your immaterial mind bring about this physical movement of your body? Or, alternatively, how can something material interact with something immaterial? When you hear a piece of music, for instance, how is it that you can experience a wave of feelings, desires, memories, or nostalgia? What sort of mental states or processes are these psychic experiences? Indeed, since these experiences occur within a brain, what exactly is thought and how is thought related to your brain state?

For Descartes, God bridged the gap. In post-Enlightenment times, however, that convenience is not available to scientists or philosophers. The result, according to one commentator, is a "residual bridgeless gap between mind and brain [that] constitutes the mind-body problem."[11]

RESPONSES TO THE MIND-BODY PROBLEM

A sizable and complex body of criticism has grown up in answer to the mind-body problem raised by Cartesian interactionism. A general familiarity with it helps in understanding the serious challenges to survivalist belief posed by some modern theories of mind.

To begin, various philosophers have categorically rejected Cartesian interactionism. Among them would be those who, like the German philosopher Gottfried Leibniz (1646–1716), have questioned the possibility of any mind-body causal interaction, or those who have doubted only that body can affect mind.

Others have cast mental states as non-causal by-products of brain states.[12] In this dualism-preserving view, termed epiphenomenalism, matter is primary and mind is a secondary phenomenon accompanying some bodily processes. This gives body mental as well as physical attributes. Mental states, then, are by-products of brain activity, but don't cause or affect its activity. In short: no mental states without brain states. How, then, could brain-dependent mind survive death? It couldn't. That's why, if correct, epiphenomenalism would rule out virtually all survival theories.

There is, additionally, the view of those who simply refuse to engage interactionism as a meaningful, philosophical problem. The Austrian philosopher Ludwig Wittgenstein (1889–1951), for example, treated it as basically a linguistic problem. Instead of being drawn into the centuries-old debate about whether minds and mental states are real, Wittgenstein chose to examine the circumstances under which people use words that seem to designate mental states, such as "think," "hope," "imagine," "regret," "recall," and so on. If we look closely at such terms, Wittgenstein said, they have plain, conceptual meanings without any metaphysical phenomenon at all. Presto! The problem of dualistic interactionism vanishes.

A similar conclusion and denial of the problem was reached by another student of language and meaning, the British philosopher A. J. Ayer (1910–1989). Ayer, together with the German philosopher Rudolph Carnap (1891–1970), is associated with the twentieth century school of philosophy termed logical positivism. According to positivists, only two kinds of statements are meaningful: (1) statements that are true by definition (called tautologies), such as "Squares have four sides" or "My brother is a male"; and (2) statements of fact (called empirical statements), such as "Water boils at 212 degrees Fahrenheit at sea level" or "HIV causes AIDS." Assertions neither tautological nor empirical are meaningless, according to positivists Ayer and Carnap.

Positivists say, furthermore, that all metaphysical statements (as well as ethical, aesthetic, and theological ones) lack literal meaning. They're simply meaningless.

Significantly included would be the statement at the root of Cartesian dualism: "There is something immaterial inside a human being—a soul or mind or inner self." How could such a statement possibly be verified? How, even in theory, could it be tested? In fact, it's void of literal meaning, and, by extension, so are statements like "The soul survives death" or "At death the soul separates from the body." (By contrast, Ayer believed, the statement "Humans survive death" is at least intelligible, although altogether improbable, as is the notion of the disembodied mind.)[13]

Sharpening the criticism of Cartesian dualism in the twentieth century was the growth of a monistic position termed metaphysical materialism, also called physicalism. Monism, as opposed to dualism, is the view that reality is reducible to *one* kind of thing or principle, not two such as mind *and* spirit. Metaphysical materialism or physicalism holds that reality consists of only matter, which of course would foreclose the problem of mind-body interaction. Philosophical or metaphysical materialists reject all supernatural beliefs, including belief in spirit, soul, mind, or any other nonmaterial substance. Since reality can be explained only in terms of scientifically verifiable concepts, for strict materialists death is extinction.

In mind-body questions, materialism refers to any theory that reduces mind or mental states to bodily phenomena. Thus the label "reductive materialism," or "reductionism" for short. More than an arcane interest of brain neuroscientists and cognitive philosophers, any reductive theory of mind amounts to an overwhelming philosophical attack on afterlife belief.[14,15]

Reductive Theories of Mind

Three prominent reductive theories of mind are termed *identity, behaviorist,* and *functional.* In challenging the traditional dualism of mind and body, each also poses a challenge for philosophically based survivalist theories.

Identity Theory: The View That Mental States Are Identical to Physiochemical Brain States   In his essay "Materialism" (1963), Australian philosopher J. C. Smart undertakes to explain how a nonphysical property such as mind or consciousness suddenly could arise in the course of animal evolution.[16] There are only two possible answers, Smart proposes. The first is that nonphysical entities always accompany certain complex physical structures, an explanation he regards as unscientific and inexplicable. The second, favored by Smart as scientifically sound, is a strict materialistic conception of mind as brain. This makes "mental" states not mere attributes of the body (as in epiphenomenalism), but identical to "brain" states. Mind is brain—they are one and the same thing.

Philosophical Behaviorism: The View That Conscious States Are to Be Explained in Terms of Behavior   Behaviorists such as the British philosopher Gilbert Ryle (1900–1976) say that mental states and activities can be explained in terms of observable behaviors that are associated with the body.[17] Whatever the mental process—thinking, feeling, intending, imagining, loving—it is not to be understood only as an inner state accessible only to the person having that experience. It is also to be understood as a publicly observable behavior. When someone says, for example, "I hate spinach," "I need a vacation," or "I believe in life after death," she is not referring to some inner state of mind accessible only to her but to behavior appropriate to these expressions. "I hate spinach" expresses how she behaves or would behave under certain circumstances, for example when she finds spinach on the menu. Similarly, "I believe in life after death" is best taken to mean that she conducts herself in keeping with that belief, perhaps by following a particular code of conduct or ritual, such as praying for the dead. For behaviorists such as Ryle, who famously called the soul "the ghost in the machine," what we term "mind" is really bodily behavior. And words that describe mental characteristics and operations—"intelligent," "thoughtful," "carefree," "happy," "calculating"—apply in practice to types of human behavior or behavioral dispositions.

Functionalism: The View That Humans Are Like Complicated Computers   The view of the human as computer was foreshadowed in the mechanistic view of human nature proposed by the English philosopher Thomas Hobbes (1588–1679). In his famous work *Leviathan* (1651), he writes:

> For seeing life is but a motion of limbs, the beginning whereof is in some principal part within; why may we not say, that all *automata* (engines that move themselves by springs and wheels as does a watch) have an artificial life? For what is the *heart,* but a *spring*; and the *nerves,* but so many *strings*; and the *joints,* but so many *wheels,* giving motion to the whole body, such as was intended by the artificer?[18]

Today the machine to which the human often is analogized is the computer. Functionalist philosopher D. M. Armstrong, for example, refers to the body's "inputs" and "outputs" in referring to mental states and mental activities. And the short-lived "founder of computer science" Alan Turing (1912–1954) even envisioned a not-too-distant day when computers would be able to replicate the input-output process of the human brain, and thus, for all intents and purposes, have "minds." Defining computation in terms of manipulating binary symbols, usually zeros and ones, Turing saw no essential difference between the computer and the human mind. Both "compute," or, crudely, "figure things out."

As a result of the development of theories like these, as well as the general assault on dual-substance theory, much contemporary philosophy curiously leans toward the biblical depiction of humans as forms of finite, mortal, psychophysical life, and not as eternal souls temporarily housed in mortal bodies.[19] The body, in brief, is the soul in its outward form. This way of thinking inevitably challenges the Platonic and Neoplatonic views of death that profoundly shaped Christian theology and Western thought in general. Indeed, it not only calls into question the traditional assumption of spiritual immortality but postmortem survival itself. For in a world where mind is brain, or mental states are bodily behavior, or a human being is a complex computer, the creature possessed of a soul inevitably is swept into the dustbin of medieval superstition.

Critical Responses to Reductive Theories of Mind

The philosophical response to reductive theories of mind often begins with a litany of human qualities and behavior, such as loving and hating, dreaming and hoping, struggling and striving, imagining and inventing. The question is then asked: Can all of this and more be explained totally in terms of, say, physio-chemical processes? Can ideas and concepts? Can consciousness itself? Does reductive materialism adequately account for the experience we have of seeing something, a color, for example? Does it, *can* it, adequately explain more complex experiences, such as being in love?

The contemporary American philosopher John Searle, for one, grants that the brain produces mental states or activities. But Searle denies that these mental phenomena can be reduced to familiar physical qualities. Unique to humans, Searle believes, is consciousness. No matter how brainy a computer, for example, it does not, cannot, and will not have consciousness. If computation simply means figuring things out, then yes, we are "conscious computers." But figuring things out, zeros and ones, by themselves do not constitute consciousness or, indeed, any other mental phenomenon. "They are just zeros and ones, nothing more," Searle says.[20]

So, what is consciousness, then? Searle names what he calls three "plain facts" about consciousness. (1) Consciousness is a real part of the world, not an illusion; (2) consciousness is entirely caused by brain processes; (3) consciousness functions causally in our behavior. These facts place philosophical tradition and modern science at odds, Searle believes. Thus, dualism, while comfortable with 1 bristles at 2 and 3. Materialism or physicalism, on the other hand, in denying 1 denies what we know from our own experience. Searle's solution is to scrap traditional philosophical categories, "with all their accumulated barnacles of theological and metaphysical confusion, and just state the facts," (i.e., 1, 2, and 3). In other words, if we jettison the Platonic/Cartesian traditional dichotomy of mental and physical, then all the known facts of consciousness pose no problem, although exactly how the brain produces consciousness still does.

David Chalmers, another American philosopher critical of reductionism, holds that the presence of consciousness amounts to an "extra character" in the world. Viewing consciousness as a property distinct from physical properties, Chalmers contends that, while conscious experiences may depend on physical properties, they are not the same as them. He maintains that the character of the brain is not exhausted by the brain's physical facts and features. Consciousness gives it an added dimension. Chalmers's implied dualism is not Cartesian, but *property dualism. According to property dualism, mental and physical properties are genuinely different kinds of things, although properties of the same kind of objects.* This means that, although conscious properties may lawfully depend on physical properties, they are not entailed by them. I need a properly functioning brain to think, feel, and imagine. But thinking, feeling, and imagining are not identical to having a properly functioning brain. What is consciousness then? Chalmers suspects that consciousness may forever be beyond the reach of neuroscience.[21]

The distinguished British neuroscientist and Nobel Prize winner Sir John Eccles (1903–1997) was probably the foremost opponent of identity theory. Eccles thought that the reductive view fails to account for the "wonder and mystery of the human self with its spiritual values, with its creativity, and its uniqueness for each other."[22] Over the course of several decades—partly in unique collaboration with distinguished philosopher of science Karl Popper (1902–1994)[23]—Eccles developed an interactive theory of mind (i.e., a dualist-interactionism), according to which we have a nonmaterial mind or self, which acts upon and is influenced by our material brains. But Eccles didn't consider the mind a nonphysical substance the way Descartes did. For Eccles mind merely belongs to a different world, a mental world that interacts with the physical world. Each of us is a supernatural, spiritual creation—a divinely created unique self or soul. On death, our dualistic existence ends and the liberated soul, Eccles hoped, will find "another future of even deeper meaning and more entrancing experiences, perhaps in some renewed embodied existence. . . in accord with traditional Christian teaching."[24]

Eccles's faith is not shared by today's *mysterianists,* although his confidence in a future deeper understanding and meaning is. Mysterianists are mostly cognitive scientists and philosophers, notable among whom are American philosopher Thomas Nagel[25] and British philosopher Colin McGinn,[26] as well as Harvard psychologist Stephen Pinker.[27] Such scholars endorse *mysterianism,* a term invented for the distinct possibility that the mind-body problem, in the end, may turn out to be an insoluble mystery. Why the capitulation? Basically because no progress has been made in the three centuries since Descartes set the conundrum. The mind-body problem, according to mysterianism, simply may remain a mystery that, even in principle, defies solution without radically rethinking mind and brain. Is such a reconception far-fetched? Perhaps. But now that physical science has turned its attention to consciousness, Nagel, for one, confidently envisions a future reconfiguring of the link between the physical and the mental that will "transform science radically."[28]

Mysterianism not withstanding, the ongoing philosophical dispute between dualism and monistic materialism suggests a genuine dilemma, a real choice between mutually exclusive options. But not everyone views the issue in exclusive either-or terms. Given the wide range of phenomena that "mental" covers, perhaps dualism accounts for some mental phenomena and materialism for others. This is view of philosopher Paul Edwards. "Speaking for myself," he writes,

> I find it grossly implausible to identify dreams or sensations with brain states. At the same time I am convinced that an identity theory is quite defensible for feelings, for example fear or rage. Fear and rage seem to be states of the organism: they are *felt* by the person who has them and they can be *observed* by others. The content of consciousness of the person who feels the fear is different from that of the person who observes the frightened individuals, but it is arbitrary and unreasonable to confine the word "fear" to the experience of the subject. It seems much more natural to say that it is the same state, experienced in different ways by the subject and the observer. It should be noted that feelings are here identified with total states of the organism and not with brain events. Somebody who accepts dualism for some mental states and materialism for others is

committed to a view which lacks the neatness and "simplicity" of both the identity theory and of a thoroughgoing dualism; but, if it is true, this would be a small price to pay.[29]

As one who contends that "a living brain is a *necessary* condition for all mental states" ("brain-dependence theory"),[30] Edwards doesn't believe in postmortem survival. For him, survival is only possible if there can be mental states in the absence of a bodily foundation.[31]

Let's, for argument's sake, take that assumption of mind without body. Even if the possibility of postmortem survival is thereby granted, how to explain, let alone justify, the identification of this disembodied mind or spirit with the previously flesh and blood person? What exactly of the unembodied person would be the same as the deceased person to constitute one and the same person?[32]

With that question, we're brought to another major aspect of the mind-body problem that shakes survivalist belief: the persistence of personal identity.

THE PERSISTENCE OF PERSONAL IDENTITY

No matter his profound physical, emotional, intellectual, and moral transformation, Ivan Ilyich still maintained a sense of personal identity. Each of us can say the same. No matter how different we are from one another, all of us share the common experience of undergoing numerous personal changes during our lives and yet, for all of that, experiencing a persisting "self" or "I" over time. What accounts for this enduring personal identity? What does it take exactly for you to remain the same person over time? For me to have a sense of self that lasts despite myriad changes? Whatever it is, clearly it must endure after we die for us to *personally* survive death.

Over the years, a number of candidates have been proposed as accounting for enduring personal identity, notably body, soul, or memory. There is another tradition, well known in Eastern philosophy, that denies the existence of self and, thus, rejects the problem of the persistence of personal identity.

Body

Philosopher Peter Geach plainly states the position of many philosophers that it is the body that accounts for the persistence of personal identity. "When we say an old man is the same person as the baby born years before," Geach writes, "we believe that the old man has material continuity with the baby." This doesn't mean that the new body must in every way be identical with the old. But there must be "some one-one relation of material continuity between the old body and the new."[33] In other words, one baby grows up into an old man, and one old man has grown out of one baby. Otherwise there would have to be at some stage a drastic change, which we should regard as destroying personal identity. Moreover, the baby-body never coexists with the aged body, but develops into it. The clear implication of this somatic view, as it's called, is that, philosophically speaking, unembodied personal survival of death makes no sense. (It would not rule out, however, the *theological* belief that the dead can come to life again by an act of resurrection.)

Soul

Supporting the traditional Western assumption that we are the same person through time is the belief that not only does each living human have a material body but also an immaterial soul or self. While the material body changes, the immaterial soul or self does not. It is this enduring soul or self, then, that accounts for continuing self-identity, as well as survival of death; for since a person is a nonmaterial mind or soul, the person can continue to exist after the body dies.[34]

The Cartesian Interpretation   One way of showing how the belief in the enduring soul accommodates personal death survival is how Descartes did. Notice how in the following short passage from *Meditations* Descartes associates soul with thinking mind and, then, continuity of mind with enduring personal identity:

> Thinking is another attribute of the soul; and here I discover what properly belongs to myself. This alone is inseparable from me. I am—I exist: this is certain; but how often? As often as I think; for perhaps it would even happen, if I should wholly cease to think, that I should at the same time altogether cease to be.[35]

For Descartes, then, it is the immaterial mind, not the material body that makes a person continue to be the same person through time. If that's the case, then a person can continue to exist after death, since it is the material body and not the immaterial mind that dies.

The problems with Descartes' view cluster around issues of observation. Since we can't observe the immaterial or spiritual mind, how do we know it persists? Consider, for example, the common experience of recognizing someone—say, someone in a large crowd whom you haven't seen in a long time. Although you know she is the same person you've seen before, you certainly don't know that from perceiving her mind. This suggests, at least from the standpoint of the observer, that something other than the mind makes the person the same over time. Observable profound changes in mental states are no easier for Descartes' view to explain. Take the man who suddenly quits a job, leaves a marriage, or simply vanishes. What precisely of his "mind" persists to call him the same person? Then there are cases of severe brain disease. What exactly of the mind endures in the advanced Alzheimer's patient to call her the same person?

The Theological Interpretation   Perhaps a way out of these difficulties is to distinguish between "mind" and "soul," such that the mind depends on the body but the soul does not. This is the general theological view of Judaism, Christianity, and Hinduism, but also discernible in the thought of many philosophers, including Kant. The basic argument here is that while the mind dies with the body, the soul, or the "I" that "owns" body and mind, lives on.

But why posit an entity that underlies both body and mind, common expression notwithstanding?[36] Besides, if there were such a spiritual substance or metaphysical soul, it wouldn't be what we mean by "I." If it were, why do we dread death? Don't we fear death because we dread the annihilation of our empirical self? Isn't it the survival of the empirical self what we would like? Another way to pose the same objection is to imagine a case of insanity, which we attribute to brain disease. Since the metaphysical soul does not depend on the body, it presumably is untouched by the insanity. In other words, the soul remains sane even though the person is insane. But doesn't that lead to an absurd conclusion, namely, that "If I go mad and if at the same time my soul remains sane then I and my soul are not the same thing"?[37]

Eschewing body and soul, most modern philosophers believe that it is some mental feature or features that the future being inherits that best explains the persistence of personal identity. Just what this is, is disputed. Memory, however, has been a popular choice since the attention John Locke gave it in the last decade of the seventeenth century.

Memory

Even if human beings have immaterial souls or minds, Locke argued, that alone doesn't account for the persistence of identity. To prove his point, Locke set a reincarnation scenario in which the soul of someone long deceased somehow enters the body of someone alive today, presumably making the living person the same as the deceased person. But if the living person has none of the memories of the deceased one, how can he conceive of himself as the same person as the deceased? Locke concluded, in his *Essay Concerning Human Understanding* (1694), that it is not soul or mind that accounts for personal identity, not even consciousness. It is *continuity* of consciousness or, simply, memory.

While appealing, Locke's memory-based theory of personal identity has been criticized, beginning as early as the eighteenth century, along the following lines. Consider that today you probably can remember things that happened when you were ten-years-old. In this sense the person you were at ten is the same person you are today. Then again, there probably are plenty of things you *can't* remember. In this sense, you're not the same person. Isn't this at least paradoxical—that you the ten-year-old are and are not the same person as the present you? Doesn't it make you wonder about the past person who did all those things that the present you doesn't have the foggiest notion of? And what about the human tendency to rewrite personal history, embellish on the past, or selectively recall it? Is the present person to be identified by the seriously flawed memory, perhaps even to the point of delusion? Who is W. Mark Felt? "Deep Throat" of Watergate fame? Or the 91-year-old who can't recall much about being theNumber 2 official at the FBI during the Nixon years?

Although different, the preceding perspectives all share the assumption that there is something called the "self" that persists through time—body, soul, or some aspect of consciousness, notably memory. But what if the shared assumption of these perspectives is incorrect? What if there is *no enduring self,* because the whole idea of self is an illusion? What if the "true self" is "no self"?

No-Self

The belief that the self exists and persists in time has enjoyed the status of a self-evident truth for the vast majority of Western philosophers, not to say ordinary people, as much as it did for Descartes. And yet, to many of the philosophies of the East and Far East—generically termed "Eastern"—nothing could be further from the truth. According to Buddhism, for example, it is the illusion of a unique individual self that is the source of human suffering and misery.

If there is no soul or unique, discrete self, what, then, is an individual "person"? Buddhism proposes a composite of five "skandhas" or components: a body and, working with the body, four mental states: sensation, perception, mental constructs, consciousness.[38] Like everything else in existence, the aggregate or bundle of components that constitutes the "person" is constantly changing. And also like everything else, it has no permanent existence. The idea that nothing is permanent, termed *anatman,* is Buddhism's most important doctrine.

Variously translated as "egolessness," "no-self," or "non-soul," the point of *anatman* is that nothing has any substantial or perpetual reality, including the self. This makes the sense of self associated with the body-mind skandhas an illusion.

Buddhism further teaches that clinging to the idea of self and its permanence is a basic misreading of reality that is potentially harmful. Reality isn't constant, but impermanent and always in flux, much like a swiftly moving river. Adhering to a view of permanency, especially to the idea of an enduring self, we end up denying "natural truths" of existence, notably aging, illness, and death. We also make false distinctions, such as existence and non-existence, good and bad, right and wrong.[39] Such distinctions, in fact, exist only in our confused minds, according to Buddhism.

Eight centuries ago—in the same century that Thomas Aquinas was constructing his formidable summary of Christian theology—the revered and enlightened Japanese monk Dogen (1200–1253) succinctly expressed the Buddhist sentiment metaphorically:

> When someone rides in a boat, as he looks at the shore he has the illusion that the shore is moving. When he looks at the boat under him, he realizes the boat is moving. In the same way, when one takes things for granted with confused ideas of body-mind, one has the illusion that one's own mind and own nature are permanent; but if one pays close attention to one's own actions, the truth that things are not self will be clear.[40]

Although tightly connected with Buddhism and more generally with Eastern philosophies, the "true self is no self" view has had its Western devotees, the Scottish philosopher David Hume (1711–1776) among them.

Hume

As an empiricist Hume believed that all knowledge originates in and is derived from sense experience. In other words, there is no innate or *a priori* (Latin for "from former") knowledge, as Descartes and similar metaphysicians had claimed. For Hume, genuine knowledge is *a posteriori* (Latin for "from later") or knowledge stated in empirically verifiable statements.[41] This led Hume to an extreme skepticism that, among other things, denied foundational beliefs of Christianity such as miracles and personal immortality. It also turned his skeptical eye on assertions about the self.

Hume claimed that sense experiences or perceptions are resolved in the mind, as it thinks and reasons, into "impressions" and "ideas." The difference between them is merely a matter of "liveliness." An impression, said Hume, is a vivid or "lively perception," as "when we hear, or see, or feel, or love, or hate, or desire, or will." Impressions are distinguished from ideas, "which are the less lively perceptions of which we are conscious, when we reflect on any of those sensations or movements above mentioned." The sharp pain you feel with a toothache, for example, is an impression; the memory of what you felt is an idea. Again, the solemnity I experience in listening to Brahms's German *Requiem* is an impression; my recollection of that solemnity is an idea. As copies of impressions—"feeble perceptions" that are less vivid as we subsequently reflect upon them—ideas depend on impressions. There can be no ideas without impressions (although not every idea necessarily reflects an impression).

Now, with regard to self a question arises. It is this: From what impression can the idea of self be derived?

As a rationalist Descartes claimed that reason alone could arrive at certainty. And, for Descartes, there was nothing that reason made us more certain of than the existence of the "I." But empiricist Hume asked: When we think and reason, do we ever have even the faintest experience that corresponds to the "I"? Do we ever experience the 'self'? What single, identical impression does this "I" or "self" arise from? If it arises from some single, identical impression, then either (1) preposterously, the self cannot be itself any more than a toothache can be the tooth or the feeling of solemnity the *Requiem*; or (2) there is no single, identical impression, in which case the self does not exist. Adopting the latter view, Hume was led to conclude:

> . . . when I enter most intimately into what I call *myself,* I always stumble on some particular perception or other, of heat or cold, light or shade, love or hatred, pain or pleasure. I never can catch *myself* at any time without a perception, and never can observe anything but the perception. . . .
>
> I may venture to affirm of the rest of mankind, that they are nothing but a bundle or collection of different perceptions, which succeed each other with an inconceivable rapidity, and are in a perpetual flux and movement. . . . The mind is a kind of theatre, where several perceptions successively make their appearance, pass, re-pass, glide away, and mingle in an infinite variety of postures and situations.[42]

So thinking, Hume couldn't help but deny the possibility of personal immortality.[43]

As for the question he raised, that lives on, continuing to test the mettle of immortalists: *If we know existence of our personalities only in association with our bodies, what philosophical basis is there for asserting life after the death of the body?*

CONCLUSIONS

Today most people who believe in personal survival after death may not consciously wrap that belief around a notion of an immortal soul. They may simply believe that death is not the end of life, that they will continue to exist as individual personalities with their memories and self-awareness basically intact. Like Mary Follett, many take this on religious faith or other grounds. Much the same can be said of most people historically. As the authors of a recent book defending human nature as body and soul write:

> It is safe to say that throughout human history, the vast majority of people, educated and uneducated alike, have been dualists, at least in the sense that they have taken a human to be the sort of being that could enter life after death as the very same individual or as some sort of spiritual entity that merges with the All. Some form of dualism appears to be the natural response to what we seem to know about ourselves through introspection and in other ways. Many philosophers who deny dualism admit that it is the commonsense view.[44]

Indeed, this widespread assumption that human beings are not purely physical things is *philosophically* necessary for believing in personal survival after death.

Asserted in the ancient world by Plato, then reformulated in the seventeenth century by Descartes, this premise philosophically grounds the argument that life does not end with the death of the body. Call it soul, mind, consciousness, or inner self—there is something of a spiritual or immaterial nature that defines us, not our bodies, and it will persist after death. Or so Western tradition holds.

But are we, in fact, essentially immaterial, conscious beings who can exist without our bodies? Or are consciousness and mental states identical with brain states, as materialists say; or at least brain-dependent? If so, then dualism fails, and, philosophically speaking, what is variously called soul, mind, consciousness, or inner self faces extinction at death, if it wasn't an illusion to begin with.

Such matters of the self in relation to death should be kept in mind in mulling afterlife theories, such as those to be considered in the next chapter.

REFERENCES

1. Kenneth Doka, *Death and Spirituality,* Amityville, NY: Baywood Publishing Co., 1993, p. 144.
2. W. T. Jones, *Kant to Wittgenstein and Sartre,* New York: Harcourt, Brace & World, 1969, p. 33.
3. Jacques Choron, *Suicide,* New York: Charles Scribner's Sons, 1972, p. 108.
4. Arnold Toynbee and others, *Man's Concern with Death,* New York: McGraw-Hill Book Company, 1968, p. 86.
5. Plato, *Phaedo,* Benjamin Jowett, trans., in *The Harvard Classics,* vol. 2, New York: P. F. Collier & Son Company, 1909, pp. 67–68.

6. Ibid., pp. 59; 61–62.

7. Ibid., p. 72.

8. John Hick, *Philosophy of Religion*, 3rd ed., Englewood Cliffs, NJ: Prentice-Hall, 1983, p. 123.

9. Rene Descartes, *Discourse on Method*, in *The Philosophical Works of Descartes*, vol. 1, pp. 100–101, Elizabeth S. Haldane and G. R. T. Ross, trans., Cambridge: Cambridge University Press, 1911, pp. 100–101.

10. Paul Edwards, *Reincarnation: A Critical Examination*, Amherst, NY: Prometheus Books, 1996, pp. 14–15.

11. Huston Smith, *Why Religion Matters*, San Francisco: Harper San Francisco, 2001, p. 182.

12. Paul Edwards, *Immortality*, Amherst, NY: Prometheus Books, 1997, p. 31.

13. Ibid., p. 47.

14. Jonathan Shear, ed., *Explaining Consciousness: The Hard Problem*, Cambridge, MA: Bradford Books, 1999.

15. David Chalmers, *Philosophy of Mind: Classical and Contemporary Readings*, Oxford: Oxford University Press, 2002.

16. J.J.C. Smart, "Materialism," *Journal of Philosophy*, October 24, 1963, pp. 651–662.

17. Gilbert Ryle, *The Concept of Mind*, London: Hutchinson & Co., Ltd., 1949.

18. Thomas Hobbes, *Hobbes's Leviathan*, Oxford: Clarendon Press, 1909. p. 23.

19. Hick, p. 124.

20. John R. Searle, "No Ghost in the Machine," *Los Angeles Times Book Review*, October 12, 2003, p. R12.

21. David Chalmers, *The Conscious Mind*, New York: Oxford University Press, 1996.

22. John C. Eccles, *How the Self Controls Its Brain*, Berlin: Springer-Verlag Telos, 1994, p. 33.

23. Karl R. Popper and John C. Eccles, *The Self and Its Brain*, London: Routledge, 1984.

24. John C. Eccles, *Evolution of the Brain*, London: Routledge, 1989, p. 242.

25. Thomas Nagel, "What's It Like To Be a Bat?" *Philosophical Review*, vol. 83, 1974, pp. 435–450.

26. Colin McGinn, *The Mysterious Flame*, Cambridge, MA: MIT Press, 1999.

27. Stephen Pinker, *How the Mind Works*, New York: W. W. Norton & Company, 1999.

28. Smith, p. 186.

29. Edwards, *Immortality*, p. 30.

30. ——, *Reincarnation*, p. 291.

31. ——, *Immortality*, p. 31.

32. C. D. Broad, *Lectures in Psychical Research*, London: Routledge & Kegan Paul, 1962, p. 409.

33. Peter Geach, *God and the Soul*, Bristol, U.K.: Thoemmes Press, 1994, p. 26.

34. Manuel Velasquez, *Philosophy: A Text with Readings*, 8th ed., Belmont, CA: Wadsworth/Thomson Learning, 2002, p. 124.

35. Rene Descartes, *Meditations*, in *The Philosophical Works of Descartes*, pp. 115–152.

36. Paul Edwards, "The Dependence of Consciousness on the Brain," in *Immortality*, p. 307.

37. Ibid.
38. Michael Brannigan, *The Pulse of Wisdom*, Belmont, CA: Wadsworth Publishing Company, 1995, p. 139.
39. *The Teaching of Buddha*, Tokyo: Bukkyo Dendo Kyokai, 1966, p. 53.
40. *Shobogenzo: Zen Essays by Dogen*, Thomas Cleary, trans., Honolulu: University of Hawaii Press, 1986, p. 33.
41. Velasquez, p. 717.
42. David Hume, *A Treatise of Human Nature*, L. A. Selby-Bigge, ed., Oxford: Clarendon Press, 1896, p. 6.
43. "On the Immortality of the Soul," in *Of the Standard of Taste and Other Essays*, John W. Lenz, ed., Indianapolis: Bobbs-Merrill Educational Publishing, 1965, pp. 161–167.
44. J. P. Moreland & Scott B. Rae, *Body & Soul: Human Nature & the Crisis in Ethics*, Downers Grove, IL: InterVarsity Press, 2000, p. 17.

6

Survival Hypotheses

A significant part of any culture's orientation is its death ethos or guiding beliefs about death. The place and circumstances of mortality, the disposition of the corpse, the various postmortem rituals and expressions of mourning and grief, these and other matters reflect a culture's death ethos.

However, a culture does more than tell its members what to do and how to behave when death comes. Its death ethos also helps people comprehend and temper the fact of death. This is achieved mainly through religion. Primarily through its predominant religious beliefs, a culture gives answers to the ultimate mystery of death. *What happens to us when we die? Is the death of the body the end of life, or is there life after death? If there is, what's it like? Do we survive death as individuals, perhaps to be eventually annihilated? Do we go on existing forever? Do we survive death not as individuals but possibly as part of a higher spiritual reality?* An important part of a culture's death ethos, then, is its religious views about the sequel to death.

The vast majority of cultures have taught that there is life after death, although they have differed on its nature. For some, typically Western, postmortem life means that the individual survives as a personality. Eastern traditions, by contrast, generally teach an impersonal survival in which the individual merges (or re-merges) with an ultimate spiritual reality. Unlike the Eastern tradition, the Western has persistently pursued the problems of death and eternity, beginning with the deaths of Socrates and Jesus.[1] From these philosophical and religious influences, the Western world receives its evolutionary creation story whereby life has a beginning and not an end but a goal, death. Death in the West thus becomes the gateway to a new existence. In stark contrast stands the prevailing Eastern idea of death as a means to the end of rebirths so that a melting into an impersonal oneness with a static, self-contained, meaningless universe can be attained.

Four principal afterlife perspectives operate within these two great traditions. Two of them—disembodied mind and resurrection—often are associated with Western culture. Reincarnation and mystical union, the other two, are considered more typically Eastern.

But caution is called for, since these perspectives on afterlife often cross cultures. The idea of reincarnation, for example, has figured prominently in the afterlife philosophies of many Westerners; and the idea that, though disembodied, one lives on after death, is a basic teaching of Confucianism.[2] What's more, these afterlife views are not always mutually exclusive, with some reincarnationists, for instance, also believing in disembodied mind. Also worth remembering is that, despite its powerful influence, culture doesn't entirely determine an afterlife orientation. Countless individuals, no doubt, have arrived at considered afterlife opinions quite different from the one generally prescribed by their culture's death ethos. Some we'll meet in this chapter.

DISEMBODIED OR PURE INDIVIDUAL MIND

Recall from the preceding chapter that, although their philosophies spanned about 2,000 years and differed in important ways, Plato and Descartes shared basically the same view of human nature. Both believed we have bodies, but that our bodies are not what we are essentially. We have a spiritual or immaterial aspect, a mind or soul associated with consciousness. While body and mind interact, mind is *not* dependent on body for its existence. This view of human beings accommodates the belief that the mind can continue to exist after the death of the body, even if it no longer interacts with a body as it once did. Such an afterlife view is termed disembodied or pure individual mind.

Plato and Descartes aren't the only philosophers associated with the idea of disembodied or pure mind. Locke, Spinoza, Kant, and the French philosopher Henri Bergson (1859–1941) also are. Even disbelievers in postmortem life, such as Hume and the British philosopher Bertrand Russell (1872–1970), respected this view, but, admittedly, not enough to embrace it.

In the West, though, it's Plato who champions the idea of disembodied mind. Thus, the body belongs to the world known to us through our physical senses, and shares the nature of this world: change, impermanence, death. On the other hand, the soul or inner self is related to the permanent unchanging realities we are aware of when contemplating not particular things but universal, eternal Forms. Being related to this higher and lasting realm, the soul, unlike the body, is immortal. Upon death, therefore, those who have contemplated the eternal realities rather than indulged the desires of the body will discover that, although their bodies have returned to dust, their souls will gravitate to the world of eternal Forms. The soul will continue to exist in the realm of the unchanging and the immortal, *without the body.*

But how can disembodied spirits have sensations and feelings, or thought and will? After all, according to the pure mind view, we will have the same sorts of experiences after death as before. How can this be if we have no bodies? How can an immaterial being experience emotion, anger, or joy, for example; how can it see or hear? How can a disembodied mind think and choose when thought and choice are inseparable from mental images and emotions? Any satisfactory answer to these questions, even if possible, would raise the persistence of personal identity problem. Thus: In what sense could a disembodied mind, something alien to the whole experience of human life, remain the same person? Beyond this, pure individual mind theory leaves us puzzling over what kind of consciousness survives death. This general question has specific relevancy to those whose minds have been destroyed by disease or those who, like infants and children, haven't even matured.

All of these difficulties, broadly associated with the "mind-body problem" of the preceding chapter, turn some away from disembodied mind to resurrection as the vehicle of survival.

RESURRECTION

Likely as not, if you asked someone if he'd ever heard of Zoroastrianism, he'd probably say no. And if he had, he probably couldn't tell you much about this ancient religion. Yet Zoroastrianism, the oldest of revealed world-religions, has had, perhaps, more influence on humankind than any other single faith.[3]

Founded by the Persian Zarathusthra (also Zoroaster or Zarthoght) sometime between 1500 and 1000 BCE, Zoroastrianism includes articles of faith that have become staples in the world's three main monotheistic religions—Judaism, Christianity, and Islam. Chief among those teachings is a future resurrection and life everlasting for the reunited soul and body.[4]

In general, Western religions not only teach immortality of the soul (that is, that we will go on living forever) but often the resurrected body as well. They tend to frame death not as the end of life but as its goal—the portal to eternity, the final test, the ultimate dread and suffering before divine judgment of one's life. In this fashion, the soul will live on as a separate, recognizable, communicative entity in a place where it awaits resurrection and judgment by God, who will deal with all according to their actions, punishing the bad and rewarding the good.

Judaism

The Jewish tradition contains a range of beliefs about life after death, from no view of an afterlife to a belief in the resurrection of the body and the immortality of the soul. The one constant among the different views is the desire of the survival of the Jewish people as a whole. Importantly this desire for communal immortality exists beside any view of personal immortality.

The earlier Jewish attitudes toward death did not include a return to God. All that remained after death was a "shadow" or "shade," something like an "impermanent residue" in *sheol,* Hebrew for "underworld" or "non-land." It is only later that the human soul or *ruah* was conceived as having memory and personality, and *sheol* became the abode of disembodied souls, both good and wicked.[5]

The *Book of Daniel* (165/164 BCE) contains what is thought to be the oldest and only reference in Hebrew scriptures to the resurrection of the dead:

> At that time Michael will stand up, the great prince who mounts guard over your people. There is going to be a time of great distress, unparalleled since nations first came into existence. When that time comes, your own people will be spared, all those whose names are found written in the Book. Of those who lie sleeping in the dust of the earth many will awake, some to everlasting life, some to shame and everlasting disgrace (Dan. 12: 1–2).[6]

Significantly, in this apocalyptic vision the dead will arise not as disembodied souls but as "animated body-souls," or "body-forms animated by the life-force *(ruah)*"[7] to be with God eternally. Passages with similar implications can be found elsewhere in the later biblical or Old Testament period, such as Isaiah (xxvi: 7–19) and Ezekiel (xxxvii).[8] Later still, during the compilation of Oral Law termed the Talmudic Period, taken from the second to the sixth centuries CE, Jewish tradition became more specific about resurrection, heaven, hell, and judgment.[9] Still, to repeat, belief in the resurrection of the dead did not undermine the early Hebraic desire for communal immortality or the continuous survival of the Jewish people.[10]

Unlike the Platonic conception of the immortality of the soul, then, Judaic belief in the resurrection of the body postulates a special divine act of re-creation. Typical of the three great Semitic, monotheistic religions, Judaism leaves us utterly dependent upon God in the hour of death. Without divine intervention, death would bring personal extinction. But through "the sovereign creative love of God" there is hope for personal survival and even immortal existence beyond the grave.[11]

Islam

Resurrection is a universally accepted doctrine of Islam that is proclaimed literally on the first page of the Qur'an (or Koran), the holy book for Muslims and the basic source of Islamic teachings and law. There we find the following portrayal of creation:

> Then we made the sperm
> Into a clot of congealed blood;
> Then of that clot We made
> A (foetus) lump; then We
> Made out of that lump
> Bones and clothed the bones
> With flesh; then We developed

Out of it another creature.
So blessed be god
The Best to create!
After that, at length
Ye will die.
Again, on the day
Of judgment, will ye be
Raised up (The Holy Qur'an, Sura 23:14–16).

Prior to that day of judgment, according to the Qur'an, the souls of the departed gather in a place called *barzakh,* a barrier that separates the land of the living from the dead (Sura 23:100). Here the dead await restoration to their (uncremated) bodies on Judgment Day.

According to tradition, upon death the soul separates from the body and journeys heavenward for a vision of God, after which it returns to the grave to await judgment day. On the Day of Judgment, the Qur'an teaches, "Those who have practiced good deeds the angels will descend upon" and escort to paradise (Sura 41:30–31; 6:32). The wicked, on the other hand, will "taste the punishment of the fire" (Sura 8:50–51). This makes life on earth the determinant of an eternal future. One best prepares for eternity, according to the Sufi mystics, by practicing *fana* (extinction) or "passing away into God, and dying to the self."[12]

Christianity

Although both Judaism and Islam teach resurrection theory, belief in a resurrected body is the cornerstone Christian doctrine taught by virtually all Christian churches. Of the New Testament writers, none states the centrality of resurrection doctrine more powerfully than St. Paul in his "First Letter to the Corinthians," who, as Greeks, had little difficulty grasping the immortality of the soul, but not a resurrected body (see 1 Cor. 15:12–26).

Paul and all the other New Testament writers agree that we will have bodies in the afterlife. But what will they be like? Since the exact disposition and nature of the afterlife body remains an unsettled problem for all resurrection theories, it's worth our attention.

The Nature of the Resurrection Body   Traditional religious teaching holds that we'll have the same bodies we had in life. But the obvious problems presented by decay and deterioration of corpses, not to mention cremation and possibly dispersion of ashes, have led some Christians to believe that immediately after death the soul is given a new body and lives in a spiritual realm. For proof they refer to a parable of St. Luke, in which a rich man and a poor one evidently are given bodies immediately after their deaths (see Luke 16:19–31).

Thomas Aquinas, on the other hand, apparently believed that the soul continues to exist for some time without the body until ultimately being reunited with it. As for the location of the soul immediately after death, his understanding of the scriptures and the teachings of the early Church led the "Angelic Doctor" to posit as an article of faith a tripartite supernatural realm consisting of heaven, hell, and an intermediate venue of purification termed purgatory.

Recognizing the inherent doctrinal problems raised by body decay or cremation, contemporary philosopher Peter van Inwagen concedes that the bodies somehow must be preserved for Judgment Day, otherwise there's no hope of resurrection. How, then, might an almighty being accomplish the feat of resurrection? Perhaps, van Inwagen suggests, "God preserves our corpses contrary to all appearance. . . ." As he writes:

> Perhaps at the moment of each man's death, God removes his corpse and replaces it with a simulacrum which is what is burned or rots. Or perhaps God is not quite so wholesale as this: perhaps He removes for "safekeeping" only the "core person"—the brain and central nervous system—or even some special part of it. These are details.[13]

The tricky problems of the soul's postmortem embodiment and location aside, what kind of bodies can we expect to have in the afterlife? If the same as in this life, at what stage (or age) of our lives? Maybe we will have "new and improved" bodies, idealized ones. But if so, what about individuals who died at birth, in infancy, or childhood? What kind of bodies will they have?

Unfortunately, scriptures don't provide a clear, unequivocal answer to these questions. Indeed, a reading of the New Testament turns up conflicting depictions of the resurrection body. In some accounts Jesus has a clearly recognizable body when he appears to the apostles after his death, elsewhere not (see John 21:4–6; Luke 24:36–43). Recognizable or not, the resurrection body doesn't seem limited like other bodies. The resurrected Jesus, for example, walks through walls or suddenly appears in houses with doors shut (John 20:19).

Uncomfortable with the problems raised by traditional resurrectionism but wanting to preserve the doctrine of a risen body and with it mind/body dependence, some Christians have turned to an alternative version of resurrection termed "replica theory."

Replica Theory   Replica theory postulates that, instead of carrying over into the afterlife the actual body we had in this life, we will have a *replica* of our human body, perhaps an idealized version of it.

Some replica theorists believe that the New Testament provides a basis for their belief. For example, in the aforementioned letter from St. Paul to the Greeks at Corinth, Paul makes the point that there are many kinds of "bodies," and that the resurrection body will be a new body, not physical or perishable, which God will provide (1 Cor. 15:35–38).

Drawing on St. Paul, philosopher of religion John Hick says resurrection of the dead has nothing to do with the resuscitation of corpses in a cemetery. Rather, "It concerns God's re-creation or reconstitution of the human psychophysical individual, not as the organism that has died but as a *soma pneumatikon,* a spiritual body inhabiting a spiritual world as the physical body inhabits our present world."[14] This world of replicas, the theologian speculates,

...occupies its own space distinct from that with which we are now familiar. That is to say, an object in the resurrection world is not situated at any distance or in any direction from the objects in our present world, although each object in either world is spatially related to every other object in the same world.

This supposition provides a model by which one may conceive of the divine re-creation of the embodied human personality. In this model, the element of the strange and mysterious has been reduced to a minimum by following the view of some of the early Church Fathers that the resurrection body has the same shape as the physical body, and ignoring Paul's own hint it may be as unlike the physical body as a full grain of wheat differs from the wheat seed.[15]

Since the next life supposedly begins immediately after death, replica theory such as Hick's does provide answers to two questions that trouble the literal version of resurrection theory: (1) where exactly are the disembodied souls while they're awaiting their resurrected bodies?; and (2) how is a body that has decayed or been cremated resurrected?

Still puzzling, though, is exactly how a replica can be identical to the original body. Paul Edwards, for one, believes that Hick is using the word "resurrection" in a highly misleading way. Edwards explains:

> "Resurrection" in its original and literal sense means bringing a dead body back to life, and in such a case we could have no identity problem. If we accept the New Testament account, then Jesus resurrects Lazarus in this literal sense [see John 11]. If instead of bringing the body of Lazarus back to life Jesus had allowed it to remain a corpse and created a duplicate, this would no doubt have been a stunning miracle but it could hardly be counted as a resurrection.[16]

Beyond this, replica theory still must deal with the "age-stage" problems that hound literal resurrection theory, as well as disembodied mind.[17]

Of course, none of these objections shakes the conviction of believers in a divinely orchestrated resurrection, for in God all things are possible. Indeed, it is the seeming impossible that makes possible faith in the supernatural. In the words of St. Augustine: "Faith is to believe what you do not yet see; the reward for this faith is to see what you believe." Or as literal resurrectionist Peter Geach puts it:

> The traditional faith of Christianity, inherited from Judaism, is that at the end of this age Messiah will come and men rise from their graves to die no more. That faith is not going to be shaken by inquiries about bodies burned to ashes or eaten by beasts; those who might well suffer just such death in martyrdom were those who were most confident of a glorious reward in the resurrection. One who shares that hope will hardly wish to take out an occultist or philosophical insurance policy, to guarantee some sort of survival as an annuity, in case God's promise of resurrection should fail.[18]

But other survivalists can't so easily hurdle the paradoxes of resurrectionism, or disembodied soul for that matter. As an alternative, some of them turn to the oldest afterlife hypothesis with the broadest cross-cultural reach: reincarnation theory.

REINCARNATION

Reincarnation, also termed metempsychosis (from the Greek *meta,* after, + *empsukhos,* animate) or transmigration, is the belief in rebirth of the soul or spirit in another form, a new embodiment.

Like resurrection theory, then, the doctrine of reincarnation includes the belief that the disembodied soul will be restored to a new bodily existence. But where resurrection theory generally attributes re-embodiment to a divine collective miracle "at the last day" (John 11:24), reincarnation theory depicts it as ongoing in the divine plan of creation. Specifically in contrast to Christian resurrection doctrine, where God creates an immortal human soul out of nothing or from His eternal being, reincarnation theory steers clear of absolute origins. It prefers instead to think of the soul as evolving from more primitive stages in the infinite past to more advanced stages into the infinite future. Furthermore, whereas it is fundamental to almost all versions of Christianity that this life here and now determines one's eternal destiny, reincarnationism views the present life as one in, perhaps, a long succession of earthly lives. Each of these existences represents a kind of school for learning and developing, for growing in wisdom and maturing spiritually.

Depending on the particular reincarnation theory, the form of embodiment will vary. Many reincarnation theories believe that humans may be reborn as animals, while others contend that, once in human form, the soul does not reanimate as an animal. Then there is the time interval between two incarnations. Depending on the version of reincarnationism, this can vary from centuries to reincarnation immediately after death. Believing the latter, for example, Tibetan Lamas limit the search for a successor to their spiritual leader, the Dalai Lama, to infants born at the time of the Dalai's death. Presumably, his spirit is immediately reincarnated as a newborn baby.

Although probably perplexing to most Westerners, no afterlife doctrine has exerted more influence on the peoples of the world than the doctrine of reincarnation. Not only does it continue to enjoy a huge following throughout Asia, it maintains significant appeal to many persons in the West as well.

Hinduism

According to one important version of Hindu teaching, the soul of each person is reborn into another body on earth after death. The basis for this belief is found in the Bhagavad Gita, the Hindu holy book.

The Gita, as it's sometimes called, centers around a discussion between Lord Krishna and the warrior Arjuna, who is despondent about soon having to shed the blood of relatives in battle, albeit a righteous one. In the book's second chapter, Krishna, who is a god in disguise, comforts Arjuna by reminding him that the *atman*—the genuine self or soul—cannot die because it is spiritual and eternal. The soul's vehicle, the body, on the other hand, being material and finite, will die, whereupon the released soul will receive a new body-vehicle.

Technically, according to Hinduism, the soul is covered by two bodies, one physical and perishable, the other subtle and immortal. It's the subtle body that stores all the thoughts, desires, and experiences one has had in every single life one has lived, and that carries the soul to its next destination at the time of death. "From the time of the soul's original embodiment in matter," writes Hindu philosopher Prasannatma Das, "it has possessed the same subtle body regardless of the external body it had. At death the physical body changes, but the subtle body continues with the soul."[19] This makes us eternal souls within perishable bodies.[20]

What determines the soul's destination at the time of death is one's actions or deeds in life, termed "karma" (literally "action" or "deed"). Karma is one's fate—what one deserves or is due according to how one has lived. What we are is largely the result of past karma.

Sometimes our karmic destiny takes us to a higher plane of existence, sometimes to a lower. If, for example, just prior to death my mind focuses on an activity that is very ignorant, I will be reenacted as a lower species of life, perhaps a plant, fish, tree, or an animal. If my mind turns to an activity that is passionate, I will take a human form. And if I contemplate an activity that is primarily within the mode of goodness, I will receive the body of one of the higher planets.

The point is: We die as we live. We reap what we sow. "Only by having one's mind focused on Brahman can one return to Brahman,"[21] that is, World Spirit, ultimate Reality, or universal soul, of which Krishna is an aspect. The aim of the whole evolutionary process—the point to the long succession of earthly lives—is for the individual soul or *atman* to understand its identity with Brahman. When we realize *atman* as Brahman, we have attained *moksha,* the state of personal insight and enlightenment.[22]

Ideally, then, according to Hinduism, we do not reincarnate. Having attained enlightenment, we have arrived at the supreme destination. There is, therefore, no need to return to the world. As Krishna tells Arjuna: "From the highest planet in the material world down to the lowest, all are places of misery wherein repeated birth and death take place. But one who attains to My abode...never takes birth again."[23]

Buddhism

While their various interpretations make it risky to summarize Buddhist and Hindu teachings about life after death, some careful statements are possible.

In contrast to Hinduism, Shakyamuni Buddha, the founder of Buddhism who was born as Siddhartha Gautama (563–483 BCE), taught that rebirth was due not to *karma* but to *tanha*. *Tanha* is the wish or desire to be a separate self at the expense, if need be, of all other life forms. In a word, *tanha* is selfishness and it is selfishness that causes rebirth. If it is selfish desire that consigns us to re-embodiment, it is sincere wish that allows us at any point to step permanently out of the cycle of rebirth.[24]

Another difference is that, unlike Hindus, most Buddhists don't believe in a spiritual, eternal *atman* or soul. One of Buddha's chief teachings was the *anatta* doctrine. According to the *anatta* teaching, there is no permanent *atman* or ego and, therefore, no rebirth of a permanent self.

On the other hand, like Hindus, Tibetan Buddhists, at least, hold that regardless of religion or belief, preparation in life for death can help anyone. The *Tibetan Book of the Dead,* whose eighth century CE legendary author and teacher Padmasambhava (also: Guru Rinpoche) converted Tibet to Buddhism, deals in part with that preparation. If adequately prepared, Padmasambhava says, at the moment of death I will abandon grasping and attachment, and see reality for what it is: illusion. This profound realization, according to teaching, is liberating. It frees me from attachment and aversion, and extinguishes the illusion of some eternal, personal self. Realizing the idea of an individual soul as illusory is essential for being released from the wheel of rebirths and for attaining enlightenment, or *nirvana*. If, however, I remain unenlightened—still believing in an independent self—then I am destined to be reborn.

Buddhism, then, shares with Hinduism: (1) a reincarnation belief, or belief in a continual succession of rebirths; and the view that (2) rebirth is a greater evil than death. The difference is that for Buddhists it isn't a reborn *atman;* for, according to Buddha, there is no soul, only a series of discontinuous psychic states. What is reborn is some karmic stream of consciousness.

Unlike the karma of Hinduism, however, which is the destiny one generates for oneself by one's own thoughts, words, acts, and attitudes, the karma of Buddhism is more likened to indelible, influential traces that one inevitably leaves behind in living. Buddha expressed his view of reincarnation and karma in the image of a flame being passed from candle to candle. The first candle's flame doesn't pass to subsequent candles, but its light does. The final candle isn't the same as the original, but it was influenced by it. In this sense, according to religious scholar Kenneth Kramer, for Buddhists "rebirth is the on-going process of the transmission of the entire evolutionary process and in all its possibilities and probabilities."[25] Still, even though each of us is the product of all the influences, near and far, that have helped shape us, we aren't predetermined to mechanically pass on to others our legacies. Within the chain of causation, each of us can help determine the future through our own choices and actions.

As for the afterlife, Buddhism teaches that most of us live on in the strands of desire we leave behind that can only be realized in other incarnations.[26] These *skandhas* or forces holding life together have been likened to black holes, which we never see but whose effects, for example gravitational fields, are powerfully evident in space when a star implodes. Despite the nonexistence of the star, it has left behind something tangible and verifiable. Similarly, something lives on after we die, after the material aspect of our personhood has disappeared.[27] Some term it "invisible mental energy." This energy supposedly carries its "karmic residue" to a new form that subsequently affects the development of the senses, mental activities, and even desires. All of this leaves death the mere passing of a particular phase within the ongoing process of existence.[28]

Christianity

Although not ordinarily associated with Christianity, belief in reincarnation is traceable to some of the earliest Christian theologians. Origen (185–254), for example, next to Augustine the most prominent of the Church founders, evidently believed in repeated lives for the soul until fully purified to enter heaven. Three centuries after Origen's death, the reincarantion doctrine he seemingly espoused was officially condemned by the second Council of Constantinople (553 CE). Earlier, in the fourth century CE, the emperor Constantine (285–337), who made Christianity the official religion of the Roman Empire in 325, had references to reincarnation removed from the New Testament. In this fashion, according to some, the idea of reincarnation was suppressed in the West in favor of theological and later scientific dualism, leaving life and death in an unbridgeable antagonism.[29]

In the seventeenth century reincarnation theory figured prominently in the philosophy of the Christian Anne Conway (1631–1679), who believed that divine justice requires a kind of reincarnation whereby the good will be made better, and the evil made worse. Decades before Conway, some Christian thinkers of the fifteenth and sixteenth centuries evidently found support for their own reincarnation beliefs in ancient Hebrew mystical teachings called cabala (also "kabala" or "kabbalah," from the Hebrew *qabbala* for "received doctrine"). Following its earliest formulation in eleventh-century France, cabala spread throughout Europe, notably to Spain. Significant among its doctrines was transmigration of souls, which some scholars think was borrowed from the Neoplatonists.

Today a reincarnation belief is evident in the theologies of some prominent Christians, such as the physicist and parapsychologist Raynor Johnson (1901–1987). And, according to George Barna, former minister and head of Barna Research Group, one out of ten born-again Christians—"those who believe entry into heaven is solely based on confessing of sins and faith in Jesus Christ"—also believe in reincarnation, even though it violates Christian tenets.[30] In theory, that would put the number of American Christian reincarnationists in the millions, given that nearly 50% of Americans say they are evangelical or born-again Christians (according to a December 2003 Gallup Poll). (Born-again Christians have experienced a dramatic conversion to faith in Jesus that is associated with salvation, conversion, and spiritual rebirth.)

Some of these individuals have confidently asserted a biblical basis for reincarnationism. There is, they say, the fact that Jesus never denied reincarnation when given the opportunity (see, for example, John 9:1–3). But more important to Christian reincarnationists is what Jesus did say, such as the times he asserted that John the Baptist was the prophet Elijah (see Matthew 13:10–13). It was one such occasion that led the renowned English writer and poet Robert Graves (1895–1985) to conclude: "No honest theologian therefore can deny that his acceptance of Jesus as Christ logically binds every Christian to a belief in reincarnation—in Elias case at least."[31]

Some fundamentalist Christians also submit non-canonical gospel support for reincarnationism, such as the Gnostic text *Pistis Sophia* (250–300 CE). There it is written: "Souls are poured from one into another of different kinds of bodies of the world." For others the seemingly Taoist and Buddhist concepts in *The Gospel of Mary Magdalene* are reason to infer an early Christian reincarnation view.

Western Philosophy

Of the doctrine of reincarnation and its origins, the fifth century BCE Greek historian Herodotus writes in his *History*:

> The Egyptians were the first who maintained the following doctrine...
> that the human soul is immortal, and at the death of the body enters into
> some other living thing then coming to birth; and after passing through
> all creatures of land, sea, and air, it enters once more into a human body at
> birth, a cycle that it completes in three thousand years.
>
> There are Greeks who have used this doctrine, some earlier and some
> later, as if it were their own; I know their names, but do not record
> them.[32]

Pythagoras likely was one of the famed historian's unnamed Greeks.

As noted in the preceding chapter, Pythagoras taught the doctrine of the transmigration of the soul through successive incarnations. For Pythagoreans, theoretical thinking—pure science and pure mathematics—was how to purify the soul. Through those disciplines, individuals could turn their thinking from particular things to the permanent and ordered world of numbers. With this intellectual purification came liberation from the "the wheel of birth" or the migration of the soul to animal and other forms in the constant process of death and birth. In this manner, according to Pythagoreans, individuals could achieve unity with God and share divine immortality.[33]

Of the Greek philosophers who taught preexistence and successive lives through which individuals progress, Plato, of course, was the most renowned. Both his *Phaedo* and *Phaedrus* echo the Pythagorean notion that the soul's fate hinges on its degree of purity in life. Impure souls may be reincarnated as animals, and those who never see the truth will never pass into human form. Only the purest souls can escape further reincarnation and enjoy the company of the gods. The kind of human body a moderately virtuous soul can expect depends upon how much progress toward truth it has made in its former incarnation. With startling specificity, Plato has Socrates delineate nine degrees of probation from philosophers to tyrants, in *descending* order of enlightenment, happy to say.[34]

The Neoplatonist Plotinus not only reaffirmed Plato's doctrine of the preexistence of the soul but also his belief that the soul survives the death of the body. Through a series of rebirths or transmigrations from one body to another, it is ultimately purified and educated to Plato's vision of truth: the intelligible world of ideals or perfect forms.

In *A Critical Examination of the Belief in a Life After Death* (1961), the French philosopher C. J. Ducasse (1881–1969) identifies numerous other Western philosophers who have befriended the idea of reincarnation: Hume, Kant, Johann Fichte (1762–1814), and Arthur Schopenhauer (1788–1860) among them.

Himself a confirmed reincarnationist, Ducasse distinguished between personality and individuality. Personality, he said, is what we acquire during our lifetime, such as knowledge, character, and memories. Individuality, on the other hand, are our native aptitudes and dispositions, such as our intellectual or aesthetic inclinations and even, perhaps, aptitudes persistently striven for in previous incarnations. It is individuality, our "stock of innate latent capacities and incapacities," that is reborn, according to Ducasse.[35]

Despite its diverse, widespread appeal, reincarnation theory has numerous skeptics. Some simply assert that survival of death demands a "relation of material continuity." In other words, no matter how strong the mental or memory connections, there must be bodily continuity. Others puzzle over verification issues. How, they wonder, could the idea of reincarnation be proved? How, even in theory, could it be tested?[36] Reincarnation skeptics also say that it clashes not only with some highly regarded scientific theories such as biological evolution but with established facts. For example, according to reincarnationism the earth's population should be either stationary or decreasing as personal enlightenment is attained. In fact, notes reincarnation critic Paul Edwards, the earth has shown enormous increase throughout recorded history.[37] Edwards further asserts that alleged cases of reincarnation fail to meet the two criteria for personal identity: bodily continuity and memory.[38] Another loose end concerns the location of the dead awaiting new bodies. If, as most reincarnationists hold, death is not immediately followed by rebirth, where, then, are the individuals in between, and what are they like?

Reincarnation beliefs, by definition, posit *personal* survival, that is, that human beings will survive as individuals. But some ideas of reincarnation also include impersonal or depersonalized survival. This means that, ultimately, we will not continue to survive as individuals but will merge or remerge into an impersonal oneness with the universe. It is to this idea of "mystical union" that we now turn.

MYSTICAL UNION

Although Hinduism and Buddhism believe in reincarnation, they also believe in an ultimate end to rebirths and an absorption in Brahman (in Hinduism) or attainment of Nirvana (in Buddhism). In this sense, they combine both a belief in personal survival *and* impersonal survival. But their overarching afterlife view is *mystical union*. This is a continued existence, not as an individual personality, but as a oneness with the divine.

Hinduism

Recall that, according to Hinduism, the only way to end the round of rebirths is to attain *moksha* or enlightenment. Although there are several paths to enlightenment, common to each is cultivating spiritual knowledge and remembering Krishna at the time of death.

Attaining *moksha* or enlightenment means that one is freed of the external covering of the body and thus from the wheel of birth, death, and rebirth. In this way one shares in divine immortality. But the immortality won is not of the body, since the body isn't actually alive at any time, according to orthodox Hindu teaching. Nor is it the immortality of the individual personality with, say, personal consciousness, or memories intact. Rather, the immortality promised by Hinduism (at least the Vedanta version) is an impersonal merging with or absorption into the divine essence, at the heart of which is the realization of the soul's eternal blissful nature. "That art Thou" sums up what *moksha* or enlightenment brings—"that" meaning ultimate reality, and thou "a human soul."

Taoism

Taoism, together with Confucianism and Buddhism, constitutes one of the three great religions of China. According to tradition its founder was Lao Tzu, who probably lived during the time of Confucius (551–479 BCE). Another eminent figure in early Taoism was Chuang Tzu (c. 369–286 BCE).

In classical Chinese Taoism, immortality doesn't exist because life and death are but phases in the cycle of change, itself part of *tao. Tao,* or "way," has been described as "the all-pervading principle that exists prior to the existence of the universe, and is to be found in everything, no matter how trivial or base."[39] The manifestation of *tao* in every individual thing is termed *te,* meaning virtue or power. *Te* is the share of *tao* deposited in each essence. To the extent that all things have *te,* they partake of *tao.* This means that there is no essential difference between one thing and another. All distinctions are human-made and transitory. It follows that any distinction between life and death is artificial or false. There is really no difference, therefore, between the living and dead, between mortal and immortal. Death is already in life, life is already in death. To separate one from the other renders each incomplete.[40]

Accordingly, treating life and death as equal manifestations of *tao,* of a single reality, Chuang Tzu expressed an affirmative attitude toward death reminiscent of Epicurus:

> Life is the companion of death, death is the beginning of life. Who understand their workings? Man's life is a coming together of breath. If it comes together, there is life; if it scatters, there is death. And if life and death are companions to each other, then what is there for us to be anxious about?[41]

By this account, death is "the natural and necessary transition from a conscious state to an unconscious one, from a life-body to a death-body."[42] If we fear death and yearn for personal immortality, it's because we don't understand nature's way. If we did and embraced *tao,* then we would understand that while our bodies die, we live as long as *tao* lives, that is, forever—not as individual personalities but as part of the universal essence.[43] "Man may die indeed," it is written in *Chuanag Tzu,* "but his essence as part of the universal essence lives on forever."

Buddhism

According to Buddhism, it is the realization that soul or personal self is an illusion that in large part constitutes enlightenment or *nirvana,* the extinction from desires. An ineffable state that baffles the imagination and defies thought and word, *nirvana* often is loosely described as release from the clinging, grasping self. Extinguished in *nirvana* is desire and craving. Freed of attachment to objects, thoughts, and desire, a person fully realizes the impermanent nature of things, including the illusion of self and ego. In this way, death is seen for what it is, not as the greatest evil, but as "an expression of being's pulse."[44] In an apt analogy, Kramer asks us to consider a motion picture.

> Just as each frame is similar to, yet slightly different from the one before it, and just as action occurs when the frames change rapidly, Buddhists believe in a moment-to-moment birth and death. Like the unrolling of a film, human life is seen as a continuous process of birth and death, birth and death, in every millionth of a second.[45]

Similarly, any particular death is viewed as one of a succession of deaths.

As for the postmortem state of the individual who reaches nirvana, the so-called *arhat,* early Buddhism offers little insight. When asked, the Buddha is said to have responded with silence.[46]

Western Philosophy

The long-lived American philosopher Charles Hartshorne (1897–2000) has been called "one of the few great Western philosophers to discuss and debate Eastern systems and ideas as philosophy."[47] In fact, Hartshorne (pronounced as if "Heershorne") shared the Buddhist view of reality, including the constantly changing personality. He was also sympathetic to the Buddhist notion of "dependent origination," according to which all things that exist and cease to exist are mutually determined by other things that exist and cease to exist.[48,49] In other words, all things change because all things are interdependent. It is for this reason that Hartshorne, like Buddhists, denied the existence of a permanent, continuing self and with it postmortem survival of personality.

At the center of this process of change and interdependence is God. Hartshorne's God, however, is not the personal God of theism. Nor is it the God of pantheism, which is the doctrine that God is in everything and is, therefore, indistinguishable from the universe and its phenomena. For Hartshorne God encompasses everything, or is panentheistic.

Panenetheism (from the Greek *pan,* all, + *en,* in, + *theos,* God) is the belief in a fixed and unchanging God who includes all possibilities. This means that, while God is not identifiable with the world, (1) everything is immediately experienced by God; and (2) God responds to the world so that every part of it experiences the consequences of divine choice.[50] God is endless cosmic life. We die, our only immortality the sharing of deathless divine life through the good we've done and the love we've shown to all life.[51]

Hartshorne's thought reflects many influences, including the American philosopher Charles Peirce (1839–1914) and some of the greatest idealistic minds of the nineteenth century, such as the transcendentalist Ralph Waldo Emerson (1803–1882). Emerson passionately embraced a view of depersonalized survival or union with absolute mind he termed the "over-soul."[52]

CONCLUSIONS

No one knows for sure what happens after death. That death brings annihilation is the considered opinion of the Stoics, Epicureans, Hume, and many people today. But, undoubtedly, survival hypotheses are more popular. Millions of Christians, Muslims, and Jews believe that death brings personal immortality with bodily resurrection; and even larger numbers of Buddhists and Hindus hold that ultimately, perhaps after many lives, we are destined for an impersonal mystical union with the divine.

Although Western and Eastern beliefs in life after death differ, they do share a notable feature that anticipates the interest of the next chapter. Each tells us how to die in the best possible spiritual state and, therefore, how best to live. To know how to live is one powerful reason for afterlife belief. But it's only one reason, we're about to see, as we now consider why people believe they will survive death.

REFERENCES

1. Nagatomo Shigenori, "Contemporary Japanese Philosophy," in *A Companion to World Philosophies,* Eliot Deutsch and Ron Bontekoe, eds., Oxford: Blackwell Publishers Ltd., 1999, p. 528.

2. Jingpan Chen (or C. P. Joseph), *Confucius as a Teacher,* Beijing: Foreign Languages Press, 1990, p. 357.

3. Mary Boyce, *Zoroastrians: Their Religious Beliefs and Practices,* London: Routledge & Kegan Paul, 1979, p. 1.

4. Ibid., p. 29.

5. Kenneth Kramer, *The Sacred Art of Dying,* Mahwah, NJ: Paulist Press, 1988, pp. 123–133.

6. Ibid., pp. 133–134.

7. Ibid., p. 125.

8. John Bowker, *The Meanings of Death,* Canto edition, Cambridge, MA: Cambridge University Press, 1991, p. 359.

9. Kramer, p. 134.

10. Arnold Toynbee and others, *Man's Concern with Death,* New York: McGraw-Hill Book Company, 1968, p. 78.

11. John Hick, *Philosophy of Religion,* 3rd ed., Englewood Cliffs, NJ: Prentice-Hall, 1983, p. 123.

12. Kramer, p. 163.

13. Peter Van Inwagen, "The Possibility of Resurrection," in Paul Edwards, *Immortality*, Amherst, NY: Prometheus Books, 1997, pp. 245–246.

14. Hick, p. 125.

15. Ibid., p. 126.

16. Edwards, *Immortality*, p. 57.

17. Ibid., p. 60.

18. Peter Geach, *God and the Soul*, Bristol, U.K.: Thoemmes Press, 1994, p. 234.

19. Prasannatma Das, "A Hindu Theory of Life and Death," in *Life and Death*, 2nd ed., Louis P. Pojman, ed., Belmont, CA: Wadsworth Publishing Company, 2000, p. 132.

20. Ibid., p. 133.

21. Michael Brannigan, *The Pulse of Wisdom*, Belmont, CA: Wadsworth Publishing Company, 1995, p. 322.

22. Ibid., p. 22.

23. Prasannatma Das, p. 133.

24. Huston Smith, *The Religions of Man*, New York: Harper & Row, Publishers, 1958, p. 360.

25. Kramer, p. 51.

26. Smith, p. 360.

27. Stephen Richards, "Immorality and Life after Death—Problems," 2004. Retrieved March 1, 2005, from http://www.faithnet.org.uk/A2%20Subjects/Philosophyo freligion/immortalityproblems.htm.

28. Brannigan, p. 329.

29. Christian Bodhi, "The Christ is back and lives in London," September 4, 2004, *Worldless.com*. Retrieved December 15, 2005, from http://www.abilityoflove.com/cgi/news.asp?NewsID=7.

30. Connie K. Kang, "Next Stop, the Pearly Gates," *Los Angeles Times*, October 24, 2003, p. A 18.

31. William House, *Science Mysteries*, "Life After Death." Retrieved June 20, 2005, from http://www.world-mysteries.com/sci_3_3.htm.

32. Herodotus, *The History of Herodotus*, A. D. Godley, trans. Retrieved June 1, 2005, from http://www.perseus.tufts.edu/cgiin/ptext?doc+Perseus%3Atext%3A1999.01. 0126&layout+&loc+2.123.1.

33. Samuel Stumpf, *Philosophy: History & Problems*, 3rd ed., New York: McGraw-Hill Book Company, 1983, p. 10.

34. Plato, *Phaedrus*, Benjamin Jowett, trans. Retrieved May 25, 2005, from http://ccat. sas.upenn.edu/jod/texts/phaedrus.html.

35. C. J. Ducasse, *A Critical Examination of the Belief in a Life After Death*, Springfield, IL: Charles C. Thomas Pub. Ltd., 1974. Retrieved June 1, 2005, from http://www. survivalafterdeath.org/books/ducasse/critical/contents.htm.

36. Edwards, *Immortality*, p. 8.

37. Ibid., p. 16.

38. Paul Edwards, *Reincarnation: A Critical Examination*, Amherst, NY: Prometheus Books, 1996, p. 8.

39. Frank Magill, ed., *Masterpieces of World Philosophy*, New York: HarperCollins Publishers, 1990, p. 97.

40. Kramer, p. 85.

41. Chuang Tzu, *The Complete Works of Chuang Tzu,* Burton Watson, trans., New York: Columbia University Press, 1968, p. 235.

42. Kramer, p. 85.

43. Magill, p. 99.

44. Brannigan, p. 237.

45. Kramer, p. 51.

46. Brannigan, p. 327.

47. John B. Cobb, Jr., "Charles Hartshorne: The Einstein of Religious Thought," Claremont, CA: Center for Process Studies. Retrieved February 1, 2005, from http://www.harvardsquarelibrary.org/unitarians/hartshorne.html.

48. Charles Hartshorne, *Omnipotence and Other Theological Mistakes,* Albany, NY: SUNY Press, 1984.

49. Charles Hartshorne and William L. Reese, *Philosophers Speak of God,* Albany, NY: SUNY Press, 2000.

50. Wesley J. Wildman, "The Thought of Charles Hartshorne," *Wildman's Weird Wild Web,* Spring, 1988. Retrieved February 7, 2005, from http://people.bu.edu/wwildman/ Weird WildWeb/courses/mwt/dictionary/mwt_themes_842_hartshorne.htm.

51. John Cobb and Franklin I. Gamwell, *Conversations with Charles Hartshorne,* Chicago: University of Chicago Press, 1984.

52. Ralph Waldo Emerson, "The Over-Soul," *Selected Writings of Ralph Waldo Emerson,* William H. Gilman, ed., New York: Signet Classic, 1965, p. 286–301.

7

Bases for Afterlife Belief

A new field of research—"After-Death Communication"—claims that life and love are eternal. That reassurance is based upon thousands of firsthand accounts from people who believe they have been contacted by a dead loved one.

"AFTER-DEATH.COM" AND LIFE EVERLASTING

"After-Death.Com" is dedicated to "After-Death Communication experiences and bereavement support for those grieving the death of a loved one." The founders of this popular website describe an "after-death communication" (ADC) as a "spiritual experience, which occurs when you are contacted directly and spontaneously by a deceased family member or friend, *without* the use of psychics, mediums, rituals, or devices of any kind." It is estimated that 50–100 million Americans—that's 20%–40% of the U.S. population—have had one or more ADC experiences.

Undoubtedly, "After-Death.Com" is a source of comfort to those who wish to believe that not only does life continue after bodily death, but that communication between the living and the dead is possible. In the U.S. alone, such individuals must number in the tens of millions. After all, for well over a half-century public opinion sampling has consistently reported that at least three-quarters of Americans believe in life after death. How this belief touches people's lives, we don't exactly know. However, we do know that, historically, afterlife belief has affected what people do and why they do it. As the authors of *Heaven: A History* (2001) point out: "In the hope of reaching heaven and its rewards, people have endured poverty and exploitation, trials, and suffering, even persecution and martyrdom."[1]

There is no doubt, then, that belief in afterlife can be a great source of hope and comfort, reassurance and motivation. But is that all it is? That's the question. Is belief in life after death no more than a psychological touchstone that we adhere to to ward off death anxiety or to endure the trials and tribulations of life? Is it merely wishful thinking? Or, psychological need aside, is there good reason to believe that there is life after death? Many people believe there is. This chapter considers the main reasons for believing in personal survival of death.

Our coverage will be restricted to belief in *personal* survival, because it is the personal, rather than the impersonal, that has been methodically defended. In examining the reasons for belief in personal survival, we'll focus on four key arguments. Three of them—from theology, morality, and human development—are non-empirical. This means that they rely primarily on reason, not sense experience, for their force. Those who use them are saying, in effect: "Afterlife belief is *logical*." But increasingly popular is an empirical argument, which is an argument that appeals to sense experience. This fourth argument, which drives fascination with ADC experiences, gets its strength from parapsychological phenomena.

THE ARGUMENT FROM THEOLOGY

The confidence of many survivalists often is buoyed by their faith in theism. Theism is belief in an all-good, all-powerful, personal God. The existence of God, say theists, implies the survival of at least some human beings. In the Jewish and Christian traditions, for example, it is argued that since God made humans for ultimate existence with him, it would be contradictory if he allowed humans to pass out of existence.[2]

But does a belief in God necessitate a belief in survival? In "Theism," a scathing attack on the proposition "If God exists, there must be life after death," John Stuart Mill argued that actually nothing can be deduced about survival from the existence of God. The theological argument fails, Mill said, because it contradicts itself. It proposes that an all-powerful God is constrained or limited by his goodness to grant humans eternal life. But if God is all-powerful, there's nothing he *must* do—not even grant us afterlife. In order to avoid the contradiction, limitations on either or both God's power and goodness are in order. But once that's done, what logical grounds are there to assert that God *must* grant us eternal life?

His reservations notwithstanding, Mill didn't see any harm in someone's indulging the hope for a postmortem state as a possibility, although only based upon express revelation.

THE ARGUMENT FROM MORALITY

The book of Job does not attempt to explain the mystery of suffering but to probe the depths of faith in spite of suffering. As such, the ancient parable of a long-suffering man provides one of the most poignant philosophical arguments for postmortem existence. The basic idea is that there must be an afterlife to offset the unequal distribution of suffering in this life. Without it, humanity would be left to echo Job's bitterest plaint:

"Let the day perish wherein I was born,
And the night which said,
'A man-child is conceived'" (Job 3:1–3).

Again, if there were no hope of an ultimate balancing of the scales of justice, we would be abandoned to lament with the reflective author of Ecclesiastes, possibly Solomon (970–928 BCE):

> ... I saw all the oppressions that are practiced under the sun. And behold, the tears of the oppressed, and they had no one to comfort them! On the side of their oppressors there was power, and there was no one to contain them. And I thought the dead who are already dead more fortunate than the living who are still alive; but better than both is he who has not yet been, and has not seen the evil deeds that are done under the sun (Ecclesiastes 4:1–3).

It is precisely life's unrelieved suffering and unrighted injustice that persuades many individuals of life after death.

Philosophically, the idea that justice demands an afterlife was given its most compelling analysis by Kant. In his *Critique of Practical Reason*, Kant observed a sad fact of life: Bad things happen to good people. That doesn't seem fair. Nor does it seem fair that liars and thieves sometimes not only go undiscovered or unpunished, they're rewarded. Good things happen to bad people.

Most of us probably would agree that it ought not be this way. In fact, many of us work hard to ensure a better world, a more equitable society. We may even feel obligated to believe in the possibility of a fair and just world, what Kant called a "*summum bonum*," a "supremely good" state of affairs. But such an idyllic state, which Kant believed we were duty-bound to pursue, is not possible in this life. It's only possible, he writes, "on the supposition of an endless duration of the existence and personality of the same rational being." In other words, the supremely good is only possible if the soul is immortal. And, therefore, "immortality, being inseparably connected with the moral law, is a postulate of pure practical reason."[3] Perfect justice, in brief, requires immortality.

Granting its psychological appeal, does the cherished belief in a sort of ultimate court of perfect justice make it so? Simply because the physical universe may exhibit uniformity and regularity, does that mean that a like kind of balance and harmony must exist in the moral sense? No, say skeptics, who generally chalk up the argument for postmortem life from moral consciousness to wishful thinking, gently chiding, perhaps: "If wishes were horses, beggars would ride." To which theistic survivalists might reply: "But God wouldn't have given us this particular wish of immortality if it weren't so." But such reasoning left Mill unimpressed. As he wryly observes in "Theism," "Many a man would like to be a [prosperous King] Croesus or an Augustus Caesar, but has his wishes gratified only to the moderate extent of a pound a week or the Secretaryship of his trades union."[4]

In the midst of all this philosophical jousting, the argument from morality seems to morph seamlessly into a theological argument. This needn't be, though. For example, many reincarnationists who aren't theists base their reincarnation belief on the injustice found in the world. Raynor Johnson, for example, claims that reincarnation is the *only* afterlife view that "carries with it the reasonable assurance that we live in a just world."[5] Still, to most of its adherents the argument from justice probably draws its force from theology. Where it does, then like the theological argument, it is open to challenges to its theistic assumptions, the most basic one being the existence of a personal God.

THE ARGUMENT FROM GLOBALISM

It's a truism that people have always believed in life after death. Not everyone, of course, but an overwhelming number of diverse peoples down through time undoubtedly have gone to their graves, tombs, or pyres absolutely persuaded that their lives were not over.

It's well known, for example, that the ancient Egyptians regarded death as a temporary interruption, not an end to life. To insure their survival after death, they honored gods. And to preserve the body so that the soul could return to it and reanimate or bring it to life, they mummified the corpse. The belief in the continuity of life after death was also basic to ancient Indian teachings, as expressed in the Vedas and developed more fully in the Upanishads. Similarly, for centuries before it was put into written form, *The Tibetan Book of the Dead* was passed down orally, evidence that for Tibetans a belief in life after death stretched back into the indefinite past.

The point of these historic examples, which easily could be multiplied, is that even if the idea of an eternal afterlife wasn't fully developed until the advent of Christian and Islamic religions, the more we learn about past civilizations the more it reveals the global appeal of the belief in some kind of life after death. Also included in the list, incidentally, would be civilizations with no apparent contact with Christian or Islamic cultures. The Aztecs, for example, mistook the conquistador Hernando Cortes (1485–1547) for an incarnation of Quetzalcoatl, the Aztec god of *resurrection*.

Those who make the historical argument for an afterlife—let's call them "globalists"—often point out that it isn't until the modern age, specifically the twentieth century, that the widespread belief in afterlife comes under attack. It was then, they say, that scientific materialism reduced consciousness (mind, soul, inner self) to brain activity, thereby reducing afterlife belief to pre-scientific thinking.

But critics demur. They say that numbers of themselves don't mean anything. The pages of history are littered with pandemic false, albeit cherished beliefs. Furthermore, they point out that the scientific materialism of the modern age, in fact, had its counterpart in ancient and primitive societies, such as the Hebrews, the Chinese, and the Greeks. In other words, although perhaps widespread, the belief in an afterlife was by no means universal.

Perhaps so, say globalists, but the larger point is that scientific materialism mischaracterizes consciousness as only the product of dead matter, whereas what we are conscious of is life. If on the deepest psychic level death is not acknowl-edged, it is for the reason that death does not exist, at least not as the permanent end of life. In what Tolstoy called the "invisible consciousness," we know our life doesn't end with bodily death.[6] For globalists, then, the widespread belief in afterlife is more than wishful thinking or terror management. It reflects a true self-understanding that we bear within ourselves.

THE ARGUMENT FROM HUMAN DEVELOPMENT

The argument from human development begins with the observation that development has always occurred in nature. Clearly discernible among organisms is a progression from lesser life forms to higher ones and ultimately to humans. Why, it is then asked, assume that human development ceases with the death of the body? Isn't a life after death more likely, where humans will progress to a higher condition? No, critics flatly answer, there is actually nothing in nature for either deducing an afterlife from human development or for considering such a post-mortem future probable. Undaunted, philosopher John Hick, for one, has given a religious spin to the argument from human development in his "Irenaean theodicy."

Irenaean Theodicy

"Theodicy" (from the Greek *theo*, god, + *dike*, justice or order) is the traditional theological term for a reasoned attempt to vindicate God's goodness and justice in the face of evil. Recall from Chapter 2 that the Augustinian type of theodicy involves a fall from grace of free finite creatures, resulting in a disharmony of nature and misuse of human freedom. As a direct consequence, we experience natural disasters such as tsunamis and hurricanes, beastly human misconduct such as genocide, unrelenting diseases such as cancer, and, ultimately, death. According to this traditional and extant Christian cosmogony, all this evil is the result of a human fall from grace or the fall of a band of angels who now wreak evil on earth.

Although a Christian, Hick finds this "pre-scientific world view"[7] implausible. So, he has turned to an alternative theodicy, one he reads in the teachings of Irenaeus (120–202), an early founder of the Church. Irenaeus's teachings were developed by subsequent scholars, most notably the romantic German theologian Friedrich Schleiermacher (1768–1834). A key source of modern Protestant thought, Schleiermacher set the foundation for modern theology's emphasis on the living experience of God, as opposed to doctrines that don't arise out of that experience.[8] Basic to this personal relationship with the divine is trust in eternal life. As kindred theologian Edward Schillebeeckx writes:

> The breeding ground of belief in life after death . . . was always seen in a communion of life between God and man . . . Living communion with God, attested as the meaning, the foundation and the inspiring content of

human existence is the only climate in which the believer's trust in a life after death comes, and evidently can come, to historical fruition.[9]

Hick's Irenaean theodicy, then, trades on this "communion of life between God and man" by casting the goal of struggling humanity, individually and collectively, as turning from self-centeredness to God-centeredness. Hick believes that we were created to be "perfect finite personal beings in filial relationship with their Maker."[10]

That we were created *to be,* not *as,* such beings explains why we begin as spiritually and morally immature creatures at the beginning of a long process of growth and development.[11] Necessary to this developmental process, Hick believes, is the presence of evil, both natural (e.g., so-called acts of God) and moral (i.e., human made). In this view, evil is necessary because only by freely choosing good over evil, "coming freely to an uncoerced consciousness of God," can we become perfected finite persons. This means that through our uncoerced choices and actions favoring good over evil, we are being perfected by gradually developing into likenesses of the divine.

Although all of us are involved in this process here on earth, Hick believes that very few of us, saints perhaps, complete it before we die. Thus, fundamental to his Irenaean theodicy is life after death, where this process of becoming children of God can be completed in *everyone.* Everyone must participate in this process so that evil and sin are not made unending, as they would be if part of humanity were condemned to hell for eternity.

Hick's conception of afterlife is as unorthodox as his account of evil and his belief that all people will be saved. He finds a series of lives probable, each with its own beginning and end.[12] Separately these finite lives are part of a spiritual progress towards the ultimate state that lies beyond them. Theologian Paul Badham interprets Hick's proposal as providing "a global approach to the theology of death," meaning:

> It attempts to draw the major speculations about our possible destiny from the philosophical and religious writings of both east and west into a coherent and unified hypothesis. For it equates both resurrection and reincarnation with the notion of the conscious personal self surviving bodily death and subsequently receiving a new embodiment for life in another space.[13]

Since any theistic theodicy both begins with and tests a belief in God, any challenge to Hick's theodicy will be a challenge to theistic belief itself. But beyond that, because his requires postmortem life, in which we are perfected or made into children of God, objections to an Irenaean theodicy controvert afterlife belief itself. Thus: How can an all-good, all-powerful God permit the sheer amount and intensity of evil, of seemingly unnecessary and useless pain over millions of years? How can such a God allow it as demonstration of human love?[14] How can he or she suffer so many obstacles in the path of the human journey that the belief in a limitless-good, limitless-powerful God strikes many as fantastical? Such questions of Hick's Irenaean theodicy disputes not only its assumption that a personal God exists but that an afterlife is inevitable.

Still, an important strength of an Irenaean theodicy, according to Hick, is its view of humans initially created through the evolutionary process.[15] This, he feels, makes his depiction more plausible than the biblical account of creation. True, for fundamental and many traditional Christians, the biblical formulation sets the stage for the great drama of life, death, and redemption—of paradise lost and regained. But, in fact, that may be its problem, Hick suggests. The Bible's poetic and dramatic values strike many people today as more myth than history. An Irenaean theodicy, by contrast, compliments science, Hick contends, specifically evolutionary theory. But, ironically, it is this boast of scientific respectability that has invited the most biting objections to an Irenaean theodicy and, more generally, to religious developmentalism.

Their detractors accuse religious developmentalists of injecting metaphysics into science, of giving a supernatural account of what can be construed naturalistically. Human development, they say, like all other phenomena, can be explained in terms of natural causes and laws without attributing moral, spiritual, or transcendental significance to them. So why do that? Applying Ockham's razor (see Chapter 2), that long-established hallmark of scientific elegance, critics ask: Why posit more when less will do? Besides, proposing that life continues after death—that life is going somewhere, as it were—strikes skeptics as implausible, if not impossible.

But such withering criticism does not deter religious developmentalists. Indeed, they respond with their own brand of naturalism.

According to *religious* naturalism, religious truths can be derived from nature and natural causes, apart from revelation. In this view, there is a divine presence, plan, and direction in evolution. Some go even further. The French paleontologist Pierre Teilhard de Chardin (1881–1955), for example, envisioned divinely directed nature moving toward higher forms of consciousness. Thus, in *The Phenomenon of Man* (1955), Teilhard writes: "I believe I can see a direction and a line of progress for life, a line and a direction which are in fact so well marked that I am convinced their reality will be universally admitted by the science of tomorrow."[16]

Teilhard, who was a Jesuit priest and spent a lifetime attempting to reconstruct Christian doctrines from the viewpoint of science, was inspired by the thought of Henri Bergson (1859–1941), whose *Creative Evolution*[17] he studied in his twenties. The French philosopher claimed that Darwin had provided an incomplete description of evolution, accounting for mutations, for example, but not for why such changes occurred in the first place. For Bergson a creative impulse, what he termed *elan vital*, was at the heart of evolution, not Darwinian natural selection or survival of the fittest. Although Bergson never intended his notion of *elan vital* to support afterlife belief, some developmentalists have, nonetheless, appropriated it for that cause. So, it's worth briefly considering.

Bergson's *Elan Vital*

Literally "vital urge," Bergson's *elan vital* is the basic reality. It is the "procreant urge of the world," its creative force that moves through and motivates all organic things. The *elan* is at once the impulse and desire of all life to act in its evolution; what drives it toward increasing complexity. It is the life force that we discover first, not through the intellect, but the intuition. As Bergson writes: "through the immediate awareness of our continuous self: we discover that we *endure*."[18]

Elan vital, then, is the positive power that moves us forward and upward by motivating and enabling us, through acts of free choice, to shape body, matter, and world to our intellect and will. More than a mere mechanism of biological evolution, the *elan* resembles consciousness, from which emerges life, action, freedom, creativity—in a word, possibility. Little wonder that Bergson likened this protean life impulse as being "of God, if is not God himself." Thus defined, God has nothing of the already made. "He is unceasing life, action, freedom. Creation, so conceived, is not a mystery; we experience it in ourselves when we act freely."[19]

Bergson's bold, poetic vision has invited some developmentalists to assert that human beings are the final stage of evolution. As such, they say that it's reasonable to speculate that individual development does not end with death. Human beings, in short, will survive bodily death and continue to develop in ways unspecified, in places unknown.

But why does evolution have to stop with human beings? In fact, doesn't positing a final end contradict any philosophy of evolution?[20] Furthermore, Bergson's version of evolution could imply only that *some* but not necessarily *all* human beings would have life after death. Beyond this, attaching Bergson's evolutionary vision to survivalist belief raises other concerns.

Although Bergson didn't offer his alternative theory of evolution in support of afterlife belief, that partly seems to explain the early celebrity he enjoyed.[21] Bergson's religious views actually listed more toward mysticism. His vision of the *elan*, accordingly, seems to say more of the cosmos than of its human occupants, since what endures, evidently, is the *elan*, not any individual. Indeed, even if there is a future life, there is nothing about *elan vital* as duration that supports a personal rather than an impersonal afterlife. In other words, nothing in Bergson's view, or in developmental theory for that matter, precludes a Hindu or Buddhist version of survival. (In, perhaps, a revealing footnote, Bergson writes of the passing of an individual life: "Everything is *as if* this death had been willed, or at least accepted, for the greater progress of life in general.")[22]

None of this, however, should be taken to mean that Bergson's mind was closed to the possibility of personal survival. Indeed, sounding as much a romantic poet as a philosopher-scientist, he writes almost wistfully:

> The animal takes its stand on the plant, man bestrides animality, and the whole of humanity, in space and time, is one immense army galloping beside and before and behind each of us in an overwhelming charge able to beat down every resistance and clear the most formidable obstacles, perhaps even death.[23]

For Bergson, personally, that most "formidable obstacle," death, was at least unsettled if not removed by, of all things, telepathy.

Actually a curiosity among many intellectuals of Bergson's day, telepathy remains of keen interest not only to students of parapsychological phenomena but to many laypeople who are fully persuaded that it provides *empirical* evidence for life after death.

THE ARGUMENT FROM PARAPSYCHOLOGICAL PHENOMENA

Today the possibility of life after death gets impetus from parapsychology, the study of phenomena that go beyond the range of normal experience or scientific explanation, such as extrasensory perception (ESP) or having experiences without relying on the normal senses.

Although the first controlled parapsychological experiment appears to have occurred in sixth century BCE Greece and involved telepathy, just how telepathic communication works is still unknown. Some believe that, although on the conscious level our minds are exclusive of one another's, on the unconscious level we are constantly interacting. It is on this unconscious level that telepathy might occur, particularly through the link of emotion or common interest that may exist between two especially close people.

The phenomenon of telepathy would not of itself establish life after death. But it could suggest an incomplete picture of the world that requires the addition of another dimension for a unified explanation. Such a possibility is thought by its believers to gain strength when other ESP phenomena are taken into account, such as spontaneous foreknowledge (precognition) or non-spatial perceptions (clairvoyance). Taken collectively, these ESP phenomena strike some as a strong empirical argument for the existence of a paranormal dimension and, thus, for at least postmortem survival, if not immortality.

Past Life

Despite its contemporary fascination, the belief in past lives is hardly new. Plato tells of a boy who knows what he's never learned, at least not in this life.[24] Today the Canadian psychiatrist Ian Stevenson, a leading parapsychologist and reincarnationist, has assembled thousands of cases of children who, without hypnosis, supposedly remember past lives.[25]

If belief in past lives is ancient, so is skepticism. Democritus, for example, could account for the child prodigy in terms of a crude atomic theory. Not only does everything consist of atoms moving through space, he taught, but all objects emit representative atomic particles, something like images of themselves. With people, these images are the mental activities of those associated with them—their thoughts, feelings, emotions, characters. When persons are impassioned, their images can "leap out," thereby transmitting something of their opinions and impulses to recipients. For Democritus, then, knowledge, literally, could be catching.

Today's scientifically minded might attribute extraordinary feats of knowing to cryptomnesia or extraordinary memory. Under hypnosis, for example, some people can recall in exquisite detail an experience they don't consciously remember. The brain, apparently, retained the experience in the subconscious, from which it was recaptured under hypnosis.[26] But believers in past lives dismiss such explanations.

Raynor Johnson, for one, insists that pre-existence best accounts for phenomena such as child prodigies—Mozart or Chopin, for example, composing great symphonies at an early age; or mere children performing complex mathematical operations. Johnson also points to pre-existence to explain the commonplace matter of family difference. "The soul determines the heredity," he says, "not the heredity the soul."[27]

For their part, skeptics can point to the many stories that, upon investigation, turn out to be false or fraudulent, if in fact they can be checked for accuracy at all. The phenomenon of child prodigies, they say, can be or eventually will be accounted for by brain research. Then there's the matter of cultural bias. Is it a mere coincidence, for example, that the majority of past-life examples originate in cultures deeply ingrained with reincarnation belief, such as India? So, perhaps social psychology, not parapsychology, best accounts for these phenomena.[28]

Near Death Experiences

Today medical science makes it possible to resuscitate patients from clinical death. Some of the resuscitated report startling and similar experiences, such as passing through a tunnel, seeing a radiant light or figure, or being greeted or welcomed by deceased loved ones. Some even report seeing individuals they couldn't have known had died. In most instances, the subject's experience is positive and reassuring. This is true even when the subject is a child, according to pediatrician Melvin Morse, who did the first serious study of the near death experience (NDE) among children.[29]

Accounts of NDEs ordinarily are met with disdain by most scientists, who offer biochemical and neurochemical explanations for the phenomena. But not all experts agree. Recently the prestigious British medical journal *The Lancet* published an extensive NDE study of Dutch cardiologist Pim van Lommel. It concluded: "NDE pushes the limits of medical ideas about the range of human consciousness and the mind-brain relation."[30]

Do NDEs point to a death-surviving soul, inner self, or mind leaving the body? Or are they merely manifestations of the brain trying to make sense of a most unusual event? One thing's certain: Such questions recall the mind-body problem taken up in Chapter 5, specifically whether the mind or consciousness is produced from the brain. If it is, then life ends with death because essentially we are conscious beings. But if the brain is like an intermediary that manifests the mind, as a TV manifests waves in the air into a picture or sound, then the mind is still there after the brain is dead.

Deathbed Visions

Although history is full of accounts of deathbed visions, the phenomenon wasn't seriously studied until the twentieth century when physics professor William Barrett (1844–1925) assembled his collection of case studies titled *Death Bed Visions* (1926). French physiologist and Nobel Laureate in Medicine (1913)

Charles Richet (1850–1935) shared Barrett's interest in psychical research and was equally impressed by deathbed visions.

In 1986 psychologist and ESP authority Karlis Osis (1917–1997) co-authored (with psychologist Erlendur Haraldsson) a book titled *At the Hour of Death*. In it are presented the ostensibly paranormal deathbed observations of over 1,000 health care personnel. Other works bear accounts of patients nearing death who speak of traveling, even asking for maps. The authors of *Final Gifts* (1992), for example, both longtime hospice nurses, claim that they have witnessed this phenomenon so often that they invented a name for it: "nearing death awareness."[31]

No one knows why dying patients sometimes speak of taking journeys. Drugs don't seem to play a part in it, since the phenomenon occurs in the mildly medicated as well as those taking powerful painkillers. Robert Fulton, a pioneer in the study of death and bereavement in the 1960s, speculates that the dying may be experiencing visions like those in a dream. But what about dream images of immortality, such as heaven and hell or reincarnation? "The mind has it own set of analgesics," Fulton says, adding: "The mind itself is well capable of drugging itself. In a dream, there might be the euphoria of meeting a dead friend and having a conversation .... The brain is kind of cleaning itself up, like a computer downloading."[32]

Hospice nurse Patricia Kelley believes otherwise. She thinks the dying recognize that they're going from one world to another one.[33] Other commentators suggest that such dreams are reality based, that these patients *are* going on a journey or *are* being visited by deceased loved ones. This would make nearing death awareness evidence, not of cerebral housecleaning, but of postmortem survival. Even so, the so-called self could still perish shortly after bodily death, its separation from its normal embodiment notwithstanding.

Apparitions and Materializations

Osis defines an apparition experience as "awareness of the presence of a personal being whose physical body is not in the area of the experiencer, provided the experiencer is sane and in a normal waking state of consciousness."[34] Contrary to ESP, the apparition, itself, is felt in the immediate vicinity of the experiencer. Sometimes the ghostly presence is defined in terms of a "materialization" whereby the presence of a dead person supposedly is made manifest visibly (as in the form of ectoplasm or through messages on a computer screen) or audially (as on recording devices or on telephone calls).

Well-organized, systematic studies of apparitions started shortly after the founding of the Society for Psychical Research in England in 1882. The basic idea was to apply scientific method to the collection, evaluation, and interpretation of psychic phenomena.

In one of the earliest collections of cases, *Human Personality and Its Survival of Bodily Death* (1903), pioneer psychical researcher and founder of the Society F. W. H. Myers (1843–1901) maintained that the human personality is composed of "two active coherent streams of thoughts and feelings." He labeled those lying above the ordinary threshold of consciousness "supraliminal" and those remaining submerged beneath consciousness "subliminal." Evidence for the latter, he felt, derived from such phenomena as automatic writing, multiple personalities, dreams, and hypnosis. Myers, who introduced the term "telepathy," believed it is the subliminal layers of personality that live on after the death of the body.[35]

In the ancient world, only theoretical explanations could be offered for apparitions and materializations. Democritus, again, attempted to account for specters, visions, and dreams in terms of the soul's nimble and fiery molecules leaving the body at death. Today's methods of research bring to bear experts from various disciplines, including psychology, sociology, and forensics. Skeptics, accordingly, often cite grief-induced hallucination as well as the vivid recollection of forgotten memories as explanations that cover the vast majority of communications with the dead, especially when the purported communication is through a third party, such as a medium.

Out-of-Body Experiences

In the last chapter of *The Republic*, where he is discussing the rewards of justice after death, Plato tells the story of a young soldier named Er, who lay on a battlefield for ten days presumed dead before being picked up and prepared for burial. But before burial, Er returned to life and reported what he had seen in the postmortem world, including a way station for souls choosing their next incarnations. According to Er, souls experience a thousand years of reward or punishment depending on the deeds of previous lives, after which they are brought to a place where they choose their next embodiments.

In early 1944, as he was recovering from a nearly fatal heart attack, Carl Jung experienced deliriums and visions, which included fantastic out-of-body experiences. Soaring a thousand miles high up in space, bathed in a "gloriously blue light," Jung writes about how he saw "the deep blue sea and the continents"; Ceylon and India; the Arabian desert; the Red Sea; the snow-covered Himalayas. In the midst of this phantasmagoria, there floated up, "from the direction of Europe," an image of his physician "framed by a golden chain or a golden laurel wreath," which identified him as the temporal embodiment of the primal healer. A "mute exchange of thought" then took place between Jung and the good doctor, who told the esteemed founder of analytical psychology that he had no right to leave, that he must return to earth. Profoundly disappointed, Jung complied. His out-of-body experiences left Jung with the lasting impression that this life is "a segment of existence which is enacted in a three-dimensional boxlike universe especially set up for it."[36]

As with the mythic Er and the psychoanalyst Jung's, the main characteristic of an out-of-body experience (OBE) is the subject's feeling that his viewpoint and center of perception are located somewhere outside the body.[37] Some people have reported the experience of leaving their bodies, then observing it, perhaps lying in bed or on an operating able. But for such experiences to count for postmortem survival, specifically disembodied existence, they would have to be experienced by independent observers. Although rare, there have been reported cases of one or two external observers "seeing" the persons experiencing an OBE as an apparition at precisely the same time as that individual was experiencing himself as visiting the observers. Such parapsychological phenomena have also been reported to occur in near-death states. More interesting than compelling is an observable change in the *appearance* of the experiencer during an OBE. While Jung was "tripping," for instance, his nurse reported that he was surrounded by a bright light, something she had sometimes observed in the dying.[38]

OBEs often are counted as proof of the existence of an invisible duplicate of the physical body, a so-called astral body that survives death. But what kind of body is "invisible"? And how do we detect it? If the astral body is an *exact* duplicate of the original body, wouldn't it die along with the body?[39]

Messages from the Dead and the Beyond

Although the history and literature of all cultures contain purported messages from the dead, TV programs such as *Medium* and the "readings" of contemporary psychics—mediums such as James Van Praag, Suzanne Northrup, George Anderson, and John Edward—trace their modern roots back to the middle of the nineteenth century when the phenomenon was first seriously studied. Eusapia Palladino (1854–1918), an illiterate Neapolitan woman, was the first individual with paranormal powers who was seriously examined by eminent scientists and scholars, including Bergson. The once president of the British society for psychical research (as were other philosophers) evidently was quite impressed with the Palladino's psychic abilities.[40]

With the quickening of interest in spiritualism in the early twentieth century, British and American scholars took a special interest in other popular mediums of the day. Mediums are individuals thought to have powers to communicate with the spirit of the dead or with agents of another world or dimension. Philosopher/psychologist William James is credited with discovering perhaps the best known and most investigated medium of her day, Lenore Piper (1857–1950). Generally acquitting herself against a barrage of would-be debunkers, Piper was a rich source of revelation and enlightenment to numerous individuals seeking contact with deceased relatives and friends. Among them was Sir Oliver Lodge (1851–1940), whose son Raymond was killed during World War I. In his *Raymond or Life After Death* (1916) the renowned physicist recorded many purported channeled communications with his son.[41] (In *Spook: Science Tackles the Afterlife* [2005], author Mary Roach notes the sudden interest in the paranormal after World War I when, like Lodge, many had lost family members.)

In the 1870s, after recovering from a near life-ending breakdown in Europe in 1867, James avidly studied religion, including immortality. He also helped found the American Society for Psychical Research in 1885. Although he participated in numerous medium conducted séances, James remained to the end of his life a survival agnostic. Always curious, he asked his brother, the famous novelist Henry James (1843–1916), to occupy his (William's) house for one year after his (William's) death in order to field any messages he might send from the beyond. Henry received none.[42]

For believers, the most dramatic historical evidence of a world beyond may be the alleged postmortem communications from psychical researchers Myers, Henry Sidgwick (1838–1900), and Edmund Gurney (1847–1888). These "cross correspondences," as they are termed, came to a dozen mediums in Britain, the United States, and India over a 30-year period. Myers earlier had promised colleagues that when he died he would conduct an experiment that left no doubt as to his identity and survival. True to his word, or so believers claim, Myers and the others corresponded in fragment messages for three decades, "including fragments of classical quotations that were incomplete in themselves but when assembled at the Society for Psychical Research office in London fit together like pieces of a jigsaw puzzle."[43] For psychologist Gardner Murphy (1895–1979), who conducted the first telepathic experiments through wireless, such cross-correspondences posed the most serious challenge to the theoretical objections to afterlife that he otherwise found overwhelming.[44] Still, of the purportedly thousands of his messages from beyond the grave not a one suggests any new interest of Myers in the next life. Nor is anything said about the life that Myers supposedly is leading.[45]

Recently in Britain, a group of scientists has stirred controversy by claiming that certain mathematical discoveries, combined with results of in-depth exploration of physics and quantum mechanics, furnish fresh support for many previously well-documented scientific experiments dealing with psychic phenomena, such as the Myers case. These psychic phenomena, it's proposed, are the result of natural physical laws.

Michael Roll, for example, who heads The Campaign for Philosophical Freedom, talks in terms of "subatomic" rather than "psychic" phenomena. In Roll's view death involves a separation of the mind from the body. The mind retains all memories, emotions, and intellect it possessed on the materialistic plane, then moves on to a next level of existence. This event, says Roll, is universal and not conditioned by anyone's beliefs or past behavior or *karma*. When at death this "enteric" portion detaches from the physical, it remains energized by the same subatomic particles, which, in their new state, can now impart to it powers and abilities unknown and even unimaginable in the material world. Under certain conditions, these discarnate entities manifesting at the material plane can appear and disappear at will, speak, respond, and even be grasped and held by those present at controlled experiments. None of this is "supernatural" or "paranormal," according to Roll.[46]

Roll's view gibes with the "grid theory" of colleague R. D. Pearson, an engineer in thermodynamics and fluid mechanics. Pearson's work has been inspired by Sir William Crookes (1832–1919), the scientist whose name is synonymous with vacuum tubes and whose experiments produced photographs purported to show dead persons materializing in his laboratory. According to grid theory, postmortem survival of the human psyche is one of many functions of a multidimensional, multiuniversal subatomic grid matrix on which all forms of life exist and which sustain the etheric, as well as the physical consciousness of all living organisms. In this model, materialization of "dead" persons are but temporary mergings of two different frequencies or wavelengths from two discrete levels of the grid, somewhat like when more than one radio broadcast is picked up on the same dial setting.[47]

Unfortunately, for survivalists, neither hypothesis would ensure personal survival. They are, after all, equally compatible with extinction. As John Hick pointed out some 30 years ago in the context of reincarnation theory, any isolated postmortem cluster of memories, emotions, or dispositions would be "equally compatible with the extinction of the personality as a whole or with its continued life in some other sphere."[48]

Views such as Roll's and Pearson's do, however, make explicit two significant philosophical implications of *all* parapsychological claims. First, *if true*, they directly challenge a key ingredient of the modern naturalistic worldview that death is the end of consciousness or at least the end of its ability to manifest itself to and in the ongoing world of the living. Also, since most theories of afterlife require a dualistic view of human nature, psychic phenomena would buttress the case for future life by providing indirect evidence of individual consciousness after death.[49]

CONCLUSIONS

Kierkegaard believed that, viewed systematically, the whole question of immortality is nonsense because it defies objective proof.[50] But that doesn't mean it is unimportant *subjectively*. Indeed, he thought that immortality can only be put subjectively because it is a question of inwardness. And it is precisely as "the most passionate interest of subjectivity" where its proof lies.

What Kierkegaard was getting at serves as a counterweight to the tendency to over-intellectualize afterlife belief. He was suggesting that afterlife belief is an ethical issue, not just a metaphysical one. It affects how we live, not just what we think or believe. In this way Kierkegaard grounds a topic that, otherwise, might easily drift away on a cloud of metaphysical speculation.

The moral implications of survivalist belief that Kierkegaard was driving at are most evident in the principal vehicle for its transmission: religion. Western and Eastern traditions alike treat the future life as present-life dependent. Whether or not one is to attain the ideal postmortem state—heaven in the West, a release from the cycle of rebirth in the East—depends entirely on what one does in the present life. No wonder all the major religious traditions teach us what we need to do to be successful, and what will happen if we fail. Two examples are the Ten Commandments, prescribed by monotheistic religions as the way to salvation; and the Eight-Fold Noble path, which Buddhism prescribes for liberation from desire and suffering.

But even afterlife *skepticism* shapes one's morality. If unexamined, for example, disbelief might support thorough self-indulgence. Not believing in any future life, we might simply strive to enjoy this life fully before death snuffs it out. This attitude would marginalize ethics. It would make the treatment of others incidental and subordinate to one's own personal happiness. A principle such as the universal Golden Rule—roughly, "Treat others as you would want to be treated"—would be for using or not, depending on circumstance. Thus, if the Rule advances narrow self-interest, honor it; if not, don't.

But afterlife disbelief need not result in such crass self-absorption. When it's the examined product of philosophical thinking, survival agnosticism can be just as powerful a determinant of altruism as afterlife faith can be.

For example, not believing in a future life might make the present life that much more precious. This, in turn, could fine-tune one's appreciation, gratitude, and respect for life. It could also make one acutely sensitive to the value of the individual and the role that institutions can play in advancing human goals. True, moral positions might lack the muscle of theological threats and promises. On the other hand, it's precisely the absence of a metaphysical carrot-and-stick that might bring the disbeliever to heed, here and now, in the words of atheist Thomas Nagel: "a vigorous call to intelligent activity—activity for the sake of realizing human potentialities and for eliminating whatever stands in the way of such realization."[51] Nagel's "intelligent activity" in the cause of human betterment might be viewed as attaining, or seeking to attain, a kind of social, not individual, immortality.

Another moral aspect of immortality pertains to longevity and what we may owe future generations. Extended life may not mean much to survivalists, but it does to those who don't anticipate any postmortem existence. The latter probably would like to extend both the quantity and quality of the present life. Does it matter morally that in a near future humans may routinely live beyond a hundred years, perhaps well beyond it? In *Fantastic Voyage: Live Long Enough to Live Forever* (2004), inventor and futurist Ray Kurzwell (with co-author Terry Grossman, M.D.) envisions a time when humans will win immortality through technology. But would that necessarily be a good thing? Bioethicist Leon Kass, for one, doesn't think so.

An unflinching critic of science unchecked, Kass fears that technology is pushing humanity toward an unsavory future. In a recent book, the bioethicist, who was appointed by President Bush in 2001 to chair the President's Council on Bioethics, argues that the new technologies, specifically the genetic ones, threaten to downgrade the human condition.[52] Behind modern medicine's pursuit of disease cure and life prolongation, he thinks, is a quest for immortality. If won, this will blunt the human drive to improve. The result, Kass fears, would be a society both barren and bland.[53]

In this, Kass brings to mind the Japanese view of life's beauty as transience. Like the cherry blossom, or *sakura* in Japanese, that blooms for less than a week a year, life is more beautiful for being so fleeting. "The *sakura* reveals at least two immeasurable human truths for the Japanese," philosopher Michael Brannigan tells us: "First, life is like the *sakura*, in that what is of beauty does not last; second, the beauty of reality lies precisely in its impermanence."[54]

Does life shine brighter because it is such a brief candle? Are we driven to improve our lot, personally and collectively, because we have so little time? Such imponderables elevate immortality to a new level of moral gravity.

When we wonder about immortality, then, perhaps we shouldn't be asking about it in general because, as Kierkegaard says, "such a phantom has not existence." Maybe we should be asking: "How do I behave in order to express in existence my immortality?" In posing that question, we're really inquiring about what it means to *become* immortal, whether we are able to contribute anything to the accomplishment of this end.

And what if we never ask that question of ourselves—what then? Of that impoverished philosophical state, Kierkegaard also expressed an opinion, as if with Ivan Ilyich in mind:

> This is what is sad when one contemplates human life, that so many live out their lives in quiet lostness...they live, as it were, away from themselves and vanish like shadows. Their immortal souls are blown away, and they are not disquieted by the question of its immortality, because they are already disintegrated before they die.[55]

REFERENCES

1. Colleen McDannel and Bernhard Lang, *Heaven: A History,* 2nd ed., New Haven: Yale University Press, 2001, p. 21.

2. John Hick, *Death and Eternal Life,* London: Collins, 1976, p. 239.

3. Immanuel Kant, *Critique of Practical Reason,* T. K. Abbott, trans., London: Longmans Green, 1927, Pt. I, Bk II, Ch. 2, pp. 208–209.

4. John Stuart Mill, *Three Essays on Religion,* New York: Prometheus Books, 1998, p. 210.

5. Raynor Johnson, *The Imprisoned Splendor,* Wheaton, IL: Theosophical Publishing House, Quest edition, 1971, p. 376.

6. Leo Tolstoy, "The Fear of Death Is Only a Confession of the Unsolved Contradiction of Life," in *Life and Death,* Jonathan Westphal and Carl Levenson, eds., Indianapolis: Hackett Publishing Company, Inc., 1993, p. 160.

7. John Hick, "An Irenaean Theodicy," in *Encountering Evil,* Stephen T. Davis and others, eds., Atlanta: John Knox Press, p. 41.

8. Paul Badham and Linda Badham, *Immorality or Extinction?* Totowa, NJ: Barnes & Noble Books, 1982, p. 122; 141, fn. 27.

9. Edward Schillebeeckx, *Christ, the Christian Experience in the Modern World,* New York: Seabury Press, 1980, p. 797.

10. Hick, "An Irenaean Theodicy," p. 48.

11. Ibid., pp. 41–42.

12. Ibid., p. 65.

13. Badham and Badham, p. 122.

14. David R. Griffin, "Critique by David R. Griffin," in *Encountering Evil,* Stephen T. Davis and others, eds., Atlanta: John Knox Press, pp. 54–55.

15. Hick, "An Irenaean Theodicy," p. 48.

16. Pierre Teilhard de Chardin, *The Phenomenon of Man,* New York: Harper and Row, 1961, p. 142.

17. Henri Bergson, *Creative Evolution,* Arthur Mitchell, trans., New York: Henry Holt and Company, 1911.

18. Samuel Stumpf, *Philosophy: History & Problems,* 3rd. ed., New York: McGraw-Hill Book Company, 1983, p. 374.

19. Bergson, p. 248.

20. George Santayana, *Winds of Doctrine: Studies in Contemporary Opinion,* New York: Charles Scribner's Sons, 1913.

21. Will Durant, *The Story of Philosophy,* New York: Washington Square Press, 1953, p. 466.

22. Bergson, p. 247.

23. Ibid., p. 271.

24. Plato, "Meno," in *Dialogues of Plato,* vol. I, Benjamin Jowett, trans., Oxford: Oxford University Press, 1920.

25. Ian Stevenson, *Children Who Remember Previous Lives,* rev. ed., Jefferson, NC: McFarland & Company, 2000.

26. Paul Edwards, *Reincarnation: A Critical Examination,* Amherst, NY: Prometheus Books, 1996, pp. 8–9; 71–72.

27. Johnson, p. 380.

28. Paul Edwards, *Immortality,* Amherst, NY: Prometheus Books, 1997, p. 13.

29. Melvin Morse, *Nearer the Light,* New York: Ivy Press, 1991.

30. Pim Van Lummel and others, "Near-Death Experiences in Survivors of Cardiac Arrest: A Prospective Study in the Netherlands," *The Lancet,* December 15, 2001, p. 239.

31. Maggie Callanan and Patricia Kelley, *Final Gifts: Understanding the Special Awareness, Needs, and Communications of the Dying,* New York: Bantam Books, 1992.

32. Valerie Reitman, "Taking Life's Final Exit," *Los Angeles Times,* June 14, 2004, p. A10.

33. Ibid.

34. Karlis Osis, "Life After Death," in *Encyclopedia of Death,* Robert and Beatrice Kastenbaum, eds., Phoenix: Oryx Press, 1989, pp. 170–174. Retrieved February 1, 2005, from http://www.aspr.com/osis.html.

35. F. W. H. Myers, *Human Personality and Its Survival of Bodily Consciousness (Studies in Consciousness),* Charlottesville: Hampton Roads Publishing Company, 2001, p. 8; pp. 167–218.

36. C. G. Jung, *Memories, Dreams, Reflections,* Aniela Jaffe, ed., New York: Vintage, 1989, p. 295.

37. Michael Rogge, "Parapsychology and Personal Survival after Death," May 8, 2004. Retrieved March 15, 2005, from http://www.xs4all.nl/~wichm/paraps.html.

38. Jung, p. 289.

39. Edwards, *Immortality,* p. 22.

40. Durant, p. 462.

41. Oliver Lodge, *Raymond or Life and Death: With Examples of the Evidence for Survival of Memory and Affection After Death,* Whitefish, MT: Kessinger Publishing, 1997.

42. William James, "Human Immortality: Two Supposed Objections to the Doctrine." Retrieved March 20, 2005, from http://www.hds.harvard.edu/library/ingersoll/1897intro.html.

43. Myers, p. 10.

44. Gardner Murphy, *The Challenge of Psychical Research,* New York: Harpers, 1961.

45. Badham and Badham, p. 120.

46. J. J. Snyder, "Science Confirms Survival," *The Campaign for Philosophical Freedom,* (n.d.). Retrieved March 20, 2005, from http://www.cfpf.org.uk/articles/ background/snyder.html.

47. Ibid.

48. Hick, *Death and Eternal Life,* p. 378.

49. Badham and Badham, pp. 90–92.

50. Soren Kierkegaard, *Concluding Unscientific Postscript to the Philosophical Fragments,* D. F. Swenson, trans., Princeton, NJ: Princeton University Press, 1941.

51. Manuel Velasquez, *Philosophy: A Text with Readings,* 8th ed., Belmont, CA: Wadsworth/Thomson Learning, 2002, p. 294.

52. Leon Kass, *Life, Liberty, and the Defense of Dignity,* San Francisco: Encounter Books, 2002.

53. Dan Vergano, "To Kass, Science's Sword Cuts Both Ways," *USA Today,* October 30, 2002, p. 7D.

54. Michael Brannigan, *The Pulse of Wisdom,* Belmont, CA: Wadsworth Publishing Company, 1995, p. 338.

55. Soren Kierkegaard, "Balance between Esthetic and Ethical," in *Either/Or,* vol. II, Walter Lowrie, trans. Princeton, NJ: Princeton University Press, 1944.

Voluntary Death

Introduction: *Quinlan, Perlmutter, Cruzan*

T here are no free lunches"—that's one cliché with a knockout punch when it comes to modern medical science, where dazzling gains can come at a dizzy price. Yes, we can anticipate longer life. However, we also dread how we may die: tethered to machinery tended by strangers orchestrating our death. Modern medicine's capabilities to intervene in and redirect the natural course of disease is, indeed, awe inspiring. However, it also means that, increasingly, the health team, patients, and families must make wrenching decisions about when to throw in the towel and call it quits. The right to make these tough end-of-life decisions is sometimes referred to, broadly, as the "right to die."

To say that someone has a "right to die" basically means that there are medical circumstances when an individual should be permitted to die naturally rather than being kept alive by medical means. But precisely when this is and how much control the individual should have can still vex us. In the last quarter of the last century, U.S. courts heard many cases that bear on how much influence we can exercise over the circumstances of our deaths. None of these cases, perhaps, are more important than, chronologically: *Quinlan* (1976), *Perlmutter* (1980), and *Cruzan* (1990).

THE QUINLAN CASE

The case of Karen Ann Quinlan (1953–1985) is considered typical of the hard choices forced upon us by modern medical science. It began on the evening of April 25, 1975, when a 22-year-old woman collapsed after ingesting a mix of alcohol

141

and barbiturates. Within hours, Karen Ann Quinlan fell into a permanent, irreversible coma or persistent vegetative state (PVS). Her parents, convinced that their daughter would not want to be heroically kept alive in such a condition, sought the court's permission to remove Karen's ventilator. One year later, they received it. Citing the patient's constitutional right to privacy, the New Jersey Supreme Court said Karen's mechanical breathing machine could be turned off. Artificial feeding was continued until June 1985, when Karen Ann Quinlan died of pneumonia.

Significance

The New Jersey Supreme Court made two important points in *Quinlan* about formerly competent persons. First, they have a constitutionally protected privacy interest, based on liberty, in refusing unwanted medical care, even if that refusal leads to their deaths. Second, their interests may be represented by others, called surrogates or proxies. Beyond this, *Quinlan* has come to symbolize the dawn of a new era in medicine—one of complex, technology-driven moral, social, and legal issues; an era when patients, families, and physicians—not the courts—decide what is appropriate end-of-life treatment. It was also during this time that the phrase "right to die" came into use.

THE PERLMUTTER CASE

Seventy-three-year-old Abe Permutter (1907–1980) was hospitalized with amyotrophic lateral sclerosis (ALS or "Lou Gehrig's Disease"). Unlike Quinlan, Perlmutter was "mentally competent, terminally ill, and dependent on a ventilator."[1] Over hospital objections, he and his family petitioned for removal of his ventilator. In 1980, the Florida District Court of Appeals ruled that Perlmutter should be "allowed to make his choice to die with dignity." To deny him his request, and thus compel him to live, the court added, would invade Perlmutter's constitutional right of privacy, remove his freedom of choice, and invade his self-determination. The day after the decision, Abe Perlmutter removed his ventilator tube and died 40 hours later.

Significance

Perlmutter was the first right-to-die decision involving a competent patient. The Florida Court affirmed a competent patient's constitutionally protected privacy, liberty, and autonomy interests in removing life-sustaining treatment and in choosing "to die with dignity."

THE CRUZAN CASE

In 1983, while Karen Ann Quinlan lay in a permanent coma in a New Jersey nursing home, another young woman in PVS would help shape social policy about end-of-life decisions.

Twenty-five-year-old Nancy Cruzan (1958–1990) lost control of her car one January night on a lonely road in Missouri and crashed. After restoring her breathing and heartbeat, paramedics on the scene rushed the unconscious woman to a hospital where she was placed on life support. Her respiration and circulation continued unaided, and three weeks after the accident, her husband and father consented to have a feeding tube inserted. The catastrophic and permanent brain damage she had suffered in the accident, physicians said, meant that Nancy would remain totally helpless, paralyzed, and unaware of her surroundings except for reflexive responses to sound and possibly painful stimuli. Faced with this grim prognosis and sure that their daughter would not wish to be maintained in a vegetative state, Nancy's parents waged a prolonged legal battle that culminated in 1990 when the U.S. Supreme Court effectively allowed them to stop artificial feeding by upholding the state statute requiring "clear and convincing evidence" that the patient would want to terminate treatment. The Cruzans subsequently convinced a probate court of precisely that. Her feeding tube was removed, and Nancy languished for two weeks before dying on Christmas Day, 1990. (After unsuccessfully battling severe depression, Nancy's father took his own life on August 17, 1996.)

Significance

Cruzan was the U.S. Supreme Court's first "right-to-die" case, more accurately: the right to refuse nutrition and hydration. The court said two important things in *Cruzan* about formerly competent persons: (1) Their constitutionally protected liberty interest in refusing unwanted medical treatments such as ventilators also extends to artificial food and water; and (2) states can impose procedural safeguards.

Today, largely because of the patient rights movement and cases like the aforementioned, competent or formerly competent patients through their surrogates have a well-established right to refuse any medical treatment, even if that means allowing a disease to progress on its natural, fatal course—indeed, even if it means the death of a viable fetus (*In re Fetus Brown,* Illinois Appellate Court, 1997). Still unresolved, however, is whether a competent patient who so wishes should ever be assisted to die.

"Voluntary Death," the third and final part of this book, is so titled because its chapters share a common interest in what Albert Camus (1913–1960) famously called the "one truly serious philosophical problem": suicide.[2] Thus, Chapter 9 shows how physician-assisted suicide (PAS) is a recent turn in the long and complex history of voluntary death; while Chapters 10 and 11, in engaging individual morality and social policy, show how assisted suicide reveals our deepest personal and collective values, notably choice.

Choice—that is what everyone seems to want at the end of life. For some "choice" means the right to say "Enough, let me die" or even "Help me die." But for others it means the right to life, no matter how enfeebled, tenuous, or onerous that life may be. And along with *that* choice, presumably, comes the right to medical care—no matter the condition, no matter professional opinion. Does a patient, even one in PVS or indeterminate coma, have a right to medical care that physicians judge medically worthless? Or is there a limit to a patient's claim to scarce medical resources? And if there is such a limit, does that suggest a duty to die? Chapter 12 takes on these difficult questions at the intersection of personal and social interests.

Language clarification always being important, never more so than in matters of life and death, we begin, in Chapter 8, with some key conceptual issues that swirl around "suicide" and "euthanasia."

REFERENCES

1. Jeffrie Murphy, "Rationality and the Fear of Death," in *The Meaning of Death*, John Martin Fischer, ed., Stanford: Stanford University Press, 1993, p. 47.
2. Albert Camus, *The Myth of Sisyphus and Other Essays*, Justin O'Brien, trans., New York: Harcourt, Brace, 1969, p. 3.

8

Conceptual Issues in Suicide and Euthanasia

In the fall of 2003, renowned microbiologist Garrett Hardin (1915–2003), author of two groundbreaking essays in environmental ethics—"The Tragedy of the Commons" (1968) and "Lifeboat Ethics: The Cases Against Helping the Poor" (1974)—died with his wife in a double suicide. He was 88, she 81. Both were in poor health, members of the Hemlock Society (End-of-Life Choices), and felt very strongly about choosing their own time to die.

GARRETT HARDIN AND THE PROFILE OF SUICIDE

The Hardins were only two of thousands who die by suicide annually in the U.S. According to the National Institute of Mental Health (NIMH), 30,622 Americans died by their own hand in 2001. In that same typical year, suicides outnumbered homicides (20,308 or 3 to 2); and twice as many individuals took their own lives as died of HIV/AIDS (14,175). In general, for every female who dies by suicide, about four males do, although females attempt it three times more often than males. Suicide deaths for white men over 85 are among the highest rates when categorized for gender and race. Men 65 years or older have the highest completed or attempted incidence of suicide. Every 95 minutes one of them commits suicide in the U.S., according to the American Association of Suicidology. Suicide is also the second-ranking cause of death among college students (after accidents). No official data are available for attempted suicides, but they are estimated at 734,000 annually in the U.S.[1]

Of course, these hard, cold numbers are faceless. They reveal nothing of the impact of these deaths on the six other people each suicide is estimated to affect intimately. If, as statistics show, there is a suicide in the U.S. every 18 minutes, then there are six new survivors every 18 minutes as well. That meant 4.4 million people, or 1 for every 62 Americans affected by the 738,000 suicides in the five year run-up to 2000.

The statistics are also mute. They say nothing of why these people took their lives. Mental disorders, depression, avoidance—whatever the usual suspect, a suicide almost always is attributed to an "unconscious cry for help" rather than a carefully calculated choice of death over life. But is it that simple?

Across generations and cultures, people have taken their lives out of despair or shame; to escape pain, suffering, or illness; to get revenge; to maintain dignity; to preserve a cherished belief. Consider:

- *Suttee,* the now illegal act or practice of a Hindu widow's cremating herself on her husband's funeral pyre in order to fulfill her true role as wife.

- *Seppuku,* the antiquated Japanese ritual suicide performed to regain honor after defeat or shame, usually in battle. In 1970 Mishima Yukio (1925–1970), perhaps the greatest Japanese novelist of the last century, committed *seppuku* after a failed attempted insurgency.[2]

- The Buddhist Tendai sect's ancient running ritual in the remote Japanese mountains that covers a distance equivalent to a trip around the world. Traditionally any monk who attempts this grueling path to enlightenment and fails must take his own life, either by hanging or disembowelment.

- The suicide to demonstrate against social injustice. In the fall of 2003, a Korean protester, taking part in a global demonstration against world trade talks in Cancun, Mexico, stabbed himself to death in a clash with authorities.

Such self-elected deaths clearly suggest that suicide can be compatible with so-called ego ideals. In fact, people have been known to take their lives for almost any reason, even tedium. "Dear World," read the suicide note left by the English actor George Sanders (1906–1972), "I am leaving you because I am bored."

Once non-medicalized reasons for suicide are acknowledged, then the question arises: Can suicide ever be right? Ever moral? Can there be an honorable form of suicide—a so-called noble suicide? Some philosophers claim that suicide can be a rational, justifiable act—even the ultimate expression of individual liberty. Can it? Could the Hardins have acted *from* deliberation and not merely *with* deliberation?

Or, on the other hand, does self-killing, including physician-assisted suicide, always deserve the condemnation it generally gets from religion? (In contrast to Christianity, Judaism, and Islam's denunciation of it, Confucianism and Buddhism are open to conditional suicide, for intolerable illness, as an example). Was Spinoza right in categorically denying any natural impulse for self-destruction? Is suicide, as he claimed, always the result of physical or psychological compulsion and never a rational act?[3] Were the Hardins'?

None of these questions can be answered without first clarifying the definition of suicide. On first look this may seem unnecessary. What, after all, is more self-evident than that suicide is the intentional termination of one's own life? True enough, but "intentional" is itself, a tricky notion, wrapped in considerations of foreknowledge, desire, and freedom. Traditionally, a death caused by placing oneself in circumstances one knew to be life ending constitutes an act of suicide. But some modern philosophers have employed carefully selected cases of voluntary deaths to challenge this traditional, broad interpretation, and, thereby, narrow the scope of acts that count as suicides. Correct or not, their challenge points to the importance of conceptual clarification in dealing with what one suicide scholar terms humanity's last great taboo.[4]

SUICIDE: THE PROBLEM OF DEFINITION

Emile Durkheim (1858–1917), the French social scientist and founder of sociology, applied the term suicide to all self-administered acts, positive or negative, that result directly or indirectly in one's death. Durkheim's view has inspired broad definitions of suicide that are associated with foreknowledge. Accordingly, so long as an individual knew that an act would bring about his death that act is properly termed suicide.[5]

But is suicide properly defined so broadly? Is every act of voluntary death with foreknowledge really suicide, that is, the intentional termination of one's own life? Several kinds of examples have been proposed recently—self-sacrificial and coerced deaths among them—that challenge the breadth of the foreknowledge criterion and, with it, the conventional interpretation of "intentional" as "foreknowing."

Self-Sacrificial Deaths

In 1910, the explorer Captain Lawrence Oates set out with Robert Scott's Antarctic Expedition and was one of the parties of five to reach the South Pole on January 17, 1912. On their return trek it is believed that the confluence of two events determined the grim fate of both Oates and the party: The explorers became dangerously delayed by weather and Oates became severely lamed by frostbite. Convinced that his crippled state would pose further delays, Oates walked out into a blizzard, deliberately sacrificing his life to save his comrades. (The other two of Scott's remaining companions—Petty Officer Evans had succumbed prior to Oates—may also, in effect, have taken their own lives. In her recent, gripping account of the doomed party, author/scientist Susan Solomon speculates that Dr. Wilson and Lieutenant Bowers sealed their fates by loyally remaining behind to tend a dying Scott, himself a victim of frostbite.)[6]

Was the self-sacrificial act of the gallant captain suicide? No, some would say, because presumably Oates didn't want to die but to save his comrades. Although he knew the blizzard would claim him—he had foreknowledge—his intention was not to end his own life but to save the lives of others. And besides, it wasn't Oates who claimed his life, it was the blizzard.

Not everyone, however, finds that analysis persuasive. Philosopher Tom Beauchamp, for one, believes that Oates's heroic sacrifice was "plausibly a suicide because of the active steps that he took to bring about his death."[7] In other words,

Oates put himself in harm's way. Still, Beauchamp does think some voluntary deaths are suicides, such as those "coerced" or "forced."

Coerced Deaths

Consider the case of a captured soldier who, given a choice by the enemy of being executed by them or by himself, chooses to commit suicide. Clearly he intended to take his life. But he didn't *freely* intend to; coercion to death underlay his self-killing. This explains the reluctance of analysts such as Beauchamp to call coerced self-killings suicides.[8]

An outstanding historical example of a coerced death would be Socrates being forced to drink the poison hemlock, an instance, really, of self-administered capital punishment. By Beauchamp's account, not only are the deaths of Socrates and the soldier coerced, but so would be the voluntary deaths of persons suffering from fatal diseases who refuse treatment and, consequently, hasten their deaths. Were their conditions treatable, on the other hand, and the individuals intended to die by refusing ordinary treatment, then the resulting deaths would be suicides.

Clearly, the degree of personal autonomy or freedom a person has plays a significant role in Beauchamp's concept of suicide. But so does one's role in effecting the death-causing circumstances, as his analysis of the Oates case shows. In Beauchamp's view, then, "an act or omission is a suicide if a person intentionally brings about his or her death, unless death is (a) coerced or (b) is caused by conditions that are not specifically arranged by the agent for the purpose of bringing about the death."[9]

Representative of an opposed viewpoint, philosopher Manuel Velasquez offers the following counter instance to Beauchamp's view. Imagine a man takes his own life when threatened with exposure of a dark secret he harbors. "Is this coerced death not a suicide?" Velasquez asks. It is, Beauchamp agrees, but only if the threat is *not* death. If the threat is death, and the threat is credible and such that the threatened party cannot resist it, Beauchamp insists that the death is not a suicide. Velasquez disagrees.

Velasquez also challenges Beauchamp's characterization of Captain Oates's death as suicide. Since Oates did not intentionally walk out into the blizzard to die but to save the lives of his companions, Velasquez does not consider the death a suicide.

Velasquez is thus led to the following definition of suicide, which contains the two main elements of the traditional legal definition: intention and causation.

> Suicide is the act of bringing about a person's death, provided that:
> (1) death is brought about by that person's own acts or omission, and
> (2) those acts or omissions are (a) intentionally carried out (b) for the purpose of bringing about death by those concretely particular means that actually brought death about.[10]

By this account, Oates's death would not be a suicide because, (b), his primary intention was not to end his life but to save the lives of his party.

On the other hand, Velasquez shares the general view of philosophers that Socrates' death was not a suicide, but not because of diminished autonomy, as

Beauchamp says, but because his death is more properly assigned to his execu-tioners.[11] By the same logic, presumably, some of the traditional Christian martyrs did not commit suicide when they cooperated in their own deaths rather than renounce their religious beliefs. Nor did "certain holy women," as Augustine calls them, who took their own lives at the time of persecution.

In this vein, the "Declaration of Euthanasia" (1980) of Pope John Paul II (1920–2005) asserts: ". . . one must clearly distinguish suicide from that sacrifice of one's life whereby for a higher cause, such as God's glory, the salvation of souls or the service of one's brethren, a person offers his or her own life or puts it in danger (c.f., Jn. 15:14: *'Greater love has no man, than this, that a man lay down his life for his friends')*." In the same document, the pope condemns euthanasia but supports the right to refuse extreme measures to preserve life. This means that patients who die as a result of fatal diseases for which they refuse futile treatment are not suicides, according to the church's official teaching. Velasquez and Beauchamp would agree, but for different reasons. For Beauchamp and some other philosophers, such patients lacked full autonomy; for Velasquez and the Catholic Church, among other individuals and organized bodies, the disease and not the patient caused the death.

The modern problem of defining suicide can be viewed as an extension of the centuries-old dialogue in Western civilization about the propriety of self-killing. For over 2,000 years some of the West's greatest minds have debated the permis-sibility of suicide. As we will see in the next chapter, their views have run the gamut from outright condemnation of suicide as "self-murder" to unapologetic defense of it as a sometimes honorable act. There to be seen in the pith of this ancient debate is the contemporary challenge of defining suicide, including physician-assisted suicide (PAS), a form of euthanasia. Euthanasia, as we'll now see, raises even more conceptual issues than does suicide.

EUTHANASIA

Compassion is the ordinary motivation for assisting in the suicide of a terminally ill patient. Convinced that a patient's death is preferable to his present existence, someone—usually a physician—helps a patient to die by providing the means, such as lethal drugs and instruction for their use. The same desire for compas-sionate relief of pain and suffering of a terminally ill patient typically motivates today's act of euthanasia (from the Greek *eu*, good, *thanatos*, death). Indeed, if euthanasia is viewed informally as "help with a good death," then PAS is a form of euthanasia. The difference, which some consider morally significant, is that unlike PAS, in which the patient self-administers the physician-provided lethal means, in euthanasia the physician—or at least someone other than the patient—administers the lethal means for what is believed to be the patient's own good. In PAS the patient takes his own life; in euthanasia someone else takes the patient's life.

Among the patients for whom euthanasia is sometimes considered are: pre-mature neonates with potentially fatal medical complications; severe trauma victims in severe pain and almost certain to die; the gravely ill aged; and those dying in the last stages of incurable disease. It was the 1998 CBS *60 Minutes* broadcast of the euthanasia of 52-year-old Thomas Youk that ended the assisted-death work of Dr. Jack Kevorkian. Kevorkian was sentenced in 1999 to 10–25 years on second-degree murder charges. With individuals such as Youk, a patient with Lou Gehrig's disease, the term euthanasia carries the meaning of "mercy killing," for the purpose of ending extreme suffering. That popular label suggests the importance of distinguishing between two interpretations of euthanasia, one narrow, the other broad.

DEFINITION: NARROW AND BROAD INTERPRETATIONS

Some philosophers define euthanasia narrowly as intentional killing, which can take the form of an act, termed active or positive euthanasia; or a failure to act, termed passive or negative euthanasia.

In active euthanasia (AE), someone—ordinarily a physician—intentionally causes the patient's death by performing an action, such as administering a lethal injection. In passive euthanasia (PE), someone—again ordinarily the physician—causes the patient's death by not taking usual and customary action, such as not providing antibiotics to help a terminally ill patient survive pneumonia. AE brings on death through intervention; PE brings on death through non-intervention. In AE an action is taken that causes the death; in PE an action is not taken that would have prolonged the life. Central to both is intentionality.

According to the narrow interpretation, unless the death is intentionally caused by what was or was not done, as with Thomas Youk, there is no euthanasia. For example, suppose a doctor determines that commencing a treatment will be of no help to a dying patient or that once started the treatment will be ineffective. The physician, together with the patient and the family, decides to withhold or withdraw the treatment, knowing that death will quickly follow. It does. Now ordinarily, according to the narrow interpretation of the term, what occurred is not euthanasia but "allowing to die." As bioethicist J. Gay-Williams says, after defining euthanasia with specific reference to intentionally taking the life:

> The failure to continue treatment after it has been realized that the patient has little chance of benefiting from it has been characterized by some as "passive euthanasia." This phrase is misleading and mistaken. In such cases, the person involved is not killed . . . nor is the death of the person intended by the withholding of additional treatment. . . . The aim may be to spare the person additional and unjustifiable pain, to save him from the indignities of hopeless manipulations, and to avoid increasing the financial and emotional burden on his family. When I buy a pencil it is so that I can use it to write, not to contribute to an increase in the gross national product. This may be the unintended consequence of my action, but it is not the aim of my action. So it is with failing to continue the treatment of

a dying person. I intend his death no more than I intend to reduce the GNP by not using medical supplies. His is an unintended dying, and so-called "passive euthanasia" is not euthanasia at all.[12]

According to this narrow interpretation, euthanasia, active or passive (as well as PAS), is always to be condemned as outright killing. By contrast, allowing to die, when properly carried out, is a sound medical practice supported by law and professional ethics.

Other philosophers, however, prefer to interpret euthanasia more broadly, as including both acts of killing and allowing to die. They say that if euthanasia is always wrong, then so is allowing to die because it is a form of euthanasia. Alternatively, if allowing to die is not always wrong, then neither is euthanasia necessarily wrong.

In this broad interpretation euthanasia is not always an act of killing because it includes allowing to die. Thus, AE includes acts of painlessly and deliberately ending the lives of people suffering from terminal (or possibly incurable) conditions, such as Thomas Youk. PE includes acts of deliberately allowing such patients to die by withholding or withdrawing treatment. So, whereas the narrow interpretation always prohibits euthanasia and sometimes permits allowing to die, the broad interpretation, discarding "allowing to die" as an irrelevant artifice, can permit either form of euthanasia.

Is the distinction between "killing" and "allowing to die" a phantom, as the broad interpretation says? Or is it, as the narrow interpretation claims, a meaningful, even significant distinction?

KILLING VS. ALLOWING TO DIE

In rejecting challenges to the constitutionality of laws prohibiting physician-assisted suicide, the U.S. Supreme Court has invoked the "killing" vs. "allowing to die" distinction. In *Vacco. v. Quill* (1997), for example, the high court rejected the position of the "Philosophers Brief" that there is no moral difference between "killing" and "allowing to die."

The case involved three gravely ill patients who were prohibited by New York law from dying with the assistance of their physicians, one of whom was Dr. Timothy Quill. According to several philosophers writing in support of the patients, who had since died: "Whether a doctor turns off a respirator in accordance with the patient's request or prescribes pills that a patient may take when he is ready to kill himself, the doctor acts with the same intention: to help the patient die."[13,14] In other words, according to the philosophers, the accepted practice of knowingly administering powerful, death-hastening pain relievers to dying patients is morally no different from "killing." Earlier the Second Circuit of the U.S. Court of Appeals had ruled it discriminatory to allow a person on life support to end her life by removing such treatment, while those who are not connected to life support would be denied similar access to death. In other words, the law violated the equal protection clause of the Fourteenth Amendment. In reversing that decision, the Supreme Court, over the philosophers' objections, accepted the traditional distinction between killing and allowing to die.

Today deep divisions have formed within the medical profession over the issue of legalizing euthanasia and PAS. Still, in general, medicine, as well as the larger society, agree with the nation's high court that "killing" and "allowing to die" are morally different.

Many clinicians, for example, intuitively sense an important difference between turning off a ventilator and giving a lethal injection. "If their intuitions are confused or mistaken, however," worries Daniel P. Sulmasy, "physicians and other health care professionals will have one less reason for refraining from the practices of euthanasia and assisted suicide."[15] The philosopher/attorney's concern is shared by organized religious and professional bodies. Accordingly, in its earliest and subsequently reaffirmed statement on euthanasia, the House of Delegates of the AMA on December 4, 1973, adopted the following position:

> The intentional termination of the life of one human being by another—mercy killing—is contrary to that for which the medical profession stands and is contrary to the policy of the American Medical Association. The cessation of the employment of extraordinary means to prolong the life of the body when there is irrefutable evidence that biological death is imminent is the decision of the patient and/or his immediate family. The advice and judgment of the physician should be freely available to the patient and/or his immediate family.

The shared position of the Roman Catholic Church has been expressed more fully as follows:

> Whatever its motives and means, direct euthanasia consists in putting an end to the lives of handicapped, sick, or dying persons. It is morally unacceptable. Thus an act or omission which, of itself or by intention, causes death in order to eliminate suffering constitutes a murder gravely contrary to the dignity of the human person and to the respect due to the living God, his Creator. The error of judgement into which one can fall in good faith does not change the nature of this murderous act, which must always be forbidden and excluded. Discontinuing medical procedures that are burdensome, dangerous, extraordinary, or disproportionate to the expected outcome can be legitimated; it is the refusal of "over-zealous" treatment. Here one does not will to cause death; one's inability to impede it is merely accepted. The decisions should be made by the patient if he is competent and able or, if not, by those legally entitled to act for the patient, whose reasonable will and legitimate interests must always be respected. Even if death is thought imminent, the ordinary care owed to a sick person cannot be legitimately interrupted. The use of painkiller to alleviate the sufferings of the dying, even at the risk of shortening their days, can be moral in conformity with human dignity if death is not willed as either an end or a means, but only foreseen

and tolerated as inevitable. Palliative care is a special form of disinterested charity. As such it should be encouraged.[16]

The positions of the church and the AMA are consistent with both law and cultural tradition, which prohibit only killing, or definite actions deliberately committed or omitted in order to end the patient's life. The paradigm case of patient killing is the physician who mercifully administers a lethal injection into a consenting, terminally ill adult in order to end the patient's life; or, alternatively, intentionally causes the patient's death by withholding or withdrawing a treatment that would have saved the patient's life.

In contrast to these deliberately death-causing acts of commission and omission are ones that are not intended to cause death, although death inevitably occurs sooner because something was done or not done. For example, when the symptoms of a dying patient cannot be eliminated by other appropriate and acceptable means, drugs sometimes are used to make the patient unaware of the symptoms, a practice termed terminal or total sedation. Administering increasing dosages of regular analgesic and sedative drugs that can suppress consciousness and hasten death is legal and considered a valuable therapeutic adjunct so long as the declared intention is to ease pain and suffering. This has been the official position of the Catholic Church since Pope Pius XII (1876–1958) approved it as a last resort in 1957: "If no other means exist, and if, in the given circumstance, this does not prevent the carrying out of other religious and moral duties."[17]

Notice that the same question that arises in defining suicide may be asked of the AMA and church's official positions: "Can an outcome (death) be foreseen and foreknown without being intended?" Yes, say the Catholic Church and AMA, among others. Injecting a drug with the explicit intention of causing death is euthanasia and not permissible. But injecting a drug with the intention of relieving pain and even suppressing consciousness is *not* euthanasia and is permissible, even though it is foreseen and foreknown that, as a direct result of that act, life will be shortened.

The conventional emphasis on intention or aiming at death as the legal and moral determinant in end-of-life treatments applies equally to acts of omission. In theory, then, any end-of-life treatment that is omitted with the intention of causing the patient's death is passive euthanasia, and is not permissible. For example, had the physician in the earlier example deliberately withheld antibiotics in order to end the patient's life, that would be killing—murder, in fact, in all U.S. jurisdictions and almost all other countries. The same would apply to an instance of disconnecting a terminally ill patient from a dialysis machine or making no effort to revive one in cardiac arrest, if the intention was to cause the patient's death.

The moral significance of intention was behind Pope John Paul II's stunning pronouncement of March 20, 2004, that PVS patients should not be denied food and water.[18] To do so, he said, would amount to "euthanasia by omission," a viewpoint that contradicts existing policy followed by American Catholic hospitals. Although considered an "allocution"—an opinion rather than an encyclical—the pope's remark sent shock waves through the Catholic medical community owing to the potential complications related to do-not-resuscitate orders and medical requests to end treatment. With the installation of Pope Benedict XVI, only time will tell how John Paul's opinion will affect Catholic health policy on these matters, if at all.

In contrast to those emphasizing the manner under which a death is caused, supporters of the broad interpretation insist that what matters are the conditions of a death.[19] This makes the distinction between allowing to die and passive euthanasia a false one, an artifice for avoiding the full weight of moral intuition and analysis that supports helping consenting adult patients with a merciful death. Rather than responding honestly to the dictates of logic and morality by modifying their condemnation of euthanasia, supporters of the narrow view, charge critics, are engaging in a verbal sleight of hand. They are calling "allowing to die" what really are instances of "passive euthanasia." This allows them to have their cake and eat it, too—cause death but not intend it. They can kill but not be killers. Pope John Paul II, apparently, concurred, given his aforementioned challenge to tradition the year before his death.

A Distinction with a Difference?

Is the official distinction between euthanasia and allowing to die morally meaningful? Friends of the broad interpretation obviously don't think so. But proponents of the narrow view do.

Yes (Narrow Interpretation)

The defense of the passive euthanasia/allowing to die distinction rests on various grounds. First, say its defenders, the distinction coheres with ordinary language usage, which distinguishes between harms that are actively caused and ones that are permitted. More importantly, it identifies the cause and pinpoints responsibility. Thus, in euthanasia the physician directly causes the death; in allowing to die, the disease does. Not distinguishing between euthanasia and allowing to die would blur this important moral and legal distinction.

Additionally, its defenders say the distinction recognizes and honors the subtle but very real medical discrimination honored since the birth of medicine in the West. The Hippocratic Oath, composed some time between the sixth century BCE and the fourth century CE, enjoins physicians to do no harm. Although ancient physicians were not obligated to follow the oath, tradition teaches that there is no greater harm than to kill a patient deliberately. But deliberately to leave a patient in treatable pain is a close second, and, perhaps, a greater harm sometimes. What is the physician to do when she can't both save a life and pain? Supporters say it is exactly the distinction between (passive) euthanasia and allowing to die that captures this kind of clinical dilemma by distinguishing between permissible cases of allowing to die and impermissible cases of killing. Furthermore, it's this discrimination that enables physicians to meet their historical duty. On one hand, they are expected to avoid the harm of interfering with natural death by over treatment. On the other hand, they are expected to avoid the harm of deliberately killing the patient. Without such clear distinction, physicians would be in a moral muddle. To its defenders, then, the euthanasia/allowing to die distinction may be conceptually awkward, but it creates a needed firewall or "psychological barrier" between acts of omission and commission.[20] To remove the distinction—to treat allowing to die as a form of euthanasia—would make killing acceptable and, perhaps, active euthanasia inevitable.

No (Broad Interpretation)

The position that the euthanasia/allowing to die is a false distinction was given forceful expression more than a quarter-century ago by philosophers Michael Tooley[21] and James Rachels (1941–2003). In the latter's widely anthologized 1975 article that first appeared in *The New England Journal of Medicine,* Rachels argued that the killing/allowing to die distinction is fraught with inconsistencies and contradictions.

Consider, Rachels suggested, that if the difference between euthanasia and allowing to die is relevant anywhere, then it should be relevant everywhere. Thus, if someone saw a child drowning in a bath, wouldn't it be just as wrong to watch him drown as to push his head under water? If emphatically yes, then why isn't it wrong to allow a suffering patient dying, say, of throat cancer to die? Suppose further that such a patient is certain to die in a few days even if his present treatment is continued, but he doesn't wish to go on. So, with his family's support, he asks his physician to put an end to his pain. Now, according to the conventional doctrine—seemingly the narrow view of euthanasia—the doctor may withhold treatment because the dying patient is in terrible pain and it would be wrong to prolong his suffering needlessly. "But now notice this," Rachels wrote:

> If one simply withholds treatment it may take the patient longer to die, and so he may suffer more than he would if more direct action were taken and a lethal injection given. This fact provides strong reason for thinking that, once the initial decision not to prolong his agony has been made, active euthanasia is actually preferable to passive euthanasia [i.e., allowing to die], rather than the reverse. To say otherwise is to endorse the option that leads to more suffering rather than less, and is contrary to the humanitarian impulse that prompts the decision not to prolong his life in the first place.[22]

In other words, whether active or passive, the outcome is the same: the death of the patient on humanitarian grounds. And that—the conditions under which the patient died—is what matters, Rachels argued, not the manner in which the death was caused.[23]

While permissive of euthanasia, philosopher Philippa Foot thinks the distinction between euthanasia and allowing to die *is* relevant. In a 1977 reply to Rachels's example of the drowning boy, Foot pointed out that while both killing and allowing him to drown are iniquitous acts, they are so for different reasons, and that makes all the difference in euthanasia. Killing the child violates justice, Foot believes: No one has the right to push the child's head under water. To leave him to drown, on the other hand, violates charity or benevolence by denying the child what is good for him. In Rachels's example justice and charity happen to coincide. But this isn't always the case, as Foot ingeniously illustrated as follows:

> Suppose, for example, that a retreating army has to leave behind a wounded or exhausted soldier in the wastes of an arid or snowbound land where the only prospect is death by starvation or at the hands of an enemy notoriously cruel. It has often been the practice to accord a merciful bullet to men in such desperate straits [an act of charity]. But suppose that one of them demands that he should be left alive? It seems clear [by the requirements of justice] that his comrades have no right to kill him though it is a quite different question as to whether they should give him a life-prolonging drug.[24]

Foot's point is that although the right to life can sometimes require positive service of others, it does not in this case. In other words, justice dictates that the soldier has a right to be left alone. But considerations of charity relieve the retreating army of any obligation to give him the means to prolong his life. In other words, it matters whether they opt to kill the soldier (which Foot believes would be wrong) or whether they allow him to die (which Foot believes could be acceptable). This distinction, she feels, really matters in euthanasia.

For his part, Rachels would agree that killing the soldier would be wrong because the soldier doesn't want to be killed. But what of *voluntary* cases of euthanasia as opposed to voluntary cases of allowing to die? In such situations, the foreseen outcome, death, is the same. For Rachels this means that it is irrelevant whether the death is aimed at (euthanasia) or merely foreseen. Merely foreseeing the death as certain is enough to characterize a doctor's ceasing treatment as intentional termination of life, according to Rachels. The AMA, of course, as well as all major religions and U.S. jurisdictions, disagrees, insisting that so long as the physician does not discontinue treatment in order to end the life she did not intentionally terminate it. But Rachels has argued further that any decision to withhold extraordinary means is based precisely on the same grounds as a decision to end the patient's life: a determination of whether the patient's life should be prolonged.[25]

VOLUNTARY AND NONVOLUNTARY DECISIONS

We could easily imagine as a counterpart to Foot's suffering soldier a terminally or incurably ill patient who "for her own good" would be better off dead but wants to live. On the other hand, it's just as easy, as in Rachels's example, to imagine a terminally ill patient who wants to die because she no longer regards her life as worth living. Then there are patients whose wishes are unknown—for example, formerly competent patients now in comas, or never competent patients such as the severely mentally retarded. So, in addition to the challenges of defining euthanasia and distinguishing between killing and allowing to die, another conceptual issue in euthanasia debates involves patient wishes. Patient decisions about life and death ordinarily are characterized as voluntary and nonvoluntary.

Voluntary Decisions

Voluntary decisions about death refer to cases in which a competent adult patient requests or gives informed consent to a particular course of medical treatment or nontreatment.[26] Generally speaking, informed consent exists when patients freely give permission to a physician to do or not do something after they are made fully aware of and understand its benefits, risks, and any alternatives.

Voluntary death decisions include cases in which patients: (1) take their own lives either directly or by refusing life-sustaining treatment; (2) request that physicians either perform a procedure that will end their lives or discontinue a procedure that would save their lives; or (3) designate others, for example spouses, to act on their behalf should their medical condition leave them unable to speak for themselves. The designation could take the form of an advance medical directive, such as a Durable Power of Attorney for Health Care, in which the patient formally delegates someone to make health care decisions for him if incapacitated, and expresses his wishes and expectations to that individual in writing. The instructions can be quite general, such as "Use your own best judgment" or "Do what you think is best." In that case the designee is charged with doing what she believes is in the patient's best interests. On the other hand, the directions might be more specific: "No resuscitation if there's cardiac arrest," for example, or "Comfort care measures only." Alternatively, a patient could instruct "Keep me alive as long as possible," and, to this end, complete a relatively new document called a "Right to Life."

Whatever the patient's wishes, one thing is certain: For a death decision to be voluntary, the patient's consent must be explicit.

Nonvoluntary Decisions

Nonvoluntary decisions about death refer to cases in which the decision is not made by the person who is to die, perhaps because of age or medical condition. Of special note, given its frequency, are the many nonvoluntary cases that arise because formerly competent patients never formally deputized someone to act on their behalf and expressed unambiguously what they wished done and not done, as apparently with Quinlan, Cruzan, and Schiavo.

Inevitably such cases raise two important questions: What's best for the patient and what would the patient want if she could choose? The first is largely a medical matter, the second a moral and legal one. The Quinlans and Cruzans were persuaded that discontinuing treatments was both in the medical and moral interests of their daughters. But families aren't always unified in their understanding of a loved ones' wishes or best interests, as in the case of Terri Schiavo. Nor are physicians and families always on the same page. Generally, what competent adult patients wish or likely would wish takes moral and legal priority over their best medical interests where the two conflict. Still, as we'll see in Chapter 12, the issue is far from settled.

Even when a patient is competent, it is not always easy to determine exactly what she wishes. Mixed messages, fear or denial of death, a false sense of protecting others, reluctance to talk about imminent death, and other factors on the part of patient, physician, or family can block a clear, unambiguous expression of patient wishes. And because pain and suffering can always impede communication, former hospice physician Quill urges colleagues to distinguish between the very common "transient yearning for death as an escape from suffering" and the extremely rare "requests for a physician assisted suicide death." In other words, "I wish I were dead" doesn't always mean, "Doctor, I want to die. Will you help me?"[27]

Given the uncertainty of patient wishes, sometimes physicians are called on to use their best judgments. A 1998 study found that in one case out of six of the rare euthanasia or assisted suicide in the U.S., it is the family or physician who requests it, without the patient's knowledge or request, even though the patient is conscious.[28]

When the voluntary-nonvoluntary distinction is paired with them, the narrow and the broad interpretations of the meaning of euthanasia each yields four kinds of death decisions. For the narrow interpretation there are:

1. Voluntary euthanasia: impermissible
2. Nonvoluntary euthanasia: impermissible
3. Voluntary allowing to die: permissible
4. Nonvoluntary allowing to die: permissible

For the broad interpretation:

1. Voluntary active euthanasia: permissible
2. Nonvoluntary active euthanasia: permissible
3. Voluntary passive euthanasia: permissible
4. Nonvoluntary passive: permissible[29]

As the numbered list shows, for the broad interpreters, a deliberate action to shorten a patient's life may be right if it's in keeping with the patient's wishes. For narrow interpreters, such an act is always wrong regardless of what the patient wishes. Of overriding moral consideration to the broad interpreters is patient autonomy, while to the narrow interpreters it is the nature of the act: killing.

CONCLUSIONS

In addition to voluntary and nonvoluntary decisions, a third kind of death decision is at least theoretically possible. An *involuntary* death decision would be one that opposes the expressed wishes of the patient. Were a patient's life ended or shortened contrary to her known wishes, that would be an involuntary decision.

Overriding expressed patient wishes ordinarily has been a moral threshold that neither philosopher nor physician has dared to cross, even hypothetically. And for good reason. Whose life is it, anyway? The patient's. So shouldn't patient wishes override any other consideration? Indeed, the whole right to die movement was launched on the moral premise that individuals be permitted to determine the circumstances of their deaths. This turned existing standards, rules, practices, customs, and laws that interfered with free choice into potential instruments of involuntary decisions—that is, choices imposed on patients contrary to their expressed wishes. Consequently, over recent years most death-decision disputes have pitted the patient's right to limit or discontinue treatment and the physician's reluctance to do so. But today, backed by right-to-life or pro-life advocates, some patients are opting for life against contrary medical opinion, triggering an attack on patient autonomy.

Powerful social, economic, medical, and ethical arguments recently have been assembled for sometimes limiting individual autonomy in end-of-life decisions. In practice, this means possibly overriding the wishes of the patient. Fueling this position is the weight of professional and philosophical opinion that a patient does *not* have an unlimited right to care. In other words, as in Foot's soldier example, even if they insist on having all possible medical intervention to stay alive, there is a limit to what patients are entitled to. If there is, then physicians and medical institutions are under no moral obligation to exceed that limit. But where exactly is that limit, and who is to determine it? Most problematic of all: Does that limit to care include deliberate, life-shortening against patient wishes?

In the great, ongoing social debate about death decisions, right-to-life supporters have always feared that blurring the distinction between allowing to die and passive euthanasia would lead to active euthanasia. Now a new fear has emerged: limiting a patient's right to care will open the door to involuntary euthanasia. At the heart of this concern are profound questions of personal morality and social policy, to be taken up in Chapters 10, 11, and 12. But first, following the maxim that history is philosophy teaching by examples, let's briefly consult the past for perspective and enlightenment on the topic of suicide and euthanasia.

REFERENCES

1. "Suicide Facts and Statistics," The National Institute of Mental Health. Retrieved June 20, 2005, from http://www.nimh.nih.gov/suicideprevention/suifact.cfm.

2. Michael Brannigan, *The Pulse of Wisdom,* Belmont, CA: Wadsworth Publishing Company, 1995, p. 340.

3. Jacques Choron, *Suicide,* New York: Charles Scribner's Sons, 1972, p. 122.

4. Georges Minois, *History of Suicide: Voluntary Death in Western Culture,* Lydia G. Cochrane, trans., Baltimore: Johns Hopkins Press, 1999.

5. Manuel Velasquez, "Defining Suicide," in Tom L. Beauchamp and Robert M. Veatch, *Ethical Issues in Death and Dying,* 2nd ed., Upper Saddle River, NJ: Prentice Hall, 1996, pp. 106–111.

6. Susan Solomon, *The Coldest March,* New Haven, CT: Yale University Press, 2001.

7. Tom L. Beauchamp, "The Problem of Defining Suicide," in Tom L. Beauchamp and Robert M. Veatch, *Ethical Issues in Death and Dying,* 2nd ed., Upper Saddle River, NJ: Prentice Hall, 1996, p. 116.

8. Ibid., p. 114.

9. Ibid., p. 116.

10. Velasquez, p. 109.

11. Ibid., p. 110.

12. J. Gay-Williams, "The Wrongfulness of Euthanasia," in Jeffrey Olen, Julie C. Van Camp, and Vincent Barry, *Applying Ehics: A Text with Readings,* 8th ed., Belmont, CA: Wadsworth/Thomson Learning, 2005, p. 180.

13. John Rawls and others, "Assisted Suicide: The Philosophers' Brief," *The New York Review of Books,* March 27, 1997. Retrieved February 4, 2005, from http://www.nybooks.com/articles/1237.

14. Ronald Dworkin, "Assisted Suicide: What the Court Really Said," *The New York Review of Books,* September 25, 1997. Retrieved February 4, 2005, from http://www.nybooks.com/archives/.

15. Daniel Sulmasy, "Killing and Allowing to Die: Another Look," *Journal of Law, Medicine, and Ethics,* Spring, 1998, p. 57.

16. "Euthanasia," in *Excerpts from the Catechism of the Catholic Church on Life, Abortion, and Euthanasia,* Staten Island: Priests for Life. Retrieved February 1, 2005, from http://www.priestsforlife.org/magisterium/catechismonabortion.htm#euthanasia.

17. Pope Pius XII, "Address to a Symposium of the Italian Society of Anesthiology," February 24, 1957, *Catholic Mind,* May/June, 1957, p. 277.

18. Pope John Paul II, "Life Sustaining Treatments and Vegetative State: Scientific Advance and Ethical Dilemmas," March 20, 2004. Retrieved June 10, 2005, from http://www.lifeissues.net/writers/doc/doc_33vegetativestate.html.

19. Jeffrey Olen, Julie Van Camp, and Vincent Barry, *Applying Ethics: A Text with Readings,* 8th ed., Belmont, CA.: Wadsworth/Thomson Learning, 2005, p. 172.

20. Philippa Foot, "Euthanasia," in Olen, Van Camp, and Barry, pp. 187–201.

21. Michael Tooley, "An Irrelevant Consideration: Killing Versus Letting Die," in *Killing and Letting Die,* 2nd ed., Bonnie Steinbock and Alastair Norcross., eds., New York: Fordham University Press, 1994, pp. 103–111.

22. James Rachels, "Active and Passive Euthanasia," in Olen, Van Camp, and Barry, p. 184.

23. Olen, Van Camp, and Barry, p. 172.

24. Foot, p. 195.

25. James Rachels, "More Impertinent Distinctions and a Defense of Active Euthanasia," in *Killing and Letting Die,* 2nd ed., Bonnie Steinbock and Alastair Norcross, eds., New York: Fordham University Press, 1994, pp. 139–154.

26. Olen, Van Camp, and Barry, p. 172.

27. Timothy E. Quill, M.D., "Doctor I Want to Die, Will You Help Me?" *JAMA,* August 18, 1993, pp. 870–875.

28. Linda Emanuel and others, "The Practice of Euthanasia and Physician-Assisted Suicide in the United States," *JAMA,* August 12, 1998, pp. 507–513.

29. Olen, Van Camp, and Barry, p. 173.

9

History and Contemporary Opinion

I n the eighteenth century, David Hume made what is regarded as the first un-apologetic defense of the moral permissibility of suicide on grounds of individual autonomy and social benefit. In making his case that suicide did not violate duty to "god, our neighbor, or ourselves," Hume was directly challenging each leg of a tripod that for more than a thousand years had supported the medieval Church's categorical condemnation of suicide and euthanasia on grounds of theology, social interest, and self-preservation.

But the medieval Church was not original in its attacks on self-killing. The same arguments made by Augustine and Aquinas were first advanced in the ancient world by Plato and Aristotle. It is with this classical perspective that we begin this centuries-old and ongoing philosophical debate that has characterized suicide, variously, as being offensive, rational, sinful, beneficial, irresponsible, and socially useful. As we'll also see, the palpable Western ambivalence about voluntary death resonates today in the issue of physician-assisted suicide or PAS for short.

SUICIDE AS AN OFFENSE TO GOD, NEIGHBOR, SELF: PLATO AND ARISTOTLE

In *Phaedo* Plato has Socrates speak of a doctrine from "mystics" "who say that we men are put in a sort of lock-up, from which one must not release oneself or run away...." Of this teaching, Socrates professes no understanding, but agreement. "I believe," he affirms, "that this much is true: that we men are in the care of the gods, one of their possessions," concluding: "So...it is not unreasonable to say that we must not put an end to ourselves until God sends some necessary circumstance like the one which we are facing now [that is, his own death sentence]."[1]

Plato, to be sure, tolerated exceptions to the prohibition of suicide. Extreme misfortune and hardship, personal disgrace, and capital punishment self-administered were among them. He also permitted voluntary euthanasia of the disabled and incurable, and for eugenic reasons infanticide of defective newborns and the products of certain incestuous unions (see *The Republic,* Bk. IV, Ch. XVI). But, in general, Plato considered voluntary death an offense against God, to be punished by disgraceful burials in solitary and unmarked graves. And such would be the funerary ignominy of suicides for centuries to follow.

That it was legally prohibited figured prominently in Aristotle's condemnation of suicide. It was, in his view, a socially irresponsible act that weakened the state by depriving it of the services of a citizen. As he says in *Nicomachean Ethics,* "a certain loss of civil rights attaches to the man who destroys himself, on the ground that he is treating the state unjustly."[2] Also, according to Aristotle, the act of suicide goes against the instinct of self-preservation and, therefore, is further to be condemned as an unnatural act.

SUICIDE AS RATIONAL: THE STOICS

Many cultures, including ancient Greece and Rome, have permitted and respected so-called rational suicide, that is, ending one's life for good reasons, as opposed to emotional or psychological ones. Not surprisingly, what constituted "good reasons" varied from culture to culture, and at times even within cultures. For example, to the warrior Vikings only those who died violently—in battle or by their own hand—were worthy of paradise or Valhalla. For the elderly infirm among the ancient Scythians, suicide presented a most honorable alternative to overburdening their nomadic tribe.[3] And it was the promise of immediate heavenly reward that motivated many voluntary deaths among the early Christians.

To Plato, but not to Aristotle, crippling grief or unrelenting disease was reason enough for both voluntary death and euthanasia. On this point, incidentally, Plato differed from Pythagoras and his followers who, respecting the sanctity of life and viewing a hard death as punishment for past sins, discouraged suicide.[4] Plato also tolerated suicide for patriotism or personal honor, and the Greeks generally, as well as the Romans, believed that people should meet death with equanimity and comfort. As a rule, then, the ancients did permit suicide in the face of intolerable and irremediable life circumstances.[5]

Within a century of Socrates' death, many philosophers framed suicide as sometimes most reasonable and desirable. For example, to the Stoics, philosophers who flourished for centuries in Greece and Rome, suicide was a rational choice when life no longer seemed to accord with nature. This gave primacy to the individual rather than the community, the orientation favored earlier by both Plato and Aristotle. But just how much freedom individuals ought to have in ending their own lives remained somewhat unsettled.

Still, most Stoics believed that suicide was justified only when the individual could no longer live according to reason. They interpreted this state as a divine message to depart from life. In other words, when it was no longer possible to live the life nature intended—what today we might call poor "quality of life"—voluntary death was appropriate. Only the individual could determine when life had so deteriorated as to warrant self-killing. As Epictetus avers, "If the room is smoky, if only moderately, I will stay," but "if there is too much smoke I will go. Remember this, keep a firm hold on it, the door is always open."[6] And in a sentiment as befitting the twenty-first as the first century, Seneca writes to his friend Lucilius:

> Living is not the good, but living well. The wise man therefore lives as long as he should, not as long as he can . . . . He will always think of life in terms of quality not quantity . . . . Dying early or late is of no relevance, dying well or ill is . . . . Even if it is true [that while there is life, there is hope], life is not to be bought at all costs.[7]

True to his code, the Roman philosopher took his own life rather than endure the blood lust of the emperor Nero (37–68), himself a suicide.

SUICIDE AS SINFUL: AUGUSTINE AND AQUINAS

If the Roman Stoic could find honor and dignity in suicide, the early Christian could find in it a ticket to paradise. Indeed, the increasing popularity of suicide among early Christians as a way to heaven—and even to sainthood, as with suicidal virgins—threatened the stability of the Church so much that Augustine urged his fellow bishops to join him in condemning suicide as a violation of the Sixth Commandment. "It is significant that in Holy Scripture no passage can be found enjoining or permitting suicide either in order to hasten our entry into immortality or to void or avoid temporal evils," he writes in *The City of God*. And then, as if to dispel any doubt, he adds: "God's command, 'Thou shalt not kill,' is to be taken as forbidding self-destruction."[8]

Still, the Church's *official* condemnation of suicide would not come until over 100 years after Augustine's death when, at the Council of Braga in 562, it was pronounced a crime against God who, as creator of the universe and everything in it, was the sole determinant of death and life.

In years following, the gravity of the offense was reflected in harsh punishments instituted for suicide, such as the denial of burial rites or excommunication. Then in the thirteenth century the official position of the Catholic Church was given its most discursive voice by Aquinas, who, drawing on the three classical arguments, categorically condemned suicide as a sin against self, society, and God. Thus, he writes in *Summa Theologica*:

> It is altogether unlawful to kill oneself, for three reasons. First, because everything naturally loves itself, the result being that everything naturally

keeps itself in being, and resists corruption as far as it can. Wherefore suicide is contrary to the inclination of nature and to charity, whereby every man should love himself. Hence suicide it always a mortal sin, as being contrary to the natural law and to charity. Secondly, because every part, as such, belongs to the world. Now every man is part of the community, and so, as such, he belongs to the community. Hence by killing himself he injures the community, as the Philosopher [Aristotle] declares (*Ethic* vii). Thirdly, because life is God's gift to man and is subject to His power, Who kills and makes to live. Hence, whoever takes his own life sins against God, even as he who kills another's slave sins against the slave master and as he who usurps himself judgment of a matter not entrusted to him. For it belongs to God alone to pronounce sentence of death and life according to Deut. xxxii. 39, *I will kill and I will make to live.*[9]

It was thus, says suicide scholar A. Alvarez of the evolution of feeling about suicide from classical to medieval times, that "an act which during the first flowering of Western civilization had been tolerated, later admired, and later still sought as the supreme mark of zealotry, became finally the object of intense moral revulsion."[10]

The medieval Church's condemnation of suicide also extended to active euthanasia. What today is termed "allowing to die" by some and by others "passive euthanasia" (see Chapter 8) was tolerated as non-suicide.

SUICIDE AS BENEFICIAL TO SELF
AND OTHERS: HUME

In his 1577 description of Elizabethan England, chronicler William Harrison tartly observes: "Such as kill themselves are buried in the field with a stake driven through their bodies."[11] So suicides, apparently, fared only slightly better than witches and thieves, who, imprudently failing to kill themselves, were variously hanged, burned, or beheaded. But about the same time Harrison penned these chilling words, the Church-sponsored Elizabethan view of suicide as an unmitigated evil was about to be challenged.

In "A Custom of the Isle of Cea," an essay presenting opposed arguments on suicide, Michele de Montaigne insisted that "God gives us sufficient dispensation when he puts us in a situation where life becomes worse than death." Referring to the extension of the commandment "Thou shalt not kill" to suicide, he added: "I don't break the law made for crooks, when I take away my own property, thus I am not obliged to conform to the law made for murderers when I deprive myself of my own life." In Montaigne's view pain and "the fear of a worse death" were "excusable incitements" for suicide. In the essay's most memorable aphorisms, he wrote: "For a desperate disease a desperate cure" and "The wise man lives as long as he ought, not as long as he can."[12]

Other voices of the time echoed the sentiment, if not the eloquence, of the famed French essayist that suicide was an individual choice.

In 1516 the English humanist Sir Thomas More (1478–1535), for one, defended euthanasia in *Utopia*. Idealizing the functions of hospitals, More supported hastening the death of consenting patients with incurable illnesses, when sanctioned by a priest.[13] His pro-euthanasia stand apparently posing no obstacle to sainthood, More was canonized Saint Thomas More in 1935.

The English philosopher Francis Bacon (1561–1626), the creator of scientific induction, similarly conceived the role of physicians as "not only to restore the health, but to mitigate pain and dolors; and not only when such mitigation may conduce to recovery, but when it may serve to make a fair and easy passage" (*New Atlantis,* 1627).

Other writers employed more theological arguments to challenge the religious prohibition on suicide, notably John Donne in *Biathanatos* (1647). In that first defense of suicide in English, the metaphysical poet and cleric claimed that, while suicide often was morally wrong, it could be acceptable if performed with the intention of glorifying God, not serving self-interest. Yes, Donne conceded, prohibitions of suicide had their place, but so did exceptions that proved the rule.

On the continent, the eighteenth century French *philosophes*—Baron d'Holblach (1723–1789), Voltaire, Baron de Montesquieu (1689–1755), Rousseau—all took a generally permissive view toward suicide. Rousseau's uncommon reservation involved obligations to others such as family. The sole exception among the principal French intellectuals of the day was Diderot (1713–1784), who, in the famous *Encyclopedie* (1765), based his opposition to suicide on the three classic arguments.[14]

It was thus left to Hume in England to rebut the 2,000 year condemnation of suicide as sin against God, neighbor, and self. This he did in "On Suicide," (1777), which is considered the first substantive attempt to defend the permissibility of suicide for reasons of both self- and social-interest.

"On Suicide"

Considered by some the most compelling statement in any language of the Enlightenment's position on the subject,[15] "On Suicide" basically urges the potential suicide to decide after assessing the multiple interests and values involved. If, on balance, it's determined that either the individual or society benefits more from taking one's life than not, then the action is permissible, perhaps even praiseworthy.

In making his case, Hume used counter instances to the traditional disapproval of suicide. He submitted, for example, that if God is the creator of the universe, then in all things, great and small, his will is expressed—even in acts of self-killing. Therefore, suicide cannot be a violation of divine will but can be a rational and reasonable act that occurs within the context of a divinely ordered universe. Notice how in the following passage Hume turns the classical metaphor of the suicide being like a soldier deserting his post without orders into a devastating boomerang:

> But you are placed by providence, like a centinel in a particular station, and when you desert it without being recalled, you are equally guilty of rebellion against your almighty sovereign and have incurred his displeasure.—I ask, why do you conclude that providence has placed me in this station?

For my part, I find that I owe my birth to a long chain of causes, of which many depended upon voluntary actions of men. *But Providence guided all these causes, and nothing happens in the universe without its consent and Co-operation.* If so, then neither does my death, however voluntary, happen without its consent; and whenever pain or sorrow so far overcome my patience, as to make me tired of life, I may conclude that I am recalled from my station in the clearest and most express terms.[16]

If as an expression of liberty suicide does not necessarily offend divine will, by the same token it does not always threaten public order. It may even at times promote it, Hume thought, as it would were one to become a burden to society or family. In such cases, "my resignation of life must not only be innocent but laudable."[17] (This argument is taken up in earnest today to support a "duty to die," as we'll see in Chapter 12.) Beyond this, Hume argued that suicide can also be consistent with duty to self when "age, sickness, misfortune" renders life intolerable, "worse even than annihilation."

But not all Enlightenment thinkers were as permissive of suicide as Hume. John Locke, for one, condemned disowning one's right to life as preposterous as giving away one's inalienable and irrevocable right to liberty.[18] In Chapter 2 of his "Two Treatises of Government," Locke invoked the traditional theological anti-suicide argument such that, being "servants of one sovereign Master . . . every one . . . is bound to preserve himself, and not to quit his station willfully."

Even more effusive in his opposition than Locke, Immanuel Kant offered four arguments, three philosophical and one religious, for casting self-killing as always a violation of moral responsibility.

SUICIDE AS VIOLATING MORAL RESPONSIBILITY: KANT

Kant claimed that suicide was always wrong because it (1) involved a contradiction of free will; (2) degraded human nature; (3) was inconsistent with autonomy; and (4) violated the law of God. (Although 3 and 4 might be considered versions of 1 and 2, they'll be considered separately here.)

The Argument from Free Will

Kant believed that we can treat our bodies as we please so long as our motives are self-preservation. Consider an amputation: Part of the body is intentionally sacrificed for the preservation of the body as a whole. In contrast, since in taking one's life one obviously does not preserve one's person, suicide always involves the intention to destroy oneself. It robs oneself of one's person, thereby making it for Kant:

> Contrary to the highest duty we have towards ourselves, for it annuls the condition of all other duties; it goes beyond the limits of the use of

free will, for this use is possible only through the existence of the Subject.

In terms of Kant's ultimate rule of morality, the categorical imperative (see Chapter 2), the maxim that would permit suicide would be self-contradictory, since it would permit the power of will to destroy itself.

The Argument from Human Nature

Kant believed that there are many circumstances when life ought to be sacrificed, chief among them whenever life conflicts with duty. Thus, "If I cannot preserve my life except by violating duties toward myself, I am bound to sacrifice my life rather than violate these duties." But suicide never qualifies as a justifiable sacrifice of life because life is the condition of everything else. Conscious that life is a trust reposed in us, we should recoil at the thought of breaking this trust by turning our lives against ourselves. An act of suicide, then, doesn't merely devalue life, it degrades human worth and human nature. In his *Lectures on Ethics*, Kant writes:

> Suicide is not abominable and inadmissible because life should be highly prized; were it so, we could each have our own opinion of how highly we should prize it, and the rule of prudence would often indicate suicide as the best means. But the rule of morality does not admit of it under any condition because it degrades human nature below the level of animal nature and destroys it. Yet there is much in the world far more important than life. To observe morality is far more important. It is better to sacrifice one's life than one's morality. To live is not a necessity; but to live honorably while life lasts is a necessity. We can at all times go on living and doing our duty towards ourselves without having to do violence to ourselves. But he who is prepared to take his own life is no longer worthy to live at all. The pragmatic ground of impulse to live is happiness. Can I then take my own life because I cannot live happily? No! It is not necessary that whilst I live I should live happily; but it is necessary that so long as I live I should live honorably. Misery gives no right to any man to take his own life, for then we should all be entitled to take our lives for lack of pleasure. All our duties towards ourselves would then be directed towards pleasure; but the fulfillment of those duties may demand that we should even sacrifice our life.[19]

Suicide violates the categorical imperative, therefore, because it is not treating humanity (i.e., one's own person) as an end in itself, but simply as a means to pleasure or the avoidance of pain.

Alternately, in Chapter 2 of his *Principles of Morals*, Kant famously depicts the objectionable maxim of a person who commits suicide as follows:

> A man reduced to despair by a series of misfortunes feels wearied of life, but is still so far in possession of his reason that he can ask himself whether it

would not be contrary to his duty to himself to take his own life. Now he inquires whether the maxim of his action could become a universal law of nature his maxim is: From self-love, I adopt it as a principle to shorten my life when its longer duration is likely to bring more evil than satisfaction. It is asked then simply whether this principle founded on self love can become a universal law of nature. Now we see at once that a system of nature of which it should be a law to destroy life by means of the very feeling whose special nature it is to impel to the improvement of life would contradict itself, and therefore could not exist as a system of nature; hence that maxim cannot possibly exist as a universal law of nature, and consequently would be wholly inconsistent with the supreme principle of all duty.[20]

The Argument from Autonomy

According to Kant and contrary to the Stoics and Hume, autonomy, properly understood, disallows suicide. Kant did not share the Stoic and Humean view that a self-killing may be the justifiable act of a rational choice to die according to one's values and principles. On the contrary, he held that autonomy, properly understood, argues against using one's freedom self-destructively. To do so would be to destroy the very existence that is necessary for freedom.

In the context of the categorical imperative, a maxim that would allow a person to use freedom to end her life would be self-contradictory since it would allow something external to limit that freedom. A simpler understanding is to view suicide as violating Kant's principle of humanity, which forbids intentionally using a person as a means to an end rather than as an end in himself. As Kant writes, similarly to his argument from free will:

> He who contemplates suicide should ask himself whether his action can be consistent with the idea of humanity *as an end in itself*. If he destroys himself to escape from painful circumstances, he uses a person merely as *a means* to maintain a tolerable condition up to the end of life. But a man is not a thing, that is to say, something which can be used merely as means, but must in all his actions be always considered as an end in himself. I cannot, therefore, dispose in any way of a man in my own person so as to mutilate him, to damage or kill him.[21]

Argument from Divine Will

Finally, Kant believed that suicide opposes God's purpose and design, and, therefore, is always wrong. In reviving the classic appeal to divine will, Kant even borrowed the soldier and chattel metaphor of Plato. The suicide is, thus, classically depicted as a deserter of his post, deserving God's wrath.

Despite the obvious religious nature of this argument, for Kant suicide is not wrong because God forbids it, but rather because it degrades and destroys human nature. In reducing one's inner worth to a sub-animal level, suicide is an abomination that properly warrants the divine condemnation it gets. Kant's argument from divine will, then, could be read as a religious version of the argument from human nature. For Kant—as well as for Georg W. F. Hegel (1770–1831)—the imperatives of reason validate the traditional religious condemnation of suicide and euthanasia.

The recurrence of the theological argument in the battle between traditional prohibition and enlightened permissiveness recalls the tension between faith and reason in the Age of Enlightenment (see Chapter 2) that profoundly shaped views of the nature and purpose of morality. Thus, for Aquinas, Augustine, and their descendants in faith, morality was all about obeying the will of God. This view led them to an unqualified disapproval of suicide and euthanasia. For philosophers such as Hume and Kant, in contrast, morality was about following reason, and reason did not entail a single moral judgment about suicide. As it happened, reason led Hume to permissiveness, Kant to prohibition. The larger point, though, is that as reason, itself, gained cachet in moral discourse, the theological case against suicide weakened and its permissibility strengthened. Another and related factor that came into play was the maturing of scientific medicine in the nineteenth century.

SUICIDE AS A SOCIAL UTILITY:
BENTHAM AND MILL

Medical ethicist Andrew Papanikitas points out, "It is generally regarded that the medical profession overtook the theological monopoly on death in the nineteenth century." Specifically, the ascent of scientific medicine made it possible to pinpoint incurable or terminal patients, and thus candidates for euthanasia in the modern usage of the term. As a result, says Papanikitas, "Until the end of the nineteenth century euthanasia was regarded as a peaceful death, and the art of its accomplishment."[22]

The toleration of suicide and euthanasia was given additional impetus by the philosophical movement known as "utilitarianism," which substituted the greatest possible creature happiness for divine will or abstract imperatives as a test of morality. Do what likely will yield the most utility, that is, the greatest happiness for the greatest number. So advised British reformer Jeremy Bentham (1748–1832). Central to this "utility principle" was liberty, without which individuals lacked a, if not *the*, key ingredient of happiness. Along with compatriot John Stuart Mill and other utilitarians, Bentham pressed for minimal state intrusion into demonstrably private affairs, notably suicide and euthanasia.

What business is it of government if the individual wishes to end his or her life rather than suffer an agonizing death? On what moral grounds can state interference that extends pain and suffering at the end of life be justified when the alternative, hastening death, promises an end to individual suffering? Whose interests are mainly at issue—the individual's or the society's? With such questions, utilitarians launched a blistering, still heard liberty-interest case for permissive euthanasia legislation.

But the impact of scientific medicine and utilitarianism was felt well beyond philosophical circles. Throughout the nineteenth century, the medical profession increasingly addressed the subject of euthanasia. For example, "Medical Euthanasia," a lecture delivered by a physician, stressed the importance of treating patients, not just their diseases. Its author, Dr. Carl F. H. Marx, reminded his colleagues that a physician "is not expected to have a remedy for death, but for the skillful alleviation of suffering," before adding pregnantly, "and he should know how to apply it when all hope has departed."[23]

Interestingly, the first popular advocate of active euthanasia in the nineteenth century was not a physician or philosopher. He was a schoolmaster. In the first paper (1870) to deal with the concept of "medical" euthanasia, Samuel Williams wrote:

> In all cases it should be the duty of the medical attendant, whenever so desired by the patient, to administer chloroform, or any other such anaesthetics as may by and by supersede chloroform, so as to destroy consciousness at once, and put the suffer at once to a quick and painless death; precautions being adopted to prevent any possible abuse of such duty; and means being taken to establish beyond any possibility of doubt or question, that the remedy was applied at the express wish of the patient.[24]

Though widely printed, Williams's view apparently was ignored by the British medical profession. Still, under the influence of utilitarianism and social Darwinism—the belief that society's strongest and fittest should survive, while the weakest and unfit be allowed to die—the argument made the incurably sick dispensable.

Feeding into the nascent tendency to marginalize the socially "undesirable" were related ideas that were emerging with the new science of eugenics. Among the most controversial proposals was sterilization of the disabled, the mentally ill, and those with hereditary disorders. The "social burden" depiction of such individuals reached a grisly climax in the twentieth century with the mass involuntary deaths that occurred in Nazi Germany. Among them were thousands of disabled people, as Hugh Gallagher horrifyingly shows in *Betrayed By Trust* (1995). And should the practice leave physicians of that day squeamish, they could always borrow strength from a little book published in Germany in 1920 titled *Consent to the Extermination of Life Unworthy To Be Lived*. In it was provided a rationale for ending lives thought unworthy to preserve.[25]

As this overview has shown, the ethics of suicide and euthanasia has occupied philosophers and others for centuries. Central to the colloquy are broad principles about duties to self and to society, as well as fundamental beliefs about the value of human life, including its nature, purpose, and divine origins. A list of the principals engaged in the debate has been likened to a "Who's Who?" of Western intellectual history, "ranging from Plato and Aristotle in ancient Greece to Augustine and Thomas Aquinas in the Middle Ages, and Locke, Hume, and Kant in more modern times."[26]

This mix of religious and secular belief, modified by cultural conditions and demands, has shaped law, morality, and feeling about suicide. What once was a crime that brought punishment—loss of family inheritance for suicides or punishment for attempted suicide—today is decriminalized. But assistance in suicide remains a crime, and has become the front in the contemporary battle over voluntary death.

ASSISTED SUICIDE:
THE CONTEMPORARY PICTURE

In the next chapter we'll consider the morality of assisted suicide. Here, where we sample world and domestic opinion, it's enough to note that for someone who believes that suicide is never morally permissible, assisting a death—by providing lethal drugs, for example—would be equally wrong. But if suicide is sometimes a morally justifiable act, then assisted suicide could be permissible, as with the "terminally ill," taken to denote individuals with an incurable or irreversible disease that will, by reasonable medical judgment, produce death within six months.

Supporters of assisted suicide argue that a competent terminally ill adult is entitled not only to refuse life-sustaining treatment—a well-established patient right—but to end her own life and to be supported in her death decision. But while agreeing in general that a dying person should have the right to determine how and when to end her own life, supporters of assisted suicide can and do differ on details. Who should assist, when, under what circumstances—these and other matters often lead to significantly nuanced positions among those who favor assisted suicide.

Physician Assistance

In the ongoing national and world debate, "assisted suicide" ordinarily is taken to mean physician- or doctor-assisted suicide (PAS or DAS). In PAS the physician provides the means—for example, lethal drugs—with which the dying person takes his or her own life. Physicians are involved because of their knowledge and control of drugs and because they're trusted not to misuse the practice of assisted suicide.[27]

In the U.S., the California State Bar Conference was the first public body to approve of physician aid in dying, when it passed a PAS resolution on March 4, 1987. In 1988, the Unitarian Universality Association of Congregations became the first religious body to do so when it passed a resolution favoring aid in dying for the terminally ill. Then in 1990, partly as a response to the momentum-gathering right-to-die movement, the American Medical Association (AMA) adopted the formal position that, while not condoning PAS, permits a physician, with patient consent, to withhold or withdraw treatment from a patient who is close to death, and to discontinue life support of a patient in a permanent coma. In that same year: (1) the U.S. Supreme Court in *Cruzan*, its first ruling on the right to refuse medical treatment, recognized that competent adults have a constitutionally protected liberty interest in refusing medical treatment; and (2) the U.S. Congress passed the Patient Self-Determination Act, requiring hospitals that receive federal funds to tell patients about the legal options in their state.

With advances in physician-directed life support technologies and patient insistence on ever greater control over medical treatment, the controversy over PAS has intensified worldwide, both within and outside medical professions.

World Legal Opinion

Today most countries and American states prohibit assisting suicide. Where it is permitted, medical tradition opposes it. In the world's developing nations, debates about PAS are as rare as their populations are rich. Nevertheless, a look at laws around the world turns up a mixed and ambivalent body of opinion concerning assisted suicide.[28]

Europe Europe is the only place outside Oregon where assisted suicide is legal. Since 1941 Switzerland has permitted both physician- and non–physician-assisted suicide, uniquely today with no resident requirements. Holland officially sanctioned assisted death, as well as voluntary euthanasia, in 2002, although it had been permitted since 1984 and practiced in the Netherlands well before then. Since 1975, public opinion polls have shown that a large majority of the Dutch population across the religious spectrum believes that physicians should be permitted to carry out euthanasia.[29] In 2002, Belgium became the world's second country to allow euthanasia, despite the considerable outrage of its influential Roman Catholic clergy. Sweden and Norway don't prohibit suicide but have prosecuted assisters as accessories to murder, albeit lightly.[30]

Asia In Asia and the Pacific, aging populations, especially in developed countries, are pressing medicine to address quality of end-of-life issues, including suicide. Although assisting suicide is generally illegal, penalties for it tend to be lenient. In some instances the whole matter is complicated by a mix of ambiguous law and long-standing custom.

In Japan, for example, assisted suicide is illegal. At the same time, rulings from earlier times seem to permit it by distinguishing PAS from assisted killing. Further complicating the Japanese picture are traditional taboos on suicide, dying, and death, and the fact that patients frequently are not told they are terminally ill.

In 1994, delegates from the National People's Congress (NPC) in the Republic of China proposed a law in support of euthanasia, and in 1995 thirty delegates again urged passage after the imprisonment of a man who assisted his terminally ill wife to commit suicide. Despite these efforts, euthanasia remains illegal in China. Still, given the challenges of providing quality care to burgeoning elderly populations there and throughout the Far East, the issue is unlikely to fade.

The only place in the area where PAS was ever legal was in the sparsely populated Northern Territory of Australia, and there only for a nine-month period ending in March 1997. Interest in permissive legislation, however, has spawned the lobby group Exit International, founded by Dr. Philip Nitschke.

U.S. Public and Professional Opinion

Sampling opinion is always tricky, no more so than on an issue as controversial as PAS/euthanasia, where conceptual clarity, information about correspondents, and provisions for maintaining confidentiality can be problematic. Incompleteness also is a concern. Physicians' attitudes toward PAS and alternatives, for example, still need thorough studying.[31] These and other cautions notwithstanding, recent polls and surveys can give us a sense of popular and professional sentiment within the U.S. at present.

According to *Issues and Controversies on File,* during the last quarter of the twentieth century, public opinion polls consistently showed that between two-thirds and three-quarters of Americans approved of doctors' helping terminally ill patients to end their lives. This is a marked increase since 1973, when about half did. A 2002 Harris poll puts the number of approving PAS at 65%, disapproving 29%.[32]

When accounted for age, however, the polls show a different picture of opinion. For example, according to an *AARP/Modern Maturity* survey of Americans 45 and older reported in September 2000, about 50% agreed that PAS should be allowed for terminally ill patients. And a Zogby poll reported in 2000 that only one-in-three Americans if stricken with a painful fatal disease would prefer a suicide to "letting nature take its course." Both the AARP and Zogby polls turned up a correlation between age and opinion such that respondents between 30 and 64 years old were most likely to support PAS for terminally ill patients. Support was significantly weaker among those 18 to 29, and 65 and older.

Also noteworthy is that support for assisted suicide seemingly increases if the questions avoid the word "suicide" and includes "wishes of a dying patient." For example, a 1997 Princeton Survey Research poll asked respondents: "Do you think it should be legal for a doctor to help a terminally ill patient commit suicide, or not?" Forty-five percent answered "Yes, it should be legal." In the same year, however, 69% responded "Yes" to the following question posed in a Louis Harris and Associates Poll: "Do you think that the law should allow doctors to comply with the wishes of a dying patient in severe distress who ask to have his or her life ended, or not?" This higher figure roughly corresponds with results of a December 2001 Harris poll question that described safeguards along the lines that have been instituted in Oregon.[33]

A survey of cancer patients and their doctors by researchers at Dana Farber Cancer Institute in Boston that was released in 1997 sheds further light on PAS opinion.[34] With respect to cancer patients, the study found:

- more than one-quarter (27.3%) had "seriously thought about" requesting PAS or euthanasia
- about 12% had discussed the matter with a doctor or family member
- a small number, 3.4%, had saved up drugs with the intent of taking an overdose
- 1.3% had read *Final Exit* (itself an indication of interest if not opinion, Derek Humphry's how-to-book on "self-deliverance" had sold more than one-half million copies and topped best-seller lists within 18 months of its publication in 1991)

Of the surveyed oncologists (cancer specialists):

- 57.2% said that they had received requests for assisted suicide from patients
- 13.6% said they had granted patients requests for assisted suicide
- a majority could not agree on any conditions outlined by researchers—not even serious, unrelievable pain—that would morally warrant the legalization of PAS or euthanasia

The study also found that more than 90% of patients, physicians, and the general public believed it was ethical for a doctor to give consenting dying patients enough morphine to control their pain "even if premature death likely would result."[35]

In the first nationwide survey of its kind, conducted by Baylor University and reported in 2001, 45% of rank-and-file physicians said doctor-assisted suicide should probably or definitely be legal, a rate that is about twice as high as the AMA's House of Delegates. But both physicians and delegates agreed that that any decision on assisted suicide should be strictly between physician and patient and not structured by law or medical guidelines.[36]

Fewer cancer doctors were reported supporting the idea of assisted suicide in 1998 (22%) compared to 1995 (45%). But, according to the survey conducted by the American Society of Clinical Oncology, while doctors are less willing to help end the life of terminally ill patients, the majority of oncologists, 64%, said they had received requests for PAS or euthanasia, and about 13% said they had performed PAS or euthanasia during their careers.[37] This contrasts with a similar survey published earlier in the prestigious *New England Journal of Medicine* that reported on doctors in all fields. Of the 18% of them who had received a request for assisted suicide, 3% had complied; and of the approximately 11% who had received a request for euthanasia, 4.7% had acceded.[38] In 2003, the *Archives of Internal Medicine* reported one in five U.S. physicians had received at least one request to assist a terminally ill patient to die, and approximately 3%–18% reportedly agreed to these requests, even though the practice is illegal in all but one state.[39]

As with the general public, political orientation and religion seem to be the key indicators of professional opinion. Physicians and laypeople alike who say they are politically conservative or that religion is "very important" to them are more likely to oppose PAS than those who consider themselves politically liberal and those for whom religion is "not at all important."[40]

Initiatives and Legislation

Voting results and proposed laws provide another gauge of public opinion. In general, when given the opportunity voters have rejected the legalization of assisted suicide, sometimes by lopsided margins, other times razor-thin ones. In 1998, for example, one month after Dr. Kevorkian's conviction, voters in Michigan rejected an assisted-suicide referendum by a margin of 71% to 29%. But a similar initiative was defeated in Maine in 2000 by a margin of only 51%–49%. Like initiatives have been rejected elsewhere, in Washington state in 1990 and in California in 1992, both by identical 54%–46% margins.

Oregon's Death with Dignity Act

Today Oregon is the only state in the U.S. with legalized PAS. (Previous attempts at permissive legislation failed: in Ohio in 1906, in Nebraska in 1937, and in New York in 1939.) Twice Oregonians voted in favor of legalized PAS, first in 1994 (51%–49%), then again in 1997 (60%–40%) after the Death with Dignity Act had survived a constitutional challenge.

According to the law, a physician may legally prescribe lethal drugs for mentally competent terminally ill Oregon residents 18 or older who want to end their own lives—the law does not permit euthanasia—provided: the patient is expected to die of a terminal illness within six months and diagnosis and prognosis are confirmed by a consulting physician. Additionally under the law:

1. the patient must make his or her requests at 15-day intervals, one of which must be a written request supported by two witnesses

2. before writing the prescription the physician must wait at least 15 days after the patient's initial request and at least 48 hours after the written request

3. the physician must fully inform the patient about the diagnosis and prognosis, as well as feasible alternatives such as comfort care, hospice, or pain control

4. both the attending physician and consulting physician must certify that the patient is mentally competent, is acting voluntarily, and has made an informed choice

5. if either physician believes that the patient's judgment might be impaired, the patient must be referred for counseling

Although Oregon's criteria resemble Holland's, they differ significantly. Unlike Oregon, the Dutch do not require "witness support," thereby granting a larger measure of patient freedom. In fact, in 1984 when the Dutch Medical Association compiled its requirements for doctors to follow in order for euthanasia to be acceptable, it stated that "the patient must experience his suffering as unacceptable for *him*" (italics added).[41] Also notable: The "suffering," although unbearable and hopeless, need not be physical pain; and Dutch law has no life expectancy requirement.

Through 2004, 208 people, representing 1 in 1,000 deaths, had used the Oregon law to take their lives.[42] Most were cancer patients. The top reasons given by patients for wanting to end their lives are: losing autonomy (84%), decreasing ability to participate in activities they enjoyed (84%), and losing control of bodily functions (47%).[43] There has not been widespread abuse, as feared, in part apparently because doctors and nurses have done a good job on end-of-life palliative or comfort care.

Meanwhile, bills modeled after Oregon's Death with Dignity Act were introduced in four states in 2003—Arizona, Hawaii, Wisconsin, and Vermont—and one stalled in committee in California in 2005. In North Carolina two physician legislators introduced a bill calling for banning such legislation, which 38 states already have done so. Seven states have either adopted case law or interpreted homicide statutes to criminalize PAS. Its legal status remains undetermined in Nevada, Utah, Wyoming, and Hawaii.

CONCLUSIONS

Kant writes (in *Perpetual Peace,* Appendix I, 1775): "Policy says, 'Be wise as serpents'; morality adds thereto the restrict: 'and harmless (without falsehood) as doves.'" Is PAS wise social policy? Is it harmless—even helpful in saving suffering and enlarging liberty? Or is PAS potentially dangerous public policy, perhaps even a threat to some of the most vulnerable members of society? Whatever one's personal or professional opinion, one thing is certain: These questions, and Kant's directive, are at the heart of the public debate about how much control we can exercise over how we die.

Before considering what society has a right to expect of us (in Chapter 11), let's first inquire (in Chapter 10) what we should expect of ourselves in the matter of voluntary death decisions. Both concerns, social- and self-expectation, often are determined by common moral principles, such as autonomy or sanctity of life. Sometimes what any one of us expects of ourselves morally is what we believe society has a right to expect of all its members, and vice versa. But, as we'll see in the next two chapters, what any one of us expects of ourselves morally is not always what we believe society has a right to expect of all its members. And, by the same token, what we believe society should expect of all of its members, we personally may not expect of ourselves.

REFERENCES

1. Plato, *Phaedo,* Benjamin Jowett, trans., in *The Harvard Classics,* New York: P. F. Collier & Company, 1909, pp. 121–122.

2. Aristotle, *Nicomachean Ethics,* R. D. Ross, trans. Retrieved June 1, 2005, from http://www.ethics.sandiego.edu/theories/Aristotle.

3. A. Alvarez, *The Savage God: A Study of Suicide,* New York: Bantam Books, 1971, pp. 52–53.

4. Ron P. Hamel, *Choosing Death: Active Euthanasia, Religion, and the Public Debate,* Harrisburg PA: Trinity Press International, 1991.

5. Jacques Choron, *Suicide,* New York: Charles Scribner's Sons, 1972, p. 116.

6. Choron, p. 118.

7. Seneca, "Letter to Lucilius, No. 70," in *The Stoic Philosophy of Seneca,* Moses Hadas, trans., Garden City, NJ: Doubleday, 1987, p. 202.

8. St. Augustine, *City of God,* Gerald G. Walsh and others, trans., Bk. I, Ch. 20, New York: Image Books, 1958, p. 55.

9. Thomas Aquinas, *Summa Theologica,* Father of the English Dominican Province, trans., Benziger 1947 Edition. Second Part of the Second Part, Q. 64, Art. 5. Retrieved May 1, 2005, from http://www.ccel.org/a/aquinas/summa/home.html.

10. Alvarez, p. 71.

11. William Harrison, "A Description of Elizabethan England," *Hollinshed's Chronicles,* in *The Harvard Classics,* vol. 35, Charles W. Eliot, ed., New York: P. F. Collier & Son Company, 1910, p. 366.

12. Michele de Montaigne, "A Custom of the Isle of Cea," in *The Essays of Montaigne,* E. J. Trechmann, trans., London: Oxford University Press, vol. I, bk. II, 1927, pp. 336–351.

13. Thomas More, *Utopia,* in *The Harvard Classics,* vol. 36, New York: P. F. Collier & Son Company, 1910, p. 208.

14. Choron, p. 125.

15. Ibid., p. 127.

16. David Hume, "On Suicide," in *Of the Standard of Taste and Other Essays,* John Lenz, ed., Indianapolis: Bobbs-Merrill Educational Publishing, 1965, p. 157.

17. Hume, p. 159.

18. G. B. Ferngren, "The Ethics of Suicide in the Renaissance and Reformation," in *Suicide and Euthanasia,* B. A. Brody, ed., Dordrecht, Germany: Kluwer Academic Publishers, 1989, pp. 173–175.

19. Immanuel Kant, *Lectures on Ethics,* Louis Infield, trans., New York: Harper & Row Publishers/Harper Torchbooks, 1963, pp. 151–152.

20. Immanuel Kant, *Fundamental Principles of the Metaphysic of Morals,* T. K. Åbbott, trans., in *Harvard Classics,* vol. 32, New York: P. F. Collier & Son, 1910, p. 332.

21. Ibid., p. 340.

22. Andrew Papanikitas, "Is It Historically Possible for a Consensus to Be Reached on the Subject of Euthanasia, Voluntary or Otherwise?" *Catholic Medical Quarterly,* February 2000. Retrieved March 15, 2005, from http://www.catholicdocors.org. uk/CMQ/FEB_2000/consensus_on_euthanasia.htm.

23. Derek Humphry, *The Right to Die,* New York: Harper and Row, 1986, p. 10.

24. Papanikitas.

25. "When Death is Sought: Assisted Suicide in the Medical Context," Ch. 5, *The New York Task Force on Life & the Law,* October, 2001. Retrieved February 7, 2005, from, http:/www.health.state.ny.us/nysdoh/provider/death.htm.

26. Ibid., pp. 77–78.

27. Samia Hurst and Alex Mauron, "Assisted Suicide and Euthanasia in Switzerland: Allowing a Role for Non-Physicians," *BMJ,* February 1, 2003, pp. 271–273. Retrieved February 1, 2005, from http://bmj.bmjjournals.com/cgi/content/full/ 326/7383/271.

28. "Assisted Suicide Laws around the World," *ERGO,* November 22, 2004. Retrieved May 1, 2005, from http://www.assistedsuicide.org/suicide_laws.html.

29. John Griffiths, Alex Bood, and Heleen Weyers, *Euthanasia and Law in the Netherlands,* Amsterdam: Amsterdam University Press, 1998.

30. "Assisted Suicide Laws around the World."

31. Kathleen Foley and Herbert Hendin, eds., *The Case Against Assisted Suicide,* Baltimore: Johns Hopkins Press, 2002, p. 140.

32. "Issues and Controversies: Assisted Suicide Update," *Facts on File News Service,* November 21, 1997. Retrieved February 1, 2005, from http://www.facts.com/icof/ i00057.htm.

33. Humphrey Taylor, "2-to-1 Majorities Continue To Support Rights to Both Euthanasia and Doctor-Assisted Suicide," January 9, 2005. Retrieved February 2, 2005, from http://www.harrisinteractive.com/harris_poll/index.asp?PID=278.

34. "Issues and Controversies: Assisted Suicide Update."

35. Ibid.

36. Simon Whitney and others, "Views of the United States Physicians and Members of the American Medical Association House of Delegates on Physician-Assisted Suicide," *Journal of General Internal Medicine,* May 2001, pp. 290–296.

37. Ezekiel Emmanuel and others, "Attitudes and Practices of U.S. Oncologists regarding Euthanasia and Physician-Assisted Suicide," *Annals of Internal Medicine,* October 3, 2000, pp. 527–532.

38. "Fewer Doctors Support Assisted Suicide Poll Says," *Pro-Life Info net,* 1998. Retrieved February 1, 2005, from http://www.euthanasia.com/docs.html.

39. Diane Meier and others, "Characteristics of Patients Requesting and Receiving Physician Assisted Death," *Archives of Internal Medicine,* July 14, 2003, pp. 1537–1542.

40. Whitney and others.

41. Griffiths, Bood, and Weyers, p. 68.

42. Brad Cain, "High Court To Hear Challenge to Oregon's Suicide Law," *Santa Barbara News-Press,* September 29, 2005, p. B2.

43. "Assisted-Suicide Numbers Continue to Rise in Oregon," *American Medical News,* March 24/31, 2003. Retrieved February 3, 2005, from http://www.ama-assn.org/amednews/2003/03/24/prsc0324.htm.

10

Individual Morality

Fighting the ravages of Lou Gehrig's disease, fearing the prospect of choking on her own saliva, unwilling to linger for months in steady decline, Velma Howard, 76, of Belleville, Illinois, made a decision.

THE ASSISTED DEATH OF VELMA HOWARD

Velma decided to hasten her death. So, she and her husband, also 76, together with their two sons—one a Texas businessman, the other a Kansas judge—gathered at a convenient central point, a motel in Joplin, Missouri. There, after a day spent reminiscing, Velma took her life with the assistance of her family.

Although her death was swift and peaceful, it hardly passed unnoticed by local authorities. Both husband and a son were charged with felonies, the one for providing the poison-laced orange juice Velma drank, the other for reading from a book containing instructions on self-killing. When asked by a reporter if the case wasn't really a moral issue, the prosecutor replied: "This case doesn't have anything to do with whether it's right or wrong to commit suicide. It just happens to be illegal in Missouri to help somebody to do so." He didn't say why.

In fact, it is the widely held assumption that physician-assisted suicide (PAS) and voluntary-active euthanasia (VAE) are immoral that drives their prohibition. Any intelligent analysis of law and social policy regarding voluntary-death decisions, therefore, best begins with the question: Is PAS or VAE ever morally acceptable?

Journalist and assisted-suicide activist Derek Humphry has no doubt of the rectitude of what occurred that Sunday morning in a hotel in Joplin. He describes the Howards as "solid citizens, unanimous in their decision, with no hint of impropriety." They were "decent people trying to handle a difficult situation,"[1] says the author of the book used in the death.

Was the assisted death of Velma Howard a moral action of compassion and love, as Humphry and many others say it was? Or was it a perversion of compassion and love—an action, in the view of the Catholic Church, AMA, and National Right to Life, morally akin to murder?

For our moral guidance in such matters, many of us turn to some principle or rule. What honors the principle or rule, we consider right; what doesn't, we consider wrong. Others of us view morality as less about rules and principles than about character. For us the good action is not so much the one that conforms to some norm, but the one performed by a good person. As we'll soon see, these two traditional approaches to individual morality—principle and virtue—play leading, if morally ambiguous, roles today in the great drama of assisted death.

PRINCIPLES

Moral principles, rules, or laws conceive of moral judgments and actions in terms of the question "What ought I do?" To that question, each offers an answer. "Do what will maximize happiness," for example, or "Do what God wants you to do." Whatever the answer, it takes the form of a principle (rule or law) of conduct. Although the principles vary, the underlying assumption of all principle-based morality is that a "What ought I do?" question has an answer. This means that a question such as "Ought I ever practice assisted death or have it practiced on me?" can be answered, once and for all, as yes or no, according to the principle.

But is it that easy? In fact, an application of the three most prominent moral principles—utility, respect, and natural law—turns up morally ambiguous answers about the propriety of assisted death. They seem to say not yes *or* no, but yes *and* no.

Utility/Happiness

When her family acted to relieve the pain and suffering of Velma Howard, they acted on one of the most enduring of human impulses, powerfully captured in the opening of Jeremy Bentham's *Introduction to the Principles of Morals and Legislation*:

> Nature has placed mankind under the governance of two sovereign masters, *pain* and *pleasure*. It is for them alone to point out what we ought to do, as well as to determine what we shall do. On the one hand the standard of right and wrong, on the other the chain of causes and effects, are fastened to their throne. They govern us in all we do, in all we say, in all we think: every effort we can make to throw off our subjection, will serve but to demonstrate and confirm it. In words a man may pretend to abjure their empire: but in reality he will remain subject to it all the while.[2]

So thinking, Bentham said the purpose of morality is to maximize human happiness. This makes the morality of an action dependent on its utility or tendency to increase or decrease happiness.

Philosophers such as Bentham, who believe that the value of something depends on its utility, are called utilitarians. In doing ethics utilitarians follow the "greatest happiness" or utility principle. In answer to the "What ought I do?" question, utilitarians reply: "Do what likely will yield the greatest net happiness."

But in the pleasure/pain calculation, a question naturally arises as to whose interest is to be considered—the individual's or the society's? Is the yardstick of utility to be applied to individual or group net happiness? In fact, Bentham allowed for either depending on circumstances. Accordingly, a utility argument for PAS has been made on both self- and social-interest.

Self-Interest   As we saw in the preceding chapter, utilitarians such as Bentham argue that a death decision by a consenting adult is largely a private and personal affair, one whose outcome is limited to the interests of the patient and perhaps a few others. Therefore, PAS (or even VAE) is basically the patient's call. (Perhaps true to his position, Bentham is rumored to have requested euthanasia at the end of his life, although it's not known whether it was administered.)[3]

The self-interest argument is given a curious turn today by some who argue that having PAS available might, in fact, help patients choose life. The idea is that given the PAS option, patients are less likely to fear and thus avoid aggressive medical treatments that, while risky and painful, could extend their lives.[4] They may also be relieved of anxiety and put at ease over their worsening condition and the prospect of uncontrolled pain and suffering.[5]

Physician Timothy Quill echoes this point in describing his assisted death of a leukemia patient he calls "Diane." In his controversial admission, Quill writes:

> ... it was ... evident that the security of having enough barbiturates available to commit suicide when and if the time came would leave her secure enough to live fully and concentrate on the present.[6]

Some other prominent American physicians have expressed a similar view. Marcia Angell, for example, in recalling the self-inflicted death of her terminally ill father, writes:

> If patients have access to drugs they can take when they choose, they will not feel they must commit suicide early, while they are still able to do it on their own. They would probably live longer and certainly more peacefully, and they might not even use the drugs.[7]

Such sentiments are summed up in the words of one patient who says, "I'm so afraid of pain and being dependent, of not having my body parts work. I don't know if I could do it or would do it [commit suicide]. But I want the feeling of having a choice of ending what may be a horrible situation."[8]

Like this one, many patients today—and non-patients, for that matter—assume that a quick and painless death is always in their best interests. To them that's reason enough for having PAS available. But is the quick and painless death brought by PAS or VAE always in one's best interests? Some think not.

"Because death is final and irreversible," worries philosopher J. Gay-Williams, "euthanasia contains within it the possibility that we will work against our own interest if we practice it or allow it to be practiced on us."[9] Although directed specifically at voluntary euthanasia defined as intentional killing, Gay-Williams's argument seems equally relevant to PAS.

For example, since medicine doesn't have complete and perfect knowledge, mistaken diagnoses and prognoses are possible. We may think we're dying when we're not, or believe we have a disease when we don't. Beyond this, we may have more life than reasonable medical judgment would expect. Federal officials note, for instance, that about 10% of patients live longer than the anticipated six-month life expectancy that in part defines "terminal" under Oregon's assisted-suicide permit.[10] Moreover, according to a 1999 study, more than one-quarter of Oregon physicians willing to write a lethal prescription for a patient request they'd received were not confident they could determine when a patient had less than six months to live.[11]

But the argument from self-interest *against* assisted death goes well beyond considerations of diagnosis or prognosis. Assisted death, say some of its opponents, precludes the potential benefits of therapeutic experimental procedures, not to mention possible cure from spontaneous remission. Also, if knowing assisted death is available might bring comfort, might not the same knowledge incline one to give up too easily or because of concern for others? Then there's the matter of clinical depression, which might be driving a suicide decision. Beyond this, some opponents, such as M. Scott Peck, view dying as potentially "the opportunity of a lifetime for learning and soul development."[12] To them, assisted death may prematurely end this divinely decreed, developmental process.

For their part, supporters of assisted death from self-interest willingly concede all these points. Yes, they say, sometimes, though rarely, a terminal diagnosis is mistaken and an experimental procedure is lost. And, yes, more needs be done of a psychiatric and psychological nature to rule out volition-limiting depression, although depression of itself doesn't make a decision irrational. (As Angell says, "Some of the vegetative symptoms of depression are similar to the symptoms of terminal illness.") But what weight any of these improbable factors carries in an end-of-life decision is, ultimately, the patient's call. And that is at the heart of the matter. If self-interest is to be the determinant, then we need to trust to self-interest to sort out these essentially personal and private matters. For defenders of assisted death, then, the liberty argument is as fresh today as when Bentham made it more than a century-and-a-half ago.

Social Interest   Of course, unlike suicide, assisted death is not a wholly private act. In both PAS or VAE at least one person is facilitating the death of another. This makes assisted deaths matters of public concern.

Although early utilitarianism readily acknowledged a sphere of inviolable private affairs and decisions, it was mainly driven by community interest. For Bentham and Mill, for example, morality was about maximizing collective pleasure and minimizing collective pain. This meant we should look beyond self-interest—beyond the pleasure/pain calculation for self—and consider the impact of our act on others, now and in the future. By this measure, the right act is the one that likely will yield the greatest happiness for the greatest number. Subsequently, some utilitarians (termed *rule* as opposed to *act*) ask us to go beyond the isolated act and inquire: What if everyone in a similar circumstance did this? What would the social impact be? If, from this bird's-eye perspective, more happiness and less pain would result than from everyone's doing the alternative, then we should adopt that rule. Otherwise, we shouldn't.

The act/rule distinction can make a significant difference in the morality of voluntary-death decisions. In its report on the topic, for example, the 2001 New York Task Force on Life and Law judged assisted suicide as "ethically acceptable" in exceptional cases. But all 24 members—physicians, bioethicists, lawyers, clergy, civil libertarians, and government officials—agreed that, as heart wrenching as individual cases can be, they do not justify changes in the law owing to potential "error and abuse for all members of society, not only for those who are disadvantaged."[13] In the language of utilitarian theory, the Task Force was saying "Yes" to PAS, considered as an act, and "No" to PAS, considered as a rule.

Still, according to traditional utilitarian theory, the moral determinant is the act, not the rule. And by that standard, for utilitarians such as Bentham and Mill the issue comes down to whether or not a particular act of assisted death increases or decreases human happiness. Viewed that way, the consequences of such an act, as even the Task Force admitted, may well decrease the amount of misery in the world. If so, it is a morally right act.

But before so concluding, say opponents, consider the potential corrupting influence on medicine of acts of physician-assisted death. After all, aren't physicians supposed to be guardians of life, not purveyors of death? Doesn't PAS violate the special moral character of the medical profession and ethical obligations that it entails?[14] Most worrisome to some is that PAS gives too much power to physicians, allowing them to stray dangerously outside their traditional role of protecting and preserving health to become promoters of individualistic pursuit of happiness.[15]

Former Surgeon General Everett Koop sums up the opposition to the arguments for assisted death from both self- and other-regarding interests when he warns:

> . . . we must be wary of those who are too willing to end the lives of the elderly and the ill. If we ever decide that a poor quality of life justifies ending that life, we have taken a step down a slippery slope that places all of us in danger. There is a difference between allowing nature to take its course and actively assisting death. The call for euthanasia surfaces in our society periodically, as it is doing now under the guise of "death with dignity" or assisted suicide. Euthanasia is a concept, it seems to me, that is in direct conflict with a religious and ethical tradition in which the human race is presented with "a blessing and a curse, life and death," and we are instructed ". . . therefore, to choose life." I believe "euthanasia" lies outside the commonly held life-centered values of the West and cannot be allowed without incurring great social and personal tragedy. This is not merely an intellectual conundrum. This issue involves actual human beings at risk . . . .[16]

But would permitting assisted suicide place us on the "slippery slope" feared by Koop and others? Angell, the former editor-in-chief of the *New England Journal of Medicine,* says it's impossible to avoid the slippery slope in medicine, or anywhere else for that matter. Consider proxies to terminate life-sustaining treatment. They can be abused, but is that reason not to have them? "The question," Angell writes, "is not whether a perfect system can be devised, but whether abuses are likely to be sufficiently rare to be offset by the benefits to patients who otherwise would be condemned to face the end of their lives in protracted agony."[17]

Respect for Persons

For many moralists, it isn't utility or happiness that should govern morality but the respect for persons that Kant had in mind when he wrote that rational nature exists as an end in itself. In practice, this means that we are never to use each other merely as a means to our own selfish ends but always as ends in themselves. So, to the question "What ought I do?" one version of Kant's answer is: "Always treat others as ends in themselves, never merely as means to ends." This makes Kantian respect all about honoring autonomy, reciprocity, and dignity. Applying these three ideals to assisted suicide, however, turns up the same moral ambiguity as implementing social interest does.

Autonomy   In Chapter 9 we saw that, according to Kant, we should never allow anything to condition our freedom. But this is precisely what we do, he said, when we use our freedom against ourselves to take our own lives. For Kant, then, irreversibly relinquishing autonomy is simply not consistent with autonomy itself.

Curiously, the utilitarian Mill makes a similar argument. Not all voluntary acts, he writes in his famous essay *On Liberty,* are justified by autonomy. Take slavery, for example. The slave

> . . . by selling himself for a slave . . . abdicates his liberty; he forgoes any further use of it beyond that single act. He therefore defeats, in his own case, the very purpose which is the justification of allowing him to dispose of himself. . . . The principle of freedom cannot require that he should be free not to be free. It is not freedom to be allowed to alienate his freedom.

Some philosophers have extended this analysis of individual freedom and autonomy to euthanasia. They argue that, like slavery, "death irreversibly alienates autonomy and cannot be condoned by appeal to autonomy."[18]

But the reason we can't sell ourselves into slavery, goes an objection, has less to do with the nature of autonomy than the sheer social costs of slavery. The same applies to authorizing another to end my life. By this account, context and cost are the only terms for considering the morality of euthanasia. That, in turn, requires a sensible analysis of autonomy itself.[19] For assisted death advocates, being autonomous or self-determining means choosing for ourselves. It means acting for our own reasons or based upon our own goals and aspirations. Given the great variability among individuals about the matter, it's most important that they themselves control how and when they die.[20]

But what about the complex frame of mind of many patients with advance disease and the lack of personnel trained in the care of the dying? Such concerns lead neurologist Kathleen Foley to doubt that a suicide decision in these cases is ever the end product of a competent person making a rational, autonomous decision.[21] Some studies support her view.[22]

Other critics of assisted death offer still another take on autonomy in end-of-life decisions. They cast self-determination not as the right to die but to refuse disproportionate treatment. Additionally, they say autonomy is not the only relevant right in assisted-suicide cases. The good of the community, both medical and social, is also relevant. And the good of the community is never merely the aggregate of self-directing individuals.[23]

Reciprocity   Besides autonomy, Kantian respect for persons is commonly associated with the principle of reciprocity, whereby, in the fashion of the Golden Rule, we treat others as we would want to be treated. This prompts a pro-PAS argument: If involuntary euthanasia is objectionable because it goes against a person's will, then why, by the same token (of reciprocity), isn't it equally objectionable to go against the will of a person who wants to die?

Consider, too, what appears to be another double standard at the end of life. Most everyone would agree that the dying ought to be treated alike. Are they? Terminally ill patients are permitted to refuse life-*preserving* treatment, but they are not permitted life-*ending* treatment. And yet, in both cases the foreseen outcome is identical: death. Isn't that unequal and, therefore, unfair treatment?

No, it's not, say critics of assisted death. Simply because we may want to die doesn't mean we have the right to die. A killer who has acted with full knowledge of the consequences of his act is effectively saying: "Since I don't mind you're killing me, it's okay for me to kill you." Does that make killing right? Of course not. Also, there's a big moral difference, say PAS opponents, between suspending life-prolonging treatment and intentionally hastening death. The first is permitting nature to take its course or "allowing to die"; the latter is interfering with that natural process, or killing. For the many who make such distinctions, legitimating conditions under which one person can kill another is not only wrong, it represents still another way that life is cheapened and made expendable in contemporary society.

Dignity   Kantian respect for persons also means that we allow them to live with dignity, as they see fit. For one person that may include fighting for the last breath of life. For another, lying in a hospital bed, wasting away to something hardly recognizable as human, let alone one's former self, is the ultimate indignity.

"Death with dignity" makes perfect sense, assisted-death opponents say, in the context of a "natural death." In other words, it is a gross indignity to thwart nature by artificially maintaining life instead of allowing someone to die. PAS and VAE, by contrast, are actually avoiding a natural death rather than facing it. Killing the patient is the real indignity.

But assisted-death supporters call "killing" a loaded term. They point out that unlike the other two methods of hastening death—withdrawing life-sustaining treatment and euthanasia, both of which can be performed even if the patient is unaware of the decision—assisted suicide requires the patient's knowledge and participation. Where, then, is the indignity with PAS? Isn't the real indignity thwarting an informed choice for an assisted suicide?

As for those who say such a choice can never be voluntary, what about requests made earlier in life in advance directives and then repeated when desperately ill? As one Oregon cancer specialist says: "I think there are people who are perfectly sane, who know what their future holds for them, and then don't want that. Those are the ones who want the death with dignity."[24] This view is supported by studies showing that most patients who have chosen suicide under the Oregon permit have not been depressed and socially vulnerable, with untreated pain and without access to good hospice care. They have been individuals for whom being in control and not dependent are their most important values when dying.[25,26]

Natural Law

Whichever its many forms, natural law ethics, true to its ancient Greek origins, teaches that we should live according to nature. Its core idea, rooted in the philosophy of Aristotle, is that everything in nature, including humans, has natural tendencies. From this notion of natural dispositions springs the prescription or rule for living and answer to the "What ought I do?" question: "Always act according to nature" (i.e., built-in or natural tendencies). Thus, the right action conforms to natural dispositions, the wrong action does not.

Underlying natural law ethics are two critical assumptions: (1) there are tendencies or propensities built into human nature and the mind; and, therefore, (2) the mind can discover them.

Both of these assumptions figure in the traditional natural law argument against assisted death, euthanasia in particular. Thus, from the observation that every human being has a natural inclination to continue living, it is then asserted that reason alone tells us that euthanasia sets us against our own nature. Additionally, it is said that euthanasia does violence to our dignity as conscious beings who are not only naturally disposed towards survival but also are aware of this disposition.[27]

But critics are quick to hoist natural law proponents by their own theory. On the assumption that it is rationality that makes us fully human, natural law enjoins us to use reason, to act rationally. Why at the end of life, then, are we to suspend the use of the very faculty that is the essence of our humanity? If natural law suggests anything, say friends of PAS, it is that competent individuals be left free to decide such matters for themselves.

The *religious* version of natural law attempts to overcome this objection by interpreting nature's law in terms of divine will.

The Will of God   In the context of revealed religion, natural law is treated as a reflection of divine mind and plan. Aquinas, for example, taught that natural law is God's moral plan for human beings. Unlike legislatively enacted conventional law, natural law is divinely embedded in nature, just as much as scientific law is. Scientific law is descriptive, natural law prescriptive. The law of gravitation, for example, describes the natural phenomenon of attraction between massive bodies.

Its moral counterpart, natural law prescribes how humans are to conduct their lives and relate to one another. Specifically, religious natural law answers the question of obligation, "What ought I do?": "Do what God wills." We can know God's will through the divine gift of intellect. Because natural law is in human reason, then, it is not only the law of God but the law of nature and reason as well.

Aquinas taught that we can identify basic moral precepts of natural law. The relevant one here involves self-preservation. Since we have an innate disposition to preserve our lives and avoid what destroys it, our reason tells us that life is a basic good that we should not deliberately destroy. To do so, as with acts of assisted suicide, for example, is an offense against God, reason, and nature.

Still, determining appropriate treatment for the dying often poses conflicts between goods we're naturally disposed towards. What to do, for example, when the goods and goals of saving life and saving suffering conflict? To reconcile the tension of conflicting dispositions, Aquinas proposed what today is called the "principle of double effect."

Principle of Double Effect   The principle of double effect recognizes that actions sometimes have more than a single outcome; that sometimes, for example, bad things must come with good things. Dousing a dying patient with pain-relieving opiates saves pain, a good effect, *and* inevitably it hastens death, presumably a bad effect. What morally matters in such cases, according to Aquinas, is intention. If the physician's intention is to save pain and not end life, under the principle of double effect it would permissible to "allow" death to occur. But it would be wrong to provide a large amount of opiate for the purpose of killing the patient.

The same reasoning applies to a decision to discontinue "disproportionate," "extraordinary," or "heroic" life-prolonging measures. These are medicines, treatments, and procedures that don't offer any reasonable hope of benefit to the patient and involve excessive pain, expense, or other significant burdens. What constitutes disproportionate treatment in a clinical setting and who is to say aren't always easy to determine. Still, the consensus of moral opinion, both religious and secular, invests in these distinctions enough to base moral judgments upon them.[28,29]

But sorting out actions by intention is tricky. For example, when a dying patient is sedated, can the physician really limit her intention to a single good—saving pain and suffering—while not intending to destroy the other good, life itself? When a physician knows that a massive dose of opiate will end life along with pain, doesn't he really intend both? The significance of this question is that if double effect doesn't work, then the unsettled conflict between fundamental goods may end up undermining natural law theory.[30]

There's another difficulty with double effect and, implicatively, natural law. If we're naturally inclined to live, we are also naturally inclined to live free of pain. Saving pain, in short, is a natural human disposition that the application of double effect to end-of-life cases implicitly acknowledges. But where death may be hastened to relieve suffering, albeit not intentionally, isn't relief of suffering being given a higher moral priority than the maintenance of life? Aren't we actually saying, "To maintain life under these circumstances would be injurious"?

Now, if life saving can be "injurious," life saving can also be "non-injurious." According to double effect and natural law, we are always morally obligated to support non-injurious life saving (call it "proportionate" or "ordinary" treatment); but we're not morally obligated to support injurious life saving ("disproportionate" or "extraordinary" treatment). Usually, according to both religious and secular natural law, we may deliberately take measures to avoid injurious prolongation of life for reasons of burden and consent. In practice this simply means that a patient *may* heroically endure, but is not obligated to. He may opt out when he judges the burden to be too great. The general obligation to preserve life, then, may be overridden if doing so results in disproportionate burden or, simply, is injurious. But if prolongation of life can be injurious or non-injurious, doesn't that imply that killing can be?

Consider the example of a cat writhing in pain after being mangled by a dog attack. In putting the cat out of its misery, philosopher Richard Brandt suggests that he has indeed killed the cat "but surely not *injured* it." Why? Because, says Brandt, we don't injure something by relieving its pain. "If someone is being tortured and roasted to death and I know he wishes nothing more than a merciful termination of life, I have not injured him if I shoot him; I have done him a favor."[31] More generally, "I have not injured a person if I treat him in a way in which he would want me to treat him if he were fully rational, or in a way to which he would be indifferent."[32]

If Brandt is correct in his analysis, then the basic principle about killing needs to be phrased in such a way as to take into account (1) whether the killing would be an injury; and (2) the person's own wishes and directives. More important, the unqualified commandment "thou shalt not kill" cannot be taken as a correct extension of natural law. It needs to be shaped by relevant considerations in assisted deaths, specifically considerations of autonomy and burden.

To the question of whether there's an obligation to sustain the life and suffering of a patient against his autonomous request for a termination of his existence, Brandt writes, "Surely not." And he denies an obligation to refuse the patient death support. As he says, "What possible reason could be offered to justify the claim that [there is such an obligation] beyond theological ones about God's will and our being bound to stay alive at His pleasure?"[33] That, of course, is precisely the reason given by religious natural law.

VIRTUE

That the preceding principles don't yield unambiguous moral direction is one reason that many philosophers are more inclined to focus on character than conduct. Identifying desirable character traits is more important to them than identifying principles. They prefer to ask "What ought I be?" than "What ought I do?"

For character ethicists, then, the question "Ought I ever practice assisted death or allow it to be practiced on me?" can only be answered in reference to what it means to be a morally good person. Once we know that, then we should act accordingly. In the West, the tradition that associates individual morality with character strengths or virtues goes back to Aristotle.

The Aristotelian Good   Aristotle characterized good acts as those acts performed by the good person. The good person, in turn, is the virtuous person, that is, one who is reasonable in her actions, desires, and emotions. The point of life, according to Aristotle, is to fulfill ourselves through the development of moral character or reason.

Elaborating on the Aristotelian good, some contemporary virtue ethicists identify the good or virtuous person variously with self-discipline, courage, compassion, flexibility, open-mindedness, even intuition. Above all, the good person is thought to possess Aristotle's *phronesis* or practical wisdom, which has been associated with applying lessons learned to new situations in, perhaps, novel and creative ways. Thus, according to Joseph DesJardins, *phronesis* "requires us to fit our reasoning to the situation and to avoid forcing the situation into preconceived categories."[34] This makes the morally permissible action one that a person of *phronesis* or practical wisdom would perform in the circumstances. What makes the action permissible is not that a virtuous person would perform it, but certain other characteristics of the act, such as its being courageous or compassionate. What a virtuous person does suggests that an action is permissible, although it doesn't establish it as so.

Would a virtuous person—a person of *phronesis* or practical wisdom—ever assist death? In one sense, no. If, after all, the point of life is to fulfill ourselves through the development of our character (or in any other way, for that matter), then, obviously, acts of suicide make that impossible.[35] Certainly this is a significant consideration for virtue ethics, which is profoundly concerned with the affect of what we do on what we become.

But virtue ethics is also about how what we do *reflects* what we are. So, it can be asked: What does an assisted-death decision say of one's moral character? What sort of people generally practice PAS/VAE or have it practiced on them? Do they tend to be virtuous—for example, temperate, persevering, honest, rational, and compassionate? Why do they choose to end their own lives or help others do so? Are their reasons selfish or unselfish? Well considered or rationalizing? Have their lives, in general, exhibited characteristics we admire, or not?

For many people, the answers to these questions are driven by the generalizations they have formed based on extensive studies of so-called suicide personalities.[36] For example, Burke Balch, who is director of the Department of Medical Ethics for the National Right to Life committee, flatly says people attempting suicide are "deranged and in need of psychological help, and, therefore, in no position to make an accurate assessment of their circumstances."[37] This leads Balch and many others like him to urge compassionate counseling, as with hospice, together with medical and psychological care as an alternative to assisted death.

But is this assessment fair and accurate? Can an assisted-death decision be rational, even courageous and compassionate? Certainly Dr. Timothy Quill thinks so.

Quill, who knew leukemia patient "Diane" over eight years, describes her as an "incredibly clear, at times brutally honest, thinker and communicator," with "a strong sense of independence and confidence." Although alternately fearful, angry, and sad upon learning she had an acute form of the blood disease, these emotions were not the main determinants of her decision. On the contrary, "...she had a remarkable grasp of the options and implications," says Quill, adding: "It was extraordinarily important to Diane to maintain in control of herself and her own dignity during the time remaining to her. When this was no longer possible, she clearly wanted to die."[38]

If virtue ethics is only about becoming a good person and cultivating morally desirable character traits, then Diane seems to have failed inasmuch as she made *her own* further moral development impossible. But from another perspective, she succeeded. According to Quill, a trained medical observer of unimpeachable character, Diane exhibited a high order of virtue. And if the virtuous life is also about teaching and inspiring and presenting ideals or models for others, then, on her physician's testimony, Diane's life and death serve as an exemplar. Thus, fully persuaded that he and her family gave Diane the best possible care, Dr. Quill says of her impact on him:

> Diane taught me about the range of help I can provide if I know people well and if I allow them to say what they really want. She taught me about life, death, and honesty. And about taking charge and facing tragedy squarely when its strikes. She taught me I can make small risks for people that I really know and care about.[39]

In a word, Diane made *Dr.* Quill a better physician, and Timothy Quill a better man.

Diane's professional impact on Dr. Quill reminds us that, beyond the general interest in moral character or integrity, some forms of virtue ethics address character strengths as they relate to particular social roles or professions. Given the physician's leading role in assisted death, this aspect of virtue ethics bears some attention.

Roles and Professions   Virtue has always been an important ingredient of the physician–patient relationship, and thus of medicine as a practice. That the Hippocratic Oath dealt not with the technical but the virtuous practice of medicine is compelling evidence that the ancients recognized that virtue sustains medicine as a social institution.

Although a list and discussion of all the virtues relevant to the physician and the practice of medicine would fill books, historically four stand out:

- respect for persons: treating competent adults autonomously while protecting those with diminished autonomy, such as children and the mentally impaired
- nonmaleficence: doing no harm or not injuring
- beneficence: maximizing benefits while minimizing harm
- justice: doing what's fair

From these, most if not all other medical virtues can be derived. Compassion, care, and concern, for example, can be derived from beneficence. Similarly, truth and honesty can be derived from respect for persons. It is also from these cornerstone virtues that some moral rules and principles have been inferred, such as informed consent from respect for persons and the prohibition of assisted suicide from nonmaleficence.

Taking their lead from the Hippocratic Oath's most important injunction—"do no harm"—many physicians and others would agree that the virtuous physician—the "good doctor"—avoids assistance in death. The AMA goes further, saying that PAS threatens the integrity of the medical profession. In the language of virtue ethics, then, the assisted-death prohibition partly defines professional excellence in end-of-life medical decisions. It is what is thought necessary both to be a good doctor and to sustain medicine as a social institution.

Not everyone, however, agrees with this interpretation of the Hippocratic Oath. Why they don't relates to an important philosophical point about virtues.

Prominent virtue theorist Alisdair MacIntyre reminds us that current standards of excellence never once-and-for-all define a socially based practice; they only *partially* do.[40] At any given moment, then, what medicine is depends on a way of understanding the practice of medicine that has developed over hundreds of years. As such, medicine's standards of excellence are subject to review, criticism, amendment, and change by its practitioners.

Historically, for example, physicians were held to the Hippocratic prohibition of abortion: "I will not give a woman an abortive remedy." But today a physician who does an abortion can still be widely considered a good or virtuous doctor who does not threaten the survival of medicine as a social institution. With respect to abortion, then, the understanding of the practice of medicine has changed. That change has effectively expanded the conception of excellence in the practice of medicine to allow for abortion.

On the other hand, the prohibition of assisted death still largely stands: "I will neither give a deadly drug to anybody if asked for it, nor will I make a suggestion to this effect." This appears, incidentally, in the same Hippocratic passage as the abortion prohibition. And even more than abortion, many today feel that this traditional prohibition needs reinterpretation in the context of the complex, technology-driven end-of-life issues that arise in a modern clinical setting. Excellent medical practice, they suggest, should include assisted death and a Dr. Quill should be considered a good or virtuous doctor. (Some scholars also point out that Hippocrates' famous injunction upon physicians was about suicide in general but not specifically PAS or VAE.)[41]

Is prolonging life the limit of a physician's responsibility to a patient, as opponents of PAS say? Or does it sometimes go beyond that to include helping patients die, as PAS advocates say? What is to be regarded professional excellence in employing life-prolonging measures?

For some the test is reasonable quality of life and level of function, defined by the patient's own life goals, supported by hospice-style terminal care. But others feel just as strongly that when suffering cannot be relieved, it would be an abrogation of medical power to abandon the patient, especially when through that same power the patient's life and suffering have been artificially extended. In the language of character ethics, not to assist the consenting patient's death can fall short of professional excellence for failing all four virtues: nonmaleficence (for extending pain or suffering), beneficence (by not conferring a benefit), respect for persons (by not respecting autonomy), and even justice (by not repairing the harm done by extending the life in the first place). To abandon such patients, in brief, can be a professional failure, whereas assisting their deaths, as with "Diane," can be professional excellence.[42]

But even granting Quill's compassion and respect for his young patient, is that enough to justify death assistance? No, say Quill's critics, who view the physician's cooperation in Diane's death as a perversion of compassion, beneficence, and autonomy. One of them, Dr. Edmund Pellegrino, writes: "The moral psychology of an act has a certain weight in assessing an agent's guilt, but not in changing the nature of the act itself."[43] Rather than improving the physician-patient relationship, and thus the practice of medicine, Pellegrino believes that Quill's misplaced compassion threatens both by presenting "opportunities for conscious or unconscious abuse of [physician] power." He warns that "[w]hen assisted suicide is legitimated, it places the patient at immense risk from the 'compassion' of others," adding darkly: "Misdirected compassion in the face of human suffering can be as dangerous as indifference." For Pellegrino, then, compassion requires the constraint of moral principle.[44]

Fair enough, but can't the same be said of principle? Uncoupled from virtue, isn't principle subject to abuse? It was Adolf Eichmann (1906–1962), after all, who deported millions of European Jews to death camps and later quoted Immanuel Kant at his trial (session 105). Is the highest ethical imperative of the physician to save life no matter what the cost in suffering? No, says physician Angell, "The highest ethical imperative of doctors should be to provide care in whatever way best serves patients' interest, in accord with each patient's wishes."[45] By that measure, assisted death is for some physicians a natural extension of the physician's calling to heal. And if healing is the highest medical imperative, then some doctors support PAS for that reason. Dr. Quill couldn't heal Diane's body, but he could heal her overwhelming sense of helplessness.

But to opponents of assisted death the proper response to such patients is sympathy and empathy, period. Patients like Diane, they say, underscore not the need for assisted death but rather the profound inadequacy of pain control and general care for the chronically ill and dying. This social and professional failure, they point out, is supported by cultural denial and avoidance of death.[46,47]

But wasn't Quill empathetic? A former hospice physician, wasn't he an expert in pain relief? Indeed, according to professor of medical ethics Nancy Jecker, the source of Quill's moral quandary was the personal relationship he'd formed with Diane over eight years. As a result, Diane wasn't merely a patient of Quill's; she was a particular person whose ends and good Quill ultimately held as his own. Were their relationship impersonal—were Diane "just another patient"—then Quill could have detached from her specific needs and invoked some abstract rule appropriate to his role as a doctor. He might have reasoned, for example, that doing PAS would undercut the trust in the medical profession, "while ignoring the actual basis of Diane's trust in him." Alternatively, he might have invoked the Hippocratic maxim "Do no harm," "while discounting what harm meant to Diane." Although such an abstract focus might be appropriate in impersonal relationships, Jecker feels it is unacceptably facile in personal ones. "Keeping an abstract and distant gaze then becomes a way of retreating and pulling back," she says. "It renders moral reasoning instrumental to the purpose of denying the moral claims personal relationships make."[48]

What Jecker is saying is that being a physician does not permit one to engage in PAS, but being a physician *in a personal relationship with a patient* may. Quill's experience, then, leads Jecker to conclude that "the love and care one harbors for a particular person may impel one to intervene and hasten death." Care and concern, in short, may make it impermissible to stand by and allow a protracted illness to run its painful course. Earlier, in Chapter 4, we saw care and concern for his family seemingly help Ivan Ilyich to die. Now we see these same virtues assisting a different kind of death.

Feminist Ethics   Jecker's emphasis on the responsibilities imposed by relationships, it's worth noting, is a way of looking at morality that has been described as being more characteristic of women than men. In her celebrated book *In a Different Voice* (1982), moral psychologist Carol Gilligan attempts to demonstrate that for women morality is mostly a matter of caring and being responsible for others with whom they are involved in personal relationships.[49] Philosopher Nel Noddings, similarly, contends that ethics is about specific individuals in actual encounters with other specific individuals, with care and concern as the major determinants of the relationship.[50] Gilligan, Noddings, and others today with an interest in "feminist ethics" are working squarely in the tradition of virtue as opposed to principle-based ethics. What they're saying and writing has powerful ramifications for the ongoing assisted-death debate. This doesn't imply, however, that the moral direction suggested by "feminist ethics" is any less ambiguous than that of virtue ethics. After all, the same considerations that argue for assisted death—loving care and concern—may also be enlisted to support life.

CONCLUSIONS

In Oregon, two groups have organized with opposed positions on PAS. The one that opposes PAS, the so-called pro-life group, calls itself "Physicians for Compassionate Care." The one that favors PAS, the so-called pro-choice group, calls itself "Compassion in Dying." That both draw their inspiration from the same virtue is emblematic not only of deep divisions about the morality of assisted death but also of the difficulty of applying virtue theory to that issue. Our examination of principle-based theory turned up exactly the same challenge. In the matter of PAS, then, neither principle nor virtue seems to yield an unambiguous answer to the question "What ought I do?" or "What ought I be?"

This inherent difficulty of implementing moral theory in real, end-of-life situations haunts the struggle to reach cultural agreement and form social policy about assisted death, as we'll see in the next chapter.

REFERENCES

1. Derek Humphry and Mary Clement, *Freedom To Die: People, Politics, and the Right-to-Die*, New York: St. Martin's Press, 1998. Retrieved February 7, 2005, from http://www.assistedsuicide.org/typical_example.html.

2. Jeremy Bentham, *Introduction of the Principles of Morals and Legislation*, Oxford: Oxford University Press, 1823, p. 1.

3. James Rachels, *The Elements of Moral Philosophy,* 4th ed., New York: McGraw-Hill, 2003, Ch. 4.

4. "Issues and Controversies: Assisted Suicide Update," *Facts on File News Services,* November 21, 1997. Retrieved February 1, 2005, from http://www.facts.com/icof/00057.htm.

5. Dan Brock, "Voluntary Active Euthanasia," *Hastings Center Report,* March–April, 1992, pp. 10–22.

6. Timothy E. Quill, "Death with Dignity: A Case of Individualized Decision Making," *The New England Journal of Medicine,* March 7, 1991, p. 692.

7. Marcia Angell, "The Supreme Court and Physician-Assisted Suicide–The Ultimate Right," *The New England Journal of Medicine,* January 2, 1997, p. 50.

8. Tomothy Egan, "Suicide Comes Full-Circle, to Oregon," *New York Times,* October 26, 1997, p. A1.

9. J. Gay-Williams, "The Wrongfulness of Euthanasia," in Jeffrey Olen, Julie C. Van Camp, and Vincent Barry, *Applying Ethics: A Text with Reading,* 8th ed., Belmont, CA: Wadsworth/Thomson Learning, 2005, pp. 180–183.

10. Jane Cys, "HCFA Won't Punish Doctors for Long Living Hospice Patients," *American Medical News,* October 9, 2000. Retrieved February 3, 2005, from http://www. ama-assn.org/amednews/2000/10/09gvsb1009.htm.

11. Linda Ganzini and others, "Oregon's Physicians' Attitudes About and Experiences With End-of-Life Care since Passage of the Oregon Death with Dignity Act," *Journal of the American Medical Association,* May 9, 2001, p. 2363.

12. M. Scott Peck, M.D., *Denial of the Soul*, New York: Harmony Books, 1997, p. 152.

13. "When Death is Sought: Assisted Suicide in the Medical Context," *The New York Task Force on Life & the Law,* October 2001. Retrieved February 7, 2005, from http://www.health.state.ny.us/nysdoh/provider/death.htm.

14. Leon Kass, "I Will Give No Deadly Drug," in *The Case Against Assisted Suicide,* Kahtleen Foley and Herbert Hendin, eds., Baltimore: Johns Hopkins Press, 2002, pp. 17–40.

15. Daniel Callahan, "When Self-Determination Runs Amok," in Ralph Baergen, *Ethics At The End Of Life,* Belmont, CA: Wadsworth/Thomson Learning, 2001, p. 223.

16. C. Everett Koop, M.D., *Koop: The Memoirs of America's Family Doctor,* New York: Random House, 1991, p. 293.

17. Angell, p. 52.

18. Ezekiel Emanuel, "Euthanasia: Historical, Ethical and Empiric Perspectives," in Ralph Baergen, *Ethics at the End of Life*, Belmont, CA: Wadsworth/Thomson Learning, 2001, p. 211.

19. John Lachs, "When Abstract Moralizing Runs Amok," in Ralph Baergen, *Ethics at the End of Life*, Belmont, CA: Wadsworth/Thomson Learning, 2001, p. 231.

20. Brock, p. 10.

21. Kathleen Foley, "Medical Issues Related to Physician Assisted Suicide," testimony before Judiciary Subcommittee on the Constitution, April 29, 1996. Retrieved February 1, 2005, from http://www.2.soros.org/death/testimony.htm.

22. James H. Brown and others, "Is It Normal for Terminally Ill Patients to Desire Death?" *American Journal of Psychiatry,* February, 1996, pp. 210–211.

23. Callahan in Ralph Baergen, *Ethics at the End of Life,* Belmont, CA: Wadsworth/Thomson, 2001, p. 223.

24. "Dying Wishes," *CBS Sunday Morning,* March 17, 2002. Retrieved March 1, 2005, from http://www.cbsnews.com/stories/2002/03/15/Sunday/main503851.shtml.

25. Linda Ganzini, "Oregon's Physicians Perceptions of Patients Who Request Assisted Suicide and Their Families," *Journal of Palliative Medicine,* June 3, 2003, pp. 381–390.

26. "Dying Wishes."

27. Gay-Williams, p. 180.

28. Pope John Paul II, "Life-Sustaining Treatments and Vegetative State: Scientific Advances and Ethical Dilemmas," March 20, 2004. Retrieved February 13, 2005, from http://www.lifeissues.net/writers/doc/doc_33vegetativestate.html.

29. E. Fritz Schmerl, "The Right to Die is Ethical," *Euthanasia: Opposing Viewpoints,* Neal Bernards, ed., San Diego: Greenhavn Press, Inc., 1989, p. 31.

30. Manuel Velasquez, *Philosophy: A Text with Readings,* 8th ed., Belmont, CA: Wadsworth/Thomson Learning, 2002, p. 521.

31. Richard B. Brandt, "A Moral Principle about Killing," in Jeffrey Olen, Julie Van Camp and Vincent Barry, *Applying Ethics,* 8th ed., Belmont, CA: Wadsworth/Thomson Learning, 2005, p. 205.

32. Ibid., p. 206.

33. Ibid., p. 205.

34. Joseph R. DesJardins, "Virtues and Business Ethics," in William H. Shaw and Vincent Barry, *Moral Issues in Business,* 9th ed., Belmont, CA: Wadsworth/Thomson Learning, 2004, pp. 90, 98.

35. Gay-Williams, p. 181.

36. Brown and others, pp. 210–211.

37. Burke J. Balch and Randall K. O'Bannon, "Why We Shouldn't Legalize Assisting Suicide," *National Right to Life.* Retrieved February 3, 2005, from http://www.nrlc.org/euthanasia/asisuid3.html.

38. Quill, p. 692.

39. Ibid.

40. Alisdair MacIntyre, *After Virtue,* Notre Dame, IN: University of Notre Dame Press, 1981.

41. Ludwig Edelstein, *Ancient Medicine,* Owsei Temkin and C. Lilian Temkin, eds., Baltimore: The John Hopkins University Press, 1967, pp. 11–12.

42. Howard Brody, "The Physician's Role In Determining Futility," in Thomas A. Mappes and David DeGrazia, *Biomedical Ethics,* 5th ed., New York: McGraw Hill, 2001, pp. 344–350.

43. Edmund Pellegrino, M.D., "Compassion Needs Reason Too," in *Dying, Death, and Bereavement* 02/03, George E. Dickinson and Michael R. Leming, eds., Guilford, CT: McGraw-Hill/Dushkin, 2002, pp. 96–97.

44. Ibid., p. 97.

45. Angell, p. 51.

46. Kathleen Foley and Herbert Hendin, eds., *The Case Against Assisted Suicide,* Baltimore: Johns Hopkins Press, 2002.

47. Diane Meier and others, "Characteristics of Patients Requesting and Receiving Physician-Assisted Death," *Archives of Internal Medicine,* July 14, 2003, pp. 1537–1542.

48. Nancy Jecker, "Giving Death a Hand: When the Dying and the Doctor Stand in a Special Relationship," in Ralph Baergen, *Ethics at the End of Life,* Belmont, CA: Wadsworth/Thomson Learning, 2001, p. 171.

49. Carol Gilligan, *In a Different Voice,* Cambridge: Harvard University Press, 1993.

50. Nel Noddings, *Caring: A Feminine Approach to Ethics and Moral Education,* Berkeley: University of California Press, 1984.

11

Social Policy and Law

Assisted death isn't only a question of personal morality but also social morality. Yes, physician-assisted suicide (PAS) and voluntary-active euthanasia (VAE) challenge us as individuals to answer the question: "Is it ever morally permissible for individuals to practice assisted death or have it practiced on them?" But assisted death also raises the social concern of the present chapter: "Should such a practice be legally permissible?" Many people think not. Indeed, at the highest levels of U.S. law enforcement, action has been taken to set aside the Oregon suicide permission (see Chapter 9).

GONZALES V. OREGON

In November 2001, U.S. Attorney General John Ashcroft, a critic of PAS, reinterpreted the Controlled Substances Act so as to nullify Oregon's Death with Dignity Act. The rule, referred to as the "Ashcroft Directive," made using a controlled substance to assist suicide illegitimate, thereby making any physician or pharmacist who acted under the act subject to revocation of her prescribing license and criminal penalties under the drug laws. A U.S. district court subsequently issued a permanent restraining order, blocking implementation of the directive; and a federal appeals court panel ruled against Ashcroft saying his efforts exceeded his authority. In January 2006, the U.S. Supreme Court upheld the lower court's decision, 6–3.

As a legal matter the case, called *Gonzales v. Oregon,* pitted the traditional power of the state to regulate medicine against the federal government's authority to regulate drugs. As a practical matter, *Gonzales v. Oregon* represents the Bush administration's unsuccessful challenge to the nation's only permission to die law.

Whether or not assisted death should be permitted is a question of collective, not individual, decision making. But like individual action, collective action can be moral or immoral. And, like individual action, whether it is one or the other depends on how well it is supported by moral principles.

Often the relevant principles are the same. For example, believing that individually *and* collectively we should be concerned with human happiness, one would understandably view utility as an important principle of social morality. Likewise, concern with fairness collectively as well as individually makes respect for persons just as important for social morality as for individual morality.

But individual morality isn't always the same as social morality. In the matter of assisted death, for example, we can hold ourselves to a prohibitive moral standard that we would not want legislated, perhaps out of respect for the rights of others. Alternatively, we might practice assisted suicide, or have it practiced on us, but still not favor a law that would allow others to assist a death, perhaps out of fear of potential abuse and social harm. It's even possible to be uncertain of our own view and tolerate either permission or prohibition, so long as everyone is treated equally. The point is that sometimes additional principles are needed to guide social policy. Whatever those principles, presumably we prefer them because they serve the social good by moving us closer to the ideal society.

Historically, when philosophers have inquired into the kind of society we should be, they inevitably have answered, a just society. But while there is widespread agreement that we are morally required to be just, there is lively disagreement about the best principles of social justice, with *individual rights, general welfare,* and *equal treatment* vying for priority. In the abstract, these principles are not controversial. But their application can be uncertain, just as we found the application of principles of individual morality to be.

In some cases, a principle of social justice may suggest an answer opposed by another principle, forcing a choice of one over the other. Consider, for example, the liberty right and general welfare. Which is to be preferred—freedom or security—if we can't have both? In other cases, conflicting policies may result from competing extensions of a single principle, forcing a choice of one interpretation over the other. For example, both retentionists—those favoring prohibition of assisted death—and abolitionists—those opposing prohibitions or favoring permissive legislation—equally appeal to rights and invoke the general welfare to support opposed positions. Whose interpretation is the more compelling? Whose vision of the ideal society? Is the best society, like Oregon's, the one that permits assisted death? Or is it the one that, like the rest of the nation, prohibits it?

Questions of social justice always involve the most practical matters that we can philosophically think about. But, as *Gonzales v. Oregon* shows, sometimes the practical turns urgent—"urgent" as in a matter of life and death.

INDIVIDUAL RIGHTS

In ethics, a right is generally considered a justified claim or entitlement to something against someone.[1] In other words, if somebody has a right to something, then somebody else has a duty, either not to interfere or possibly to help. The right to vote, for example, implies a corresponding duty of non-interference, perhaps even assistance. This basically means that others may not stop us from voting, and possibly may even be obligated to help us practice our right to vote, as by providing special assistance to the disabled, for example. It is this language of rights that dominates the assisted-death debate. It is there that "the right to die" is pitted against "the right to life" (or "sanctity of life").

Today when PAS advocates assert a right to die, they mean that certain kinds of patients, typically competent terminally ill adults, are specifically entitled to be left alone in choosing to hasten their deaths. Since rights generally imply duties imposed on other individuals, the right to die implies obligations of others. Accordingly, the right to die is advanced in both (1) a negative sense, meaning no one may interfere with the patient choice; and (2) a positive sense, meaning someone (e.g., a physician) must (i.e., is obligated to) assist the death. The just society, abolitionists argue, is the one that permits such a right to die.

For their part, those arguing the "right to life" say that everyone, but especially the most vulnerable, such as the terminally ill, are entitled to have the sanctity of their lives protected. This means a ban on all forms of assisted death, whose very existence is a threat to the existence of the gravely ill. This makes the just society the one that bans assisted death, according to retentionists.

For their philosophical force, both sides—right-to-die abolitionists and right-to-life retentionists—invoke two categories of general rights in making their cases: human (or natural) rights and welfare (or moral) rights.

Human Rights

A human right is considered a natural right, not in the sense that it can be derived from a study of human nature but in that it does not depend upon human institutions the way legal rights do. Human rights are entitlements we, presumably, have simply because we are human beings, not because some authoritative body has assigned us these rights.

Although some would deny the existence of human rights, the United States has a long and proud tradition of acknowledging and, in many cases, explicitly protecting them. Consider the claim of the Declaration of Independence that all human beings have certain inalienable rights, among them "life, liberty, and the pursuit of happiness." In general practice, this is taken to mean that we are entitled to make critical choices of our lives, regardless of what anyone else thinks so long as we don't harm anyone. That I don't agree with your religious affiliation or you don't agree with my political beliefs is irrelevant to our right of critical choice or liberty in religion and politics, and we treat interference as injury.

A "right to die," say some abolitionists, implies that determining the manner of one's own death is a critical choice for competent, terminally ill adults. In other words, such individuals have both (1) a vital liberty interest in being free from outside interference in their own death decisions; and (2) a claim to appropriate services and opportunities to make and act on this critical choice, including the assistance of appropriate parties (i.e., physicians).

But why, ask retentionists, restrict the right to die to the "competent, terminally ill adult"? Don't people act from an array of complex motives, some of which, at least, would seem to give them a justified claim to assisted death? Incurable but not life threatening disease comes to mind, as do severely life-limiting disabilities. Couldn't these be as plausible for justifying PAS as physical pain or debilitation? Its implications, in short, lead retentionists to doubt there is a human right to die.[2]

Supporting this criticism are two important 1997 U.S. Supreme Court decisions, both of which reversed rulings by courts of appeal that a terminally ill and mentally competent patient's "right to die" was constitutionally protected. In *Washington v. Glucksberg* and aforementioned *Vacco v. Quill* (see Chapter 8), the nation's high court found that the right of assistance in committing suicide is not a fundamental liberty interest protected by the Constitution, and that states, in fact, may protect the sanctity of life by banning PAS/VAE.

The rulings, of course, also allow states to *permit* PAS, as human rights activists are quick to point out. And of themselves the decisions don't prove that assistance in dying is not a human right, only that it is not a constitutionally protected one, and that only for now. Another court may rule otherwise. Besides, the right to assisted death, like any other human right, does not originate in law, although the law's protection is always welcome. Basic human rights—from speech to religion to political assembly—are flouted throughout the world. For all of that, they are no less human rights, since human rights derive from the assumption that all human beings, merely by virtue of their being human, have certain inviolable entitlements. Assisted death is one such entitlement, say abolitionists. Therefore, the society that interferes with this human right is unjust.

Retentionists—at least those of them who believe in the existence of human rights—concede that judicial opinion, in the end, is just that—*opinion*. Nevertheless, they believe that judicial opinion currently casts a grave shadow of doubt over the charge that PAS prohibition is a social injustice. In fact, they note, in both decisions the court properly specified a constitutionally guarded human entitlement: the right to discontinue or never initiate heroic life-prolonging measures. *Glucksberg* and *Vacco* also reaffirmed another human right: the basic right of competent patients to refuse medical treatment, in general, and to receive adequate pain relief at the end of life, *even if so doing hastens death*. The moral right a patient has, then, is to risk his life, not to take it. The just society makes this distinction, and thereby strikes a proper balance between individual liberty and the sanctity of life, according to retentionists.

"Irrelevant," abolitionists fire back, invoking *Compassion in Dying v. Washington* (1996). There the Ninth Circuit Court of Appeals found (8 to 3) "no ethical or constitutionally cognizable difference between a doctor's pulling the plug on a respirator and his prescribing drugs which will permit a terminally ill patient to end his own life." Abolitionists use this ruling to support their position: If a patient has a right to withhold life support, she has an equal right to have her life actively shortened, since the result is the same, death.

But do the identical outcomes imply identical constitutional concerns? Quoting various court rulings, constitutional law expert Yale Kamisar explains why he thinks not:

> The right to terminate life support grows out of the doctrine of informed consent, a doctrine "firmly entrenched in American tort law." "The logical

corollary," of that doctrine, of course is "the right to consent, that is to refuse treatment." The other tradition, which has "long existed alongside" the first one, is the anti-suicide tradition. This is evidenced by society's discouragement of suicide (indeed, by the state's power to prevent suicide, by force if necessary) and by the many laws criminalizing assisted suicide.[3]

In other words, according to Kamisar, the right to end life support is a clinical extension of the fundamental right of informed consent, whereas intentionally hastening death is not. In fact, tradition opposes it.

Taking another tack, abolitionists say the right to refuse treatment implies a right to assisted death because refusal of treatment is an extension of a well-established right of privacy, specifically bodily determination. Since you have the right to determine what happens to your own body, you can refuse treatment. From there it's easy to infer that you have the right to choose to end your life and to have support in so doing.

The right to refuse treatment may derive from the right to bodily self-determination, but is it a "right to die"? True, patients may exercise the right of self-determination at the risk of death, or even in order to die. But retentionists say that the right of refusal of medical treatment is about protection from unwanted interference, not permission to decide whether to live or die. As Bonnie Steinbock points out, "There can be a reason for terminating life-prolonging treatment other than 'to bring about the patient's death.'"[4]

Retentionists and abolitionists agree, then, that the just society is one that protects and does not interfere with a human right, while the society that fails to is unjust. But where abolitionists see a human right in assisted suicide, retentionists see a human right in the protection of life. For the one, abolitionists, the just society protects and doesn't interfere with the right to die, and the society that prohibits PAS is unjust. For the other, retentionists, the just society protects and doesn't interfere with the sanctity of life, and the one that permits PAS is unjust.

Welfare Rights

An alternative, more conservative rights argument holds that, even if assisted death isn't a human right, it is nevertheless a welfare or moral right, as much as medical care itself is. By this is meant that the special circumstances or situations of the competent, terminally ill patients support a right to PAS that the just society would recognize. Therefore, a society that doesn't is unjust—not because it's denying individuals something they are entitled to as human beings (i.e., a human right) but something they're entitled to as a *special* category of human beings (i.e., a welfare right).

Skeptics readily admit the cruelty of any patient's suffering needless pain. One researcher even terms the often inadequate pain treatment for the dying "the most prevalent crime in medicine today."[5] But that merely argues for improved palliative care, retentionists say, including relief from emotional and spiritual suffering as well as physical pain. The welfare right here is to adequate care, not suicide.

But what about those patients, even if few, with unrelievable physical pain? Or worse, those with severe physical disabilities in emotional pain, suffering with no hope of relief and simply not wanting to go on? Take, for example, the case of Elizabeth Bouvia, the young woman who by her own assessment felt trapped in a useless body.

Back in 1983, 26-year-old quadriplegic with cerebral palsy Elizabeth Bouvia wanted doctors to help her in dying. Specifically, she sought admission to a hospital to be given painkillers while she starved herself to death. When the hospital refused, Bouvia sued. A California Superior Court ultimately rejected her request. Later, in 1986, she was admitted to a hospital and was tube-fed against her will and contrary to her written instructions. She successfully sued to have the tubes removed, but she did not die and still lives.

Then there are patients who, like Janet Adkins (1936–1990), make a personal and informed decision to end their lives before being overtaken by the ravages of an incurable disease. Diagnosed with probable Alzheimer's disease in 1990, Adkins became Michigan pathologist Jack Kevorkian's first assisted-death client, even though at the time of her death in the same year, the 54-year-old was still active and mentally coherent. (Adkins is one of the early cases in the Kevorkian file that reporter Michael Betzold documents in *Appointment with Death,* 1993).

Many abolitionists believe that society should grant such patients the (welfare) right to voluntary death. They say that the society that does not is unjust for its cruelty and inhumanity by making people needlessly suffer.

Abolitionists also find another injustice in denying individuals the full measure of personal autonomy. Even if autonomy in decisions to die can't be justified as a human right, they insist that it can be defended as a welfare right in the context of political theory. After all, our capacity to reflect about our deepest convictions and goals is the basis of a democratic system of government. What area of critical choice, they then ask, is more basic an expression of autonomy, of personal morality and self-definition, than how we're going to die? Doesn't an Elizabeth Bouvia have the right to say, "Enough is enough, help me die"? Isn't a Janet Adkins entitled to choose whether or not to let a disease take her mind and body? Isn't it their call when to exit life? To abolitionists, then, the fully democratic society allows (at least carefully regulated) assisted death as part of its commitment to their members' dignity and autonomy.[6]

Retentionists admit that people have a critical interest in living their lives according to their own beliefs about what is good. And if it were strictly a matter of suicide, self-determination might be pertinent as a negative right, or a sphere of liberty that should not be interfered with. But assisted suicide, by definition, is proposed as a *positive* right. It's an entitlement to aid and assistance in the act of self-killing. Bouvia and Adkins were not just asking to die, but to have physician assistance in so doing. That makes assisted suicide "no longer a matter of only self-determination, but of a mutual, social decision between two people, the one to be killed and the other to do the killing,"[7] according to bioethicist Daniel Callahan.

But patients like Bouvia and Adkins seek medical assistance in dying because they can't end their own lives. They need help to do it. But even if they don't need help, that doesn't take medicine off the hook, since it has a protected monopoly on, perhaps, the most expedient means of death: drugs.

Abolitionists say that the medical profession and its supporters can't have it both ways. They can't insist on controlling access to lethal drugs, on one hand; while, on the other hand, say: "Let the patient do the deed herself." Respect for patient autonomy, in short, requires legal access to deadly drugs. As abolitionist John Lachs writes:

> This restriction of human autonomy is due to the social power of medicine; it is neither surprising nor morally wrong, therefore, to ask those responsible for this limitation to undo some of its most noxious effects. If the medical profession relinquishes its hold on drugs, people could make effective choices about their future without the assistance of physicians. Even limited access to deadly drugs, restricted to single doses for those who desire them and who are certified to be of sound mind and near the end of life, would keep physicians away from dealing with death.[8]

For abolitionists such as Lachs, then, even if self-determination in the context of assisted death cannot be shown to be a human right, it certainly stands as a legitimate welfare right. The just, democratic society recognizes that, specifically by relaxing drug laws and, thereby, enlarging personal freedom.

But for retentionists such as Callahan, self-determination in the context of assisted suicide is not a welfare right and the society that thinks and acts otherwise is unjust. While granting the significance of self-determination, they say that when public cooperation is requested, autonomy must bow to a broader notion of the public good. Individual valuations of the quality of life must never be permitted to trump the sanctity of life.

EQUALITY

A society that doesn't treat all its citizens equally isn't just. But what exactly does equal treatment require of the just society? About that there is as much disagreement as there is on the requirements of justice itself.

A fruitful entry point into the complex topic of equality as it applies to assisted suicide is with the notion of "equal treatment under the law." To many people, equality under the law is strictly a procedural matter. Thus, equal treatment means treatment according to the same laws and legal procedures.[9] By this account, so long as like patients are treated alike, they are treated equally. In other words, whatever the laws allow in end-of-life decision making—medical directives, withholding/withdrawing life-prolonging measures, terminal sedation—so long as all like patients are permitted the full measure of these rights and privileges, they are being treated equally.

Equal treatment as strictly procedural often is used to support a retentionist view of PAS. The argument here might go something like: "The laws governing end-of-life care are fine as they are. Don't change a thing. Just make sure that everyone gets the full benefit of what's permitted and is disallowed what is not."

But procedural equality isn't only a prop for retentionism. It can also bolster an abolitionist position.

The abolitionist argument from proceduralism might begin with the observation that not all laws are fair and just. Obvious examples would be laws that unfairly discriminate, for example on the basis of color, ethnicity, religion, sex, age, or disability. Such laws would be unfair and unjust because they harm individuals simply because of their membership in a certain group. "Equal treatment" under such laws, then, doesn't mean much; in fact, it's masking and perpetuating deep social injustice. The same, abolitionists could say, applies to competent terminally ill who desire assisted suicide, as well as willing physicians. Elizabeth Bouvia, Dr. Timothy Quill, "Diane," such individuals do not enjoy the same measure of freedom as their non-death-desiring and -assisting counterparts. Nor do Kevorkian and his clients.

For support abolitionists might cite the social justice theory of the American philosopher John Rawls (1921–2002). Rawlsian justice requires that every person has a right to the greatest basic freedom compatible with a like freedom for all. In other words, social justice demands equal freedom for everyone. If freedom can be increased without violating that requirement, it must be.

Currently, it could be argued, pro-life patients and their physicians have more freedom of conscience, choice, and action than pro-choice patients and their physicians. Only by abolishing assisted-suicide prohibitions, therefore, can the latter group have an equal measure of freedom as the former and enjoy real "equal treatment under the law." Absent that, pro-choice patients and physicians no more enjoy procedural equality than did any African American who ever had to sit in the back of a bus. Pro-choice patients and their physicians are *de facto* second-class citizens. In this most critical area of personal and professional choice, they are victims of discrimination.

But would permitting PSA truly enlarge patient and physician freedom while not interfering with others? Retentionists think not. They warn of an unequal or *disparate* impact on members of vulnerable groups such as the elderly, the poor, minorities, and the undiagnosed but treatably depressed.[10]

Even allowing for ambiguity of definition, in 1997 there were approximately 35 million "disabled" Americans, alone, currently being "maintained" at tremendous expense, according to the National Health Interview Survey. (More than half of Kevorkian's patients were disabled, not terminally ill.) "Being maintained" does not always mean getting the health care, personal assistance, housing, or other supports needed. Nevertheless, cost conscious health care providers, insurers, and taxpayers are aware of the huge costs of maintaining the disabled. It's a safe bet that some of them are wondering whether it's worth it. Where dollars are scarce, aren't they best spent on the "socially productive" or at least those with the potential to be? Can we afford to drain our nation's treasure on individuals whose survival doesn't enrich anyone? Sensing in such thinking a growing danger to the disabled, Not Dead Yet (NDY), a vocal disability organization, formed in 1996 to oppose legalized suicide.

According to a 1995 Harris poll, two-thirds of people with disabilities support the right of assisted suicide. Members of NDY aren't among them. Indeed, they fear that were assisted death legalized, the disabled and the socially disadvantaged could be pressured into choosing death because of economic circumstances, low-quality health care, or limited availability to medical services. The rationale could be akin to the one provided by Dr. Kevorkian to a Michigan court in 1990: "The voluntary self-elimination of individual mortally diseased or crippled lives, taken collectively, can only enhance the preservation of public health and welfare." If coerced to choose death, then such individuals would lose, not gain, personal freedom.[11] They would be discriminated against, which might make legalized assisted death a violation of the Americans with Disabilities Act of 1990. The state can't allow this to happen, says law professor and retentionist Carl Coleman, given its strong interests in protecting vulnerable populations, especially those that society does not guarantee access to adequate health care.[12] It follows that any society that erects a framework for individuals' reluctantly choosing an option they don't really want would be presumptively unjust.

But can't legislation be crafted to preclude the feared injustice, as it has been with refusing disproportionate life-prolonging measures? For example, predictions to the contrary notwithstanding, in the 20-odd years that most states have permitted withdrawing life-sustaining medical treatment, there is no evidence that that right has been abused. Nor in Oregon, where PAS is restricted to competent, fully informed persons whose requests are voluntary and enduring, has any coercion been reported.

Furthermore, who's to say that members of at-risk groups can't make informed, voluntary death decisions? As abolitionist Ronald A. Lindsay points out: "If assisted suicide can be a rational, moral choice for competent persons, then the disparate impact argument (if accepted) erects a barrier to the exercise of this rational, moral choice by anyone, *including* members of disadvantaged groups."[13] In other words, according to this attorney who views assisted suicide as a fundamental constitutional right, the prohibition of PAS could just as easily result in unequal treatment for high-risk groups as its legalization could. Unfair discrimination, in short, can be argued by abolitionists as well as retentionists.

Some abolitionists go further, claiming that legalizing assisted suicide actually might prevent some patients from seeking to end their lives, because most suicide decisions today are done in private, without any possible controls, such as counseling or referrals to hospice.[14] Who can say if these patients really wanted to die? Properly regulated PAS, as in Oregon, at least would remove any lingering doubt about a patient's suicide decision.

Still, retentionists worry about the capacity of our medical system to implement even a carefully fashioned law. They fear it may not be equipped to make assisted death available, while insuring that it is restricted to competent persons experiencing unrelenting suffering who have made a voluntary, informed, and settled decision to die. The danger lies in the systemic inadequacies in end-of-life care. Cost considerations may drive assisted-death decisions, leaving unsettled such questions as: *Have all the options been spelled out to the patient? Does she fully understand them? Is he making a formal request to die or simply expressing a fleeting desire to.*[15]

Fodder for the retentionist concern about hasty or ill-considered death decisions is a study reported in *The New England Journal of Medicine* (1996) citing widespread abuses in Holland, including the deaths of competent patients without their express consent.[16] Then there are the patients of Dr. Kevorkian who weren't terminal, and the five autopsies that turned up no existent pathologies.

These developments at home and abroad are enough for retentionists to conclude that permitting assisted death will inevitably increase the risk borne by patients whose lives already are treated with less respect and dignity in a medical context. Such disparate or unequal impact a just society ought never permit, let alone foster with misguided social policy.

Abolitionists are quick to return fire. The U.S. isn't Holland, they remind us, and Kevorkian acted without professional or legal oversight. So, isn't it premature to cry "disparate impact" prior to permissive legislation? First legalize PAS, they suggest; if it's then found that a group of people, say the disabled, is choosing assisted suicide in significantly greater numbers than would be expected, revisit the procedures in place for assisted death.[17]

THE GENERAL WELFARE

Together with natural rights and equality, the just society is thought to be one that promotes the general welfare or the common good. But what is in the "public interest" and how the government can rightly promote it are not always easy to ascertain.

Consider that approximately 20% of voters in the 2004 presidential election said that "values" were important to them. Of these, an overwhelming majority voted for President Bush over Senator John Kerry. Abortion, gay marriage, the general "coarseness" of the culture, all probably were among the "value issues" that these voters felt the government should act to end, prevent, or ameliorate. Apparently, these voters felt that the incumbent, more than the challenger, was more likely to address these matters.

In feeling that the general welfare includes a wholesome moral environment (whatever that is), these voters probably weren't any different from most of the approximately 100 million other voters. What distinguished them, however, was that they most likely believed that a wholesome moral environment includes restrictions on certain private behaviors. In the matters of abortion and gay marriage (and sometimes even homosexual civil unions), for example, they likely support state paternalism.

State Paternalism

State paternalism refers to actions taken by government bodies or agencies over particular kinds of actions or procedures. Usually such controls take the form of government-enacted laws and regulations purportedly for the good of individuals or the society, regardless of individual preference.

Sometimes the harm that individuals are being paternalistically protected from is obvious. Without most licensing and technical specifications, for example, both patients and the medical profession itself could be harmed. Other times the harm is less clear, and so the liberty limitation of the paternalistic intervention is more controversial. Thus, while licensing and drug standards may protect the patient-consumer and the medical profession, they also limit the variety of medical viewpoints, therapies, and medications that both consumers and physicians can choose from. In such cases, it's more difficult to discern the harm that individuals are supposedly being protected from. Many today would say that the largely prohibited access to cheaper Canadian drugs or to medical marijuana are cases of illegitimate state paternalism by the U.S. government in the health care and market choices of individual Americans. So, too, is assisted suicide, say abolitionists, who want to know: "What exactly is the harm that a competent terminally ill adult voluntarily requesting assisted death is being protected from? What harm is the society being protected from?"

Self-Regarding vs. Other Regarding Virtues and Vices

Relevant to the proper reach of state interference (or, alternatively, the proper limits on self-determination) in personal decision is the distinction that utilitarian Mill made between "self-regarding" and "other-regarding" virtues and vices.[18] For example, drinking to intoxication in the privacy of one's own home is, arguably, a self-regarding vice in that it might directly harm the individual but not anyone else. Drinking and driving, on the other hand, is an example of an "other-regarding" vice because it threatens direct harm to others.

Now, there's no dispute about laws against drinking and driving, because the harm that the government is protecting us from is clear and present. But imagine the furor that would erupt were the private act of drinking alcohol banned. Where, most people would ask, is the direct *public* harm? Which of our rights is being violated by the individual act of private intoxication? Why ought the government interfere with what appears to be, in Mill's terms, not an "other-regarding" but a "self-regarding" vice? So also with assisted suicide, say abolitionists, who insist that if an individual wants to die a quick, painless death rather than a lingering, painful one, it's no one's business but his own. It's strictly up to Janet Adkins, for example, whether to die before losing her mind and being reduced to infant dependency.

But even if assisted death is a "self-regarding" act, is it really a harmless one? Is Adkins's self-regarding suicide harmless? Recalling those value-oriented voters, let's suppose many of them believe that, even if abortion and homosexuality are self-regarding acts, such acts cause moral harm to those who engage in them. Therefore, government interference is justified in order to protect individuals from themselves, as it were. Likewise with assisted death. Individuals like Adkins and her family need to be saved from the moral harm of assisted death. Therefore, the government that limits individual freedom to practice assisted suicide or have it practiced on oneself promotes the general welfare, and, therefore, is just.

For their part, utilitarians would remind us that the only freedom that will not maximize happiness is the freedom to harm others. And since assisted suicide does not directly harm others, and individual patients and their families are in a better position to know what is best for them in these matters than paternalistic governments are, prohibitions are unjustified.

Even granting no direct harm to others, might assisted suicide cause *indirect* harm? Might it devalue life, for example, or invite abuses?

The Case for Indirect Harm

The great slippery slope fear that continues to dog the right-to-die movement is that were PAS legitimated euthanasia will inevitably follow. And with time it will extend to the disabled, the clinically depressed, the chronically debilitated, even to the elderly and deformed newborns.[19] The current cost-conscious, market-driven medical environment does little to allay this fear of runaway abuse. As avid retentionist Wesley Smith chillingly warns, "When people learn that the drugs used in assisted suicide cost only $40 but it could take $40,000 to treat a patient properly so that they don't want a 'choice' of assisted suicide, the financial forces at work become clear."[20]

The fear of retentionists such as Smith is that legalizing voluntary assisted suicide will lead to a perversion of nonvoluntary euthanasia. Once it's considered "medical treatment," for example, it could be argued, under the Fourteenth Amendment, that it would be discriminatory to deny it to those too young or incapacitated to request it. (Oregon Medicaid already pays for assisted suicide for poor residents as a means of "comfort care.") What's stopping the suicide permission from being extended to the mentally incompetent? Why, under the "substitute judgment" doctrine, couldn't surrogates choose what the person would want if competent? Retentionists imagine a culture where infants, the mentally ill and retarded, the confused and senile elderly, all would be considered "entitled" to have someone else enforce their "right to die." Where's the freedom to choose if you can be killed even though you never expressed a wish to be?

Adding heft to the retentionist doomsday scenario are bioethicists who express other concerns about legalizing assisted death, such as the harmful effect on the physician–patient relationship; the diversion of resources from comfort care; and the adverse impact on families, health care, and medical services, including hospice.[21,22,23] Why change current law, they ask, when proper pain management can alleviate a patient's desire for a hastened death; and life can be shortened through permissible terminal sedation and dehydration? Such analysts worry that relaxing current prohibitions on assisted suicide will only serve to encourage a "culture of death." (That's a popular catchphrase for beginning and end-of-life decisions and policies that countenance death, as with abortion or euthanasia.)

Still, what about those patients who might be delivered from agony and indignity were the assisted death that they desire permitted? The Dutch people, evidently, identify with such a plight more than with being a possible victim of abuse. So do abolitionists in the U.S., who methodically muffle each retentionist alarm as they make their case *against* indirect harm.

The Case Against Indirect Harm

Regarding the potential for abuse, abolitionists cite recent reports that suggest widespread abuses in Holland have been exaggerated.[24] But it's mainly here at home, in Oregon, where abolitionists take their stand against charges of potential abuse. To them the experience of that pioneering northwestern state belies the spectre of a slippery slope.

Oregon's law clearly safeguards against coercion and requires the PAS process be stopped if any is detected. So far, there's been no indication of jeopardy for members of the most vulnerable groups.

For example, according to Oregon's Department of Human Services, between 1998 and 2003 rates of participation in PAS actually *decreased* with age and were highest among the better educated and those with killing conditions, specifically terminal cancer or amyotrophic lateral sclerosis (Lou Gehrig's disease). What's more, referrals to hospice *increased* to about 32%, which is almost double the national average and higher than any other state. Overall, one-third of Oregonians who die are enrolled in a hospice program and two-thirds have completed an advance directive before death, versus the national average of about 20%.[25,26] Far from being coerced by a flawed system, economic necessity, or rapacious health maintenance organizations (HMOs), (who, incidentally, never get involved in a PAS decision in Oregon), patients opting for PAS in 2002 gave as their top reasons: losing autonomy (84%), decreasing ability to participate in activities they enjoyed (84%), and losing control of bodily functions (47%).[27] As for the Death with Dignity Act's impact on the physician-patient relationships, PAS has been utilized so infrequently that it's currently impossible to calculate the law's effects on clinical practice.[28] But so far there's no evidence of a toxic effect. If anything, the encouraging figures on the utilization of medical directives and hospice suggest more honest and open physician-patient communication.

The abolitionist case for indirect harm then turns to alternatives to PAS, specifically pain control and terminal sedation. They point out that statistically at least 5% of terminally ill people will still die suffering even with the best pain care. But the other 95% also risk not getting good pain control because of stringent regulations of the Drug Enforcement Agency (DEA), which leave doctors fearing investigation and worse.[29] What's more, dying of starvation and dehydration while heavily sedated, though legal in all the states, is unpredictable. It can take up to two weeks, as with Terri Schiavo (see Chapter 1). The prescription used under Oregon's law, by contrast, usually renders the patient asleep within a few minutes and dead within a few hours. Beyond this, the wishes of the dying who prefer comfort care are fully respected, which tends to underscore Dr. Angell's observation that "good comfort care and the availability of physician-assisted suicide are no more mutually exclusive than good cardiologic care and the availability of heart transplantation."[30]

Finally, some abolitionists on utilitarian principle would oppose collective action to protect the public morality. They believe that in a free society the general welfare is never advanced at the cost of individual freedom that does no *direct* harm to anyone else.

Such are the profound disagreements about the nature and likelihood of indirect harm that leave retentionists and abolitionists predictably divided about the sheer possibility of writing or enforcing a suicide permit. Retentionists doubt that a meaningful law can be written or enforced that guarantees safeguards because PAS occurs in the context of private and confidential doctor-patient relationship. Abolitionists say that it is precisely the sacredness of the physician-patient relationship that can and should serve as the foundation for a "safe law."

Absent that, they believe that society will continue to abandon patients to their suffering, cruelly leaving them to devise ways and means to take their own lives, perhaps like Percy Bridgman. In 1961 the Nobel laureate in physics shot himself rather than die of metastatic cancer. His suicide note read: "It is not decent for Society to make a man do this to himself."[31]

CONCLUSIONS

After years of debate and legal wrangling, as a society we have reached some areas of social agreement on the care and treatment of the terminally ill. Today, for example, physicians honor the resuscitation wishes of patients. This means that should they suffer cardiac or respiratory arrest while hospitalized, the terminally ill or very old who so desire will not be revived. Patients also have the right to refuse life-sustaining treatment, including IVs, food, and water. Although undertreating end-of-life pain is still a serious lapse, pain relief is a top priority. The law, as well as a moral and professional consensus, recognizes a right to the most powerful analgesics, even if they shorten life.

Agreement eludes us, however, on the issue of assisted suicide. In the preceding chapter, we saw how the same principles of individual morality can be used to support or oppose the morality of voluntary death. Now we see that powerful moral arguments from identical principles of social justice can be made for the opposed propositions: "The just society permits assisted death" vs. "The just society does not permit assisted death." It is within this moral impasse that we must fashion social policy regarding assisted death. What to do?

We could do nothing. We could maintain the status quo, which seems to be a policy of toleration without legalization. Then again, we could respond aggressively.

On one hand, we could ban assisted death on the federal level, including any initiatives such as Oregon's Death with Dignity Act. Any physicians who didn't comply could be prosecuted and, conceivably, sued for malpractice. On the other hand, we could legitimate PAS. As in Oregon, strict rules could be formulated specifying the conditions under which assisted death could be permitted. Tests of mental competency, insurance of adequate comfort care, and, if we follow the lead of Dr. Quill, "a meaningful doctor-patient relationship" could be among the necessary criteria.[32]

Whichever option we choose, especially the liberty-limiting prohibition, ethicists are increasingly recognizing the moral importance of providing quality end-of-life care. From the patient's perspective, research shows that this includes five focal points: adequate pain and symptom management, avoiding inappropriate prolongation of dying, achieving a sense of control, relieving burden, and strengthening relationships with loved ones.[33,34]

Here isn't the place for discussing these patient interests. But it is appropriate to suggest constituents of a genuine moral commitment on the part of society and the medical profession to meeting these elements of quality end-of-life care.[35]

Required is a substantial investment of human and financial resources in research and development that address not only the physical needs of dying patients but also their psychological, spiritual, and emotional requirements, as well as those of their families. At minimum, this calls for the removal of irrational barriers to effective pain management, such as cruelly restrictive regulation of narcotics. Also, patients and families need to be encouraged to issue directives, not just preferences. Most important, quality care at life's end must be based on need not affordability. It must be seen as a universal right, not a privilege of wealth. And since none of this is possible without a cast of professionals who by inclination, training, and character can offer quality care to the dying and their families, reforms in medical education already underway must keep apace.[36]

Anything less than these social and professional developments would make the society that preaches life and prohibits assisted death heartless, and the one that preaches choice and permits assisted death dangerous—and both breathtakingly hypocritical. We may be understandably divided on whether the just society is the one that prohibits or permits assisted death. There can be no reasonable disagreement that the just society insures the highest quality end-of-life care, and by that measure we have a long way to go.

REFERENCES

1. Manuel Velasquez, *Philosophy: Text with Readings,* 8th ed., Belmont, CA: Wadsworth/Thomson Learning, 2002, p. 638.

2. Yale Kamisar, "The Reasons So Many People Support Physician-Assisted Suicide— And Why These Reasons Are Not Convincing," in Ralph Baergen, *Ethics at the End of Life,* Belmont, CA: Wadsworth/Thomson Learning, 2001, p. 183.

3. Ibid., p. 180.

4. Bonnie Seinbock, "The Intentional Termination of Life," in *Killing and Letting Die,* 2nd ed., Bonnie Steinbock and Alastair Norcross, eds., New York: Fordham University Press, 1992, p. 123.

5. Ronald Melzak, "The Tragedy of Needless Pain," *Scientific American,* February, 1990, p. 27.

6. John Lachs, "When Abstract Moralizing Runs Amok," in Ralph Baergen, *Ethics at the End of Life,* Belmont, CA: Wadswoth/Thomson Learning, 2001, p. 232.

7. Daniel Callahan, "When Self-Determination Runs Amok," in Ralph Baergen, *Ethics at the End of Life,* Belmont, CA: Wadsworth/Thomson Learning, 2001, p. 224.

8. Lachs, p. 230.

9. Jeffrey Olen, Julie C. Van Camp, and Vincent Barry, *Applying Ethics: A Text with Readings,* 8th ed., Belmont, CA: Wadsworth/Thomson Learning, 2005, p. 18.

10. George Annas, "Assisted Suicide—Michigan's Temporary Solution," *The New England Journal of Medicine,* May 27, 1993, p. 1575.

11. "When Death Is Sought: Assisted Suicide in the Medical Context," *The New York Task Force on Life & the Law,* October, 2001. Retrieved February 1, 2005, from http://www.health.state.ny.us/nysdoh/provider/death.htm.

12. Carl Coleman and Tracy H. Miller, "Stemming the Tide: Assisted Suicide and the Constitution," *Journal of Law, Medicine & Ethics,* Winter, 1995, p. 393.

13. Ronald A. Lindsay, "Should We Impose Quotas? Evaluating the 'Disparate Impact' Argument Against Legalizing Assisted Suicide," *Journal of Law, Medicine & Ethics,* Spring, 2002, p. 7.

14. Stephen Jamison, *Final Acts of Love: Families, Friends and Assisted Dying,* Los Angeles: Jeremy P. Tarcher, 1996.

15. Coleman, p. 19.

16. Marcia Angell, "Euthanasia in the Netherlands, Good News or Bad?" *The New England Journal of Medicine,* November 28, 1996, pp. 1676–1678.

17. Lindsay, p. 14.

18. Olen, Van Camp, and Barry, pp. 19–20.

19. Ian Dowbiggin, *A Merciful End: The Euthanasia Movement in Modern America,* New York: Oxford University Press, 2003.

20. Wesley Smith, "Dying Cause," *National Review Online,* May 20, 2003. Retrieved February 3, 2005, from http://www.nationalreview.com/comment/comment-smith052003.asp.

21. Peter Singler and M. Siegler, "Euthanasia—a critique," *The New England Journal of Medicine,* June 28, 1990, pp. 1881–1883.

22. Arthur Caplan, "Will Assisted Suicide Kill Hospice?" in *Ethics in Hospice Care,* Bruce Jennings, ed., Binghampton, NY: Haworth Press, 1997.

23. James Bernat, "The Problem of Physician-Assisted Suicide," *Seminars in Neurology,* 17, 1997, pp. 271–279.

24. Angell, "Euthanasia in the Netherlands, Good News or Bad?" *The New England Journal of Medicine,* November 28, 1996, pp. 1676–1678.

25. S. W. Tolle, "Care of the Dying: Clinical and Financial Lessons from the Oregon Experience," *Annals of Internal Medicine,* 1998, vol. 128, pp. 567–568.

26. S. W. Tolle, A. G. Rosenfield, V. P. Tilden, and Y. Park, "Oregon's low-in-hospital death rates: What determines where people die and satisfaction with decisions on place of death?" *Annals of Internal Medicine,* 1999, vol. 130, pp. 681–685.

27. "Assisted-suicide Number Continue to Rise in Oregon," *American Medical News,* March 24/32/2003. Retrieved February 3, 2005, from http://www.ama-assn.org/amednews/2003/03/24/prs0324.htm.

28. Linda Ganzini and others, "Oregon's Physicians' Attitudes About and Experiences With End-of-Life Care Since Passage of the Oregon Death with Dignity Act," *Journal of the American Medical Association,* May 9, 2001, pp. 2263–2269.

29. Arthur Caplan and David Orentlicher, "The Pain Relief Promotion Act of 1999," *Journal of the American Medical Association,* January 12, 2000, pp. 255–258.

30. Marcia Angell, "The Supreme Court and Physician-Assisted Suicide—The Ultimate Right," *The New England Journal of Medicine,* January 2, 1997, pp. 50–53.

31. Sherwin Nuland, *How We Die,* New York: Alfred A. Knopf, 1994, p. 152.

32. Timothy E. Quill, "Doctor, I Want to Die, Will You Help Me?," *Journal of the American Medical Association,* August 18, 1993, p. 873.

33. Peter Singer, Douglas K. Martin, and Merijoy Kelner, "Quality End-of-Life Care," *Journal of the American Medical Association,* January 13, 1999, pp. 163–168.

34. Institute of Medicine, "Accountability and Quality in End-of-Life Care," in *Approaching Death: Improving Care at the End of Life,* Washington, D.C.: National Academy Press, 1997.

35. Last Acts, "Means to a Better End: A Report on Dying in America Today," 2002. Retrieved February 9, 2005, from http://www.americangeriatrics.org/product/positionpapers/quality.shtml.

36. Rose Virani and Dalia Sofer, "Improving Quality End-of-Life Care," *American Journal of Nursing,* May 2003, pp. 52–60.

12

Futile Treatment
and the Duty to Die

After being treated for a broken hip she suffered after a fall in her Minneapolis home in December 1989, 86-year-old Helga Wanglie was moved to a nursing home. The following month respiratory complications landed her back in the hospital where she was placed on a respirator before being transferred in May of 1990 to a long-term care facility that specialized in treating respirator-dependent patients. While there, she suffered a heart attack that left her with severe and permanent brain damage. By the end of May, she was back in the hospital, being maintained by a respirator and artificial food and liquid. She was ultimately diagnosed as persistent vegetative state (PVS).

THE CASE OF HELGA WANGLIE

Mrs. Wanglie had left no instructions about how she wished to be treated under conditions that had rendered her incapable of suffering but also of indicating preference. Given the extended care required to maintain her in PVS, medical staff were inclined to withdraw the ventilator, since it couldn't restore consciousness. But Mrs. Wanglie's husband and conservator, Oliver, 87, balked. He insisted that everything be done to keep Helga alive, over physician objections that doing so would go beyond the limits of "reasonable care."

With the family thwarting their medical judgment, hospital administrators and medical staff petitioned to appoint an independent conservator who might elect to have Mrs. Wanglie's ventilator removed. Physician Steven Miles, who served as the ethical consultant for the hospital, argued that a physician should not have to prove that medical care does not serve a patient's medical interest, whereas Oliver Wanglie insisted that all life-prolonging medical treatment be continued.

In a ruling issued July 1, 1991, the probate court rejected the hospital's position and turned over full guardianship to Oliver Wanglie. Three days later, on the Fourth of July, Helga Wanglie died of multi-system organ failure, leaving behind $750,000 in medical expenses mostly–covered by the family's health insurance.

If the case *"In Re: The Conservatorship of Helga M. Wanglie"* was strictly about guardianship not treatment, it would have passed unnoticed. But in awarding conservatorship to Oliver Wanglie, the Minnesota district court was also giving priority to a patient's right to decide over a physician's professional judgment about the treatment's futility.

Chemotherapy, mechanical ventilation, dialysis, blood transfusions, antibiotics—these and other treatments and procedures are today commonplace medical weapons in the battle to prolong life. As worthwhile as these tools can be, sometimes they offer no realistic medical hope, as with Helga Wanglie. The treatment or procedure likely won't work, yield the expected outcome, or improve the poor quality of the patient's life. Under such circumstances, the treatment might well be termed "medically futile."[1] What then?

Should treatment be ended if the physician thinks that would be best? Or should it be continued until the patient or surrogate says, "Enough"? With public and professional opinion sharply divided, and life being extended in an environment of limited resources, the whole notion of futile medical treatment has become an unexpected part of the "right to die" debate.

MEDICAL FUTILITY: PHYSICIAN BENEFICENCE VS. PATIENT AUTONOMY

As *Wanglie* shows, physicians and patients or their surrogates don't always agree about what "futile" means and when a treatment or procedure is rightly termed "futile." A physician might consider cardiopulmonary resuscitation (CPR) or artificial feeding futile because the treatment itself is useless or the condition of the patient makes it so, whereas the patient or family might disagree. Cases such as *Quinlan, Perlmutter,* and *Cruzan* could be viewed as the opposite: physicians resisting the discontinuation of treatment that patient or family deems useless and dehumanizing. In cases of medical futility, it is the patient or, more typically, the patient's surrogate resisting the physician's judgment to withhold or discontinue treatment. Either way the parties are not on the same page. Lacking is a physician/patient (and family) agreement about what represents futile treatment.

As in *Quinlan, Perlmutter,* and *Cruzan,* courts of final jurisdiction consistently have weighed in on the side of individual autonomy. This can be taken as a permission if not a "right to die" by refusing life-sustaining treatment. But does individual autonomy include a complementary "right to live" that supersedes a physician judgment to terminate treatment because of futility? Can patient autonomy compel treatment at the end of life that a physician believes is medically worthless? If the answer is yes, then patients are entitled to a certain level of health care regardless of their condition, and the physician is obligated to provide it. If the answer is no, then patients have no such claim and the physician no such obligation.

In the Wanglie case, administration and staff were following the long-established medical beneficence principle that enjoins physicians from offering treatments or procedures that do not benefit the patient. Traditionally, the rule of beneficence has directed physicians always to apply their insights and techniques only for patients' good. This standard fits in with a paternalistic style more of the past than present.

Paternalism, recall, refers to an action that is intended to advance a person's interest but goes against the person's desires or limits the person's freedom of choice. In the last chapter we discussed paternalism in the context of the relationship between individual and state. Here we're talking about the physician/patient relationship.

Acting paternalistically, for example, a physician might choose or forego a treatment without asking or even disregarding the patient's permission, then justify her action by appeal to the patient's best interests. This gives paternalistic action in medicine two noteworthy features: (1) in *intention* it is directed toward the patient's best interests; and (2) in *means* it disregards the patient's desires or limits the patient's freedom. Usually, those who act paternalistically defend their actions by appeal to their intentions to benefit the patient, which are considered to override the means.

In the traditional paternalistic medical model, applying the beneficence principle ordinarily is straightforward. Doctor is thought to know best, and patients tend to be trusting and submissive. By contrast, today's more cooperative medical model reduces physician authority, at times even to say what is "futile treatment." Increasingly, patient autonomy is balanced with paternalistic beneficence. In *Quinlan, Perlmutter,* and *Cruzan,* for example, what the patient wanted counted for more than what the physician did. Wanglie also pitted beneficence against autonomy, only this time it was the physician, but not the family, who wanted to end treatment.

Wanglie, then, is an interesting extension of the sometimes fierce contest between two legitimate principles: beneficence and autonomy. This tug-of-war was triggered more than a quarter century ago by the so-called right-to-die movement. *Quinlan, Perlmutter,* and *Cruzan* were about the patient's right to have futile medical treatment discontinued. *Wanglie* was about the patient's right to have futile medical treatment continued. In the competition between traditional physician beneficence and modern patient self-determination, Wanglie asked: *Can patient autonomy ever compel physicians to make futile interventions at the end of life? Can it make doctors give treatment they know provides no benefits and, thus, violates the beneficence principle?*

Any answer can't help but reflect a view about the legitimate reach of autonomy. An affirmative response, which fits with the cooperative model, views autonomy subjectively. It's saying, "Yes, patients and families should be the final arbiter of what 'futile' means in these end-of-life treatment decisions, medical opinion notwithstanding." An affirmative response, then, stands in favor of autonomy in violation of beneficence.

A negative response, on the other hand, is for limiting patient autonomy. It is, in effect, saying: "No, patient autonomy in end-of-life treatment decisions may be overridden by medical judgment of futility." This makes the negative response a vote for beneficence over autonomy, or a vote for medical paternalism.

ARGUMENTS FOR LIMITING PATIENT AUTONOMY

In general, the case for limiting patient autonomy (or, alternatively, for medical judgment of futility) appeals to: (1) the nature and history of medicine, including its traditional values and professional standards; and to (2) social justice. Arguments from *professionalism* have been made to support 1, while arguments from *responsible stewardship* have been made to advance 2.

Professionalism

For 2,500 years, autonomy in Western medicine has never been strictly subjective, but has always been limited by considerations of beneficence. The traditional norm of beneficence directs physicians to apply their insights and techniques only for patients' good; to provide treatment that they believe is beneficial, or at least not harmful to patients. (Non-injury or non-maleficence can be derived from beneficence.)

The celebrated Greek physician Hippocrates (460–377 BCE) urged his colleagues "to follow that system of regimen which, according to (your) ability and judgment (you) consider for the benefit of (your) patients." This exhortation, nevertheless, recognized the limitations of medicine. Thus, patients overwhelmed by disease were not to be treated, a point made by Plato. In *The Republic* the contemporary of Hippocrates has Socrates say: "[M]edicine was not meant for such people and they should not be treated though they might be richer than Midas."[2] Again, Socrates says through Plato: "... where the body was diseased through and through, [the physician] would not try by nicely calculated evacuations and doses, to prolong a miserable existence .... The physically unsound (he) will leave to die."[3]

This tradition lives on. The AMA's professional code of ethics, for example, tells physicians "not (to) provide or seek compensation for services that are known to be unreasonable and worthless." Scholarly professionals have argued similarly that physicians should not be forced to adhere to unreasonable family preferences for resuscitations.[4] In this vein, the Society of Critical Care Medicine issued a "consensus report" in 1990 asserting that health care providers have the right to refuse requested "burdensome" therapy. This includes "treatment for which they think 'loss of function' (is) ... 'disproportionate to benefit'—even though the patient thinks the 'benefit' of continued life is worth the 'loss of function.'"[5] Two years earlier, a specialist in CPR outcomes wrote in a leading medical journal that in some cases of extremely poor quality of life, for example severely demented patients, the health care team should be permitted to withhold CPR without informing patients or families.[6]

Ordinarily beneficence is best served by respecting patient autonomy. Physicians, therefore, are rightly charged with understanding patient values, feelings, and concerns.[7] Still, the argument from professionalism denies that patient and family choices are sacrosanct. On the contrary, it asserts that physicians have a right to exercise their own autonomy to practice medicine responsibly. This means that when patient and family choices or demands are unreasonable, physicians are duty-bound to set them straight, to influence patient and family to make a rational choice. To do otherwise—to accede to treatment with no medical indication or scientific validity—violates beneficence. Furthermore, as Catholic bioethicist James Drane and physician John Coulehan point out, it insults patient and family autonomy by giving the false impression that a "sphere of decision making exists where (rationally) there is none . . . ."[8] In so deceiving patients and families, physicians fail their duty to practice medicine responsibly. They violate both their own autonomy and the patient's, according to Drane and Coulehan.

The argument from professionalism, then, views the patient's right to choose as limited and properly understood only by reference to the physician's right and duty to practice medicine responsibly. "Patients should not be given treatments simply because they demand them," frankly states the AMA's Council on Ethical and Judicial Affairs. This means that physicians ought not administer treatment whose harm outweighs any foreseeable benefit, despite patient wishes. To do so is a misrepresentation of professional knowledge and skills; in a word, medical fraud.[9]

Responsible Stewardship

According to the argument from responsible stewardship, providing treatment that fails to achieve the desired physiological effects wastes scarce resources—time, equipment, even transplantable organs—that could be used to achieve desired social ends. Topping the list of scarce resources today is money.

Experts believe there may be as many as 40,000 patients in the United States in PVS, while traumatic brain injury leaves more than 75,000 people with long-term disabilities each year.[10] According to a 2005 report issued by the U.S. Government Accountability Office (GAO), as a nation we spent about $183 billion for long-term care for all ages in 2003. That's about 13% of all health care expenditures. About 69% of those expenditures for long-term care services were paid for by public programs, primarily Medicaid and Medicare. Individuals financed about 20% of these expenditures out of pocket and, less often, private insurers paid for long-term care. What the future costs of long-term care will be is uncertain. It's a safe bet, though, that they'll be considerably more than the already considerable current costs.

Now, in theory, futility and cost are separate issues, the former dealing with achieving medical goals, the latter with their price. In practice, however, at least since the early 1990s, cost and futility have been linked. That was when Dr. George Lundberg, then editor of the *JAMA,* proclaimed futile-care policies as one criterion of health care cost control, saying: "Certainly tens and probably scores of millions of dollars annually could be saved" and "major savings can be realized by eliminating futile-care and limiting unneeded care of 'medicine at the margins.'"[11] Lundberg implicatively tied the issue of medical futility to distributive justice or "the fair, equitable, and appropriate distribution of medical resources in society." Given our current health care environment of both limited resources and access, he was saying: Unreasonable medical care is simply unacceptable.

Although many find the insinuation of rationing into the futility debate crass or irrelevant—tantamount to placing a price tag on human life—Peter A. Clark and Catherine M. Mikus aren't among them. One an ethicist, the other an attorney, they point out that "medical resources in this country *are* limited and must be conserved." As a matter of justice, they say, "patients/surrogates cannot be given the absolute right to demand any medical treatment they choose...if [they were], those treatments would be given at the expense of the poor, the powerless, and the marginalized..."[12] This means that the physician has a special responsibility to avoid this injustice by practicing prudent stewardship of scarce medical resources in determining what constitutes reasonable medical treatment. For their part, patients and families "must agree to restrict their self-advocacy to what is fair and equitable for all." Patient interests, in short, must be balanced by social interests.

Taken together, the arguments from professionalism and stewardship make a powerful one-two punch for limiting autonomy. Still, equally strong positions/rebuttals have been advanced by those who oppose limiting autonomy.

ARGUMENTS AGAINST LIMITING PATIENT AUTONOMY

The proper role of physicians is to diagnose and treat, not to determine which lives are worth preserving, which not. It is upon this thesis that some within and many without the medical profession take their stand against limiting patient autonomy. Specifically, they say that (1) physician bias; (2) uncertainty of diagnosis and prognosis; (3) lack of social agreement about what futility is; and (4) physician contractual obligations decisively support patient/surrogate determination of medical futility.

Physician Bias

While endorsing medical futility, the AMA nevertheless concedes that "futility" "cannot be meaningfully defined," because it involves a judgment about which there simply is no consensus. This means that medical futility is always a subjective judgment with qualitative and quantitative aspects. Qualitatively, a judgment of futility is an opinion about what lives are worth preserving. Quantitatively, it's an opinion not only about likely outcome, but what degree of likelihood is worth pursuing. Physicians and patients (or families) sometimes will differ on these aspects of futility. They won't always give identical answers to the question, "How much of what kind of life is worth maintaining?"

A wrenching example is the celebrated case of "Baby K," an infant born with anencephaly in a Virginia hospital in 1992. Ordinarily babies like Baby K, who are missing part of their brain, are given only comfort care. Baby K's mother insisted, against physician recommendation, that more be done. A federal court in Virginia sided with her, just as the U.S. Supreme Court did with Oliver Wanglie.

For their supporters, the wisdom of these decisions recognizes that some medical situations are too complex and multilayered to be left to physician judgment alone. Physicians have their own agendas, their own professional preferences. They can be biased in determining both an acceptable quality of life and acceptable odds of pursuing it. They can and sometimes do offer options disguised as data.[13] True, families can err as well. But as Baby K and Wanglie declare: The resolution of such difficult cases are best left with the families, who are uniquely qualified to assess the emotional and symbolic value of the non-medical goals and benefits of treatment.[14]

Uncertain Prognoses/Mistaken Diagnoses

Discontinuation of treatment based on futility presupposes that the proposed treatment won't work. It won't achieve its intended outcome with respect to patient survival or quality of life. But some recent studies challenge this assumption. Specifically called into question has been the physician's ability to accurately predict short-term mortality even in gravely ill patients. Sometimes enough data can't be collected; other times applying the data to individual patients is the problem. Then there's drawing the line between "futile" and "reasonable" care. What exactly constitutes a "futile" rate for a treatment: 0%? 10%?[15] Physicians disagree. The point is that if objectively determining medical futility is tricky, on what scientific basis can physicians make a unilateral, beneficent treatment decision on grounds of futility?

Beyond the difficulties inherent in diagnosis and prognosis, there are some troubling cases of patients misdiagnosed as vegetative. A famous one involved a Tennessee police officer who, though only slightly conscious for eight years, suddenly awakened one day in 1996 to talk, joke, and reminisce coherently with family for about 18 hours. Similarly, in 2002, Terry Wallis suddenly spoke his first words after 19 years of silence, the tragic aftermath of an auto accident that left him in a deep, extended coma. Though often poignantly fleeting and exceptional, these spontaneous flashes of lucidity are for many people cautionary tales about making hasty PVS diagnoses.

Lack of Social Consensus

There is very little social debate, if any, about suspending treatment in cases when a treatment is impossible, harmful, or ineffective. For example, no one would seriously contend that a physician must honor a request to transplant a kidney into a patient who is imminently dying. On this, there is social and professional agreement.

But, as we've seen, what makes cases like Wanglie and Baby K different is that, while recognizing that medical science is powerless to improve the quality of life of their loved ones, families still insist that those lives be maintained. This, even though physicians may believe that such families not only have no right to the life support measures they are demanding but, in fact, are acting contrary to the best interests of their loved ones.

What such physician–patient/surrogate conflicts show, say defenders of strict patient autonomy, is the absence of a broad social consensus about what constitutes futility in difficult cases. In practice, this means no clear guidelines for resolving cases where physicians recommend, "Stop treatment," and patients and families say, "Not yet."

Whose wishes are to be followed? Should society favor the patient/surrogate's autonomy or the physician's in those, admittedly, rare cases where the two clash? Put into a larger context of social rules and policies, the question becomes: When there's a lack of social agreement, how ought society determine which of two competing policies to adopt?

One traditional way to resolve the conflict of competing social policies is to apply the utilitarian yardstick of the lesser harm. Thus, it could be asked here: Which is the lesser societal offense, stifling the autonomy of the patient/surrogate or the physician? The one involves a choice of life, the other a choice of treatment. So framed, life trumps treatment. To bioethicists Robert Veatch and Carol Spicer, this makes preempting physician autonomy the lesser societal offense. As they write:

> If a patient or surrogate is demanding life-prolonging care that his or her clinician believes is futile and a violation of his or her integrity to provide, we have a head-on clash between a patient's or surrogate's choice for life and the provider's autonomy. A society that forces people to die against their will produces more offense than one that forces healthcare providers to provide services that violate their consciences. If society must offend, the lesser offense is preferred.[16]

Notice how the argument from lack of social consensus not only affirms patient autonomy in futility cases, it responds to the argument from professionalism. It says regarding futile-care: Patient/surrogate autonomy matters more than the physician's right and duty to practice medicine.

Social Contract

Patient autonomy enthusiasts also say that physicians shouldn't be permitted, unilaterally, to discontinue life-sustaining treatment, because of the implied contractual relationship between them and society. They point out that physicians accept upon licensure a "public trust" to use "their monopoly on medical knowledge to preserve lives when the appropriate decision makers want them preserved."[17] Responsible stewardship, then, prefers patient choice of life to professional judgment of futility.

Another take on the social contract argument is mindful of the substantial duties to patients, legal and moral, that physicians assume when licensed to practice medicine. Among the most basic: providing patients adequate care and not abandoning them. Earlier we saw how these twin professional obligations shaped Dr. Quill's decision to help his patient "Diane" die. Here the interpretation of the same duties favors patient/surrogate choice in futile-care decisions.

But what about cases of physicians who, in good conscience, feel it's unethical to treat patients with poor quality of life? They should transfer the patient to another physician, say strict patient choice supporters, exactly as they should were their ethics challenged by the patient's refusal of life-prolonging treatment. In this way, they can honor both their conscience and the ethics of the profession.

The ongoing debate about futile-care notwithstanding, hospitals across the country are enacting polices that, while encouraging sensitivity to family senti-ment, enable physicians to override patient or family wishes on a case-by-case basis. Included in this development are institutions with historically religious affiliations that don't always accede to the faith-based feelings of their clientele. Sometimes, as with Terri Schiavo, Christian patients or their families cite religious justification for insisting on aggressive end-of-life medical care. For example, they may invoke the sanctity of life that is worth preserving at all cost, the hope for a miracle, the refusal to abandon the "God of faith," or the belief that suffering is redemptive. But for every reason given to extend treatment, an alternative reli-gious interpretation points to the legitimacy of limiting treatment.[18] These counter-interpretations are being used by many religious hospitals to justify instituting futile-care policies.

As futile-care policies proliferate at religious and non-religious institutions, a couple of ironic and related implications—one practical, the other theoretical—are become increasingly clear.

On the practical level, although the right-to-die movement was founded on the premise that patients and their families are the best judges of when it is time to die, now physicians, bioethicists, attorneys, and committees are being officially empow-ered to make that decision. In other words, in some instances the patient autonomy movement has led to a clinical setting where beneficent paternalism and responsible stewardship are outflanking patient autonomy. Some view this as a precursor to involuntary euthanasia. Wesley Smith, for example, gives the example of an elderly person's request for brain cancer surgery being rejected by physicians on grounds of risk and age. To him "this is just one example of how hospital committees are gaining more control of end-of-life decisions, and proof that if physician-assisted suicide was further legalized physicians might abuse the process."[19] Smith flatly equates futile-care theory with physician resignation to patient death.

On the theoretical level, if autonomy cannot compel futile treatment at the end of life, then not only has a patient no right to such treatment, she may have a duty to accept a limitation of treatment, even when so doing will increase the risk of death.[20] But those so arguing inevitably stop short of asserting what is, perhaps, the ultimate fear and concern of opponents of autonomy limitations and "futile-care policies." That fear is that the right to die will morph into a duty to die.

THE DUTY TO DIE

In 1984, with Karen Ann Quinlan still languishing in a New Jersey nursing home, Richard Lamm, Governor of Colorado, noticing a local reporter in the audience of health lawyers and administrators he was about to address, wondered aloud whether his remarks would get press coverage. Not likely, his press secretary confidently assured him. That turned out to be like the lookout on the *Titanic* telling the captain not to worry about the ice up ahead. The next morning Lamm found himself on a national morning news program, and two days later the subject of a press query of President Reagan.[21] What had ignited the political firestorm was the governor's widely quoted suggestion that the terminally ill elderly have "a duty to die and get out of the way...and let...our kids build a reasonable life."

Lamm's radical notion might have wilted in widespread derision had the physician-assisted suicide (PAS) movement of the early 1990s not revived some of the same concerns and fears that had initially greeted Lamm's proposal. Critics saw in both the worst of possible motives for a death decision: guilt and shame. Thus, seeing themselves as unacceptable burdens to their families, unwilling to lose their dignity to the ravages of an insidious illness, the elderly ill might demand that their physicians help them die.

Then, in 1997, with the nation's attention riveted on Dr. Jack Kevorkian and his "suicide machine," a bioethicst writing in the *Hastings Center Report,* a prestigious bioethical journal, framed all the guilt and shame as possibly a good reason to die. After all, John Hardwig wrote in his controversial essay "Is There a Duty To Die?":

> The lives of our loved ones can be seriously compromised by caring for us. The burden of providing care or even just supervision 24 hours a day, 7 days a week are often overwhelming. When this kind of care giving goes on for years, it leaves the caregiver exhausted, with no time for herself or life of her own. Ultimately, even her health is destroyed. But it can also be emotionally devastating simply to live with a spouse who is increasingly distant, uncommunicative, unresponsive, foreign, and unreachable. Other family members' needs often go unmet as the caring capacity of the family is exceeded. Social life and friendships evaporate, as there is no opportunity to go out to see friends and the home is no longer place suitable for having friends in.
>
> We must also acknowledge that the lives of our loved ones can be devastated just by having to pay for health care for us.[22]

Unlike Lamm, who 13 years earlier had made an abstract connection between patient and social interest, Hardwig was linking patients with particular others, most deeply and profoundly with family and loved ones. Whether I as an individual live or die, the philosopher was saying, only marginally affects society. But to my family whether I live or die can be the occasion of great benefit or burden, and thus the source of "my strongest obligations and also the most plausible and likeliest basis of a duty to die."[23]

Hardwig's view represented a shift of emphasis from traditional patient-centered bioethics, in which patient interests alone are considered relevant, to family-centered bioethics, in which the family matters, sometimes more than the patient. For Hardwig the autonomy of all affected by illness, not just the patient's, must be respected and promoted. So viewed, the conditions of my illness can impose so great a burden on my family that I have a duty to die, even if, tragically, I prefer to go on living.

From Patient to Family-Centered Bioethics:
The Ideas of John Hardwig

To entertain the notion of a duty to die means continuing to rethink the principle of patient autonomy initiated by futile-care theory. There, recall how physician judgment to determine and suspend futile treatment butts up against patient/surrogate choice to continue such treatment. Now we're asked to expand the circle of autonomy further, to include family members. When we do, according to Hardwig, we see that the "ethics of family life" will not condone arrangements that support the autonomy of one family member (i.e., the patient) while destroying the autonomy of the rest. And this is something he feels that patients themselves must recognize and allow to shape their own conception of self-determination. Accordingly, patient autonomy includes choosing to protect others when I am gravely ill. Sometimes those "others" are the larger society whom I can and should protect, for example by accepting limitations of resources. More often the "others" are my family members whom I can and should protect, even if that means taking my own life.

In championing family-directed ethics, Hardwig, then, is further extending the limitation to patient autonomy imposed by futile-care policies. Such policies, we saw, mean that patient preference cannot compel physicians to make medically worthless interventions at the end of life, and, implicatively, that a patient has a duty to accept a limitation of resources, and with it an increase in the risk of death. What distances Hardwig from the many bioethicists and medical professionals who accept futile-care policies, though, is the way he further limits patient autonomy by family interest. He is saying not just that patient autonomy cannot compel physicians to provide futile-care. It also cannot compel family and loved ones to endure excessive burden at the end of life. And more: In a showdown of interests, the patient has a duty to die.

Asserting that a patient may have a duty to die is one thing, saying who and when is another. Hardwig concedes that myriad details of circumstances, histories, and relationships inevitably will shape a determination of parties and situations. Additionally, and perhaps more importantly, he doesn't think that patients should decide unilaterally but, if possible, in concert with family and loved ones.

These reservations notwithstanding, Hardwig thinks that a duty to die may arise whenever the burden of caring for us seriously compromises the physical, emotional, or financial well-being of those who love us. Conversely, there is less likely to be a duty to die when we can make a good adjustment to our illness or handicapping condition and when we can still make significant contributions to the lives of others, especially our family. Even so, we must realize that some conditions—Alzheimer's and Huntington's chorea among them—will eventually exact a toll on the family, regardless of our bravest efforts to prevail. The prospect of looming mental incapacity from disease, Hardwig believes, supports a duty to end one's life before we become incompetent and can't make a decision.[24]

Hardwig admits that would society adequately provide for the debilitated, chronically ill and the elderly, there would be very rare cases of a duty to die. But he won't let our collective failed responsibility take us off the hook. Even when we are sick and debilitated, he says, we still can have personal responsibilities to protect our loved ones, sometimes even at the cost of our own lives. In bravely owning up, we define ourselves as still having "moral agency."

In ethics "moral agency" is shorthand for moral responsibility. To say that someone is a "moral agent" basically means that she is capable of making her own decisions, and that she has obligations to others based on relationships to them. Simply because someone is ill doesn't always mean she lacks moral agency. Depending on her condition, she may still be held morally accountable for the difference she makes in the lives of her loved ones. That difference may be positive or negative; she may help or harm. Which it is determines whether she dies with or without dignity, according to Hardwig.

So, whereas a purely subjective autonomy diminishes my life by disconnecting it from the well-being of others, Hardwig says that a family-directed ethics dignifies my life by connecting it to the welfare of others. I end my life to spare the futures of those I love. My death is a testimony to connection, and in that connection, I recover meaning in my death.

Despite its notoriety, Hardwig's case for a duty to die isn't philosophically unique. In theory, any argument for rational suicide can launch a case for a duty to die, as we saw with Hume in Chapter 9. A more recent example is provided by utilitarian Richard Brandt in his 1975 article defending the morality and rationality of suicide, where he writes:

> Suppose an army pilot's single-seater plane goes out of control over a heavily populated area; he has the choice of staying in the plane and bringing it down where it will do little damage but at the cost of certain death for himself, and of bailing out and letting the plane fall where it will, very possibly killing a good many civilians. Suppose he chooses to do the former, and so, by our definition, commits suicide. Does anyone want to say that his action is morally wrong?[25]

In Brandt's view, even Immanuel Kant and Thomas Aquinas would not condemn the pilot's act. For Kant, "it is no suicide to risk one's life against one's enemies, and even to sacrifice it, in order to preserve one's duties toward oneself." For Aquinas, the right intention of the pilot was to save lives, not end his own.

Brandt's point is that suicide is one of those things—like lying or breaking promises—that we always have some obligation to avoid but which, because of other morally relevant considerations, it is sometimes right or even morally obligatory to do. "The most that the moral critic of suicide could hold, then," he writes, "is that there is some moral obligation not to do what one knows will cause one's death; but he surely cannot deny that circumstances exist in which there are obligations to do things which, in fact, will result in one's death." Then Brandt adds, anticipating Hardwig: "*If so, then in principle it would be possible to argue, for instance, that in order to meet my obligation to my family, it might be right for me to take my own life as the only way to avoid catastrophic hospital expenses in a terminal illness*" (italics added).[26]

Rather than indebtedness to family, other philosophers have focused more on self-indebtedness to support a duty to die. One is Larry Churchill. Echoing the

Roman Stoics, this contemporary philosopher writes that a "proper self respect . . . seeks values roughly commensurate with my life to be displayed through my death."[27] In this sense, my death should be as much an expression of myself—"a vehicle for my self"—as any other facet of life is. The lyrical advice "To thine own self be true," then, applies as much to how I die as to how I live. I can die responsibly or irresponsibly, just as I can live one way or the other. For Churchill, honoring myself by dying responsibly may entail a duty to die.

Hardwig's Critics

It is difficult to imagine many Americans seeing a duty to die when upwards of eight-in-ten of them are estimated to believe that a family should be able to choose life support for a seriously ill patient even if the physician thinks that the patient's quality of life is too low to merit it. An even larger number, 85%, apparently feels that life support should be provided if the patient requests it,[28] and anywhere from one-third to one-half oppose PAS.[29] Popular opinion aside, Hardwig's voluntary death proposal has been widely criticized in medical and academic circles as morally unacceptable for both logical and practical reasons.

Logical Problems

Some critics find Hardwig's theory rickety, specifically his treatment of terms such as "moral agency" and "dignity," as well as the overlooked implications of the "duties" owed others.

1. *The Meanings of "Moral Agency" and "Dignity"* Hardwig writes that

   recognizing a duty to die affirms my agency and also my moral agency. I can still do things that make an important difference in the lives of my loved ones. Moreover, the fact that I can still have responsibilities keeps me within the community of moral agents. . . There is dignity, then, and a kind of meaning in moral agency, even as it forces extremely difficult decisions upon us.[30]

   Callahan, for one, finds twofold trouble with this assertion. First, he thinks that "it implies that only a decision to die would count as moral agency, not a decision to bear the illness and to allow oneself to be dependent upon one's family."[31] But if despite our debilitated state we can make a choice, then why can't the alternative—to continue to live despite the burden it creates—express moral agency? Second, according to Callahan Hardwig seems to imply, albeit unwittingly, that those choosing to live are selfish and lack dignity, while those choosing death are selfless and dignified.[32] Others say Hardwig ignores or downplays as expressing moral agency the sacrifice made by families to bear the burden of a member's illness.

2. *The Meaning of "Duty"* According to Hardwig, family hardships may provide good reasons for a duty to die. In ordinary usage, a "duty" implies a right,

such that if I have a duty to you to do something, you have a right to demand that I do it. This would mean that the duty of an ill person to relieve the family of the burden of care implies that the family or someone has a right to have that burden lifted. Fair enough, but who determines when the burden is insupportable—the patient or the family member?[33] The sacrificing party seemingly would be in a better position to determine the presence of Hardwig's circumstances-triggering duty to die. In that case, the burdened family member can rightly demand that the patient take his own life.

Critics such as Callahan claim that the logic of the relationship between duty and rights opens the door to family tyranny. That door indeed seems to fly off its hinges when we ponder, again, that in ordinary usage "duty" implies a responsibility either to do something or refrain from doing it. It implies that others shouldn't interfere with us or possibly even should assist us in carrying out our duty. Does this then mean that if I am unable to end my own life, someone else has a duty to assist me, perhaps even to kill me? If no, why not?

3.   *The Meaning of "Altruism"* Hardwig's duty to die seems to stand on an ethic of altruism, or the unselfish concern for others. A classical touchstone of all care, the ethic of altruism raises service to others as an important reason for human existence by basically construing moral actions as ones that serve the good of others. It's within this tradition of altruism that Hardwig seems to fit when he proposes that it is for the good of their families that the sick sometimes have a duty to die. But why, it could be asked initially, does anyone have a moral obligation to provide for the good of others when, according to the ethic of altruism, no one is obligated to provide for his own good?

A handier theoretical problem with altruism is one that intrudes right into the clinical setting. It is this: If the patient is obligated to act altruistically, so is the family. If the patient should act to increase the net happiness of the family exceedingly burdened by her continued existence, so, too, the family should act to increase the net happiness of the sick relative who desires to live. But doesn't this imply that, altruistically, the family has a duty to support the life of a sick relative who, altruistically, has a duty to die? In other words, the very altruistic ethic that counsels the patient to die counsels the family to keep her alive. If this is a fair application of the logic of altruism, it would suggest an unaddressed conflict of moral counsel in Hardwig's theory.

Practical Problems

Doubtless of more interest to laypeople than the preceding theoretical objections to Hardwig's proposal are two of its practical implications for the individual, family, and society.

1.   *The Sanctity of Life* It's indisputable that the presumed sacredness of life is the foundation for our religious, political, and medical traditions. But with the rise of the modern bioethics movement, the intrinsic value of life has been

challenged. Seemingly of paramount consideration today is not so much life, but life's quality. And with that the locus of ethical thought has shifted from discovering "What is right?" to determining "Who decides?" All of this, though well-intentioned, ignores God's ultimate role in life and death; mocks our noblest civic traditions; and turns the Hippocratic Oath on its head. To many, this is morally offensive.

Others fret about the social consequences of what they view as a coarsening cultural attitude toward life. This is basically a utilitarian sanctity of life objection to Hardwig's duty to die. It is captured in the following sentiments of bioethicist Felicia Cohn and geriatrician Joanne Lynn:

> Our society consistently rejects placing an explicit price on life. As a matter of practicality, we do implicitly place values on continued existence, at least considering it as one good competing among others. Accepting an explicit duty to die, however, would unmask our euphemistic discussions, which are significant for maintaining our illusion that human life is priceless. In accepting a duty to die, we would explicitly devalue life under certain circumstances and undermine an important cultural value. Society is more humane, kind, and protective when its members hold that every life is precious, even when nearing the end.[34]

2. *The Integrity of the Family* Taking a different tack, some of Hardwig's critics say that his conception of what is an unacceptable family burden is not only weak but does violence to the very meaning of "family." They charge Hardwig with turning debilitating illness into a capital offense, an attitude that is hardly the mark of a "loving" family.[35] The family is the place where crass benefit/burden calculations are left outside the door, where love is shown by burden taken up not put down. The hard death of a family member is tragic enough, they say, without making matters worse by countenancing the crushing weight of a duty to die.[36]

CONCLUSIONS

For all their differences, Hardwig and his critics agree on one thing: The debate about the duty to die matters. Whether or not I should take my life to avoid overburdening my family may not mean much to anyone else, but it makes an enormous difference in the lives of my family and me. That's what makes the decision so agonizingly difficult—it really does matter. If it didn't, the choice would be trivial, and Hardwig and his critics wouldn't even be debating it.

But *why* does it matter? In fewer years than I'd like to admit, I'll be gone—my purest intentions, best laid plans, grandest accomplishments, all devoured by the black hole of death. What difference will it make to the ages whether I killed myself and saved the family a burden or they took on the burden and supported me in a "natural" death? Indeed, in the longest run, what difference does anything ultimately make? Doesn't the brute fact that we must die make life meaningless? Doesn't it lend weight to Macbeth's verdict that life is a "tale told by an idiot, full of sound and fury, signifying nothing"?

Obviously, despite their differences, Hardwig and his critics don't share this dour outlook. How else to explain that, despite their disagreement about the duty to die, both apparently agree that death can still provide opportunities of meaningful choice, such as expressions of loving concern? For Hardwig that means patient unburdening the family; for his critics it's the family shouldering the burden. For *both* their course is sometimes the only loving thing to do.

Still, Macbeth's lament nags. For the life that love says should be surrendered is the same life that love says should be supported. When loving concern prescribes opposed actions, what sense *does* life make? What meaning *does* it have? What *does* it signify?

Many people refer such metaphysical questions of ultimate meaning to religion. Only within a theology of a God-centered universe, they say, can a life and *all* life be understood to have meaning. Others find all the meaning they need elsewhere—in their families or life's projects; in nature, the world, science, or humanity. Still others find the query of ultimate meaning pointless.

When Camus wrote that suicide is the only "truly serious philosophical problem," he didn't have in mind the duty to die to save others burden. But the debate about the duty to die ultimately leads to what Camus was talking about: "judging whether life is or is not worth living." And that, said Camus, "amounts to the fundamental question of philosophy." Why fundamental? Because it deals with the meaning of life.

It is to life's meaning that we now turn in the final chapter of philosophical thinking about death and dying.

REFERENCES

1. James F. Drane and John L. Coulehan, "The Concept of Futility: Patients Do Not Have a Right To Demand Medically Useless Treatment," in Tom L. Beauchamp and Robert M. Veatch, *Ethical Issues in Death and Dying,* 2nd ed., Upper Saddle River, NJ: Prentice Hall, 1996, pp. 385–391.

2. Plato, *The Republic of Plato,* Francis Macdonald Cornford, trans., New York: Oxford University Press, 1945, Bk. III, p. 98.

3. Ibid., p. 97.

4. T. Tomlinson and H. Brody, "Futility and the Ethics of Resuscitation," *JAMA,* September 12, 1990, pp. 1276–1290.

5. David O'Steen and Burke J. Balch, "What's Wrong With Involuntary Euthanasia?," *Pregnant Pause,* September 6, 2000. Retrieved February 3, 2005, from http://www.pregnantpause.org/euth/whyin.htm.

6. Donald Murphy, "Do-Not-Resuscitate Orders. Time for Reappraisal in Long-Term Care Institutions" *JAMA,* October 14, 1988, pp. 2098–2101.

7. Drane and Coulehan, p. 389.

8. Ibid.

9. Howard Brody, "The Physician's Role in Determining Futility," in Thomas A. Mappes and David DeGrazia, *Biomedical Ethics,* 5th ed., New York: McGraw Hill, 2001, p. 347.

10. Maura Dolan, "Out of a Coma, Into a Twilight," *Los Angeles Times,* January 2, 2001, p. 16.

11. G. D. Lundberg, "American Health Care System Management Objectives. The Aura of Inevitability becomes Incarnate," *JAMA,* May 19, 1993, pp. 2254–2555.

12. Peter A. Clark and Catherine M. Mikus, "Time for a Formalized Medical Futility Policy," *Health Progress,* July–August, 2000. Retrieved February 3, 2005, from http://www.chausa.orgPUBS/PUBSART?/ISSUE=HP0007&ARTICLE=F.

13. Stuart J. Youngner, "Who Defines Futility?" in Tom Beauchamp and Robert M. Veatch, *Ethical Issues in Death and Dying,* 2nd ed., Upper Saddle River, NJ: Prentice Hall, 1996, p. 354.

14. Mark Wicclair, "Medical Futility: A Conceptual and Ethical Analysis," in Mappes and DeGrazia, p. 343.

15. Ian Kerridge and Michael Lowe, "When treatment is futile: ethical uncertainty and clinical practice," *student BMJ,* March 1997. Retrieved February 7, 2005, from http://www.studenbmj.com/back_issues/0397/data/0397ed.2htm.

16. Robert M. Veatch and Caro Mason Spiceer, "Futile Care: Physicians Should Not Be Allowed To Refuse To Treat," in Tom Beauchamp and Robert M. Veatch, *Ethical Issues in Death and Dying,* 2nd ed., Upper Saddle River, NJ: Prentice Hall, 1996, p. 396.

17. Ibid.

18. Allan S. Brett and Paul Jersild, "'Inappropriate' Treatment Near the End of Life: Conflict Between Religious Convictions and Clinical Judgment," *Archives of Internal Medicine,* July 28, 2003, pp. 1645–1649.

19. Danielle Gillespie, "Author Warns of New Legislative Push for Doctor-Assisted Suicide," *CNSnews.com,* June 18, 2003. Retrieved February 3, 2005, from http://www.cnsnews.com/Culture/Archive/200306/Archive.asp.

20. Daniel Callahan, *Setting Limits: Medical Goals in an Aging Society,* Washington: Georgetown University Press, 1987.

21. Kristin Dizon, "Lamm's 'Duty to Die' Message Lives On,'" *Last Rights,* September 21, 1998. Retrieved February 3, 2005, from http://www.buffzone.com/extra/last-rights/21lamm.html.

22. John Hardwig and others, *Is There a Duty To Die? and Other Essays in Bioethics,* New York: Routledge, 2000, pp. 122–123.

23. Ibid., p. 122.

24. Ibid., pp. 129–130.

25. Richard B. Brandt, "The Morality and Rationality of Suicide," in Thomas A. Mappes and David DeGrazia, *Biomedical Ethics,* 5th ed., New York: McGraw Hill, 2001, p. 392.

26. Ibid.

27. Larry Churchill, "Seeking a Responsible Death," in John Hardwig and others, *Is There a Duty To Die? and Other Essays in Bioethics,* New York: Routledge, 2000, p. 162.

28. "79% of Americans Believe Doctors Should Not Veto a Family Choice for Life Support," *Wirthlin Worldwide Survey,* conducted February 5–89, 1999. Retrieved February 3, 2005, from http://www.euthanasia.com/lifepoll.html.

29. "Right to Die: Red Flags," Pew Research Center, June 2003. Retrieved February 7, 2005, from http:/www.publicagenda.org/issues/red_flags_detail.cfm?issue_type=right2die.

30. Hardwig and others, p. 133.

31. Daniel Callahan, "Our Burden upon Others: A Response to John Hardwig," in John Hardwig and others, *Is There a Duty To Die? and Other Essays in Bioethics,* New York: Routledge, 2000, p. 144.

32. Ibid.

33. Ibid., p. 140.

34. Felicia Cohn and Joanne Lynn, "A Duty To Die," in John Hardwig and others, *Is There a Duty To Die? and Other Essays in Bioethics,* New York: Routledge, 2000, pp. 146–147.

35. Felicia Ackerman, "For Now Have I My Death: The 'Duty to Die,'" in *Ethical Issues in Modern Medicine,* 6th ed., Bonnie Seinbock, John D. Arras, and Alex John London, eds., New York: McGraw-Hill, 2002, p. 427.

36. Callahan, "Our Burden upon Others: A Response to John Hardwig," in John Hardwig and others, *Is There a Duty To Die? and Other Essays in Bioethics,* New York: Routledge, 2000, p. 144.

Conclusion
Life, Death, and Meaning

At the height of his writing career, Leo Tolstoy was nearly driven mad by the conviction that life was meaningless. Since he would die, Tolstoy wondered why he should care about career, family, friends, or anything else for that matter. Of special frustration to the moralist and mystic was science's answer to his question of the meaning of life:

> "You are what you call your life; that is, a temporal, accidental conglomeration of particles. The mutual action and reaction of these particles on one another has produced what you call your life. This agglomeration will continue during a certain time; then the reciprocal action of these particles will cease, and with it will end what you call your life, and with it will end all your questions as well. You are an accidentally combined lump of something. The lump undergoes decomposition, this decomposition men call life; the lump falls asunder, decomposition ceases, and with it all doubting.". . . Such an answer proves that the answer does not answer the question. I want to know the meaning of my life; but that it is a particle of the infinite not only does not give a meaning to it, but destroys any possibility of meaning.[1]

Tolstoy has not been alone in suggesting that if death is the end of life, then life is meaningless. Arthur Schopenhauer (1788–1860), for one, called existence an error, and life no more than a process of disillusionment.[2] Although perhaps not as harsh in their assessments, others—Bertrand Russell and Richard Taylor (1920–2003) among them—have felt that, at the very least, death casts a pall over all human endeavor.[3,4] Even the Buddha, after ten years of princely "dancing and pleasure," could no longer avoid the problem of suffering as he pondered the "true meaning" of life. Contemplating all the good things of life—youth, health, riches—the

Buddha mused: "What do they mean to me?...Some day we may be sick, we shall become aged, from death there is no escape."[5]

Still, the weight of philosophical opinion does not support the view that death as annihilation or nothingness inevitably makes life meaningless. In fact, philosophers generally have believed the opposite, that death makes life meaningful. Philosopher John Çottingham, for example, has recently suggested that life's very impermanence and fragility support the quest for a "spiritual" dimension of meaning (*On the Meaning of Life,* 2002).

Though opposed, both positions—that life is meaningful or meaningless because we die—imply that it is due to death that life has the meaning it does. However, perhaps life has meaning independently of the fact that we will die. This is the view of those who believe that it is life that does or does not give meaning to death.

Life, death, and meaning—these are the concerns of this final chapter. Their interplay touches every other topic in this book—from how we define death to our awareness that we will die to whether we think death is bad to what we think happens after we die to whether we believe it's ever right to take a life out of mercy or duty. The interplay of life, death, and meaning, in short, is central to philosophical thinking about death and dying.

DEATH GIVES MEANING TO LIFE

Regardless of how they differ, all beliefs that death makes life meaningful agree that death is the distinguishing feature of human existence. This makes death an essential as well as a biological fact of human existence, ontological as well as empirical.[6] If death is properly so characterized, then death is what gives life meaning; it is the precondition for the "true" life of a human being. Through death, life is transcended.

For many this transcendence takes a religious, afterlife form along the lines sketched in Chapter 6. But it needn't. Non-religious arguments for the idea that death, even as annihilation, gives meaning to life permeate Western philosophy. It is to them that we initially turn.

The secular case for death as giving meaning to life ordinarily is made on the following grounds: (1) Death is necessary for life; (2) Death is part of the life cycle; (3) Death is ultimate affirmation; (4) Death motivates commitment and engagement; (5) Death stimulates creativity. Besides these reasons, which pertain to individual human existence, there is the proposition that death has social utility.

Death as Necessary for Life

The argument from the necessity for life is based on the fact that there can be no development of life without evolution, and evolution requires death. As professor of religion, John Bowker writes:

If you ask, 'Why is death happening to me (or to anyone)?' The answer is: because the universe is happening to you; you are an event, a happening, of the universe; you are a child of the stars, as well as of your parents, and you could not be a child in any other way. Even while you live, and certainly when you die, the atoms and molecules which are at present locked into your shape and appearance, are being unlocked and scattered into other shapes and forms of construction . . . . It is not possible to arrive at life except via the route of death. That means, in turn, that the price which has to be paid for any organization of energy in a universe of this kind is very high indeed. It is not possible to acquire new energy out of nowhere from nothing—as it is equally true that it is not possible to lose energy. What is happening is the available energy is constantly being used and reorganized to build whatever there is—planets or plants, suns or sons. But as energy *is* used, so it is increasingly unavailable to do further work.[7]

It isn't that the necessity of death makes life meaningful, but rather that without death life could have no meaning. Conversely, because the universe can only produce life through the process of death, "death receives from life the highest possible tribute and value."[8] For life as a whole, then, death is a necessary good, albeit possibly an evil from the perspective of an individual life (see Chapter 4).

Death as Part of the Life Cycle

"Life cycle" can be considered the process of aging, including the knowledge we have of our mortality as we experience getting older. It's commonly believed that our biological life cycle allows us to give meaning to time, age, and change. Without the experiential life cycle, including the prospect of death, our entire understanding of what it means to be human would be altered in fundamental and, perhaps, impoverishing ways.[9]

Akin to this notion is the idea that death is the goal of life, in the sense that, like all living things, we are naturally "programmed" to die. In *Beyond the Pleasure Principle,* for example, Freud writes:

> . . . an instinct would be a tendency in living organic matter, impelling it towards reinstatement of an earlier condition, one of which it had abandoned under the influence of external disturbing forces . . . . The rudimentary creature would from its very beginning not have wanted to change, would, if circumstances had remained the same, have always merely repeated the same course of existence . . . . It would be counter to the conservative nature of instinct if the goal of life were a state never hitherto reached. It must be the ancient starting point, which the living being left long ago and to which it harks back again by all the circuitous paths of development . . . .[10]

In a word, then, all roads lead to Rome, to the center of things, to death.

Other modern psychological theorists, such as Erik Erickson (1902–1994) and Abraham Maslow (1908–1970), have framed human development as a life-long process, which includes dying. This makes dying another stage of the human life cycle, comparable to infancy, adolescence, adulthood, or advanced aged. Like the other stages, dying often can pose task work and challenges. Some students of death and human behavior go further. Kubler-Ross, for example, as well as Dr. Ira Byock, president of the American Academy of Hospice and Palliative Medicine, say that dying can offer *unique* opportunities for individual learning, growth, and personal satisfaction. Dying and death, in brief, are part of the continuum of a person's life.

Death as Ultimate Affirmation

The argument from ultimate affirmation is simply that death gives absolute value to life. "In the face of death," writes William Barrett, "life has an absolute value and the meaning of death is precisely its revelation of this value."[11] By this measure, death affirms life by providing it with coherence and sustaining significance. Life is precious and important precisely because it is finite, fragile, and fleeting. The death of someone we love reminds us of this, as in the following tribute to a grandmother:

> People spend their entire lives searching for the meaning of life. It's heartbreaking when a 92-year-old woman looks you in the eyes and asks, "Why am I here?" Perhaps even sadder is knowing that you don't have an answer and that, especially now on her deathbed, you'll never get the chance to help her find one. In all of this, there is beauty, however. It's the realization of the fragility and uncertainty of life. Not just for one, but for all. Knowing that nobody knows the true meaning of life makes living somehow more manageable. My grandmother never found the meaning of life, but in her search for meaning, she found something more precious; she found an appreciation for life. That appreciation she passed on to me and all of those she touched.[12]

Death as Motive to Commitment and Engagement

The argument from motive to commitment and engagement is that without life's brevity we'd be less inclined to make the best use of time and accomplish something worthwhile and significant. Death's prospect motivates us to assume responsibilities and respond to the opportunities of life, suggests psychologist Lisl Goodman (in *Death and the Creative Life,* 1981).

In his classic *Man's Search for Meaning,* psychoanalyst Viktor Frankl (1905–1997) advises: "So live as if you were living already for the second time and as if you had acted the first time as wrongly as you are about to act now!" Of the value of such advice, the man who survived four Nazi death camps from 1942 to 1945 writes:

> It seems to me that there is nothing that would stimulate a man's sense of responsibleness more than this maxim, which invites him to imagine first that the present is past and, second, that the past may yet be changed and

amended. Such a precept confronts him with life's *finiteness* as well as the *finality* of what he makes out of both his life and himself.[13]

Supportive of the view of death as potential spur to self-development is this life-affirming statement from a patient dying of esophageal cancer:

> ... To live in the bright light of death is to live a life in which colors and sounds and smells are all more intense, in which smiles and laughs are irresistibly infectious, in which touches and hugs are warm and tender almost beyond belief.... I wish that the final chapter in all your stories can have a chapter in which you are given the gift of some time to live with your fatal illness.[14]

Philosopher Bernard Williams offers another slant. He believes that without death we simply wouldn't stay engaged in living. Immortality would render life intolerably boring and vapid, as in the film *Zardoz,* in which bored immortalist-survivors of a nuclear holocaust leave a safe structure to die in ecstasy.[15]

Death as Stimulus to Creativity

The Australian philosopher Julian Young says that living with his terminal illness (non-Hodgkin's lymphoma) not only gave his career focus and purpose, it ignited the creative spark that saw him write three books in three years.[16] This is more evidence, no doubt, of how death can concentrate the mind. But some students of the subject go further, viewing creativity as inextricably tied to death.

Philosopher John Morgan, for example, sees the creative process as a blend of two interconnected elements: the overwhelming awareness of death and the confrontation of our own possibilities. "As a meaning seeking, self-creative being," Morgan writes, "each human life is a compromise between what is and what might have been.... 'an intermediate step state between the fullness of ideal life and death.'"[17] To counteract the distress caused by the loss that is death, we create. By this account, death—or, more precisely, the awareness of death—provides the necessary energy for creativity, for expanding and perpetuating oneself, for challenging destiny and fighting against extinction. Death is the vehicle for satisfying what thinkers such as Kierkegaard, Rank, and Becker see as the basic human need to transcend mortality (see Chapter 3). Were we immortal we would have no such need for transcendence. So, just as freedom and dignity reside in the very act of scraping for life's meaning (rather than being told what it is), creativity resides in transcending (the knowledge of) death as the end of possibility.

Death as Socially Useful

Beyond arguments that pertain to individual human existence, such as the preceding, there is the view that death is socially useful for population control. It is suggested that were we to live an extended, let alone indefinite life span, the world would soon become a foul battleground of interests competing for sheer survival.[18] But not everyone agrees. Some view longer life spans as actually making the world a better place, since we would have to live in the environments we create, which would encourage cooperative behavior.[19]

Underlying all arguments that death makes life meaningful is the assumption that it is due to death that life has the meaning it does. This belief is shared by the opposed view: that life is meaningless due to the fact of death.

But possibly the disputants have it all wrong. Perhaps life has meaning independently of the fact that we will die, and, therefore, it is life that does or does not give meaning to death. As one philosopher says,

> A life can be made neither good nor bad by the fact that it will eventually end, any more than a car can be made good or bad by the fact that it will eventually be scrapped. A life has the value it does quite independently of the fact that it will end. In fact, *death* has the value it does due to the value of the life it ends.[20]

With that possibility—that it is life that does or does not give meaning to death—we join the question of life's meaning.

THE MEANING OF LIFE

To ask about the meaning of life usually is to wonder whether one's own life has a larger or more important purpose than merely living, possibly as part of an influential political or social movement, or simply providing for the well-being of one's immediate family and future generations. Of course, it is still possible to ask about the meaning of those things, that is, to seek a larger or more important purpose for the glorious cause or the cherished family; and then, again, to seek larger purposes for those things, and so on.

The question of the meaning of life, it seems, is like the proverbial ripple-making stone thrown into a pond. Within the innermost of the concentric circles created, our answers are relatively clear and distinct: the cause, the family, the immediate community. The farther out, the less particular our answers, until at the outer reaches we are led to the most general of possible interpretations of the question of the meaning of life: Why does anyone or anything exist? Why is there something rather than nothing?

Whatever the ultimate answer, however seemingly ironclad, one thing is clear: It cannot prove its logic from within itself. This, however, has never kept humans from speculating about life's ultimate meaning.

Traditional answers to the meaning of life appeal to some higher purpose, such as a plan operating in the universe in relation to which an individual life has meaning. Such a view can be termed objective, in the sense that it relates individual or personal meaning to something larger or more significant than the individual's life, either religious or secular. The religious "significant whole" generally is treated as *theistic,* because it includes the existence of a deity. The secular "significant whole" is treated as *non-theistic,* because it does not include such a belief, generally finding meaning instead in the structure of the universe or world.

In the postmodern age the objective mooring of meaning, both religious and secular, has been ripped away (see Chapter 2). As a result, many are left, in the words of the Buddhist monk Bhikkhu Bodhi, "with no higher purpose than the brute struggle to survive and propagate our genes before death draws the curtain closed on all our restless strivings."[21] This crisis of meaning or higher purpose is today the biggest obstacle to a coherent philosophy of death. It poses the question: If life has no ultimate meaning, what meaning can death have?

Theistic

Typical of theistic positions is the view of the universe as developing toward some end or goal established by a divine being. Within that divine plan, all things have meaning and value, especially human lives.

Recall, as a classic example, the medieval worldview depicted in Chapter 2 and its associated afterlife models in Chapter 6, which, taken together, leave no doubt as to the meaning of life:

> "[T]he stretch on earth is only a short interlude, a temporary incar- ceration of the soul in the prison of the body, a brief trial and test, fated to end in death, the release from pain and suffering. What really matters is the life after the death of the body. One's existence acquires meaning not by gaining what this life can offer but by saving one's immortal soul from death and eternal torture, by gaining eternal life and everlasting bliss."[22]

Accordingly, without the existence of God or faith that God exists, life would be meaningless.

It is precisely this sentiment that has sustained countless people down through time. It was what saved Tolstoy from suicide, and led him to generalize that it is only as a result of faith as "the knowledge of the meaning of human life" that individuals don't kill themselves. For Tolstoy that faith was the faith in the risen Christ that promises everlasting life, depicted triumphantly in the words of the apostle Paul: "When the perishable has been clothed with the imperishable, and the mortal with immortality, then the saying that is written will come true: 'Death has been swal- lowed up in victory. Where, O death, is your victory? Where, O death, is your sting?'" (1 Cor. 15:55)

As also noted in Chapter 6, some religions, Islam for one, share the Christian cosmogony, while other religions, such as Hinduism and Buddhism, radically differ. But regardless of their divergent worldviews, all religions postulate a divine reality in relation to which life in general has meaning, and individual lives in particular do. Fundamental to this view is the necessity of death. So, while the concepts and affirmations of major religious traditions, East and West, sometimes radically differ, they resemble each other in proclaiming: (1) death is not the end of life; and (2) death is necessary as a means to life. This makes death central to any religiously based theory of the meaning of life. It is also why, according to some scholars, religions generally view any attempt to marginalize the significance of death as potentially undercutting the meaning of life.[23]

Any theistic version of the meaning of life obviously will have enormous appeal to the religious minded. But to the skeptic, including most philosophers, it raises insurmountable difficulties about the existence and nature of God, the details of which lie beyond the scope of this book. Enough to say here that over the years systematic defenses for the existence of a personal God have been made and found lacking by most philosophers. Indeed, some philosophers find the notion that God uses humans as a means to some ultimate end offensive, even immoral; and the inference that life has meaning because of some "divine plan" illogical.

Still, the atheist or agnostic does not necessarily deny that life has meaning. Unable to overcome the problems inherent in theism, many of them have sought non-theistic meaning of life in the world, nature, or the universe.

Non-Theistic

The larger whole in relation to which an individual life has meaning is found not in a deity but in the natural universe. Such at least is the view of philosophers and others who, while denying or doubting the existence of God, nevertheless interpret the universe in terms of what might be termed god-equivalents. These divine surrogates are, variously, tendencies, aims, or implicit purposes upon which, in a sense, we are dependent and in relation to which a life has meaning.

One of the most common non-theistic interpretations of objective meaning is belief in orderly intelligence working in the universe. Thus, the complex laws of mathematics, physics, and biology suggest to some the presence of aesthetic intelligence, possibly a "master plan," operating within physical reality.[24] This view needs to be distinguished from "intelligent design" (ID), which is a theory that attributes the origin of life and the universe to intelligent causes. ID advocates don't only claim that there's intelligence operating in the universe or that design is empirically detectable in nature. They go further and say that this design proves that God exists (or at least some kind of super intelligent being does). The non-theist, by contrast, perceives intelligence at work but no necessary, divine hand behind it.

But even if there's non-divine intelligence at work in the universe, how does that make life meaningful? And what exactly is our point of comparison for interpreting what we perceive as "aesthetic," "orderly," and "intelligent" in the first place? Do we know "unaesthetic," "disorderly," and "unintelligent" universes by comparison to which we can tout our world? For evolutionary biologist Stephen Jay Gould (1941–2002), the jump from pattern to meaning merely reflects a need for "comforting answers." "Our error," he says, "lies not in the perception of pattern but in automatically imbuing pattern with meaning, especially with meaning that can bring us comfort, or dispel confusion."[25] In other words, to feel secure about our place in the universe, we move seamlessly from the scientific to the metaphysical (or theological), from the empirically verifiable to the purely speculative.

This is true, in the opinion represented by Gould, of any view that imbues the cosmos with meaning.

Perhaps Gould and the many like-minds are right—maybe we are seeing things more with our heart than head. Perhaps it is our need for security that inclines us to overlay pattern and meaning on what is a purely random universe. But what about progress? Can anyone doubt the evidence of progress in human development? And might not human progress be that thing outside ourselves on which we are all dependent and from which our lives, and therefore our deaths, derive meaning? Many philosophers have thought so.

PROGRESS AND MEANING

"Progress"—a word and concept with such heavy subjective overtones invites many conceptions. But two stand out in Western intellectual history. One associates progress with self-consciousness and freedom, the other with science. Each has endeared and incensed.

Self-Consciousness and Freedom

Hegel wove an important philosophy of history around the notion of progress in self-consciousness and freedom. As human beings become increasingly aware of self and world, he said, they are able to make free decisions. This exercise of human freedom is an expression of "Absolute Spirit," which Hegel believed is engaged in its own self-realization as manifested through the rise and fall of civilizations. Despite the many reversals and setbacks evident in history, Hegel was convinced that perfectibility would eventually come from the process of struggle as more and more individuals become free.[26]

While Hegel focused primarily on what he saw as the historic pattern of human development toward self-consciousness and freedom, Karl Marx, who studied Hegel, emphasized its goal: the establishment of a classless society, or one without either profit motive or private property. For Marx, the historic process is not animated by any Absolute Spirit, but merely the material and economic interests of society. Where Hegel saw transcendent entities at work in the universe's structure, Marx saw only clashing materialistic forces. Both believed that history showed progress in consciousness of freedom, and both related the meaning of life to that progress. For Hegel the meaning of one's life was determined by a personal consciousness of freedom. This made the most meaningful lives ones lived by the most historically decisive individuals—(e.g., Caesar, Alexander the Great, Napoleon)—figures whose actions attune with the will of the World Spirit or simply the larger issues of history. By contrast, for Marx, who associated individual freedom with consciousness of economic laws governing the historic process, meaning in life was to be found by actively hastening the process of human perfectibility through social pressure or revolution.

Science

For those less metaphysically, politically, or economically inclined, the progress in relation to which life has meaning often is found in the advance of science. From its beginning, science has held a basic faith in a universe of consistency, orderliness, and beauty.

The idea of inherent progress has grown with scientific knowledge of ourselves and the world. Decidedly influential has been our understanding of life as gradually evolving over millennia from single-celled microorganisms to luminous civilizations. This appreciation of biological evolution certainly offers an account of physical phenomena in terms of natural, not supernatural causes. But it does more than that. For many people biological evolution represents the means by which human beings can, through their own effort, without divine assistance, advance into the future. The practical effect of this paradigm of progress has been such an extraordinary channeling of the forces of nature for human betterment as to anoint science the "god of progress."

Many of those who associate progress with scientific advance don't stop there. From perceived law and uniformity in nature, they see an implied duty to know that order and get into harmony with it. Often this includes a moral obligation to improve the world.

The English biologist Julian Huxley (1887–1975), for example, who was known for popularizing science in books and lectures, writes of achieving

> a sense of union with something bigger than our ordinary selves, even if that something be not a god but an extension of our narrow core to include in a single grasp ranges of our outer experience and inner nature on which we do not ordinarily draw.

Dismissive of the traditional impetuses to such an achievement—beliefs in the existence of God or afterlife—Huxley professed that "without these beliefs men and women may yet possess the mainspring of full and purposive living, and just as strong a sense that existence can be worth while as is possible to the most devout believers."[27] Huxley saw progress in the greater control, knowledge, and independence that he felt biological evolution promised. For him the most tantalizing of all the potentialities of progress was "conscious evolution," which he identified with commitment to a cause. Such sentiments inevitably led him to situate immortality, not in a world to come, but squarely in the here and now.

Writing in a spiritual, even mystical context, Pierre Teilhard de Chardin shared Huxley's vision that humanity is evolution become conscious of itself. He, too, as we saw in Chapter 7, discerned in human evolution a movement in nature toward increasingly higher forms of consciousness. Departing from the atheistic Huxley, Teilhard associated ultimate consciousness with consciousness of God. This implies that God is infused in the natural world and the work of science is spiritual work. Science uncovers the divinity toward which the universe is moving. By this account, there is no need to escape the world, as the medievalists taught— no need to die to find complete communion with God. The world itself is a divine handiwork, and we can glimpse the face of God through the eyes of science, without appeal to religious authority.[28]

Critics of Progress

Most evolutionary scientists don't share a vision of purposeful nature. Gould, for instance, flatly writes, "There is no progress in evolution," adding that much of evolution is, in fact, downward.[29] Darwinian Richard Dawkins agrees, asserting in a recent book that evolution moves in no particular direction and favors no particular species.[30] Naturalist Ernst Mayr (1905–2005), the preeminent evolutionist of the last century, is another notable skeptic of progress in nature.[31]

Schopenhauer

Among philosophers, Schopenhauer was probably the harshest critic of human progress. He saw in history and evolution only a blind, relentless striving for existence of the "immanent will." The immanent will, he said, manifests itself throughout all organic life and in human beings as the "will to life," or the inherent drive to stay alive and reproduce. Schopenhauer found nothing in history to suggest "progress," but plenty to demonstrate ruthless pursuit of self-interest. As for evolution, that merely multiplies pains, he said. Self-consciousness only makes humans exquisitely more sensitive to frustration and misery. Consciousness of freedom fares no better in Schopenhauer's view. The only real freedom, he said, was moral freedom. For Schopenhauer moral freedom is the freedom we have to deny the will to live by fleeing the pleasures of life. But fleeing life's pleasures does not include suicide. While acknowledging the right to suicide, Schopenhauer opposed it as fleeing the sufferings, not the pleasures, of life, and thus in no way destroying one's will to live. Suicide, he writes in his essay on the topic, "substitutes for a true redemption from this world of misery merely an apparent one."[32]

Von Hartmann

Another German pessimist, Eduard von Hartmann (1842–1906) shared much of his compatriot's gloom, including a notion similar to Schopenhauer's immanent will. Von Hartmann termed it "the great Unconscious."[33] The so-called philosopher of the unconscious saw intelligence and purpose at work in nature and in history, a discernible progress toward a definite goal set by this great Unconscious. But that goal is the extinction of the world. As von Hartmann writes in *Ethical Studies* (1898), the final aim of the universe is "the deliverance of the absolute from transcendental misery, and the return to its painless peace by means of immanent torment of the world evolution."[34] In this view von Hartmann echoed Schopenhauer's bleak appraisal of "life as a uselessly disturbing episode in the blissful repose of nothingness."[35] Nevertheless, like Schopenhauer, he deplored suicide, which he saw as a violation of our duty to assist the "great Unconscious" to achieve self-deliverance. To help in this task is a human being's supreme duty, according to von Hartmann, since only human consciousness can make "salvation" (i.e., "Unconsciousness") possible.

Nietzsche

But the most philosophically significant dissent to the meaning of life depicted by the seers of progress is Nietzsche's doctrine of "eternal recurrence." The doctrine of eternal recurrence postulates a world of "eternal self-creation and eternal self-destruction." Simply put, all things forever return, including ourselves. (Think of Bill Murray's *Groundhog Day.*) For support, Nietzsche invoked the very activity and study in which so many others find progress: science.[36] Given the limited combinations of reality—an infinite time in which a finite energy in a finite space can combine—Nietzsche concluded that the doctrine of eternal recurrence must be accepted as "an ineluctable implication of impartial science."[37] In the words of its interpreter Zarathustra: "Everything goes, everything comes back; eternally rolls the wheel of being."[38] Especially noteworthy about Nietzsche's circular doctrine of eternal recurrence is its opposition to the traditional Western view of progress and its experience of time as linear.

Criticism of the Western Conception of "Progress"

The West has historically viewed time as a ribbon stretching into the future along which one progresses, indefinitely and without limit.[39] Nietzsche aside, this rosy view favors and leaves unexamined the understanding of "progress" as "more and better." As we saw in Chapter 2, to many postmodernists the horrific events of the twentieth century cruelly belie this glib assumption, along with the whole notion of an inherent progress in human affairs.

Author and activist Chellis Glendenning, for one, has depicted the darker side of Western civilization, from which she describes herself as recovering. Glendenning cites specific human debris that progress as "more and better" has too often left in its wake. Included in her catalogue are: gross economic injustice; widespread human exploitation; deliberate genocide; proliferation of weapons of mass destruction; wanton, planet-threatening environmental abuse; domination of peoples, cultures, and nature; and systematic manipulation of public opinion that mocks democracy and makes right and truth a function of popular will.[40]

With this analysis, Glendenning joins the ranks of social critics who trace their modern roots back to the social criticism that emerged in Germany after the shocking events of World War II. Two of that movement's luminaries were philosophers Theodor Adorno (1903–1969) and Max Horkheimer (1895–1973). In the opening words of their grim 1947 assessment of the modern West, Adorno and Horkheimer baldly state the case against the Western conception of progress:

> Enlightenment, understood in the widest sense as the advance of thought, has always aimed at liberating human beings from fear and installing them as master. Yet the wholly enlightened earth is radiant with triumphant calamity.[41]

That we term these calamitous developments "scientific progress is both a reflection and result of our irrationality," according to the authors.

Such criticism of progress leaves us wondering, first, how meaning and value can be based on historical decline and degradation. Then it raises another question: How are we to transcend our finitude? After all, any position that ties the meaning of life to some larger, *non-theistic* purpose or whole is as much offering a meaning to the fact of death as its *theistic* counterpart is. Both are claiming that life gives meaning to death. One does it by appeal to God; the other by invoking a god-equivalent, a secular goal such as progress. Both, therefore, are salvific or redemptive. Both allow us to transcend our finitude, to overcome our mortality.

Earlier we said most philosophers reject theism. Now we see serious problems with non-theistic versions of the meaning of life. But if neither position is philosophically sound, on what grounds can life and, therefore, death be said to have meaning? "None!" reverberates the reply of postmodern philosophers appropriately termed "nihilists." Nihilism is not only the greatest challenge today to a philosophy of death but to philosophy itself.

THE CHALLENGE OF NIHILISM

In philosophy nihilism is an extreme form of skepticism that condemns existence and regards all values as baseless. Nihilism denies any larger whole in relation to which life is meaningful. Nihilism, in short, is the doctrine that life has no meaning and nothing has value.

The modern root causes of nihilism have been traced to disillusionment with both religion and science. With the ascendancy of science and its Enlightenment beliefs, there has come a "religious disappointment" born from the realization that religion is no longer capable of providing a meaning for human life.[42] But neither can science, as the Tolstoy quote that began this chapter shows. What's more, as we've just seen, the "progress" of science and its technology has come at considerable cost. In the mid-twentieth century, a great American corporation (General Electric) could boast with a straight face: "Progress Is Our Most Important Product." Today only the most mealy-mouthed Babbitt would spout such a slogan. The point is that for all our Enlightenment curiosity and inquiry, we've paid dearly.

We are left with a crisis of meaning. We lack confidence, purpose, and direction. We've lost our conviction and certitude.[43] Lacking a moral compass, we don't know where to turn or what to believe. We're stranded, in short, in the world of *Thus Spake Zarathustra,* where Nietzsche introduced the theme of eternal recurrence. In that work Nietzsche also rendered nihilism less a philosophical doctrine than a psychological state of despair. And that's where we are today, according to nihilists: in a state of mind reached when we realize that all our reference points of meaning are meaningless.[44]

What if nihilists are correct? What are the death implications of recognizing the possibility of a belief in God or some god-equivalent has broken down?

The answer to that question lies in what the hypothesis of higher meaning and purpose really does, and why we need to project it. Basically, any belief in transcendent meaning or purpose carries the hope of immortality,[45] either the religious personal or the secular social. That's a big reason we need a larger whole to relate our lives to. In denying meaning to life as a whole, then, nihilism snuffs out any hope of immortality. And with that emerges the "$64,000 question": *How to transcend human finitude? How are we to find meaning in our mortality in the absence of God or god-equivalents?*

RESPONSES TO NIHILISM

In his recent analysis of this issue, philosopher Simon Critchley has summarized the possible responses to nihilism.[46] Here they will be reduced to three: refusal or rejection, acceptance, and affirmation.

Refusal or Rejection

There are various ways that the problem of nihilism can be either refused or rejected. One way to refuse it is to view nihilism as a misreading of fact. Some say, for example, that nihilists have simply distorted history. Others see in all the gloom and doom of nihilism unique opportunities for freedom and creativity.[47]

Rejecting nihilism as a problem, some faith-based fundamentalists still operate with a pre-nihilist mind-set. For them the traditional religious worldview is still in place, despite the events of the last century. On the other hand, some religionists try to fit nihilism into a preferred cosmogony. Many theologians, for instance, strive to reconcile an all-good and -powerful God and the grotesque absurdity of the Nazi extermination of 6 million Jews during World War II.[48] In this way, they cast off the problem of nihilism.

Of course, one needn't be a fundamentalist or mainstream religionist to sidestep nihilism. Just consider a cheerful, smug American, so immersed in material things that he never even poses the question of ultimate meaning.[49] Then there are logical positivists (see Chapter 6). Neither religionists who reject nihilism nor complacent affluent unaware of it, logical positivists simply consider nihilism cognitively meaningless since no evidence can be adduced for or against the meaning of life. Any response to the question, therefore, is vacuous.

Acceptance

Viewing the question of the meaning of life as at least understandable, many philosophers accept the challenge of nihilism, while disagreeing on what "acceptance" entails, a passive or an active response.

Passive   For some, accepting nihilism means reacting passively, perhaps with a sort of "don't worry, be happy" attitude. Given that nihilism cannot be overcome, philosopher Richard Rorty suggests that the best we can do is to maintain our equanimity.[50] Such seeming complacency, however, won't appeal to those attuned to the fact that, despite our inability to alter the meaninglessness of life, we absurdly keep trying to. So, for them passive acceptance might mean simply putting up with being ridiculous. True, being absurd offends human vanity. But is absurdity necessarily a bad thing? Some philosophers think not. Thomas Nagel, for example, prefers to view acting in the face of absurdity as an expression of our most advanced and curious characteristic: the capacity to live with ironic sensibility.[51] In a similar vein, Joel Feinberg asks us to imagine a person who has led "a maximally fulfilling life" until:

> in the philosophical autumn of his days [he] chances upon the legend of Sisyphus, the commentary of Camus, and the essays of Taylor and Nagel.

In a flash he sees the inanity of all his pursuits, the total permeability of his achievement by time; the lack of any long-term rationale for his purposes, in a word the absurdity of his (otherwise good) life. At first he will feel a keen twinge. But unless he be misled by the sophistries of the philosophical Pessimists [e.g., Schopenhauer] who confuse the empty ideal of long-term coherence with the Good for Man, he will soon recover. And then will come a dawning bittersweet appreciation for the cosmic incongruities first called to his attention by the philosophers. The thought that there should be a kind of joke at the heart of human existence begins to please (if not quite tickle) him. Now he can die not without a whine or a snarl but with an ironic smile.[52]

Whatever its expression, passive acceptance of nihilism is more about attitude than action.

Active   Actively accepting nihilism, on the other hand, generally supports action designed to improve life. This implies that what is meaningless can be made meaningful. Active acceptance of nihilism, then, is an attempt to overcome nihilism by restoring a new totality of meaning.

Some active nihilists propose what amounts to another transcendent narrative, a god-equivalent, as it were. Nietzsche, for example, substituted the "will to power" for the highest values he considered lost in the modern world. Practically this meant that when the will to power asserts itself, as it does in the creative, active person who trusts will and instinct, new values arise that transcend established moral codes. This rare individual of action and creativity, who occasionally appears as an accident of history (perhaps Caesar or Goethe), Nietzsche termed the "overman."

The overman, who may one day be bred and is responsible for all human progress, is distinguished from vast humanity by what he has unburdened himself of: belief in God, confidence in indefinite progress, hope for an afterlife, and most of all, the desire to overcome nihilism. For this most exceptional of individuals, there is only the truth of the eternal return of the same, in precise detail, an infinite number of times. The overman's strength, in brief, is his acceptance of "existence as it is, without meaning or aim, yet recurring inevitably without any finale of nothingness."[53] Such for Nietzsche was, at once, the new faith, the only immortality, the answer to nihilism.

The French writer Albert Camus (1913–1960) accepted Nietzsche's diagnosis that a world lacking God has no meaning. Indeed, the absurdity of such a world posed for Camus "the fundamental question of philosophy": "whether or not life is worth living."

In *The Myth of Sisyphus* (1942) Camus argues that suicidal inclinations to escape a meaningless and absurd world can (and should) be overcome by an affirmation of freedom, choice, and autonomy found in dignified defiance. For Camus, then, active acceptance of nihilism means revolt, metaphorically epitomized in the mythical Sisyphus.

Condemned by the gods to endlessly roll a rock to the top of a hill only to have it roll back of its own weight, Sisyphus takes up his burden and owns his inevitable and despicable fate. "Sisyphus teaches," writes Camus, "the higher fidelity that negates the gods and raises rocks." It is thus that to Sisyphus the godless universe seems "neither sterile nor futile." Indeed, "Each atom of that stone, each mineral flake of that night filled mountain, in itself forms a world. The struggle itself toward the heights is enough to fill a man's heart." Leaving no doubt of the legendary king's frame of mind, Camus is led to conclude: "One must imagine Sisyphus happy."[54]

Camus further developed the connection between personal freedom and meaning, on one hand, and rebellion, on the other, in *The Rebel* (1951). In that novel, he shows that the noble fight against injustice not only defines the individual but human nature as well.

Affirmation

For thinkers like Nietzsche and Camus, nihilism can at least be overcome, through sheer will to power or rebellion. But others reject any such response to nihilism as a cop-out. They point out that the crisis of nihilism is the absence of meaning, including philosophical meaning. Nietzsche and Camus, they say, are having it both ways. On one hand they declaim the absence of meaning; on the other they proclaim a new meaning. This isn't overcoming the problem of nihilism, it's evading it. As Critchely puts it:

> The world is all too easily stuffed with meaning and we risk suffocating under the combined weight of competing narratives of redemption— whether religious, socio-economic, scientific, technological, political, aesthetic, or philosophical—and hence miss the problem of nihilism in our manic desire to overcome it.[55]

For Critchley the only appropriate response to nihilism is naked refusal of meaning. This makes meaninglessness the only meaning. So, rather than offering a new totality of meaning, Critchley is setting us a task or quest. He's conceiving of meaninglessness as an achievement. It is, as he writes, "the achievement of the ordinary or the everyday without the rose-tinted spectacles of any narrative of redemption."

For models of what he means, Critchely turns to some modern artworks, especially the plays of Samuel Beckett (1906–1989), for whom "meaning nothing becomes the only meaning." In attempting to reconstruct the meaning of meaninglessness, Critchley writes that

> ... Beckett's work offers ... a radical de-creation of ... salvific narratives, an approach to meaninglessness as the achievement of the ordinary, *a redemption from redemption* .... In this way, Beckett returns us to the condition of particular objects, to their materiality, their extraordinary ordinariness: the gaff, the handkerchief, the toy dog, the sheet, the pap, the painkiller.[56]

For Critchley, then, acceptance of nihilism means affirming the ordinary, "an extraordinary ordinary, or what the [American poet] Wallace Stevens [1879–1955] calls a return to the plain sense of things."[57]

Perhaps Critchley's point finds illustration in two American classics, one a poem by Stevens, the other a play by Thornton Wilder (1897–1975). Both works deal with death, and life.

"The Emperor of Ice Cream" (1922) Stevens's, most famous poem recounts the story of a neighbor who goes to the house of a poor old woman who has died. The neighbor's task, depicted in one stanza, is to help lay out the corpse for viewing in the bedroom. Meanwhile, in the kitchen, captured in a second stanza, others are preparing foods, including ice cream, for the wake.

The two stanzas have been interpreted symbolically.[58] The kitchen where ice cream is being made represents "life as concupiscence," whereas the bedroom where the corpse awaits decent covering represents "death as final." Both symbolic kitchen and bedroom stanzas end with the same refrain: "The only emperor is the emperor of ice-cream." In other words, in the forced option between two realms, life and death, one must acquiesce in the realm of life.

Our Town (1935) In contrast to the muted affirmation it gets in "The Emperor," Wilder's wistful *Our Town* exalts the "extraordinary ordinary." Consider the third act, when we are led to the cemetery where some of the deceased inhabitants of Grover's Corners are awaiting not judgment but greater under-standing. Into their midst is led 26-year-old Emily Gibbs, who is finding the transition from life to death very difficult. When she's permitted to return to a time of her life, Emily chooses the morning of her 12th birthday. Much to her dismay (and our edification), what she discovers is how unconsciously we mortals pass through life. We hardly take notice of the ordinary, everyday things that make living extraordinary.

"I didn't realize," Emily says with amazement, "[s]o all that was going on and we never noticed!"

And then, poignantly, she says to her mother, aloofly bustling around the kitchen: "Oh, Mama, just look at me one minute as though you really see me." But sadly, Mrs. Webb, busy preparing breakfast, doesn't hear.[59]

Unable to go on, Emily asks to be taken back to her grave. But first she must have one more look. As she does, she expresses not only acquiescence, but unbridled joy in the "reign of life":

> . . . (Gently) Goodbye! (*Then passionately, her arms outflung*) Goodbye, world! (*Then lovingly, glancing at the town . . .*) Goodbye, Grover's Corners—(. . . *softly*) Mama and Papa (. . . *eyes uplifted*) Goodbye to clocks ticking—and my butternut tree! (*Her eyes follow its trunk down and she moves lovingly toward it a step or two, then gestures toward the garden*) and Mama's sunflowers—(*Her head gradually raised as the thrill grows*) and food and coffee—and new-ironed dresses

and hot baths—(*With increasing fervor*) and sleeping and waking up!—(*She flings her arms wide in an ecstasy of realization*) Oh, earth, you're too wonderful for anyone to realize you![60]

Witness to human blindness, Emily is brought to tears. The audience, as the reader of "The Emperor," is led to an appreciation and affirmation of the ordinary—the *extraordinary* ordinary.

THE EXAMINED LIFE, DEATH, AND MEANING

Are the various responses to contemporary nihilism satisfactory? Do they adequately answer the nihilistic claim that, in the absence of any credible theistic or non-theistic defense, life and, therefore, death are meaningless? The short answer is no.

Whatever the response—refusal/rejection, acceptance, affirmation—it's open to criticism. Those who view nihilism as a distortion of history, for example, seem to be as historically one-eyed as the nihilists they criticize. In this they may be likened to Emily's mother when she chides the tipsy choir conductor Simon Stimson for mocking the "happy existence" Emily wants to return to as "ignorance and blindness." "That ain't the whole truth and you know it," Mrs. Gibbs tells him, before gently turning Emily's gaze to the clearing in the sky: "Look at that star." Perhaps, like Stimson, nihilists miss the "stars" for the cynicism. Still, history is by no means all starlight and sunshine. Surely, there is enough destruction and depravity to make even a Mrs. Gibbs wince.

For its part, the religious refusal of nihilism will appeal only to believers, and be subject to criticism concerning the existence and nature of God. And those who dismiss the question of the meaning of life as meaningless, such as logical positivists, seem to be using a criterion of meaning that itself is neither self-evident nor provable.

Accepting nihilism, on the other hand, raises its own issues. Passive nihilism can lead to talk without action, and then to action that may end talk, at least free and open talk. After all, faced with uncertainty, passive nihilists tend to withdraw and disengage from the world and its problems. But doesn't that make might right? Doesn't disengagement invite the strong willed to dominate the weak willed?[61] Passive nihilism, then, seems to be Nietzsche's will to power in disguise. For their part, active nihilists see a world of freedom, but the actions they choose can lead to revolution and violence. More troubling philosophically, active nihilism seems to teach both nothing and something. If nothing matters, why the effort?

As for affirming nihilism, by perhaps embracing the ordinary, even Critchley frankly admits that isn't much.[62] What's more, intellectually affirming the "extraordinary ordinary" is one thing, living it another. Dostoyesky's prisoner couldn't do it (see Chapter 4). Nor could Emily, who asked to be to taken back to her grave. Sadder but wiser, she muses: "Do any human beings ever realize life while they live it—every, every minute?" "No—," the Stage Manager flatly tells her, "saints and poets maybe—they do some."[63]

But that none of the responses to nihilism is entirely persuasive shouldn't surprise or dismay. After all, we are dealing with an issue that cannot be resolved by either empirical science or documentary research. There is no single procedure for determining the meaning of life. Its meaning is flexible and complicated, multilayered and obscure. Why wouldn't thoughtful people disagree? Why *shouldn't* they?

Besides, amidst all the disagreement, there is at least one view around which a citadel of philosophical opinion has formed. It is this: Even if life has no meaning in an external, objective sense, that does not mean that life is not worth living. There is nothing irreconcilable about life as such being meaningless *and* many individual lives being meaningful.[64]

So, then, what gives meaning and value to the life of one who lives it? The answer, of course, depends on the interpretation the individual gives to her life as she lives it. Still, there is an ingredient common to all worthwhile lives.

If, as Socrates taught, the unexamined life is not worth living, then all worthwhile lives are examined lives. And on that point, not surprisingly, we are brought back to where we began our study: with Ivan Ilyich, the man who lived as he was supposed to but not as he should have.

If his life was not as meaningful for him as it could have been, it's because, we have reason to suspect, Ivan Ilyich lived unmindful of death. So disposed, he never examined his life until a fatal disease compelled him to confront its vacuity. Therein lies the stimulative, cyclical relationship not only between the examined life and death, but between both and the meaning of a life. Yes, an individual life can be worthwhile even though life itself may have no ultimate meaning. *But only if that life is examined,* still resonates the venerable admonition of Socrates borne on the face of the dead Ivan Ilyich—which is to say, *only if that life includes philosophical thinking about death and dying.*

REFERENCES

1. Lyof N. Tolstoi, *My Confession My Religion,* Midland, MI: Avensblume Press, 1994, pp. 26–27.

2. Arthur Schopenhauer, "On the Vanity of Existence," in *Schopenhauer—Essays and Aphorisms,* R. J. Hollingdale, trans., New York: Penguin Books, 1970, p. 54.

3. Bertrand Russell, "A Free Man's Worship," in *Why I Am Not a Christian,* New York: Simon & Schuster Touchstone, 1957, p. 107.

4. Richard Taylor, *Good and Evil: a New Direction,* New York: Prometheus Books, 1984, p. 263.

5. *The Teaching of Buddha,* Tokyo: Bukkyo Dendo Kyoki, 1966, p. 5.

6. Herbert Marcuse, "The Ideology of Death," in *The Meaning of Death,* Herman Feifel, ed., New York: McGraw-Hill Paperback Edition, 1959, p. 65.

7. John Bowker, *The Meanings of Death,* Canto edition, Cambridge, MA: Cambridge University Press, 1991, pp. 215–216.

8. Ibid., p. 218.

9. "Beyond Therapy: Biotechnology and the Pursuit of Happiness," *The President's Council on Bioethics,* October 2003. Retrieved February 4, 2005, from http://bioehicsprint.bioethics.gov/reports/byondtherapy/index.html.

10. M. V. Kamath, *Philosophy of Death & Dying,* Honesdale, PA: Himalayan International Institute of Yoga Science and Philosophy, 1978, p. 319.

11. E. D. Klemke, *The Meaning of Life,* New York: Oxford University Press, 2000, p. 4.

12. Heather Hampel, "Dagmar Zapf," in *Your True Hero.* Retrieved October 6, 2005, from http://www.yourtruehero.org/content/hero/view_hero.asp?9268.

13. Viktor Frankl, *Man's Search for Meaning,* New York: Pocket Books, 1973, p. 173.

14. Ira Byock, "The Meaning and Value of Death," *Journal of Palliative Medicine,* May, 2002, p. 282.

15. John Martin Fischer, *The Meaning of Death,* Stanford: Stanford University Press, 1993, p. 364.

16. Julian Young, *The Death of God and the Meaning of Life,* Oxford: Routledge, 2003.

17. John D. Morgan, "The Knowledge of Death as a Stimulus to Creativity," in *Death and the Quest for Meaning,* Stephen Strack, ed., Northvale, NJ: Jason Aronson, Inc., 1997, p. 357.

18. John Harris, "Intimations of Immortality," *Science,* April 7, 2000, p. 60.

19. William Faloon, "A Revolutionary Concept Slowly Gains Recognition," *Life Extension,* February, 2005, p. 7.

20. Steven Luper-Foy, "Annihilation," in John Martin Fischer, *The Meaning of Death,* Stanford: Stanford University Press, 1993, p. 280.

21. Bhikkhu Bodhi, "Navigating the New Millennium," *BPS Newsletter,* no. 44, 2000. Retrieved September 15, 2005, from http://www.accsstoinisght.org/lib/authors/bodhi/bps-essay_ 44.html.

22. Kurt Baier, "The Meaning of Life," in E. D. Klemke, *The Meaning of Life,* New York: Oxford University Press, 2000, p. 102.

23. John Bowker, *The Meanings of Death,* Canto edition, Cambridge, MA: Cambridge University Press, 1991, p. 211.

24. Ira Byock, "The Meaning and Value of Death," *Journal of Palliative Medicine,* May, 2002, p. 283.

25. Stephen Jay Gould, "The Streak of Streaks," in *Ten on Ten,* Robert Atwan, ed., Boston: Bedford Books of St. Martin's Press, 1992, p. 137.

26. Georg W. F. Hegel, *The Philosophy of History,* J. Sibree, trans., Amherst, NY: Prometheus Books, 1991.

27. Julian Huxley, "The Creed of a Scientific Humanist," in E. D. Klemke, *The Meaning of Life,* New York: Oxford University Press, 2000, p. 80.

28. Pierre Teilhard de Chardin, *The Divine Milieu: An Essay on the Interior Life,* New York: Harper and Row, 1968, p. 112.

29. Stephen Jay Gould, "The Pattern of Life's History," in John Brockman, *Third Culture: Beyond Scientific Revolution,* New York: Touchstone/Simon & Schuster, 1996, p. 51.

30. Richard Dawkins, *The Ancestor's Tale,* Boston: Houghton-Mifflin, 2004.

31. Ernst Mayr, *Systematics and the Origin of Species from the Viewpoint of a Zoologist,* Cambridge: Harvard University Press, 1999.

32. Arthur Schopenhauer, "On Suicide," in *Schopenhauer—Essays and Aphorisms,* R. J. Hollingdale, trans., New York: Penguin Books, 1970, p. 78.

33. Eduard Von Hartmann, *The Philosophy of the Unconscious,* Ludlow, England: Living Time Press, 2002.

34. Jacques Choron, *Suicide,* New York: Charles Scribner's Sons, 1972, p. 136.

35. Alain de Botton, *The Consolations of Philosophy,* New York: Vintage Books, 2001, p. 171.

36. Walter Kaufmann, *Nietzsche: Philosopher, Psychologist, Antichrist,* Princeton, NJ: Princeton University Press, 1974.

37. ———, *The Portable Nietzsche,* New York: The Viking Press, 1968, p. 111.

38. Friedrich Wilhelm Nietzsche, *Thus Spake Zarathustra,* Walter Kaufmann, trans., ed., New York: Penguin Books, 1982, p. 329.

39. Edward T. Hall, *Silent Language,* New York: Anchor Books, 1973.

40. Chellis Glendinning, "The Spell of Technology," in *Rereading America,* Gary Colombo, Robert Cullen and Bonnie Lisle, eds., New York: Bedford Book of St. Martin's Press, 1992, pp. 150–161.

41. Theodor Adorno and Max Horkheimer, *Dialectic of Enlightenment: Philosophical Fragments,* G. S. Noerr, ed., E. Jehcott, trans., Palo Alto, CA: Stanford University Press, 2002, p. 1.

42. Walter T. Stace, "Man Against Darkness," in E. D. Klemke, *The Meaning of Life,* New York: Oxford University Press, 2000, pp. 84–93.

43. Donald Crosby, *The Specter of the Absurd,* New York: State University of New York Press, 1988.

44. Simon Critchley, *Very Little . . . Almost Nothing—Death, Philosophy, Literature,* New York: Routledge, 1997, p. 8.

45. Hazel Barnes, *An Existentialist Ethics,* New York: Alfred A. Knopf, 1967, p. 102.

46. Critchley, pp. 3–11.

47. Michael Novak, *The Experience of Nothingness,* rev. ed., Somerset, NJ: Transaction Publishers, 1998.

48. Bowker, 1991.

49. William Barrett, *Irrational Man: A Study in Existential Philosophy,* New York: Anchor Books, 1962, p. 204.

50. Richard Rorty, "From Logic to Language to Play," *Proceedings and Addresses of the American Philosophical Association,* vol. 59, 1986, pp. 747–753.

51. Thomas Nagel, "The Absurd," in Klemke, p. 285.

52. Joel Feinberg, "Absurd Self-Fulfillment: An Essay on the Moral Perversity of the Gods," in *Vice & Virtue in Everyday Life,* 3rd ed., Christina Sommers and Fred Sommers, eds., Orlando, FL: Harcourt Brace Jovanovich, 1993, p. 1012.

53. Friedrch Wilhelm Nietzsche, *The Will to Power,* Walter Kaufmann and R. J. Hollingdale, trans., New York: Vintage, 1978, p. 35.

54. Albert Camus, *The Myth of Sisyphus,* trans. Justin O'Brien, London: Penguin Books, 2005, p. 119.

55. Critchley, p. 27.

56. Ibid., p. 149.

57. Ibid., p. 28.

58. Helen Vendler, "On the Emperor of Ice Cream," in *The Columbia History of American Poetry,* Jay Parini and Brett C. Miller, eds., New York: Columbia University Press, 1993. Retrieved February 2, 2005, from http://www.english.uiuc.edu/maps/poets/s_z/stevens/emperor.htm.

59. Thornton Wilder, *Our Town,* New York: Coward–McCann, Inc., in cooperation with Samuel French, Inc., 1938, p. 82.

60. Ibid. p. 83.

61. Karen Carr, *The Banalization of Nihilism: Twentieth-Century Responses to Meaninglessness,* New York: State University of New York, 1992.

62. Critchley, p. 28.

63. Wilder, p. 83.

64. Kurt Baier, "The Meaning of Life," in E. D. Klemke, *The Meaning of Life,* New York: Oxford University Press, 2000, p. 128.

Index